Causeway Math

(with answers)

JEAN HOLDERNESS

CPL

CAUSEWAY PRESS

Published by Causeway Press Ltd
PO Box 13, Ormskirk, Lancs L39 5HP

First published 1995

British Library Cataloguing-in-Publication Data
A catalogue record for this book is available from the British Library.

ISBN 1 87392945 5

This book is also available without answers.
ISBN 1 87392944 7

The Causeway Maths Series
Available now:
Causeway Maths 1 by David Alcorn
Causeway Maths 2 by David Alcorn
Causeway Maths 3 by Jean Holderness

To follow:
Causeway Maths 4 by Jean Holderness
Causeway Maths 5 by Jean Holderness
Causeway Maths 6 by Jean Holderness
Causeway Maths 7 by Jean Holderness

GCSE Series
Available now:
GCSE Maths: Level A by Jean Holderness
GCSE Maths: Level B by Jean Holderness

To follow:
GCSE Maths: Level C by Jean Holderness

Typesetting by Alden Multimedia Ltd., Northampton
Printed by Alden Press, Oxford

Preface

This book is the third book in a series written for pupils of secondary school age, where in England and Wales they will be studying Key Stage 3 or 4 of the National Curriculum. The material is also useful for pupils in Scotland (mainly at levels C/D) and in Northern Ireland (mainly at levels 5/6).

For more able pupils the book could be used as the basis for the first year's work. Other pupils could begin by using **Causeway Maths 1** or **Causeway Maths 2** and then progressing to this book later.

The main content of the book is based on covering the Programme of Study for level 5, but work from earlier levels is included where it forms a starting point for further progress. The book also includes work beyond level 5, especially in Geometry and Algebra. This is to make a more balanced and challenging mathematical course, since level 5 has so much emphasis on Arithmetic.

The teacher can decide how best to use the book with a particular class. If the easier work has already been completely understood, it can be omitted or revised quickly. With other pupils it might be better to work at a slower pace and not cover some of the later chapters. (There are some notes for teachers on page *x*.)

I have had much help and encouragement from my family and friends while I have been planning and writing this book. I would like to thank them all. Grateful thanks also go to those who have helped with the production of the book: Sue and Andrew, Mark and Alan, Dave, my brother Jim, and the staff at Alden Multimedia and Alden Press. From Causeway Press I have had great support from Mike and everyone else, and especially from David, who has given me a great amount of practical help and encouragement over several months.

Jean Holderness

To Christopher

Acknowledgements

Artwork created electronically by
Mark Andrews
Alan Fraser

Cover design
Andrew Allen

Copyright photographs
Andrew Allen
Jim Holderness

Ed Buziak pp. 217 (top), 231 (top), 285 (left), 309.

Sally and Richard Greenhill pp. 17, 36 (top), 103.

Telegraph Colour Library (cover)

Topham Picturepoint pp. 17, 37 (bottom), 64 (bottom), 84 (bottom-left), 174, 194, 211, 230 (left), 231 (bottom), 231 (right), 240 (top), 253 (right), 275.

Contents

Chapter 1 Numbers

Thinking about numbers	1
Tables	2
Numbers: even and odd, multiples of 5 and 3	4
Multiples, factors, prime numbers	4
Index notation, squares, square roots, cubes, cube roots	7
Sequences of numbers	9

Chapter 2 Multiplication and division

Thinking about multiplication and division	16
Multiplying whole numbers by 10, 100, 1000	18
Multiplying whole numbers by 20, 30, 40, ...	19
Multiplying by numbers less than 10	19
Numbers to the nearest 10, 100, 1000	20
Long multiplication	22
Dividing whole numbers by 10, 100, 1000	24
Dividing whole numbers by 20, 30, 40, ...	24
Dividing by numbers less than 10	25
Long division	27

Chapter 3 Using a calculator

Thinking about using a calculator	36
Checking calculator answers	38
To find the square, square root, cube of a number	41
To find the remainder in a division sum	41
The memory keys	43
Mixed questions and brackets	43

Chapter 4 Symmetry

Thinking about symmetry	50
Axes of symmetry	52
Planes of symmetry	54
Rotational symmetry	56

Chapter 5 Decimals

Thinking about decimals 64
Decimals 66
Multiplication and division by 10, 100, 1000, ... 67
Adding, subtracting; multiplying and dividing by small whole numbers 69
Numbers to the nearest whole number, decimal places 71
Multiplication and division by decimal numbers 73
Money 74
Reading numbers on scales 78

Chapter 6 Probability experiments

Thinking about probability 84
Probability and probability experiments 86
Experiments to try 88
Using random numbers to simulate results 89

Miscellaneous Section A

Aural practice exercises 98
Revision exercises 100
Activities 103

Chapter 7 The metric system

Thinking about the metric system 106
Length, weight, capacity 108
To change from one unit to another 109
Accuracy of measurements, readings on scales 111
Estimation 114

Chapter 8 Lines and angles

Thinking about lines and angles 118
Drawing and measuring lines 120
Angles: turn, half-turn, quarter-turn, right angles 121
Acute, obtuse and reflex angles 122
Use of a protractor: to measure or draw an angle 123
Perpendicular lines 129
Parallel lines, to draw parallel lines with a set-square 133

Chapter 9 Fractions and percentages

Thinking about fractions and percentages 140
Fractions 142
Equivalent fractions, improper fractions and mixed numbers 143
To find a fraction of a quantity 146
Percentages 149
To find a percentage of a sum of money or of a quantity 149

Chapter 10 Statistics

Thinking about statistics 158
Introduction 160
Tally tables, presenting the data in a table 160
Diagrams: pictogram, bar chart, line-graph 161
Pie charts 164
Averages: mean, median and mode 167
Range 169
Statistical investigations 171

Chapter 11 Algebra

Thinking about algebra 180
Introduction 182
Making expressions 182
Some rules: multiplication, addition and subtraction, removing brackets 184
Division 186
Making formulae 187
Substitution, using expressions and formulae 188

Chapter 12 Probability

Thinking about probability 194
Probability 196
Equally likely outcomes 196
Formula for probability 197

Miscellaneous Section B

Aural practice exercises 204
Revision exercises 206
Activities 209

Chapter 13 British units and time

Thinking about British units and time 216
Length, weight, capacity 218
Approximate comparisons with the metric system 220
Time 222

Chapter 14 Negative numbers

Thinking about negative numbers 230
Negative numbers 232
Calculations involving negative numbers 232

Chapter 15 Angles and parallel lines

Thinking about angles and parallel lines 240
Calculations with angles 242
Calculations with angles and parallel lines 245
Naming of angles 247

Chapter 16 Equations

Thinking about equations 252
Introduction 254
Solving simple equations 257
Further equations 258
Using equations to solve problems 264

Chapter 17 Frequency distributions

Thinking about frequency distributions 270
Frequency distributions, bar-line graph, histogram 272
The mean, mode, median, range 273
Grouped frequency distributions, histogram 276

Chapter 18 Triangles

Thinking about triangles 284
Acute-angled, right-angled and obtuse-angled triangles 286
Angles of a triangle 287
Scalene, isosceles and equilateral triangles 291
Angles in isosceles or equilateral triangles 292
Drawing triangles accurately 295

Miscellaneous Section C

Aural practice exercises 302
Revision exercises 304
Activities 312

Index 322

Answers 325

Topics for Activities (included in the Miscellaneous Sections)

A display of weighing and measuring instruments, 313
A mathematical game, 214
A million, 211
A number pattern, 104
A traffic survey, 213
Cube numbers, 104
Curve stitching and string art, 212
Elevens, 314
Fourteen, 315
Multiplication, 104
Nets of solid figures, 316
Planning a day's outing, 312
Planning a party, 103
Random numbers, 209
Roman numerals, 105
The cost of a child, 209
The Earth, 318
To bisect an angle, 315
To draw perpendicular lines, 210
Using a computer, 215
Using a computer database, 318

To the teacher

This book has been written for use with pupils of secondary school age. The main content of the book is based on covering the Programme of Study for level 5. However there is considerable overlap with work from earlier levels, and the book also includes some work from higher levels, particularly in Geometry and Algebra. This is because there is so much emphasis on Arithmetic in level 5, and I have tried to balance this by including more Geometry and Algebra.

For more able pupils the book could be used as the basis for the first year's work. Other pupils could begin by using **Causeway Maths 1** or **Causeway Maths 2** and then progress to this book later.

The book is organised as follows:- For each chapter there is an introductory section called 'Thinking About ... ' You could use these sections, or parts of them, for class discussion, for group work or for individual work. They could take a brief few minutes or several lessons. You might find that by extending the ideas there you are covering the work of the chapter quite adequately and very little follow-up work will be needed.

The main part of the chapter consists of bookwork and worked examples, followed by straightforward exercises. There should be no need for most pupils to have to work through the whole of any of these exercises. They are there in case practice is needed, and to give the pupils confidence in using the mathematical techniques. It is useful to have the bookwork available for reference. The teacher who has planned a good lesson may find it unnecessary to use the bookwork at all, but pupils are not always present in every lesson, and the absentees need some text to help them later.

The last exercise of each chapter is more varied, giving ideas for applications and activities of various lengths. It has not been suggested which ones should be done as group work or as a whole class activity, because the class organisation is best decided by the class teacher.

There is a short test at the end of each chapter, covering the main topics of the chapter.

The book has 18 chapters, giving roughly 6 for each term if the book is to be used for a year. After every 6 chapters there is a miscellaneous section with aural questions, revision questions and more suggestions for activities. There are puzzle questions fitted in at the ends of chapters where there is space. These are in no particular order and are there to give further interest.

The chapters are arranged in an order which interlinks Arithmetic, Geometry, Algebra, Statistics and Probability, so that there is a variety of maths in each part of the book. However, there is no reason why you should not plan your work in a different way. For example, the experimental work on probability in Chapter 6 could be followed by the theoretical probability of Chapter 12, especially if the discoveries of the class lead on naturally to it.

I have started the book with a short section on tables because I think that these are very important. Those who know the basic number facts will take a more confident part in aural work and discussion, will do written work quickly and accurately, and will find Maths more enjoyable. This will have a cumulative effect on their progress in future years.

I think that applications or activities which are related to everyday life are very useful, and many have been included in the book. However, the best topics are those which apply directly to the interests of the class, topics currently being studied in other subjects, what is happening in your school or neighbourhood, or what is currently in the news. So it is hoped that the teacher will think of the mathematical connections and introduce them.

I have also avoided use of statistics such as road accidents or deaths. They have their place but must be introduced by a teacher who knows the class. If a young child comes from a family with a recent bereavement such a lesson can be very upsetting. Similarly, I have avoided introducing social isues in the questions. A teacher can decide whether it is appropriate with a particular class at a particular time to include discussion of such matters as health topics, sex discrimination, government spending, etc.

Calculators. It would be best for the teacher to decide whether the pupils should use simple calculators or scientific calculators. In the earlier books in the series it was assumed that pupils would use simple calculators, and with some classes it would probably be better to continue to use these. For other pupils who will need scientific calculators later for trigonometry, it might be better to start using them at this stage. They can then get to know how to use them for squares, cubes and negative numbers, and there will probably be fraction keys and other useful keys.
With calculators there are so many variations. To mention all these in the text would be too confusing, and any problems are best resolved by the teacher, with the particular calculator being used.

Computers. I hope that if you have got computers you will have the software programs to go with them, and you will make good use of them. The development of computers is so rapid that detailed references and listings soon become outdated, so none have been included in this book.

Answers. This book is available either with or without answers. The answers are given to the straightforward questions, but not usually to the activities questions where it is important that the pupils make their own discoveries. The puzzle answers are not given as the puzzles are meant to be extra challenges for fun.

I hope that you and your pupils find this book useful and interesting. Enjoy your Maths.

Jean Holderness

1 Thinking about numbers

Everyday numbers

You may be having Maths as the 1st lesson of the day or it may be the 7th. How many Maths lessons do you have each week ? How long do they last ?

Now, already we have used **numbers**. Think of all other situations when you have used or been aware of numbers today.
Make a list. Have you needed to **calculate** with these numbers ?

Describe the different uses of numbers shown here.

Kinds of numbers

When we first talk about numbers we usually mean 1, 2, 3, . . . , that is, the positive whole numbers. But there are other kinds of numbers.
For instance, there is the number 0.
List all the other kinds of numbers you know about, and give examples of situations where they are used.

Patterns in numbers

In the first chapter we are using the positive whole numbers. We want to look for patterns in numbers so here is one to begin with. Copy it down and complete it.

$9 - 1 = 8$	$\frac{1}{2}$ of 8 is 4	$4 \times 4 = 16$	$(9 \times 1) + 16 = 25$
$8 - 2 = 6$	$\frac{1}{2}$ of 6 is 3	$3 \times 3 = 9$	$(8 \times 2) + 9 = 25$
$7 - 3 = 4$	$\frac{1}{2}$ of 4 is 2	. . .	
. . .			

You can try a similar pattern starting with 19 – 1, then 18 – 2.
See if you can discover a number pattern.

On the 12th day of Christmas my true love sent to me

12 drummers drumming	6 geese a-laying
11 pipers piping	5 gold rings
10 lords a-leaping	4 colly birds
9 ladies dancing	3 French hens
8 maids a-milking	2 turtle doves
7 swans a-swimming	And a partridge in a pear tree.

Over the 12 days, how many gifts altogether ?

An example of a triangular number

A number game

Have you played 'buzz' ? Try this with some of your friends. You call out numbers in turn, 1, 2, 3, etc., but whoever's turn it is when you get to 7, any multiple of 7, or any number containing a figure 7, such as 17, says 'buzz' instead of that number. Then the counting continues with the next number.

Anyone going wrong is 'out'.

When you get too good at that game, you change it to 'fizz-buzz', where you say 'fizz' for the 5's as well. For certain numbers, such as 35, you would say 'fizz-buzz'.

Of what use to you are number games ?

What other number games do you know ?

Numbers at work

Name some situations where these people would need to count or use whole numbers and explain how they would use them.

A teacher	A football referee
A nurse	A darts player
A shepherd	A shopkeeper

Think of some other people who would use counting or whole numbers in their jobs or their leisure activities and explain how they would use them.

1 Numbers

Tables

You should be able to work out simple number calculations in your head. Although you can use a calculator when necessary, it is a waste of valuable time to use it for simple questions like $8+6$, 9×7, how many 4's in 24 ?, what is twice 32 ?.

First you must check that you know your multiplication tables up to 12×12.
If you are not sure of all of them, begin by copying this chart onto squared paper.

Fill in the results of multiplication so that the first column is the 2 times table and the numbers in the first few squares are 4, 6, 8, ... from 2×2, 2×3, 2×4, ... (or 2×2, 3×2, 4×2, ... if you prefer to think of them that way).

You may not have learnt the 11 times and 12 times tables previously, but they are very useful tables to include.
The 11 times table is easy up to 11×10, then you have only 11×11 and 11×12 to learn. When you have worked out the 12 times table, notice how it relates to the 2 times and 10 times tables.

×	2	3	4	5	6	7	8	9	10	11	12
2	4										
3	6										
4	8										
5											
6											
7											
8											
9											
10											
11											
12											

When you have filled in all the squares and made sure they are correct, you must learn all the results that you do not already know.

Can you discover some number patterns in the chart ?

- Look at the units figures in each column.
- Look at the arrangement of the odd numbers.
- Look at the diagonal lines of the table.
- What is the sum of the digits (figures) in each result in the 9's column ? Are there similar patterns in other columns ?

Make another similar chart and choose spaces at random to fill in, until you can work out the results in any order.
Then test yourself by doing the questions in the next exercise.
If you still need to improve then do give yourself further practice, because it is very important **to you** that you know your tables at this stage. It will make such a difference to your chances of understanding and enjoying future work.

Exercise 1.1

1. Do these multiplication questions as quickly as you can. Work downwards in columns, and write down the answers only.

8×1	9×6	7×7	12×6	9×0
5×6	3×2	8×9	1×4	6×7
2×7	8×0	0×5	3×3	12×11
8×6	7×4	2×1	9×1	10×10
5×5	3×8	9×9	9×7	1×11
0×1	5×9	3×11	5×2	4×6
6×2	12×8	7×12	10×11	8×8
11×8	4×5	4×4	4×3	7×5
12×4	11×7	3×6	7×8	10×7
10×3	10×2	12×12	5×12	6×6

2. Write down the answers to these division questions, doing them as quickly as you can. Work downwards in columns.

$55 \div 5$	$72 \div 6$	$15 \div 3$	$81 \div 9$	$0 \div 5$
$72 \div 8$	$30 \div 5$	$49 \div 7$	$42 \div 6$	$27 \div 3$
$35 \div 7$	$77 \div 7$	$45 \div 9$	$96 \div 8$	$132 \div 12$
$36 \div 3$	$60 \div 12$	$32 \div 8$	$56 \div 7$	$60 \div 10$
$9 \div 1$	$48 \div 8$	$144 \div 12$	$33 \div 11$	$36 \div 4$

3. Write down the answers to these questions, doing them as quickly as you can.
   1 What is 8 more than 6 ?
   2 What is 12 doubled ?
   3 What must be added to 7 to make 20 ?
   4 How many times does 6 go into 54 ?
   5 What is 11 multiplied by itself ?
   6 What is half of 46 ?
   7 What number multiplied by itself makes 49 ?
   8 What is left when 15 is taken from 19 ?
   9 What is three-quarters of 24 ?
   10 What is 12 less than 30 ?

4. What is the whole number answer, and the remainder, when the first number is divided by the second one ?

1 $28 \div 5$	**3** $57 \div 11$	**5** $100 \div 12$
2 $18 \div 7$	**4** $32 \div 4$	

5. What must be added to:

1 5×11, to make 60,	**3** 9×7, to make 70,	**5** 12×3, to make 40 ?
2 6×4, to make 30,	**4** 8×6, to make 50,	

Numbers

Even and odd numbers

An **even number** is a number which divides exactly by 2. The units figure is 2, 4, 6, 8 or 0.

An **odd number** is a number which does not divide exactly by 2. The units figure is 1, 3, 5, 7 or 9.

Numbers which divide by 5

A number divides exactly by 5 if its unit figure is 5 or 0.

Numbers which divide by 3

There is a useful way to tell if a number divides exactly by 3.
Add up the digits (figures) in the number. If the answer is more than 9 then add up the digits of that answer, and repeat this until you get a 1-figure number. If this number is 3, 6 or 9, which all divide by 3, then the original number divides by 3.

e.g. $879 \rightarrow 8+7+9=24 \rightarrow 2+4=6$.
So 879 divides exactly by 3.

If the 1-figure number is 9 then the original number will also divide by 9.

e.g. $4653 \rightarrow 4+6+5+3=18 \rightarrow 1+8=9$.
So 4653 divides exactly by 9 (as well as by 3).

Multiples

Multiples of 3 are numbers which divide exactly by 3.
The first four multiples of 3 are 3, 6, 9, 12.
Some other multiples of 3 are 33, 72, 300, 1005.

Some multiples of 5 are 5, 60, 100, 205, 455.
Some multiples of 7 are 7, 14, 21, 70, 147, 1001.

Factors

Factors of 24 are numbers which divide exactly into 24.

$$\begin{aligned} 24 &= 1 \times 24 \\ &= 2 \times 12 \\ &= 3 \times 8 \\ &= 4 \times 6 \end{aligned}$$

The factors of 24 are 1, 2, 3, 4, 6, 8, 12, 24.

Every number has 1 as a factor. Every number has itself as a factor.

The factors of 70 are 1, 2, 5, 7, 10, 14, 35, 70.

Prime numbers

A number which has no factors, except 1 and itself, is called a **prime number**.
The first few prime numbers are 2, 3, 5, 7, 11, 13, 17, 19, . . .

To find whether a number is a prime number

Check that it has no factors (except itself and 1) by dividing by the first few prime numbers 2, 3, 5, 7, 11, . . .

Examples

1 Is 39 a prime number ?

Does 39 divide exactly by 2 ?
No, because it is not an even number.
Does 39 divide exactly by 3 ?
Yes. $39 \div 3 = 13$.
So 39 has a factor 3 (and a factor 13) and so it is not a prime number.

2 Is 67 a prime number ?

Does 67 divide exactly by 2 ? No.
Does 67 divide exactly by 3 ? No.
Does 67 divide exactly by 5 ? No, because it does not have a units figure of 5 or 0.
Does 67 divide exactly by 7 ? No.
There is no need to check that it divides by 11 or any greater prime number (see below).
67 has no factors (except itself and 1).
So 67 is a prime number.

Where to stop:

Divide by the prime numbers in order, first 2, then 3, then 5, . . .
Since $5 \times 5 = 25$, 25 is the smallest number which needs to be checked to see if it divides by 5.
Since $7 \times 7 = 49$, 49 is the smallest number which needs to be checked to see if it divides by 7.
Since $11 \times 11 = 121$, 121 is the smallest number which needs to be checked to see if it divides by 11.
A similar rule works if you are checking larger numbers.

Exercise 1.2

1. From the numbers 102, 213, 415, 528, 677, 717, 725, 828, 1000,
   1 which numbers are odd,
   2 which numbers divide by 5,
   3 which numbers divide by 3 ?

2. From the numbers 30, 32, 34, 35, 39, 42, 44, 45, 48, 49,
   1 which are multiples of 3,
   2 which are multiples of 5,
   3 which are multiples of 7 ?

3. List all the factors of
   1 12, **2** 30, **3** 40.

4. Write down all the numbers from 2 to 30, inclusive.
   Except for number 2, cross out all the numbers which divide by 2.
   Except for number 3, cross out all the numbers which divide by 3.
   Except for number 5, cross out all the numbers which divide by 5.
   The remaining numbers are prime numbers. Write them down in a neat list.

5. **1** List the factors of 27.
   2 List the factors of 45.
   3 List the numbers which are factors of both 27 and 45.
   4 Which number is the highest factor of both 27 and 45 ?

6. Find a number which is a factor of both these numbers. If you can find more than one, give the highest one.
   1 77, 88
   2 18, 42
   3 45, 35
   4 30, 50
   5 28, 16
   6 24, 12
   7 9, 27
   8 48, 40
   9 14, 22
   10 63, 49

7. **1** List the multiples of 3 which are less than 50.
   2 List the multiples of 7 which are less than 50.
   3 List the numbers less than 50 which are multiples of both 3 and 7.
   4 Which is the lowest number which is a multiple of both 3 and 7 ?

8. Find a number which is less than 50 and is a multiple of both these numbers. If you can find more than one, give the lowest one.

1 4, 5
2 12, 9
3 5, 7
4 8, 6
5 10, 15
6 11, 33
7 9, 6
8 2, 3
9 14, 4
10 8, 10

9. Find whether these numbers divide exactly by 2, 3, 5, 7 and then say which are prime numbers:
71, 72, 73, 75, 77, 79, 81, 85, 88, 91.

Index notation

2×2 can be written as 2^2, (read as 2 squared).

$2 \times 2 \times 2$ can be written as 2^3, (read as 2 cubed, or 2 to the power 3).

$2 \times 2 \times 2 \times 2$ can be written as 2^4, (read as 2 to the 4th, or 2 to the 4th power, or 2 to the power 4).

$2 \times 2 \times 2 \times 2 \times 2$ can be written as 2^5, (read as 2 to the 5th, or 2 to the 5th power, or 2 to the power 5).

Similarly,

$7 \times 7 \times 7 = 7^3$,

$10 \times 10 \times 10 \times 10 \times 10 \times 10 = 10^6$.

Working out the values

$2^5 = 2 \times 2 \times 2 \times 2 \times 2$ $(= 4 \times 2 \times 2 \times 2 = 8 \times 2 \times 2 = 16 \times 2)$
$= 32$

$3^3 = 3 \times 3 \times 3$ $(= 9 \times 3)$
$= 27$

$4^2 = 4 \times 4$
$= 16$

$10^6 = 10 \times 10 \times 10 \times 10 \times 10 \times 10$
$= 1\,000\,000$ (one million)

Squares of numbers

The square of a number is found by multiplying the number by itself.

The square of 7 is 7^2, which equals $7 \times 7 = 49$.

The square of 12 is 12^2, which equals $12 \times 12 = 144$.

The square of 1 is 1^2, which equals $1 \times 1 = 1$.

Square numbers are $1^2, 2^2, 3^2, 4^2, 5^2, \ldots$ which worked out are 1, 4, 9, 16, 25, ...

Square roots

The square of 8 is 64, and the **square root** of 64 is 8.
The square of 11 is 121, and the square root of 121 is 11.
The square root of 400 is 20, since $20^2 = 400$.
The square root of 25 is 5, since $5^2 = 25$.
The square root of 1 is 1, since $1^2 = 1$.

The sign for square root is $\sqrt{}$, so $\sqrt{9} = 3$.

Cubes of numbers

The cube of 5 is 5^3, which equals $5 \times 5 \times 5 = 125$.

The cube of 10 is 10^3, which equals $10 \times 10 \times 10 = 1000$.

The cube of 1 is 1^3, which equals $1 \times 1 \times 1 = 1$.

Cube numbers are $1^3, 2^3, 3^3, 4^3, 5^3, \ldots$ which worked out are 1, 8, 27, 64, 125, ...

Cube roots

The cube of 6 is 216, and the **cube root** of 216 is 6.
The cube of 10 is 1000, and the cube root of 1000 is 10.
The cube root of 64 is 4, since $4^3 = 64$.
The cube root of 8 is 2, since $2^3 = 8$.
The cube root of 1 is 1, since $1^3 = 1$.

The sign for cube root is $\sqrt[3]{}$, so $\sqrt[3]{27} = 3$.

Sequences of numbers

Many patterns involve numbers which follow a definite sequence. Here are some examples.

Whole numbers 1, 2, 3, 4, . . .

Odd numbers 1, 3, 5, 7, . . .

Even numbers 2, 4, 6, 8, . . .

Multiples of 5 5, 10, 15, 20, . . .

Square numbers 1, 4, 9, 16, . . .

Cube numbers 1, 8, 27, 64, . . .

Triangular numbers 1, 3, 6, 10, 15, . . .

Powers of 2 2, 4, 8, 16, 32, . . .

Some other sequences

11, 18, 25, 32, 39, . . .	Formed by adding 7 each time.
50, 47, 44, 41, 38, . . .	Formed by subtracting 3 each time.
3, 6, 12, 24, 48, . . .	Formed by multiplying by 2 each time.
25 000, 5000, 1000, 200, 40, . . .	Formed by dividing by 5 each time.
8, 9, 11, 14, 18, . . .	Formed by adding 1, then 2, then 3, . . .

Square numbers can be represented by arranging dots in the form of squares.

1 **4** **9** **16**

Triangular numbers can be represented by arranging dots in the form of triangles.

1 **3** (1 + 2) **6** (1 + 2 + 3) **10** (1 + 2 + 3 + 4) **15** (1 + 2 + 3 + 4 + 5)

Exercise 1.3

1. **1** Find the values of 2^3, 3^2, 5^3, 7^2, 10^4.
   2 Write in index notation $5 \times 5 \times 5 \times 5$, $2 \times 2 \times 2 \times 2 \times 2 \times 2 \times 2$, 11×11.

2. **1** Write down the squares of these numbers: 8, 12, 7, 1, 9.
   2 Write down the square roots of 36, 4, 121, 25, 100.
   3 Write down the cubes of these numbers: 4, 1, 10.

3. From the numbers 20, 23, 25, 27, 31, 36, write down:
   1 the prime numbers,
   2 the square numbers,
   3 the numbers which are multiples of 3,
   4 a cube number,
   5 a triangular number.

4. Copy and complete this number pattern.

$9 \times 1 = 21 - 12 = 9 \times (2 - 1)$
$9 \times 2 = 31 - 13 = 9 \times (3 - 1)$
...
$9 \times 8 = 91 - 19 = 9 \times (9 - 1)$

5. Continue these sequences for three more terms each.
   1 3, 6, 9, 12, ...
   2 64, 56, 48, 40, ...
   3 1, 3, 9, 27, ...
   4 1, 2, 5, 10, 17, ...
   5 1, 8, 27, 64, ...
   6 100, 94, 88, 82, 76, ...
   7 100, 99, 97, 94, 90, ...
   8 5, 10, 20, 40, 80, ...
   9 16 384, 4096, 1024, 256, 64, ...
   10 2, 5, 11, 20, 32, ...

Exercise 1.4 Applications and Activities

1. **1** I think of a number, multiply it by itself and add 8. The result is 44. What was the original number ?
   2 I think of a number, divide it by 3 and add 12. The result is 20. What was the number ?
   3 I think of a number, subtract 5 and then divide by 4. The result is 9. What was the number ?
   4 I think of a number, add 3 and then multiply by 5. The result is 100. What was the number ?
   5 I think of a number, divide by 4 and then subtract 10. The result is 20. What was the number ?

2. **1** Start from 1 and keep adding 6's until you reach a number greater than 50. What number is this ?

2 Start from 100 and keep subtracting 9's until you reach a number less than 10. What number is this ?

3 Start from 3 and keep doubling the number until you reach a number greater than 100. What number is this ?

4 Start from 240 and keep halving the number until you reach a number less than 20. What number is this ?

5 Start from 1458 and keep dividing by 3 until you reach a number less than 10. What number is this ?

3. Represent some number patterns by drawings, and make some discoveries about them. Here are two ideas using drawings on isometric paper.

Hexagonal numbers

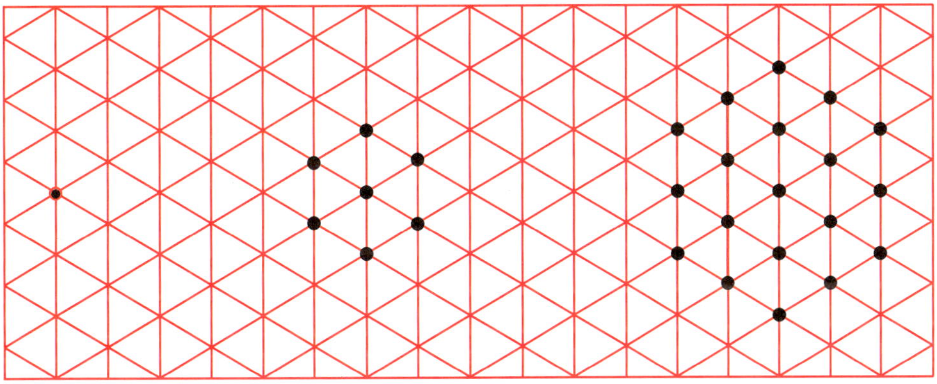

1 **7** **19**

Cube numbers

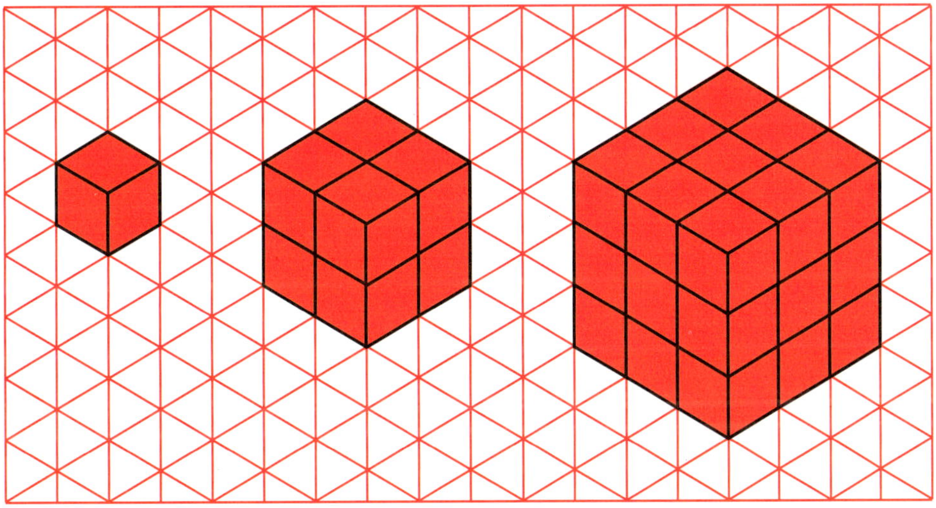

1 **8** **27**

4. Number chains

These change a number into another number by a certain rule. Then the new number is changed, and the process is repeated.
Here is an example.

Rule: For 2-figure numbers, multiply the 10's digit by 3 and add to the units digit. Stop the chain when you get to a single figure.

So 29 $\rightarrow 2 \times 3 + 9 = 15 \rightarrow 1 \times 3 + 5 = 8$.
54 $\rightarrow 5 \times 3 + 4 = 19 \rightarrow 1 \times 3 + 9 = 12 \rightarrow 1 \times 3 + 2 = 5$.

To investigate this chain, make a grid of 2-figure numbers.

10	11	12	13	14	15	16	17	18	19
20	21	22	·	·	·				
30	31	·	·	·					
·									
·									
·									

With a felt-tip or crayon, circle round each number which leads to a single figure of 8. In other colours, circle numbers which lead to each of the other single figure numbers. See what discoveries you can make. Could you adapt the rule for 3-figure numbers ?

Here is another rule:

If the number is even, divide it by 2.
If the number is odd, add 3 and then divide by 2.
Stop if a number reappears for a second time.

Investigate this chain.

Make other number chains using different rules and investigate them.

5. The Sieve of Eratosthenes

Write down the numbers 2 to 50 inclusive. Draw a circle round 2 and then cross out every other number which divides by 2. The 1st number not circled or crossed out is 3. Draw a circle round 3 and then cross out every other number which divides by 3. The next number not crossed out or circled is 5. Draw a circle round 5 and then cross out every other number which divides by 5. The next number not crossed out is 7. Draw a circle round 7 and then cross out every other number which divides by 7. Now draw a circle round all the remaining numbers which are not crossed out. The circled numbers are the prime numbers. Write them down in a list.

Why was it sufficient to stop at 7 ? If we had made a list up to 125 what other number would need to be crossed out ?

This method can be used to find the prime numbers up to any large number. It is useful to set the numbers down on squared paper in neat columns and then a pattern can be seen as you cross out the numbers. Extend the list using numbers from 1 to 100.

Set out in columns of 10,

1	2	3	4	5	6	7	8	9	10
11	12	13	14	15	16	17	18	19	20
21	22	.	.	.					

or try other columns, especially columns of 6.

1	2	3	4	5	6
7	8	9	10	11	12
13	14	15	16	17	18
19	20	.	.	.	

1 is a special number, so mark it in a different way. It is not counted as a prime number although it has no factors other than itself.

This method is known as 'The Sieve of Eratosthenes'. See if you can find out anything about Eratosthenes who lived a long time ago.

6. Make a list showing numbers and all their factors, and see what discoveries you can make. (Perhaps you might choose to begin with numbers up to 50.)

Number	Factors	Number of factors	Sum of factors, excluding the number itself
1	1	1	–
2	1, 2	2	1
3	1, 3	2	1
4	1, 2, 4	3	3
5	1, 5	2	1
6	1, 2, 3, 6	4	6
. . .			

Here are some questions to consider, but you may think of others.

1 What is special about numbers with just two factors ?

2 What is special about numbers with an odd number of factors ?

3 What do you notice about the sum of factors of the numbers which are powers of 2, i.e. 2, 4, 8, 16, . . . ?

4 If the sum of the factors, excluding the number itself, is equal to the number, then the number is called a perfect number. So 6 is a perfect number. What is the next smallest perfect number ?

7. This diagram shows a number grid with 10 columns, and a cross shown on it. We can describe this cross as 'centred at 32'. The cross can be centred at other numbers on the grid.
You can make some discoveries about the numbers in the cross.

1	2	3	4	5	6	7	8	9	10
11	12	13	14	15	16	17	18	19	20
21	22	23	24	25	26	27	28	29	30
31	32	33	34	35	36	37	38	39	40
41	42	43	44	45	46	47	48	49	50
51	52	53	54	55	56	57	58	59	60
61	62	63	64	65	66	67	68	69	70
71	72	73	74	75	76	77	78	79	80
81	82	83	84	85	86	87	88	89	90
91	92	93	94	95	96	97	98	99	100

Here are some ideas to think about:
Which numbers can the cross not be centred at ?
Is there any connection between the sum of the numbers in the cross, and the centre number ?
Is there any connection between the product of the top and bottom numbers in the cross (i.e. the numbers multiplied together), or of the two side numbers, and the centre number ?

You can extend this investigation by making a new grid with a different number of columns.
You can also investigate different shapes on the grid, such as

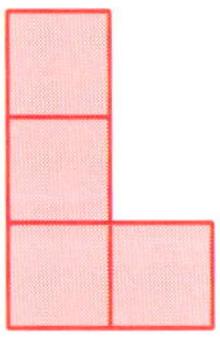

or

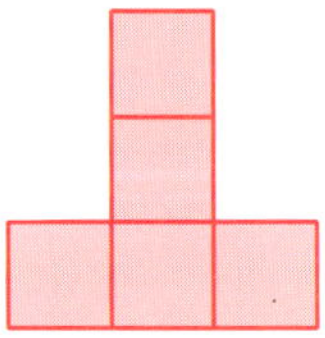

Chapter 1 test

1. **1** What is 12 more than 8 ?
   2 What is 15 doubled ?
   3 What must be added to 39 to make 50 ?
   4 What is 9 multiplied by itself ?
   5 What is half of 68 ?

2. **1** How many more 4's than 6's are there in 48 ?
2 How many more 9's than 12's are there in 72 ?
3 How many more 3's than 4's are there in 36 ?
4 How many more 10's than 12's are there in 60 ?
5 How many more 4's than 10's are there in 20 ?

3. From the numbers 21, 33, 48, 55, 66, 75, 77,
1 which numbers are odd,
2 which numbers are divisible by 5,
3 which numbers are divisible by 3,
4 which numbers are divisible by 7,
5 which numbers are divisible by 11 ?

4. List all the factors of 42.

5. Find the values of 2^4, 3^3, 5^2, 10^5.

6. Write in index notation,
7×7, $3 \times 3 \times 3 \times 3$, $2 \times 2 \times 2 \times 2 \times 2$.

7. **1** Write down the squares of 6, 11, 1, 10.
2 Write down the square roots of 25, 81, 16, 9.

8. From the numbers 11, 12, 13, 14, 15, 16, 17, 18, 19, 20, write down
1 the even numbers,
2 a square number,
3 the numbers which are multiples of 5,
4 the prime numbers,
5 the numbers which are factors of 60.

9. Continue these sequences for 3 more terms.
1 4, 8, 12, 16, ...
2 80, 71, 62, 53, ...
3 1, 2, 4, 8, 16, ...
4 729, 243, 81, 27, ...
5 1, 2, 4, 7, 11, ...

10. Write down in a list the first ten triangular numbers.
Find the sums of every two consecutive triangular numbers in your list,
e.g. $1 + 3 = 4$, $3 + 6 = 9$, ...
What do you notice about the sums ?

2 Thinking about multiplication and

What is multiplication ?

Well, it's really only repeated addition.

About 30 years ago, small calculating machines were produced and these were sometimes bought by schools. To multiply 64 by 35, you put 64 on the levers of the machine, turned the handle 5 times, which meant it added 64 five times, then moved up one place and turned the handle 3 times. Nowadays, your calculator will do it as quickly as you can enter the numbers.
However, you cannot always rely on having your calculator handy, so in case of emergency, you must be able to find the answer without it.

What is the cost of feeding your pet cat for a year ?
What is the weight of food it eats in a year ?

Calculating at work

Have you needed to do any calculating today ? If so, for what purpose ?
We use calculations continually, with money, time, lengths, weights, as well as with numbers. Think of situations where these people need to calculate, probably without using a calculator.

A teacher planning a school trip
A householder going shopping for food
The driver of a bus, who also has to collect the fares
A farmer who keeps a herd of cows for milking

You can probably think of more than one kind of calculation in each case.

Mark uses his moped to travel to school. How can he estimate how many miles he will travel in a year ?

division

How many cakes can be made from 1 bag of flour if the recipe uses 300 g of flour for each cake ?

Methods of division

A coach holds 54 passengers.
There are 918 people going on a school outing. How many coaches would be needed ?
Don't use your calculator to do this question. We must have a different method for times when the calculator is not handy.
So work it out, writing down the steps in your working so that you can explain how you did it.
(Having worked it out, how can you check that your answer is correct ?)
Now compare your method with other people's and see how many different ways of working it out you can use, and which method seems best.

If you had £40 to spend on a children's party, and the costs were £2.50 per child, how many children could you invite ?

2 Multiplication and division

Multiplying whole numbers by 10

$7 \times 10 = 70$
$87 \times 10 = 870$
$987 \times 10 = 9870$
$980 \times 10 = 9800$
$900 \times 10 = 9000$

The figures 7 units, 8 tens and 9 hundreds have all become ten times bigger by moving up one place to become 7 tens, 8 hundreds and 9 thousands. 0's are used to fill the empty spaces.

Multiplying whole numbers by 100 or 1000

To multiply by 100 is simply the same as multiplying by 10 and then by 10 again, so the figures move up two places.
To multiply by 1000 is the same as multiplying by 10, by 10 again and then by 10 again, so the figures move up three places.

$8 \times 100 = 800$
$78 \times 100 = 7800$
$678 \times 100 = 67\,800$
$5670 \times 100 = 567\,000$
$5000 \times 100 = 500\,000$

$23 \times 1000 = 23\,000$
$123 \times 1000 = 123\,000$
$4020 \times 1000 = 4\,020\,000$

Multiplying powers of 10

$10 \times 10 = 100$
$100 \times 10 = 1000$
$1000 \times 10 = 10\,000$

$100 \times 100 = 10\,000$
$1000 \times 100 = 100\,000$
$1000 \times 1000 = 1\,000\,000$

Multiplying whole numbers by 20, 30, 40, . . . , 200, 300, 400, . . . , 2000, 3000, 4000, . . .

$$70 \times 500 = 7 \times 10 \times 5 \times 100 = 7 \times 5 \times 10 \times 100 = 35 \times 1000 = 35\,000$$

or

$$70 \times 500 = 500 \times 70 = 500 \times 7 \times 10 = 3500 \times 10 = 35\,000$$

$$800 \times 20 = 8 \times 2 \times 1000 = 16\,000$$

or

$$800 \times 20 = 800 \times 2 \times 10 = 1600 \times 10 = 16\,000$$

$$5000 \times 20 = 5 \times 2 \times 10\,000 = 100\,000$$

or

$$5000 \times 20 = 5000 \times 2 \times 10 = 10\,000 \times 10 = 100\,000$$

$$9000 \times 3000 = 9 \times 3 \times 1\,000\,000 = 27\,000\,000$$

or

$$9000 \times 3000 = 9000 \times 3 \times 1000 = 27\,000 \times 1000 = 27\,000\,000$$

Multiplying by numbers less than 10

Examples

1 Work out 728 × 6.

```
   728
 ×   6
  4368
```

8 × 6 = 48. Write down 8 and carry 4 to the 10's column.
2 × 6 = 12, and 4 makes 16. Write down 6 and carry 1 to the 100's column.
7 × 6 = 42, and 1 makes 43. Write down 3, and write down 4 in the 1000's column.

2 Work out 5907 × 4.

```
   5907
 ×    4
  23628
```

7 × 4 = 28. Write down 8 and carry 2.
0 × 4 = 0, and 2 makes 2. Write down 2.
9 × 4 = 36. Write down 6 and carry 3.
5 × 4 = 20, and 3 makes 23. Write down 3, and write down 2 in the 10 000's column.

Numbers to the nearest ten

e.g. For numbers between 50 and 60.
Any number less than 55 is given as 50, to the nearest ten.
Any number from 55 upwards is given as 60, to the nearest ten.
(Actually, 55 is exactly halfway between 50 and 60 but it is usual to correct it **up** to 60.)

So, if the units figure is 5 or more, correct **up** to the next ten.

Examples

64 = 60, to the nearest ten.
78 = 80, to the nearest ten.
85 is halfway between 80 and 90, but it is usual to give it as 90, to the nearest ten.

Numbers to the nearest hundred

e.g. For numbers between 200 and 300.
Any number less than 250 is given as 200, to the nearest hundred.
Any number from 250 upwards is given as 300, to the nearest hundred.
You will notice that it does not matter what the units figure is, it is the tens figure you must look at, when rounding to the nearest hundred.

So, if the tens figure is 5 or more, correct up to the next 100.

Examples

264 = 300, to the nearest hundred, since the 10's figure is 6.
246 = 200, to the nearest hundred, since the 10's figure is 4.

Numbers to the nearest thousand

e.g. For numbers between 7000 and 8000.
Any number less than 7500 is given as 7000, to the nearest thousand.
Any number from 7500 upwards is given as 8000, to the nearest thousand.

Here you must look at the hundreds figure. If this is 5 or more, correct up to the next 1000.

Examples

9264 = 9000, to the nearest thousand, since the 100's figure is 2.
5721 = 6000, to the nearest thousand, since the 100's figure is 7.
9721 = 10 000, to the nearest thousand. Here, 9 has been corrected up to 10.

Exercise 2.1

Work out the answers to these questions without using a calculator.

1\.
1 47 × 10
2 840 × 100
3 601 × 1000
4 12 × 10
5 135 × 100
6 38 × 1000
7 100 × 10
8 80 × 100
9 100 × 1000
10 99 × 10

2\.
1 7 × 30
2 50 × 60
3 300 × 90
4 40 × 20
5 700 × 3000
6 9000 × 50
7 200 × 800
8 60 × 5000
9 7000 × 40
10 80 × 300

3\.
1 56 × 3
2 802 × 5
3 43 × 8
4 164 × 6
5 523 × 7
6 190 × 4
7 743 × 9
8 705 × 6
9 936 × 7
10 380 × 5

4\. Write these numbers to the nearest ten.

59 503 129 1043 286 94 1427 581 97 206

5\. Write these numbers to the nearest hundred.

643 481 506 1058 1038 3105 9091 449 786 20 997

6\. Write these numbers to the nearest thousand.

4273 14 691 2723 27 857 3634 55 881 9108 81 164 3935 10 487

7\. On an excursion there were 20 coaches, each carrying 40 passengers. How many passengers were there altogether ?

8\. 71 lampposts are placed along a road at intervals of 30 m. What is the total distance between the first and the last one ?

9\. What is the total cost of 500 chairs each costing £30, and 200 tables each costing £40 ?

10\. Araf and Habib worked on two machines. Araf produced 40 components each hour, Habib produced 50 per hour. They worked for 8 hours each day. How many extra components had Habib produced after 30 working days ?

11\. The number of insects in a colony doubles each week. If there were 36 insects there at first, how many would there be after 6 weeks ?
How many would there be, to the nearest 100 ?

12. Each side of this hexagon is 28 cm long.
What is the total length of the 6 sides ?

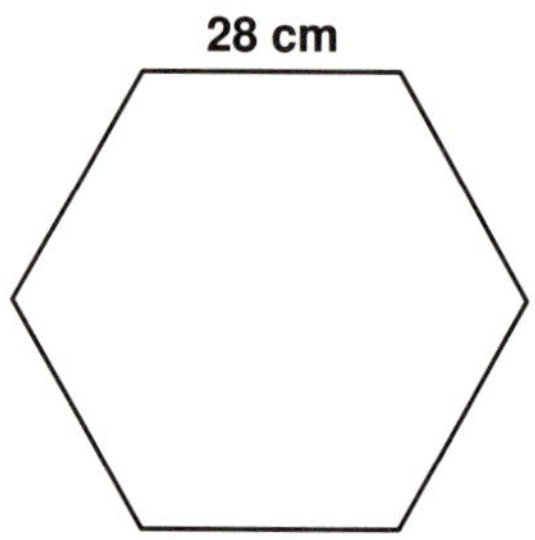

13. A cyclist rides, on average, 37 miles each day. How far will he ride in 8 days, to the nearest 10 miles ?

14. 1 nautical mile is 6080 feet. How many feet are there in 10 nautical miles ?

15. A stove burns 148 kg of fuel each day. How much fuel is used in a week (7 days) ?

16. Pieces of ribbon are each 243 cm long. If 9 pieces are joined together, what will be the total length ? What is this length to the nearest 10 cm ?

Long multiplication

To multiply by a number between 10 and 100

Examples

1 328×46

First multiply 328 by 6, then multiply 328 by 40, and add the results together.

$328 \times 6 = 1968$
$328 \times 4 = 1312$ so $328 \times 40 = 13\,120$
Finally $328 \times 46 = (328 \times 6) + (328 \times 40) = 1968 + 13\,120 = 15\,088$

However, this looks much simpler set down like this:

```
   328
×   46
  1968
 13120  ← Write down the 0 first
 15088    because this comes
          from multiplying by
          10, then multiply
          328 by 4.
```

or

```
   328
×   46
 13120   } if you prefer to
  1968   } multiply by 40
 15088   } before you
           multiply by 6.
```

2 173 × 91

$$\begin{array}{r} 173 \\ \times \quad 91 \\ \hline 173 \\ 15570 \\ \hline 15743 \\ \hline \end{array} \quad \text{or} \quad \begin{array}{r} 173 \\ \times \quad 91 \\ \hline 15570 \\ 173 \\ \hline 15743 \\ \hline \end{array}$$

Normally you would use your calculator to do such questions but it is essential to know how to work out the answers yourself as you cannot always rely on having a calculator handy.

This method is called **long multiplication**. There are other methods of working and you can use any method you prefer, as long as it gives the correct answer.

Exercise 2.2

Work out the answers to these questions without using a calculator.

1. **1** 49 × 28
   2 403 × 37
   3 654 × 51
   4 170 × 26
   5 343 × 66
   6 64 × 45
   7 517 × 86
   8 726 × 29
   9 905 × 91
   10 183 × 54

2. There are 48 drawing pins in each new box. A secretary orders 12 dozen boxes. How many drawing pins will there be altogether ?

3. The distance round a playing-field is 815 m. Laura goes round it 16 times on a sponsored run. How far has she run altogether ? How far is this to the nearest 1000 m ?

4. There are 24 bottles in a crate of milk bottles. Edward has 125 full crates on his lorry. How many bottles are there ?

5. Wire is wound round a reel 65 times, the distance round the reel being 124 cm. What is the total length of the wire ?

6. If a household uses 25 kg of solid fuel each day in winter, how much should be bought to last from 1st November to 31st March (151 days), to the nearest 100 kg ?

7. A glacier is moving at the rate of 32 cm per day.

   1 How far will it move in a week ?
   2 Give the answer to part **1** to the nearest 10 cm.
   3 How far will it move in a year (365 days) ?
   4 Give the answer to part **3** to the nearest 100 cm.

Dividing whole numbers by 10, 100 or 1000

$900 \div 10 = 90$
$6800 \div 10 = 680$
$6850 \div 10 = 685$

The figures have all become ten times smaller by moving down one place. 0's no longer needed disappear.

$9300 \div 100 = 93$
$800 \div 100 = 8$

To divide by 100 is the same as dividing by 10 and then by 10 again, so the figures move down 2 places.

$3000 \div 1000 = 3$
$34\,000 \div 1000 = 34$
$534\,000 \div 1000 = 534$

To divide by 1000 is the same as dividing by 10, by 10 again and then by 10 again, so the figures move down 3 places.

Dividing powers of 10

$10\,000 \div 10 = 1000$
$1000 \div 10 = 100$
$100 \div 10 = 10$
$10 \div 10 = 1$

$10\,000 \div 100 = 100$
$1000 \div 100 = 10$
$100 \div 100 = 1$
$10\,000 \div 1000 = 10$

Dividing whole numbers by 20, 30, 40, . . . , 200, 300, 400, . . . , 2000, 3000, 4000, . . .

$$6000 \div 30 = \frac{600\not{0}}{3\not{0}} = \frac{600}{3} = 200$$

The 0's are crossed out because we are dividing both numbers by 10. (This can be called **cancelling**.)

What we are doing is
$6000 \div 30 = (6000 \div 10) \div 3 = 600 \div 3 = 200$

$$800 \div 400 = \frac{8\cancel{0}\cancel{0}}{4\cancel{0}\cancel{0}} = \frac{8}{4} = 2$$

(We have divided both numbers by 10, and then by 10 again.)

$$30\,000 \div 5000 = \frac{30\,\cancel{0}\cancel{0}\cancel{0}}{5\cancel{0}\cancel{0}\cancel{0}} = \frac{30}{5} = 6$$

$$7200 \div 60 = \frac{720\cancel{0}}{6\cancel{0}} = \frac{720}{6} = 120$$

$$3500 \div 700 = \frac{35\cancel{0}\cancel{0}}{7\cancel{0}\cancel{0}} = \frac{35}{7} = 5$$

You can still use this method without writing anything down, if you have to do it in your head.
e.g. 40 000 ÷ 800 equals 400 ÷ 8 which is 50, (mentally dividing by 100 first).

Dividing by numbers less than 10

Examples

1 You buy 4 similar cakes and they cost £1.48. Your friend wants to buy one from you. What does it cost ?

You must divide £1.48 by 4. This is 148 pence ÷ 4.
Set it down like this.

$$\begin{array}{r} 37 \text{ Answer} \\ 4\overline{)148} \end{array}$$

They cost 37 pence each.

The working is:
4's into 1 will not go.
4's into 14 go 3 times, remainder 2. Write 3 in the answer above the 4 of 14. Carry the 2 (tens) to the next figure, making it 28.
In the next place, 4's into 28 go 7 times exactly. Write 7 in the answer above the 8.
The answer is 37 and there is no remainder.
One cake costs 37p.

If you cannot do some of the working in your head you can set it down like this:

$$\begin{array}{r} 37 \text{ Answer} \\ 4\overline{)148} \\ \underline{12} \\ 28 \\ \underline{28} \\ 0 \end{array}$$

2 966 ÷ 7

```
  138 Answer                 138 Answer
7)966              or      7)966
                             7
                             26
                             21
                              56
                              56
                               0
```

If the numbers do not divide exactly, it may be appropriate to leave a remainder, or alternatively you can continue the division using decimal places. (See Chapter 5.)

Exercise 2.3

Work out the answers to these questions without using a calculator.

1.
1 5000 ÷ 10
2 700 ÷ 100
3 90 000 ÷ 1000
4 6000 ÷ 100
5 550 ÷ 10
6 12 000 ÷ 100
7 10 000 ÷ 10
8 1960 ÷ 10
9 1000 ÷ 100
10 25 000 ÷ 1000

2.
1 600 ÷ 20
2 4000 ÷ 500
3 1500 ÷ 300
4 240 ÷ 20
5 800 ÷ 200
6 90 000 ÷ 30
7 4000 ÷ 200
8 6000 ÷ 50
9 20 000 ÷ 400
10 7000 ÷ 20

3.
1 72 ÷ 3
2 225 ÷ 5
3 472 ÷ 8
4 203 ÷ 7
5 984 ÷ 6
6 765 ÷ 9
7 912 ÷ 4
8 728 ÷ 7
9 305 ÷ 5
10 528 ÷ 8

4. Work out the answers to these questions and also give the remainder.
1 95 ÷ 8
2 127 ÷ 5
3 254 ÷ 7
4 609 ÷ 4
5 420 ÷ 9
6 146 ÷ 7
7 214 ÷ 6
8 730 ÷ 8
9 283 ÷ 5
10 506 ÷ 3

5. There are 800 children in a school and 40 teachers. What is the average number of children per teacher ?

6. Write down any number less than 10, add 2 to it and square the result. Then add 5 and multiply by 10. Take 100 away. Divide by 2, add 5 and divide by the number you started with. Subtract 20 and double the result. Divide by 10 and subtract the number you started with. What is your answer ?

7. A typist agrees to type 480 pages in 15 days. In the first four days she does 50 pages each day. Then she is ill and does none for the next three days. How many pages will she have to do, on average, each day to finish the work on time ?

8. 320 kg of apples were packed into boxes, with 7 kg of apples in each box. How many boxes were used and what weight of apples was left over ?

9. The product of two numbers is 585. (This means that the two numbers multiplied together make 585.)
One of the numbers is 9. Find the other number.

10. 6 people had a meal at a restaurant. They shared the bill of £228 equally among themselves. How much did each person pay ?

Long division

To divide by a number between 10 and 100

Examples

1 14 similar machines together weigh 826 kg. What is the weight of one ?

You must divide 826 by 14.

First, 14 into 8 will not go.
14's into 82 go 5 times. Put 5 in the answer above the 2 of 82.
Multiply 14 by 5 (= 70) and write this under the 82.
Subtract 70 from 82 leaving 12.
Bring down the next figure, 6, making 126.
14's into 126 go 9 times. Put 9 in the answer above the 6.
Multiply 14 by 9 (= 126) and write this under the 126.
Subtracting leaves 0 so there is no remainder. The answer is 59.
Each machine weighs 59 kg.

```
     59  Answer
14)826
   70
   126
   126
     0
```

The difficult part of such a question is deciding how many times 14 goes into 82, and into 126. You can do it the long way by working out the 14 times table until you get far enough: $14 \times 1 = 14$, $14 \times 2 = 28$, $14 \times 3 = 42$, and so on.
You could make a rough guess instead.
$14 \times 10 = 140$ so half of that, $14 \times 5 = \frac{1}{2}$ of $140 = 70$. Then $14 \times 6 = 70 + 14 = 84$, so 14 goes into 82 five times.

2 $988 \div 19$

```
19)988
```

First, think of 19 as nearly 20.
How many 20's in 98 ? Nearly 5.
Check whether 19×5 is less than 98. Yes, it is, so the first part of the answer is a five.

```
   5
19)988
   95
    38
```

$19 \times 5 = 95$. Put the 5 above the 8 of 98.

To find the remainder, write 95 below 98, and subtract 95 from 98. This leaves 3, which is written below. Bring down the next figure, which is 8.

```
    52 Answer
19)988
   95
    38
    38
     0
```

How many 19's in 38 ? (How many 20's ?)
There are nearly 2 20's, and there are exactly 2 19's.
$19 \times 2 = 38$. Write 2 in the answer above the 8 of 38.

Write 38 below 38 and subtract, leaving 0 so there is no remainder. The answer is 52.

So $988 \div 19 = 52$.

3 One morning a school ordered 919 bottles of milk. The milk is delivered in crates which hold 24 bottles. How many crates were delivered ?

Do a division question, and find the remainder.

```
    38
24)919
   72
   199
   192
     7      Answer 38, remainder 7.
```

The milkman will leave 38 full crates, and also 7 extra bottles which he may also leave in a crate.

There are other methods of working and you can use any method you prefer as long as it gives you the correct answer.

Exercise 2.4

Work out the answers to these questions without using a calculator.

1. **1** $819 \div 21$
   2 $986 \div 17$
   3 $1120 \div 35$
   4 $936 \div 13$
   5 $954 \div 18$
   6 $987 \div 47$
   7 $972 \div 54$
   8 $949 \div 73$
   9 $682 \div 31$
   10 $992 \div 16$

2. Work out the answers to these questions and also give the remainder.
   1 $980 \div 75$
   2 $857 \div 61$
   3 $988 \div 34$
   4 $900 \div 27$
   5 $602 \div 17$
   6 $801 \div 26$
   7 $376 \div 15$
   8 $759 \div 22$
   9 $638 \div 17$
   10 $523 \div 41$

3. 624 children went on a school outing. There were 48 children on each coach. How many coaches were needed ?

4. A length of ribbon 896 cm long was cut into 32 strips. How long was each strip ?

5. A length of wire 1360 cm long had to be cut into pieces each of length 25 cm. How many pieces could be made, and what length of wire remained ?

6. A group of boys went looking for conkers and collected 490. When they shared them out they got 35 each. How many boys were there ?

7. A fence round some gardens cost £2025. If 27 householders agreed to share the cost equally, how much had they each to pay ?

8. A group of people shared a prize of £3060. If they each got £85, how many people were there ?

Exercise 2.5 Applications and Activities

Other methods for multiplication

1. Instead of multiplying as in long multiplication, another way to work out the answers is to split both the numbers into separate parts and write the results down in a rectangular grid.

e.g. 243 × 75
Split 243 into 200 + 40 + 3, and 75 into 70 + 5.

	200	40	3
70	14 000	2800	210
5	1000	200	15

Multiply the number above the rectangle by the number at the side of the rectangle. Do this for each of the six rectangles.

Write the numbers in the rectangles down in a neat column and add them together. Any order will do but it is probably easier if you put the larger numbers first.

$$\begin{array}{r} 14000 \\ 2800 \\ 1000 \\ 210 \\ 200 \\ 15 \\ \hline 18225 \\ \hline \end{array}$$

So 243 × 75 = 18 225.

Try some of the questions from Exercise 2.2 again using the rectangle method, and if you prefer to use it then make up other questions for practice, and then check the answers on your calculator.

Note that a question such as 403 × 37 only needs four compartments in the rectangle.

	400	3
30		
7		

2. If you have to multiply by a number which has 1-figure factors, such as 48 which has factors 6×8, you can use another method.

e.g. $528 \times 48 = 528 \times 6 \times 8$

First multiply 528 by 6, and then multiply the answer by 8.

$$\begin{array}{r} 528 \\ \times \quad 6 \\ \hline 3168 \\ \times \quad 8 \\ \hline 25344 \\ \hline \end{array}$$

Practise this method with these questions.

1 129×35 $(35 = 5 \times 7)$
2 256×36 $(36 = 6 \times 6 \text{ or } 4 \times 9)$
3 817×28
4 345×72
5 550×49

3. If you have to multiply by 25, because 25 is one-quarter of 100, you can multiply by 100 and then divide by 4.

e.g. 385×25
$= 385 \times 100 \div 4$
$= 38\,500 \div 4$
$= 9625$

$$4\overline{)38500} = 9625$$

Multiply these numbers by 25.

1 244 **2** 128 **3** 451 **4** 670 **5** 529

4. To multiply by 15.

First, multiply by 10. Next multiply by 5 by finding half of the previous result. Add the two numbers together.

e.g. 596×15

$596 \times 10 = 5960$
$596 \times \ \ 5 = 2980$ (By dividing 5960 by 2.)
$596 \times 15 = 8940$

Multiply these numbers by 15.

1 134 **2** 325 **3** 810 **4** 509 **5** 618

5. To multiply by 99.

Multiply by 100 and then subtract the original number, since 99 = 100 − 1.

e.g. 186 × 99

$$\begin{array}{rr} 186 \times 100 = & 18600 \\ - & 186 \\ \hline & 18414 \end{array}$$

(subtracting the original number)

Multiply these numbers by 99.

1 528 **2** 481 **3** 370 **4** 239 **5** 112

6. **Multiplication practice**

Write down 143.
Then choose any 2-figure number to multiply it by.
Multiply that result by 7.
By investigation, can you discover the connection between the number you chose and the final answer ?

Other methods for division

7. You may prefer to do division using rectangles. The answer is the sum of the numbers at the side of the rectangle.

e.g. 312 ÷ 13

	13
10	130
10	130
4	52
24	Answer

$$\begin{array}{r} 312 \\ \underline{130} \\ 182 \\ \underline{130} \\ 52 \\ \underline{52} \\ 0 \end{array}$$

13 × 10 = 130. Subtract 130 twice, leaving 52.
13 × 4 = 52.

So 312 ÷ 13 = 24

$952 \div 34$

	34
10	340
10	340
5	170
2	68
1	34
28 Answer	

$$\begin{array}{r} 952 \\ \underline{340} \\ 512 \\ \underline{340} \\ 272 \\ \underline{170} \\ 102 \\ \underline{68} \\ 34 \\ \underline{34} \\ 0 \end{array}$$

$34 \times \underline{10} = 340$. Subtract 340 twice, leaving 272.
$34 \times \underline{5} = \frac{1}{2}$ of $340 = 170$. Subtract 170, leaving 102.
$34 \times \underline{2} = 68$. Subtract 68, leaving 34.
$34 \times \underline{1} = 34$.

So $952 \div 34 = 28$.

Try some of the questions from Exercise 2.4 again using the rectangle method, and if you prefer to use it make up other questions for practice, and then check the answers on your calculator.

8. If you have to divide by a number which has 1-figure factors, such as 48 which has factors 6×8, you can use another method.

   e.g. $912 \div 48 = (912 \div 6) \div 8$

   First divide 912 by 6, and then divide the answer by 8.

   $6\overline{)912}$
   $8\overline{)152}$
   $\underline{19}$ Answer

   Practise this method with these questions.

   1 $832 \div 32$ $(32 = 4 \times 8)$
   2 $684 \div 36$
   3 $621 \div 27$
   4 $882 \div 49$
   5 $765 \div 45$

9. If you have to divide by 25, because 25 is one-quarter of 100, you can multiply by 4 and then divide by 100.

e.g. $675 \div 25 = (675 \times 4) \div 100$
$= 2700 \div 100$
$= 27$

$123 \div 25 = (123 \times 4) \div 100$
$= 492 \div 100$
$= 4.92$

Divide these numbers by 25, giving the answers correct to 2 decimal places as shown in the example if they do not divide exactly.

1 525 **2** 375 **3** 450 **4** 836 **5** 912

Number patterns

10. Copy and complete this number pattern to the line which includes +0.

$0 \times 9 + 8 = 8$
$9 \times 9 + 7 = 88$
$98 \times 9 + 6 =$
$987 \times 9 + 5 =$
...

11. Copy and complete this number pattern to the line which begins with 90×100.

$(10 \times 20 + 21) \div 13 =$
$(20 \times 30 + 21) \div 23 =$
$(30 \times 40 + 21) \div 33 =$
...

Chapter 2 test

Work out the answers to these questions without using your calculator.

1. If Helena cycles on average 40 km a day for 60 days, how far does she ride altogether ?

2. A carton holds 30 tins.
   1 How many tins are there in 20 cartons ?
   2 How many cartons must be used to pack 480 tins ?

3. Find the total cost of 145 books at £9 each.

4. 322 kg of brass is melted down and used to make brass models each weighing 7 kg. How many models can be made ?

Show your working in questions 5 to 8.

5. From Doncaster to London is 159 miles by road. Peter makes the return journey once each month. How many miles in a year is this ?

6. A train takes 392 passengers on an excursion. They have paid £18 each. How much have they paid altogether ?

7. Two numbers multiplied together make 832 and one of the numbers is 26. Find the other number.

8. How many containers, each holding 13 litres of liquid, can be filled from a tank containing 500 litres, and how much liquid will be left over ?

PUZZLES

1. If it takes 3 minutes to boil 2 eggs, how long will it take to boil 4 eggs ?

2. Four forms had two representatives each, and had to send one representative to each of three meetings.
   At the 1st meeting, Adam (from 7P), Bimal (from 7Q), Carole (from 7R) and Davina (from 7S) attended.
   At the second meeting, Edward, Bimal, Francis and Davina were present.
   At the third meeting, Adam, Edward, Bimal and Gillian were present.
   (Heidi could not attend any of the meetings as she was ill.)
   Find the names of the second representatives from each form.

3 Thinking about using a calculator

Calculating instruments

The pictures show calculating instruments. You are lucky in having one of the latest models, unknown 30 years ago.

Calculators save a lot of time, so you can spend the time saved on doing more interesting Mathematics.

You may have a simple calculator. This has only a few keys, and is very easy to use for straightforward calculations.

A scientific calculator has many more function keys and it is needed for more advanced mathematical work.

Your teacher will tell you which type of calculator is more suitable for you to use at the present time.

A Chinese abacus, which is an ancient calculating instrument, still in use nowadays.
Did you ever use a similar counting frame ?

Engineers may still use slide rules. Logarithm tables were used in schools, for calculating, until very recently.

An old adding machine

Name some of the uses of present-day computers.

One of the first computers, in Moscow in 1955. Notice how huge it was. It could perform about 7500 arithmetical operations per second.

3 Using a calculator

What a wonderful little machine this is ! Maybe you have a fairly simple calculator, which will do addition, subtraction, multiplication and division, and probably find square roots as well, or maybe you have a scientific calculator which seems quite complicated.

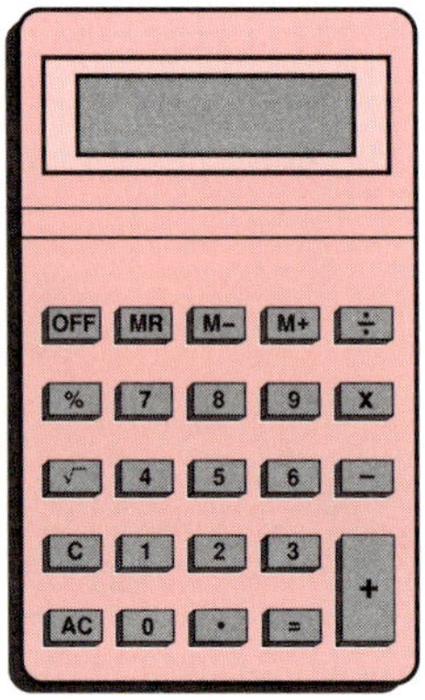

Simple calculator

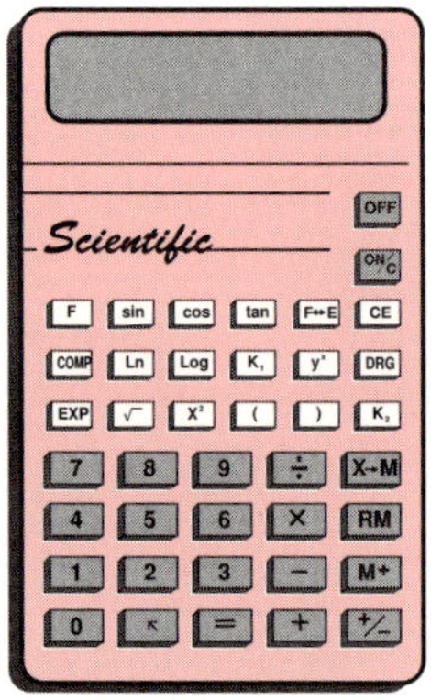

Scientific calculator

Make sure your calculator is working properly, and learn how to use it.
Not all calculators work in the same way.

It is advisable to start every new calculation by pressing the [C] key (for CLEAR), but you may find that on your calculator this is unnecessary if you have just pressed the [=] key.

Read the instruction booklet for your own calculator and try the examples shown there. You may find that there are quicker ways than you normally use to do some calculations.

Checking calculator answers

It is easy to get a wrong answer using a calculator by pressing the wrong keys, so look at the answer and see if it seems right.
You could also do the calculation twice, possibly entering the numbers in reverse order, to see if you get the same result.

Check the size of the answer

$5813 + 1967$
The numbers are approximately 6000 and 2000.
The answer should be approximately $6000 + 2000 = 8000$.
(The exact answer is 7780.)

5813×2
The answer should be approximately $6000 \times 2 = 12\,000$.
(The exact answer is 11 626.)

$5813 - 1967$
The answer should be approximately $6000 - 2000 = 4000$.
(The exact answer is 3846.)

$5813 \div 2$
The answer should be approximately $6000 \div 2 = 3000$.
(The exact answer is 2906.5.)

Check the units figure

$5813 + 1967$
The units figures are 3 and 7.
$3 + 7 = 10$ so the units figure in the answer should be 0.
(The answer is 7780.)

13×67
$3 \times 7 = 21$ so the units figure in the answer should be 1.
(The answer is 871.)

$5813 - 1967$
You cannot use $3 - 7$ so use $13 - 7 = 6$ and the units figure in the answer should be 6.
(The answer is 3846.)

You cannot do a similar check for division.

Check by doing the reverse operation

To check $5813 - 1967 = 3846$, do the calculation $3846 + 1967$ and you will get 5813.
To check $5813 \div 2 = 2906.5$, do the calculation 2906.5×2 and you will get 5813.

Exercise 3.1

1. Use your calculator to find the answers to the following.

1	$1424 + 1086 + 243 + 573$	**6**	$5328 \div 148$
2	$587 - 367$	**7**	$5236 + 408 - 3865$
3	325×1068	**8**	3415×99
4	$24\,650 \div 425$	**9**	$2873 \div 13$
5	229×28	**10**	$2000 - 528 - 659 - 715$

2. By using approximate values, estimate answers for these calculations. Then find the correct answers, using your calculator.

1	2873 − 1235	**6**	49 × 61
2	26 931 − 4188	**7**	495 ÷ 22
3	6009 − 3246 + 1896	**8**	62 × 52 × 42
4	514 × 83	**9**	817 ÷ 38
5	1764 ÷ 63	**10**	72 × 416 ÷ 104

3. Say what the units figure will be in each of these calculations. Then do the questions on your calculator, checking that the units figures are correct.

1	132 + 250 + 379	**4**	685 × 52
2	2103 − 519	**5**	775 − 696 + 317
3	324 × 89		

4. Use your calculator to find the numbers represented by □ in these statements. Then repeat each calculation in its normal order to check your answer.

1	□ + 225 = 1030.	**6**	850 − □ = 490
2	□ × 17 = 221	**7**	124 × □ = 1364
3	□ − 53 = 127	**8**	1368 ÷ □ = 152
4	□ ÷ 24 = 15	**9**	□ + 54 = 166 ÷ 2
5	1967 + □ = 1990	**10**	51 × □ = 264 + 93

5. Subtract the smallest number of the following from the largest number.

26 581 28 561 26 851 28 615 26 518 28 651

6. The answer to 384 × 97 is one of the following numbers. Without using your calculator, decide which is the correct answer.

36 249 3248 37 249 37 248 370 248

7. What is the total cost of 3 dozen chairs at £57 each ?

8. A man walks for 1 km (100 000 cm).
If the length of his step is 83 cm,
how many steps does he take ?
Give your answer to the nearest 10 steps.

9. How many fence posts will be needed for a straight length of 910 m, if the posts are placed 14 m apart ?

10. Write down any two numbers less than 100, one underneath the other.
Add them together and write the sum underneath the second number.
Add up all these three numbers together and write the sum underneath the third number.
Add up all the four numbers together and write the sum underneath the fourth number.
Continue similarly until you have 9 numbers altogether.
Divide the 9th number by the 3rd number. What is your answer ?

To find the square of a number

To find 13^2.

You can press 13 [×] 13 [=] (and you will get 169).

Try pressing 13 [×] [=] (and if you get 169, this works on your calculator and is quicker).

If there is a key [x^2], press 13 [x^2].

To find the square root of a number

To find the square root of 169, press 169 [√] (and you will get 13).

If you find the square root of a number on your calculator and the result is not an exact whole number then the original number is not a square number.

To find the cube of a number

To find 7^3.

You can press 7 [×] 7 [×] 7 [=] and you will get 343.

Try pressing 7 [×] [x^2] [=] or 7 [×] [=] [=] (and if you get 343, this works on your calculator and is quicker).

If there is a key [y^x], then here $y = 7$ and $x = 3$. Press 7 [y^x] 3 [=].

To find the remainder in a division sum

e.g. 79 ÷ 19.

Press 79 [÷] 19 [=] getting 4.157... So 19 divided into 79 goes 4 times.

Method 1

Now find out what 4 × 19 equals.
4 × 19 = 76 and 79 − 76 = 3, so the remainder is 3.

Method 2

Leaving the answer on your calculator, subtract 4 and press [=].
This leaves 0.157 ...
Multiply this decimal by 19 and this gives 3. This is the remainder.
Due to rounding errors on the calculator, instead of getting 3 exactly you might get something like 3.0000001 or 2.9999999. Count either of these as 3.

Exercise 3.2

1. Use your calculator to find
   1 the squares of 25, 52, 106, 111.
   2 the square roots of 676, 961, 2025, 7744,
   3 the cubes of 11, 53, 64, 95.

2. Find the values of

   1 47^2
   2 $\sqrt{1024}$
   3 28^3
   4 $\sqrt{529} + \sqrt{169}$
   5 $15^3 - 15^2$

3. Which of these numbers are not square numbers ?
   Give the square roots of the numbers which **are** square numbers.

   1 476
   2 576
   3 676
   4 776
   5 15 376

4. Do these division questions using your calculator. Find the answer and the remainder, if any.

   1 $300 \div 9$
   2 $8164 \div 17$
   3 $1800 \div 28$
   4 $610 \div 45$
   5 $708 \div 12$

5. Copy and complete this number pattern to the row which begins 1×9^2.

   $9 \times 1^2 + 1^3 = 10 = 1^2 \times 10$
   $8 \times 2^2 + 2^3 = 40 = 2^2 \times 10$
   $7 \times 3^2 + 3^3 = \dots$
   $\dots$

6. Multiply the sum of 65 and 25 by their difference. Then find the value of $65^2 - 25^2$. What do you notice ? Try this for other pairs of numbers.

7. Find the least number which must be added to 800 so that the sum will divide exactly by 52.

The memory keys

You can store a number in the calculator by using the memory keys.

[M +] puts a number into the memory, or adds a number to any number already stored in the memory.

[M −] subtracts a number from the number stored in the memory.

[MR] or [R.CM] displays the number stored in the memory.

To cancel the memory press [MR] [M −] or [MC].

If the memory is cleared then [MR] will display 0.

(Your calculator might have different keys. Refer to the instruction book if necessary.)

Mixed questions and brackets

If someone says to you '6 plus 4 multiplied by 5', what would be your answer ?
It depends on whether they mean

6 + 4 worked out, then multiplied by 5;

or

6 plus the answer to 4 multiplied by 5.

In a written question it can be made absolutely clear by using brackets.
The part in brackets must be worked out first.

$(6 + 4) \times 5 = 10 \times 5 = 50$
$6 + (4 \times 5) = 6 + 20 = 26$
$8 \times (10 - 6) = 8 \times 4 = 32$
$30 \div (3 + 2) = 30 \div 5 = 6$
$(15 + 40) \div 5 = 55 \div 5 = 11$

If the question was written without brackets, then we would have to have a rule to use.
Our rule is that:

1 brackets must be worked out first,
2 multiplication and division are worked out next,
3 addition and subtraction are worked out last.

So $6 + 4 \times 5$ means the same as $6 + (4 \times 5)$, since if there are no brackets, multiplication must be done before addition.

$8 \times 10 - 6 = (8 \times 10) - 6 = 80 - 6 = 74$
$30 \div 3 + 2 = (30 \div 3) + 2 = 10 + 2 = 12$
$15 + 40 \div 5 = 15 + (40 \div 5) = 15 + 8 = 23$

A fraction line can also act as a bracket.

$\frac{30}{3 + 2}$ means $30 \div (3 + 2) = 30 \div 5 = 6$.

$\frac{15 + 40}{5}$ means $(15 + 40) \div 5 = 55 \div 5 = 11$.

Be careful when you use your calculator for mixed operations

There are different methods for the two types of calculator. Enter 6 [+] 4 [×] 5 [=] and you will get either of the answers 26 or 50. If you get the answer 26, read the first set of instructions. It is probably a scientific calculator. If you get the answer 50, read the instructions for a simpler calculator.

Scientific calculators, or those giving the answer 26.

The calculator will treat 6 [+] 4 [×] 5 [=] as $6 + (4 \times 5)$ and give the answer 26.
Try 15 [+] 40 [÷] 5 [=] and it will treat it as $15 + (40 \div 5)$ and give the answer 23. In other words, it keeps to the rules and does multiplication and division as if they were in brackets, and there is no need to use brackets round them.
But, if you really intend it to do $(6 + 4) \times 5$ or $(15 + 40) \div 5$, you must either use brackets, which you will find on your calculator, **or** work out the answer to the bracket by pressing [=] before carrying on.

So press [(] 6 [+] 4 [)] [×] 5 [=] or 6 [+] 4 [=] [×] 5 [=],

and [(] 15 [+] 40 [)] [÷] 5 [=] or 15 [+] 40 [=] [÷] 5 [=].

Simpler calculators, or those giving the answer 50.

The calculator is reading all the operations in the order in which you enter them.
So for 6 [+] 4 [×] 5 [=] it will do it as if it was $(6 + 4) \times 5$ and give the answer 50, and for 15 [+] 40 [÷] 5 [=] it will read it as $(15 + 40) \div 5$ and give the answer 11.
But, if you really want to do $6 + (4 \times 5)$ then either turn it round to do $(4 \times 5) + 6$ which it will do properly, or press 6 and put it into the memory, then work out 4×5 and add this to the memory. Then press [MR] for the complete answer.
This is 6 [M+] 4 [×] 5 [=] [M+] [MR] and you will get the answer 26.
Now cancel the memory before you forget !

Exercise 3.3

1. Find the answers to these questions without using your calculator.
   Then repeat the questions using your calculator, making sure that you get the same results.

1 $(5 \times 3) - 2$
2 $(8 - 2) \times 4$
3 $17 - (3 \times 4)$
4 $12 \times (5 - 2)$
5 $36 \div (5 + 4)$
6 $(36 \div 4) + 5$
7 $(23 + 7) \div 6$
8 $18 - (12 \div 6)$
9 $(9 \times 8) - (7 \times 6)$
10 $12 + (3 \times 5) - 2$

2. By using approximate values, estimate answers for these calculations. Then find the correct answers, using your calculator.

1	$119 + (11 \times 19)$	**6**	$671 \div (23 + 38)$
2	$39^2 - 22 \times 28$	**7**	$(52 \times 118) + (28 \times 82)$
3	$(228 - 52) \times 17$	**8**	$48^2 - 31 \times 29$
4	$33 + (8 \times 11) - 13$	**9**	$(18 + 49) \times 3 \times 7$
5	$\frac{23 + 89}{32 - 18}$	**10**	$(128 + 87) \div 43$

3. 15 plots of land each of area 263 m^2 are sold from a total estate of 4000 m^2. How much land remains unsold ?

4. A rectangular piece of ground, 50 m long and 26 m wide, is to be surrounded by a fence. If the fencing costs £14 per metre, find the total cost.

5. £843 is divided among 15 people. One person gets £6 more than each of the others. How much do they each get ?

6. A bag of 50 pence coins weighs 950 g. How much are the contents worth, if the bag weighs 5 g and two 50 pence coins together weigh 27 g ?

Exercise 3.4 Applications and Activities

1. **The constant function**

If you want to repeat an operation several times, there is a method you can use to simplify the process.
For example, if you want to add 16 to several numbers in turn then you are using the function 'add 16'.

Using a simple calculator

Press [1st number] [+] 16 [=].
Then press [2nd number] [=],
[3rd number] [=],
and so on.

A similar method works if you want to subtract a number or divide by a number, several times.
For multiplication (by 16) you have to press
16 [×] [1st number] [=] [2nd number] [=] [3rd number] [=]...

Using a scientific calculator

To add 16 to several numbers in turn, press
16 [+] [+] [1st number] [=] [2nd number] [=] [3rd number] [=] ...

To subtract 16 from several numbers in turn, begin by pressing 16 [−] [−].

To multiply by 16, begin by pressing 16 [×] [×].

To divide by 16, begin by pressing 16 [÷] [÷].

If these methods do not work with your calculator, try to discover similar methods. You may have to use the key labelled k.

Use your calculator to work out these questions, using the constant function method.

1 Start with these numbers:

28 56 77 105 294

(1) Add 215 to each number,
(2) subtract 8 from each number,
(3) multiply each number by 15,
(4) divide each number by 7.

2 Find how much these people earn in a year (52 weeks).

(1) Mrs Clarke earns £160 per week,
(2) Mr Clarke earns £225 per week,
(3) Jayne Clarke earns £84 per week,
(4) Patsy Clarke earns £26 per week, doing part-time work,
(5) Bobby Clarke earns £7 per week, doing a paper round.

3 There are 1760 yards in a mile. How many miles are there in these distances ?

(1) 5280 yards
(2) 21 120 yards
(3) 61 600 yards
(4) 35 200 yards
(5) 86 240 yards

2. **Making number patterns with your calculator**

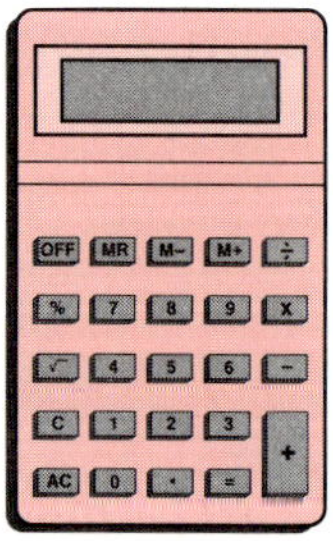

Press 2 [×] [=] [=] [=] ... and see what you get.
(On some calculators you may have to press
2 [×] [×] [=] [=] [=] ..., or use the key marked k.)

Try 7 [+] [=] [=] [=] ... (or 7 [+] [+] [=] [=] [=] ...).

Try 1 [+] 7 [=] [=] [=] ... (or 7 [+] [+] 1 [=] [=] [=] ...).

Try 100 [−] 6 [=] [=] [=] ... (or 6 [−] [−] 100 [=] [=] [=] ...).

Investigate to find other patterns.

3. **Squares of numbers**

Can you discover a number pattern involving the squares of numbers from 50 to 59 ?

number	square
50	25 ¦ 00
51	26 ¦ 01
...	

You could then investigate the squares of numbers from 41 to 49.

4. **Numbers, squares and cubes**

Copy and complete this table.

1 Is there any pattern in the unit figures in the squares column ?

2 Is there any pattern in the unit figures in the cubes column?

(It would be useful to memorise some of these results.)

number	square	cube
1	1	1
2	4	8
3	9	
⋮		
10		

5. **Sixes and sevens**

Use your calculator to find the squares of 7, 67, 667 and 6667.
Using the pattern of your answers, copy and complete this number pattern.

$7^2 =$
$67^2 =$
$667^2 =$
$6667^2 =$
$66667^2 =$
$666667^2 =$

6. **Triangular numbers**

Work out the first 10 triangular numbers.
Copy and complete this pattern using these triangular numbers, up to the 9th row.

$(\text{2nd number})^2 - (\text{1st number})^2 = 9 - 1 = 8 = 2^3$
$(\text{3rd number})^2 - (\text{2nd number})^2 = \ldots$
$(\text{4th number})^2 - (\text{3rd number})^2 =$
...

7. **Magic squares**

Rearrange these numbers so that each row, each column and each diagonal add up to 15.
(Leave 5 in the centre.)

1	2	3
4	5	6
7	8	9

In the magic square, find the sum of the squares of the numbers in the 1st row and of the numbers in the 3rd row; and also the sum of the squares of the numbers in the 1st column and of the numbers in the 3rd column.
Comment on these answers.

Copy and complete this magic square which uses numbers 1 to 16.
All rows, columns and the main diagonals add up to 34.

			12
3	16		
15	4	14	

In the magic square, find the sum of the squares of the numbers in each row and in each column. Then find the sum of the squares of the numbers in the first two rows together, the last two rows together, the first two columns together, and the last two columns together.
Comment on the answers.

Chapter 3 test

You may use your calculator in this test.

1. Write down all the different 3-figure numbers which can be made using all the three figures 4, 7, 9.
   Find the sum of these numbers.

2. The mileage readings on a car at the beginning and end of a year were 5476 and 21389. How far did the car travel in the year ?

3. What is the total weekly wage bill for 137 workers who are each paid £178 per week ?

4. A sheet of A4 paper is 210 mm wide and 297 mm long. The paper is to be ruled into squares. If each square is 15 mm wide, how many squares are there along the top row ? How many rows of squares are there ? What are the measurements of the small strip of paper left at the bottom of the sheet ?

5. Instead of writing down $(10+6)\times(3+7)$, Stephen wrote down $10+(6\times 3)+7$ by mistake.

1 What is the answer to the correct question ?
2 What is the answer to the question Stephen wrote down ?

6. Find the values of the following.

1 $(6\times 5)+8$
2 $6\times(5+8)$
3 $6+(5\times 8)$
4 $(6+5)\times 8$
5 $6\times 5\times 8$

7. Find the values of the following.

1 $(23+79)\times 187$
2 $(15^3-15)\div 14$
3 $\sqrt{41^2-9^2}$
4 $(57\times 5)+(62\times 2)$
5 $\dfrac{931}{121-72}$

8. Copy and complete this number pattern to the line beginning with 9×30.

$(0\times 30+3\times 9)\times 37=$
$(1\times 30+3\times 8)\times 37=$
$(2\times 30+3\times 7)\times 37=$
. . .

PUZZLE

3. How many mathematical words can you find reading horizontally, vertically or diagonally, in both directions ?

S	T	A	T	I	S	T	I	C	S	Y
N	O	D	R	E	M	I	R	P	A	L
E	Q	U	I	L	A	T	E	R	A	L
T	W	O	A	S	E	R	C	A	S	A
U	E	E	N	D	T	R	T	T	M	C
C	R	N	G	I	D	A	A	D	E	I
A	A	I	L	R	R	E	N	I	T	T
R	U	L	E	R	A	Y	G	C	R	R
E	Q	U	A	L	T	M	L	E	E	E
I	S	O	S	C	E	L	E	S	P	V

4 Thinking about symmetry

Making 'butterflies'

Fold a small piece of paper in half.
Open it up and put a blob of wet paint on one half or on the fold line.
Then fold it again and press hard so that the wet paint is transferred to the other half.
Open it again.

Making doyleys

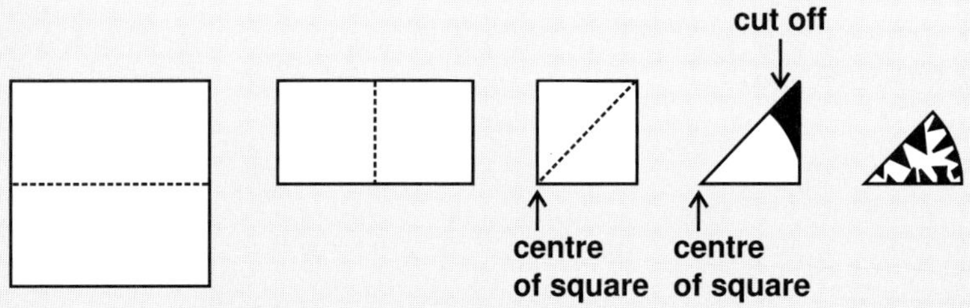

Fold a square piece of paper in half, then in half again, and then cornerways into half again. Cut the edge to make a curve and then cut bits out of all three edges. Open it out.

Letters of the alphabet

Which capital letters in the alphabet have a horizontal axis of symmetry, a vertical axis of symmetry, other axes of symmetry or two axes of symmetry ?
Which letters have rotational symmetry ?
Find some words which have a vertical axis of symmetry, e.g. **MUM**, a horizontal axis of symmetry, e.g. **BED**, rotational symmetry, e.g. **NON**, or words which have a vertical axis of symmetry when written vertically e.g.

M
A
I

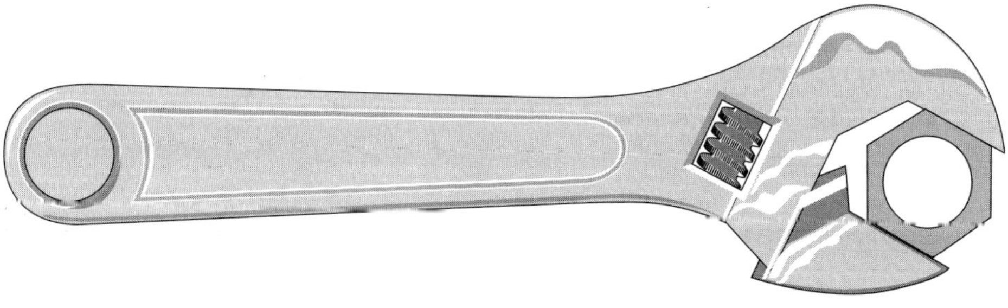

Describe the symmetry of the nut. Why are nuts made symmetrical ?

Compare these three cards and describe their symmetries, ignoring the numbers and letters.

Symmetry around you

Look around you in the room. What examples can you see of symmetrical objects ? List or sketch other examples of symmetrical objects seen in daily life, and say what kind of symmetry they have. Some will be objects found in nature, such as birds, animals, flowers, etc, and others will be man-made objects. Why have the different man-made objects been made symmetrically ? There may be different reasons for different objects. Look for examples of symmetry in art, and in patterns on such things as wallpaper and carpets.

Describe the symmetry of this circular symbol.

4 Symmetry

Axes of symmetry

These diagrams show **axes of symmetry**, marked by dotted lines.

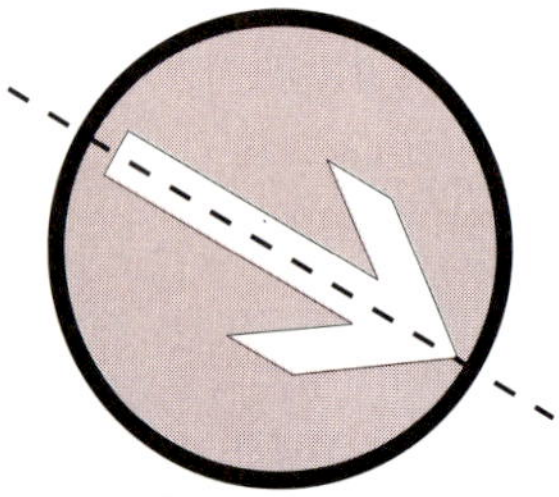

Half of the diagram is a **reflection** of the other half.
If you place a mirror along the axis of symmetry and look into it, you will see the whole shape.
The axis of symmetry can be called a **line of symmetry**, or a **mirror line**.

Some shapes have more than one axis of symmetry.
The plural of axis is axes.

This diagram has 2 axes of symmetry.

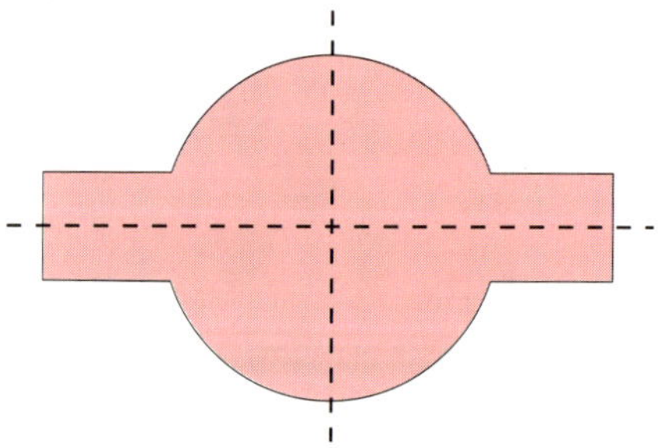

This diagram has 3 axes of symmetry.

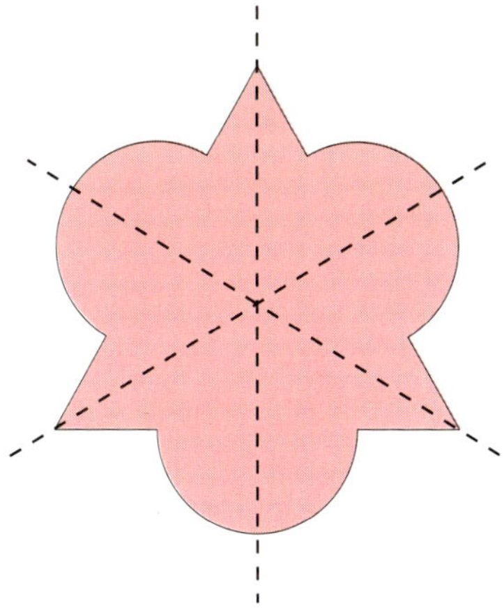

Axes of symmetry for a circle

The diagram shows a diameter of a circle, and it is an axis of symmetry.

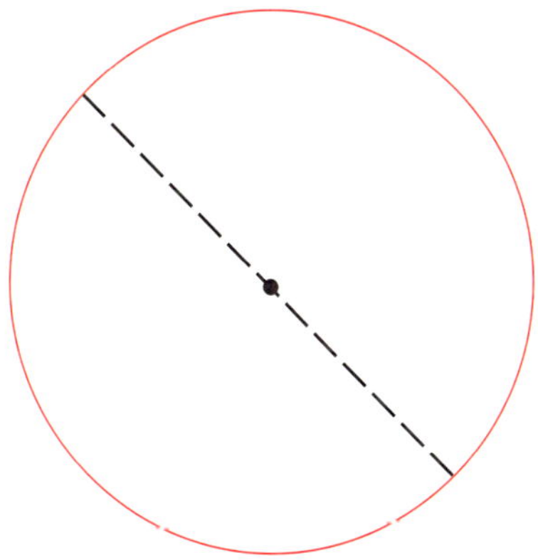

A circle has an **infinite number** of diameters. (This means that if we try to count them we never get to the end of the counting.) They are all axes of symmetry, so a circle has an infinite number of axes of symmetry.

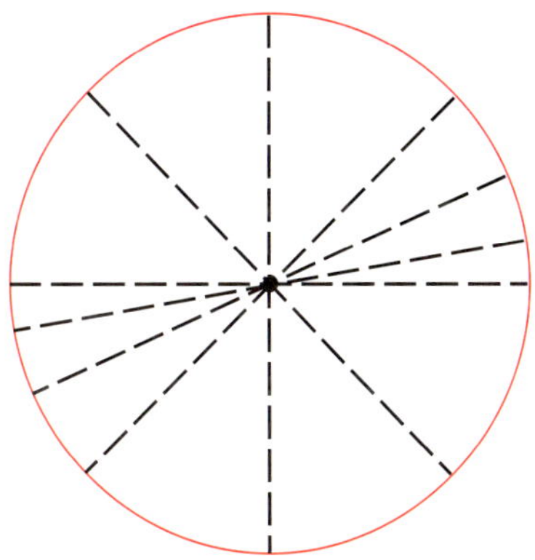

Planes of symmetry

A plane of symmetry slices through a 3-dimensional shape.

If an object is 3-dimensional, its 2-dimensional picture may show an axis of symmetry when it actually has a plane of symmetry.

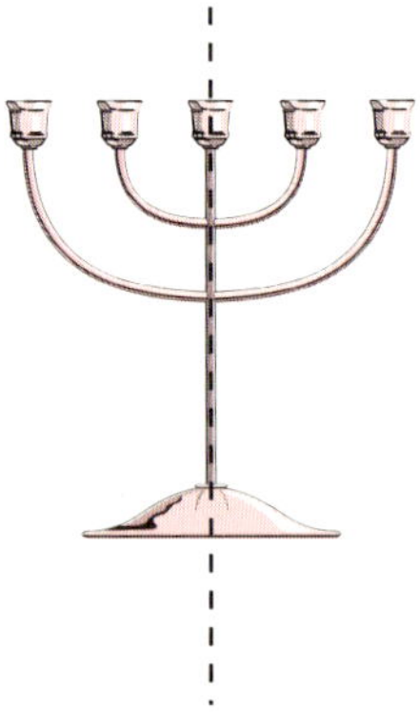

Exercise 4.1

1. Sketch these capital letters and mark in any axes of symmetry.

C N T X

2. Sketch these figures and mark in any axes of symmetry.

1

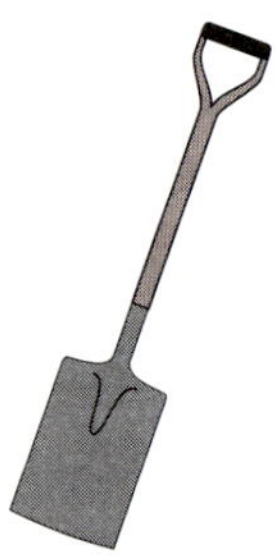

2

3

3. An isosceles triangle has one axis of symmetry. Sketch these triangles or draw them on tracing paper and mark on your diagrams the axes of symmetry. (An isosceles triangle has two equal sides.)

1

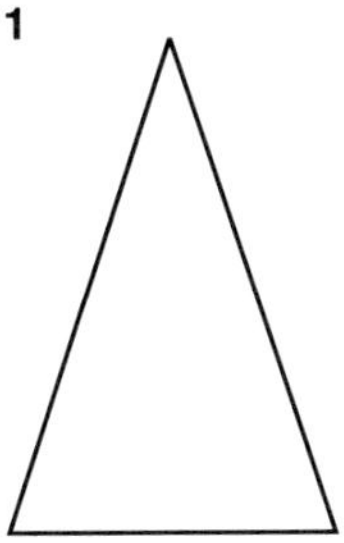

2

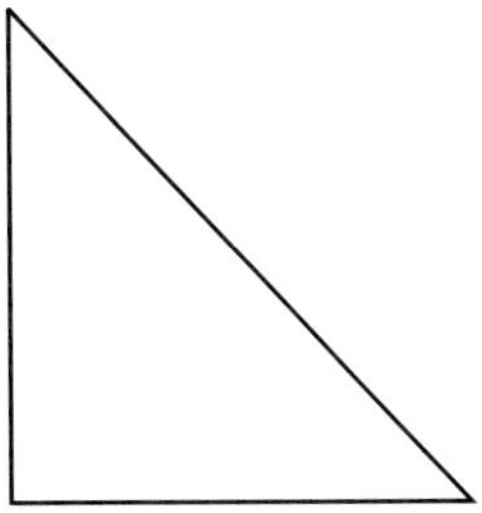

3

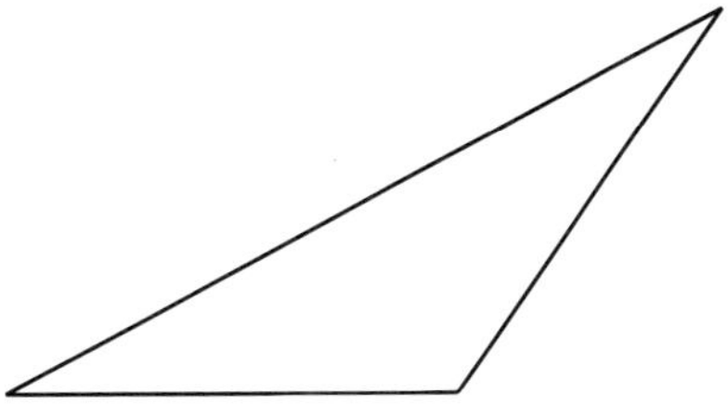

4. An equilateral triangle has 3 axes of symmetry. Sketch these triangles or draw them on tracing paper and mark on your diagrams the axes of symmetry. (An equilateral triangle has all three sides equal.)

1

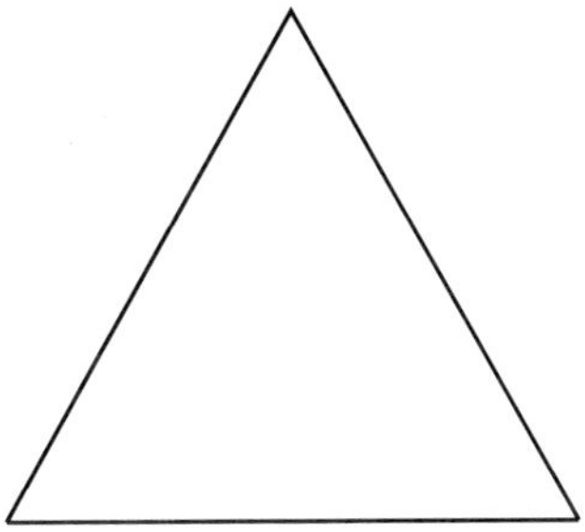

2

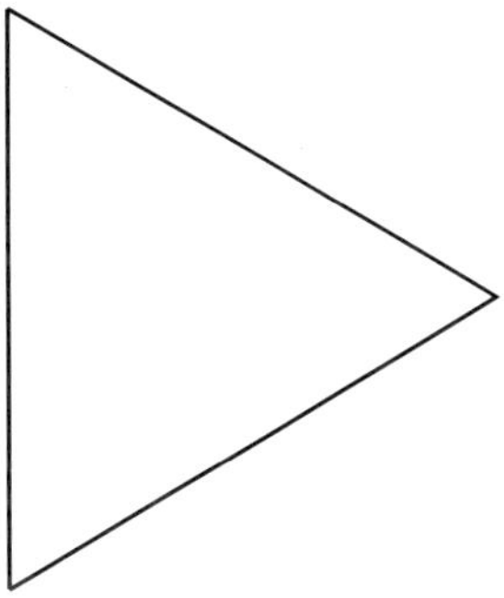

5. Sketch these figures and mark in all axes of symmetry.

1

isosceles trapezium

2

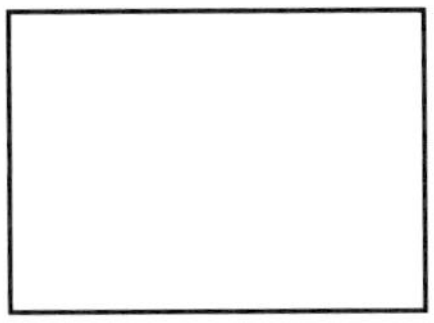

rectangle

3

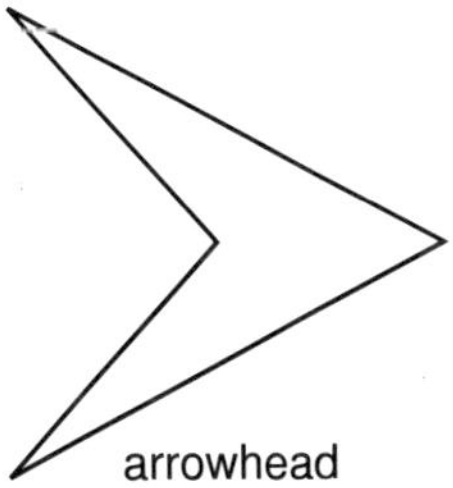

arrowhead

4

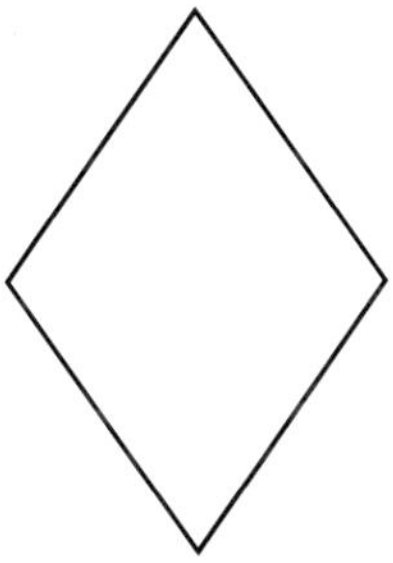

rhombus

5

square

6

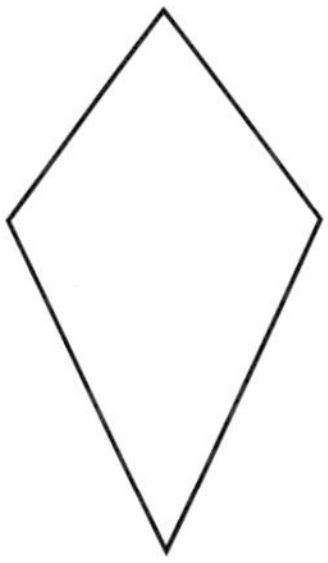

kite

6. These solid figures have planes of symmetry. How many planes of symmetry do they have ?

1

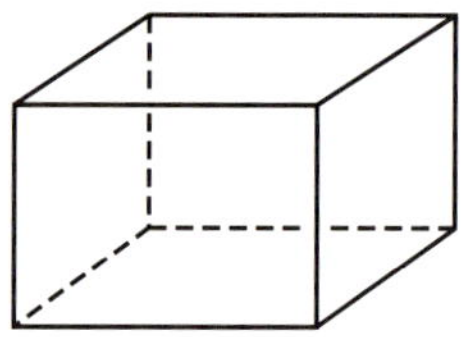

cuboid with all faces rectangular

2

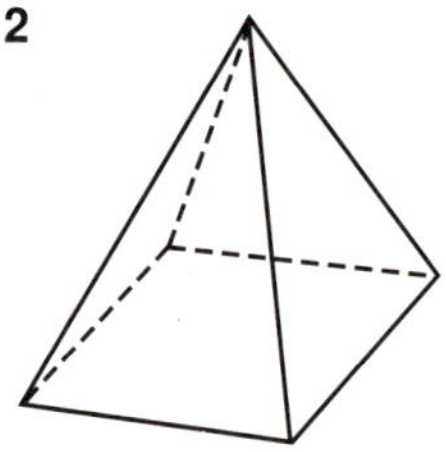

pyramid with square base

3

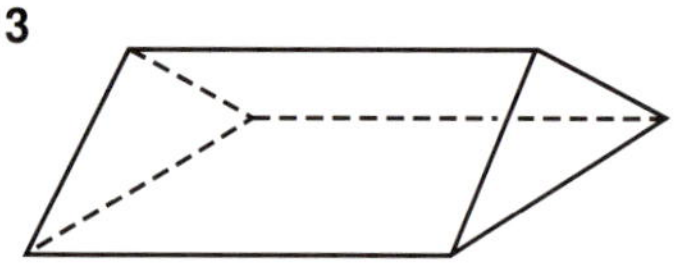

triangular prism (with isosceles triangle ends)

Rotational symmetry

These diagrams have rotational symmetry of order 2. The centre of rotational symmetry is marked by •.

If the object is turned through 180° (a half-turn), its shape is unchanged. (Look at it upside down.)

A 2nd turn brings it back to its original position.

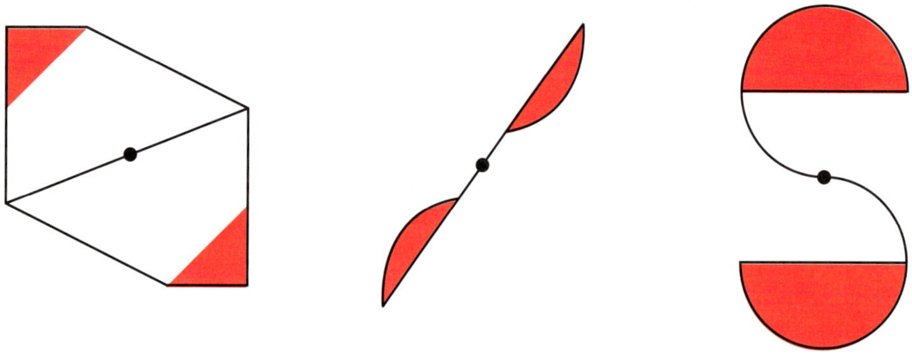

This equilateral triangle has rotational symmetry of order 3.
If it is turned through 120°, and then 120° again, it is unchanged.
A 3rd turn brings it back to its original position.
The • is the centre of rotational symmetry.

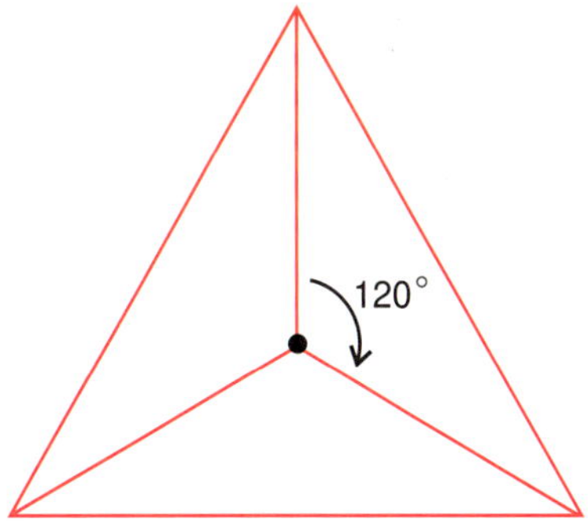

This tile has rotational symmetry of order 4.
It can be turned through 90°, four times and it is unchanged.
The • is the centre of rotational symmetry.

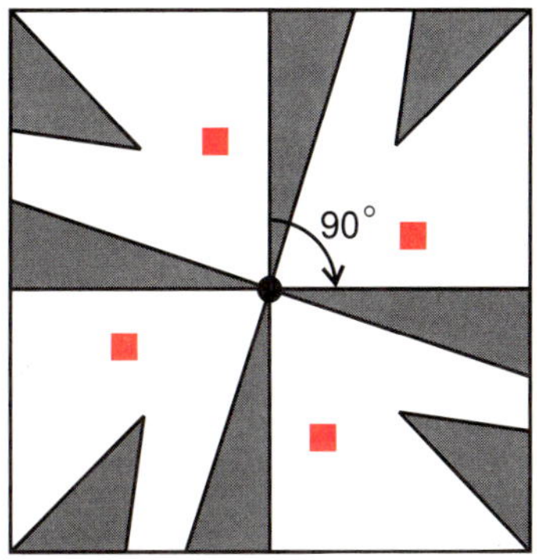

Some figures have axes of symmetry and rotational symmetry.

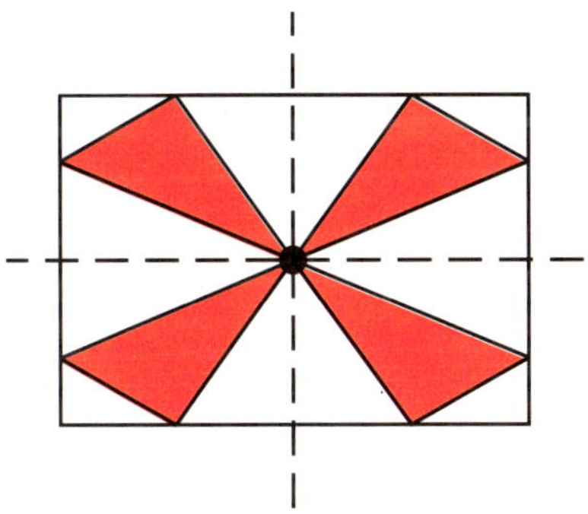

2 axes of symmetry.
Rotational symmetry of order 2.

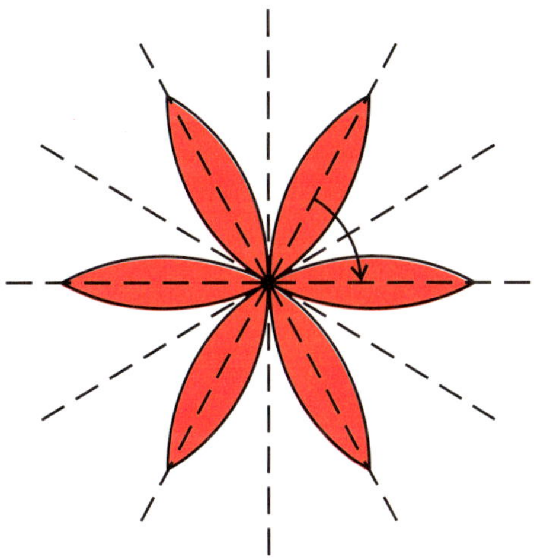

6 axes of symmetry.
Rotational symmetry of order 6.

Exercise 4.2

1. These figures have rotational symmetry about the centre of rotation marked •. State the orders of rotational symmetry.

1

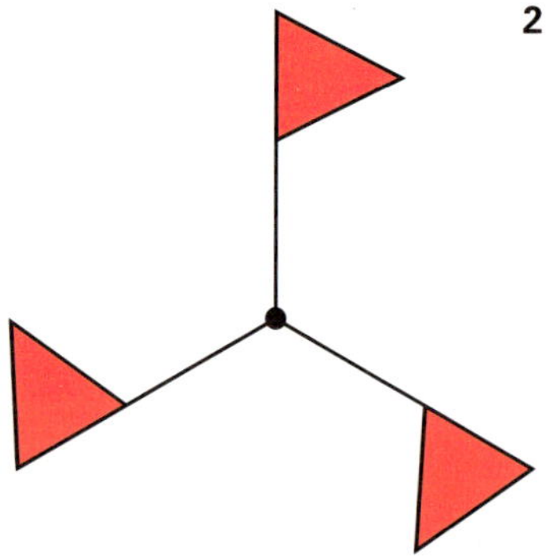

2

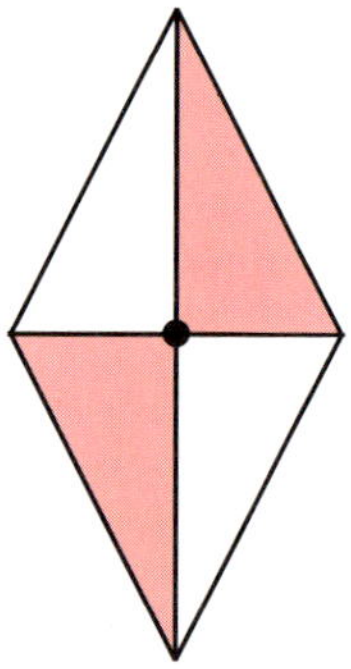

3

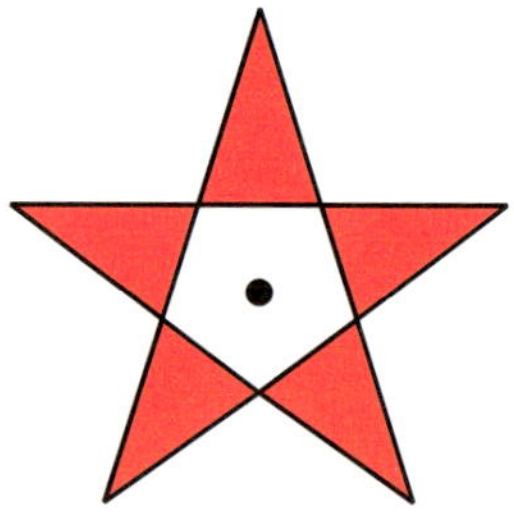

2. Sketch these figures and mark in the centres of rotational symmetry. State the orders of rotational symmetry.

1

rectangle

2

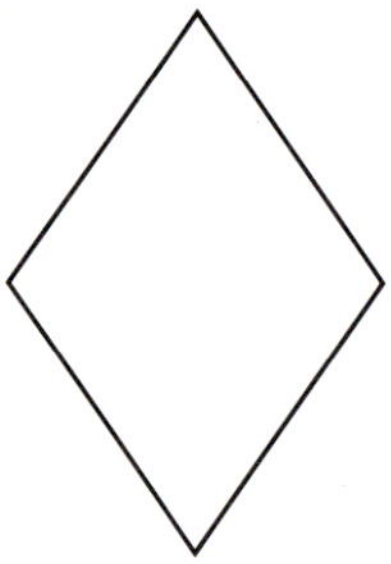

rhombus

3

square

3. Sketch these figures and mark in the centres of rotational symmetry. State the orders of rotational symmetry.

1

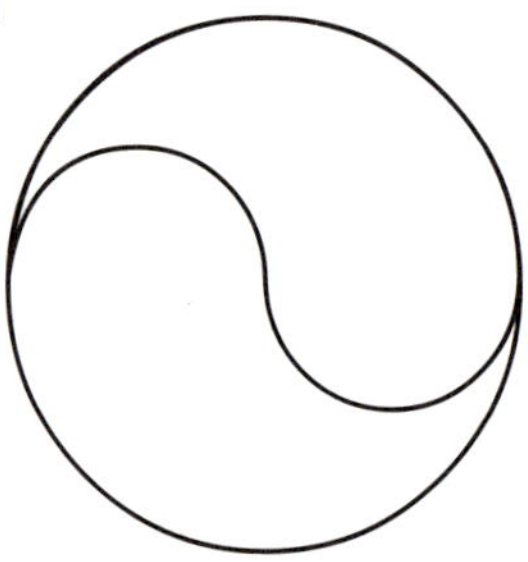

2

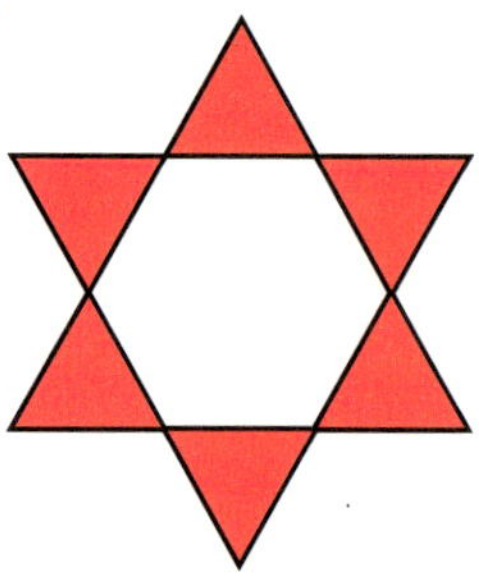

3

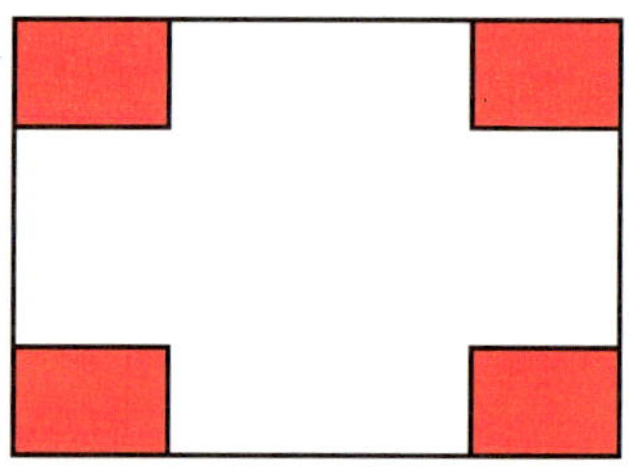

4. For each of these diagrams, state how many axes of symmetry there are.

1

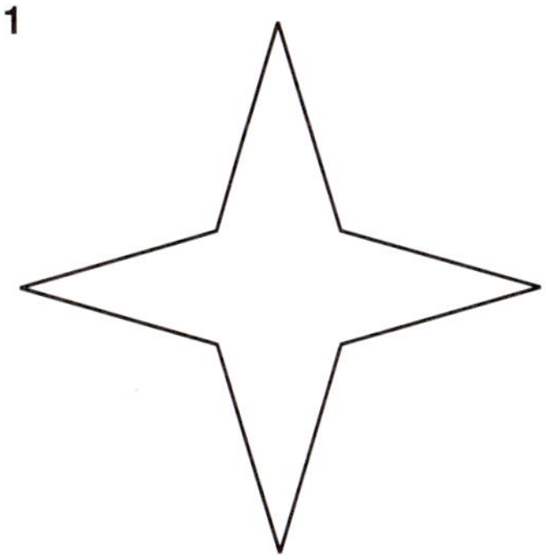

2

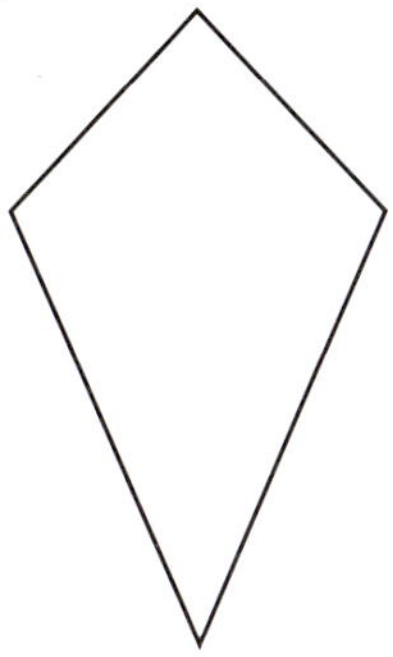

3

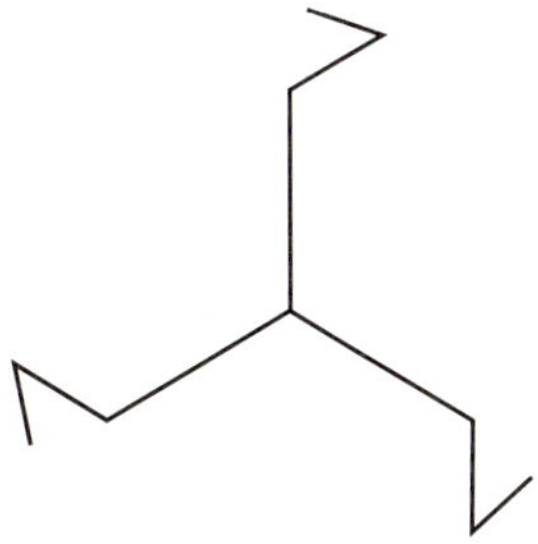

4

5

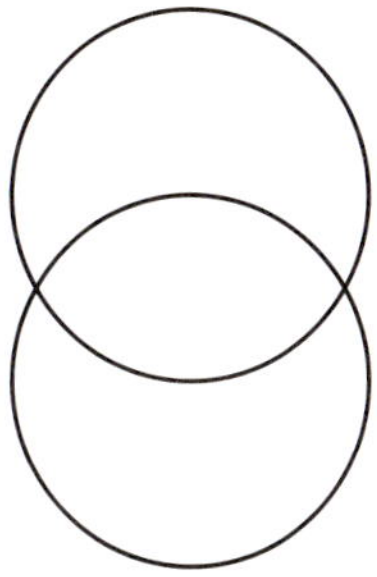

6

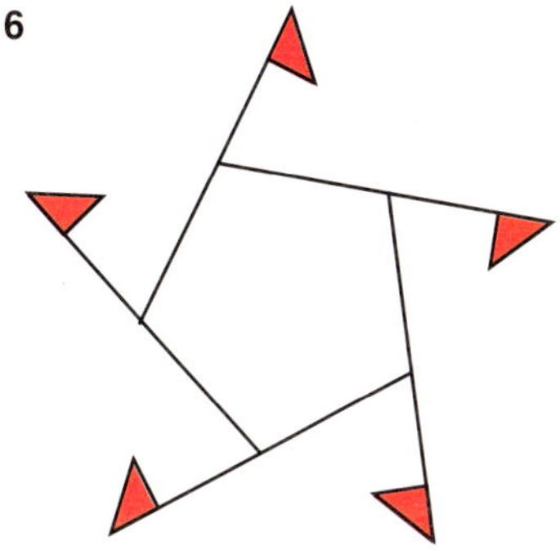

5. Say which of the figures in question 4 have rotational symmetry, and state the order of rotational symmetry.

6. This figure is a parallelogram.
Sketch it.

1 Has it any axes of symmetry ? If so, show them on your sketch.

2 Has it rotational symmetry ? If so, show the centre of rotational symmetry and state the order of rotational symmetry.

7. Begin with 5 squares joined together as shown.
On separate diagrams sketch the figure and add 1 extra square so that the complete figure has

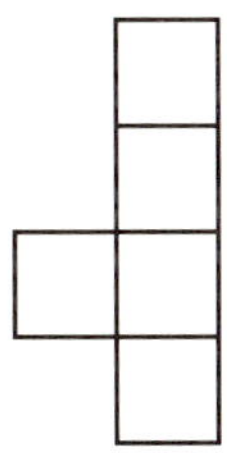

1 an axis of symmetry,

2 a different axis of symmetry to that of part **1**,

3 rotational symmetry of order 2.

8. On 6 separate diagrams, copy and shade the smallest number of squares, so that the pattern has

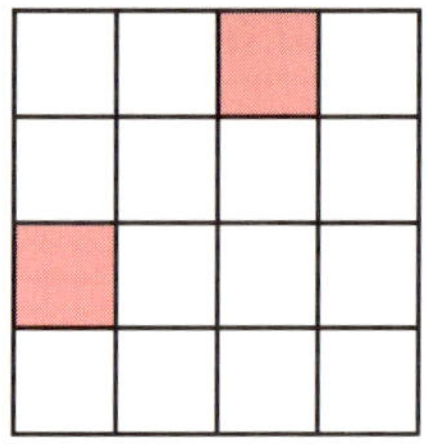

1 a vertical axis of symmetry,
2 a horizontal axis of symmetry,
3 rotational symmetry of order 2,
4 an axis of symmetry along one diagonal of the pattern,
5 an axis of symmetry along the other diagonal of the pattern,
6 2 axes of symmetry along both diagonals.
In this diagram, how many axes of symmetry are there altogether? What is the order of rotational symmetry?

Exercise 4.3 Applications and Activities

1. **Symmetrical patterns**

Here is one quarter of a symmetrical pattern. Copy it and complete the other three quarters so that the dotted lines are axes of symmetry.

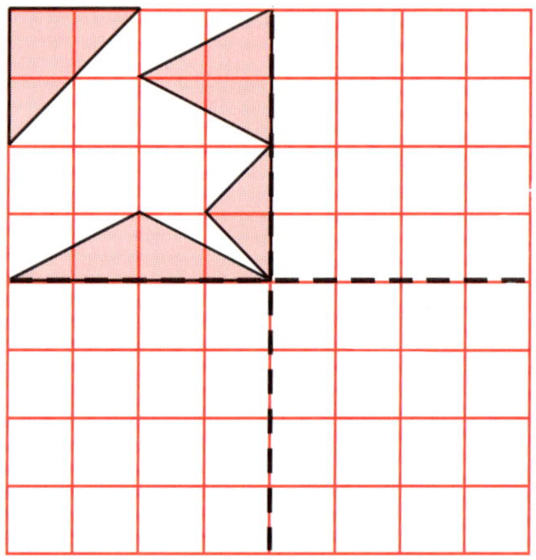

2. **Calculator displays**

Look at the figures produced on a calculator display. Ignore the fact that they may be slightly slanted,

e.g. regard 8 as  rather than 

1 Which figures have a horizontal line of symmetry?
2 Which figures have a vertical line of symmetry?
3 Which figures have rotational symmetry?
4 Which two-figure numbers have a horizontal line of symmetry?
5 Which two-figure numbers have a vertical line of symmetry?
6 Which two-figure numbers have rotational symmetry?

You can also investigate three-figure or four-figure numbers.

3. Drawing symmetrical patterns

Begin with a symmetrical figure such as an equilateral triangle, square or circle. In this equilateral triangle the mid-points and quarter-way points were marked. By joining these a pattern is formed.

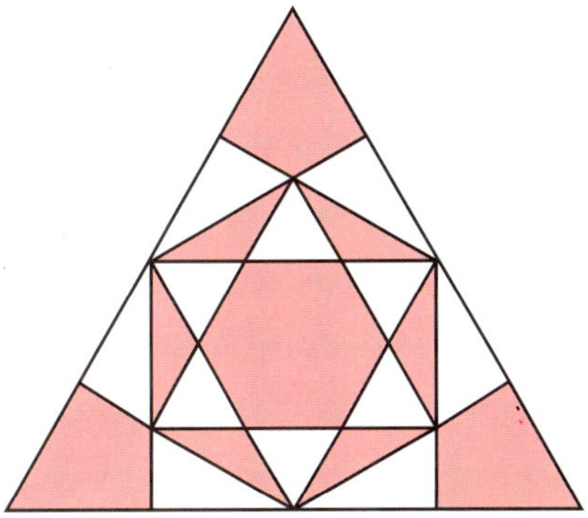

You can use isometric paper to draw the equilateral triangle.

This is a similar idea, starting with a square. Points are marked $\frac{1}{3}$ and $\frac{2}{3}$ of the way along each side of the square.

You can use a piece of squared paper divided into 4 quarters. Draw a design in the 1st quarter and then complete the pattern so that there are two axes of symmetry.

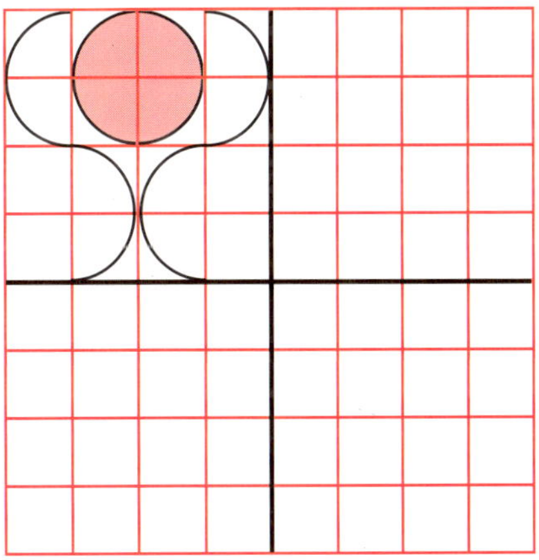

Here are some symmetrical patterns originally drawn on isometric paper.

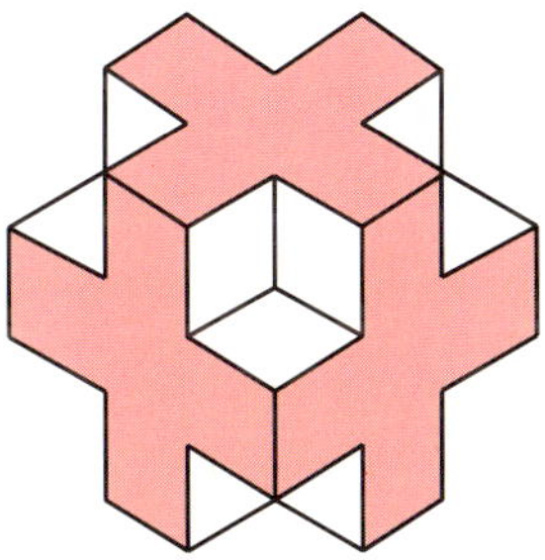

4. **Flags**

Has the Union Jack a symmetrical design ?

If you have a chart of the national flags of several countries, you can study the symmetry of the designs. You can list those which have 1 axis of symmetry or 2 axes of symmetry, and which have rotational symmetry.

You can also look separately at the symmetry of some of the symbols on the flags, which include crosses, stars, crescents, the sun, crowns, etc.

Chapter 4 test

1. Copy and complete the figure so that PQ is a line of symmetry.

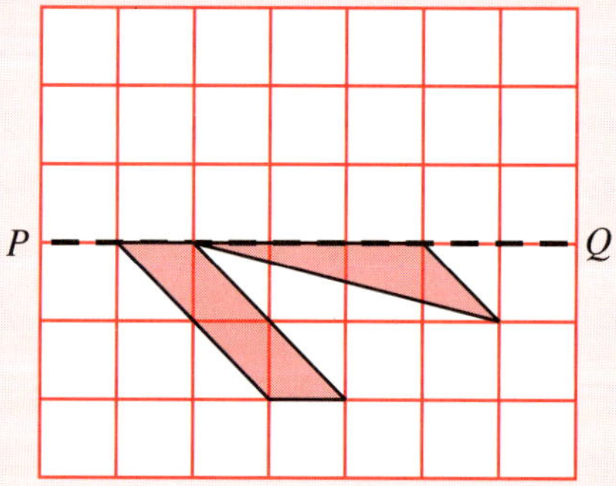

2. Look at these diagrams.

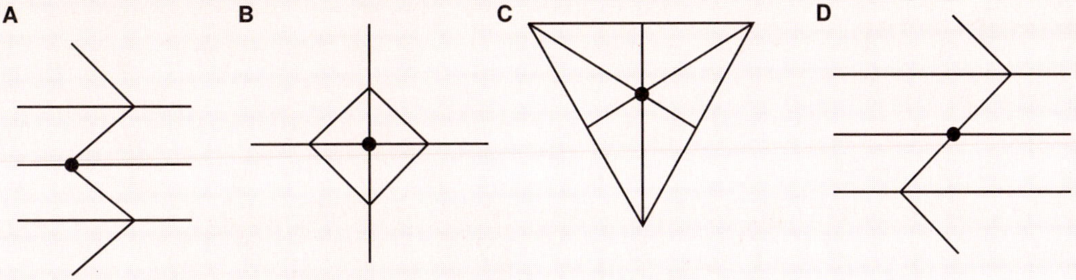

1 How many axes of symmetry has each diagram ?

2 Which diagrams have rotational symmetry about the point marked • ?
For these diagrams, state the order of rotational symmetry.

3. The diagrams show the arrangements of spots on the faces of a die.

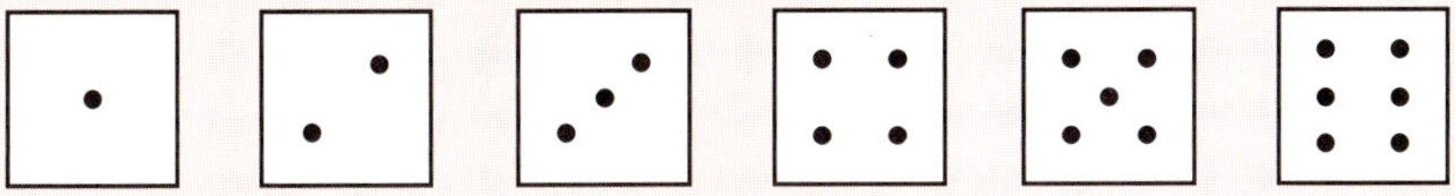

Sketch the diagrams and mark in

1 all axes of symmetry,

2 any centres of rotational symmetry.

3 Which diagrams have rotational symmetry of order 2, but not of order 4 ?

4 Which diagrams have rotational symmetry of order 4 ?

PUZZLE

4. A spy smuggled two messages to his leader.
One said '3263426 702 2498 729841'.

The other had this division sum:

```
       E P F
Y P)D R I O
    F D
     A I
     P I
     Y O O
       I Y
         I
```

Decode the sum and then find what the first message was.

5 Thinking about decimals

Decimals today

In these days of calculators and computers, decimals are used more and more. They are used in cases where we want accurate figures, rather than approximate ones.
Look in a newspaper and cut out examples of decimals being used.
Have you used decimals yourself recently, possibly in lessons in other subjects such as science or technology ? If so, for what purposes were they used ?
Name some people who will use decimals in their work, and say for what purposes they are used ?

The car has gone 5570 miles altogether, but the lower reading shows that since that scale was re-set to zero, it has travelled 134.2 miles.

USA runner Sydney Maree setting the 1500 m world record in 3 min 31.23 sec at Cologne, in 1983. Why is the time measured so accurately ? What is the world record now, and who holds it ?

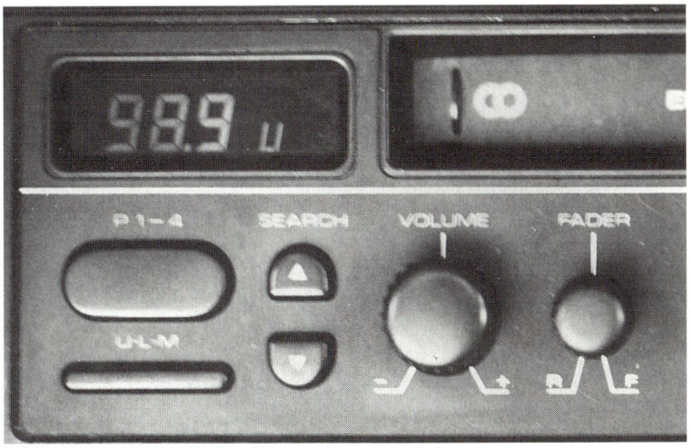

This car radio is set to get Radio 1, on the 98.9 MHz wavelength.

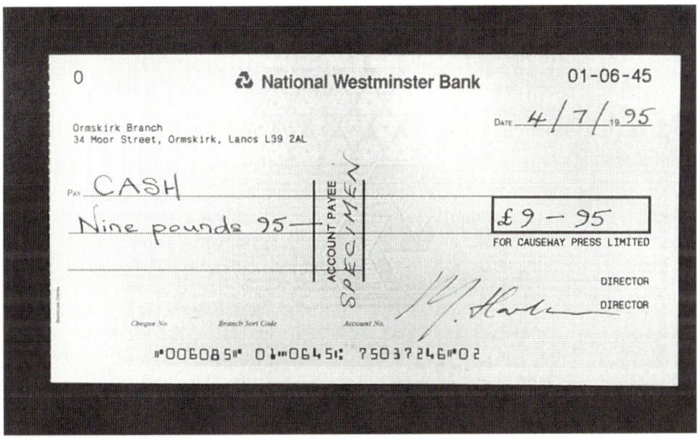

What is the amount shown on this cheque ?
Why is a dash written instead of a decimal point ?

A radio requires 6 volts. How many of these batteries are needed ?

A decimal problem

Mr Briden was planning to put fencing along the end of his garden.
He measured the length, which was 18 m.
He decided to have 5 posts, so he needed 4 spaces in between them, with wire stretched across.

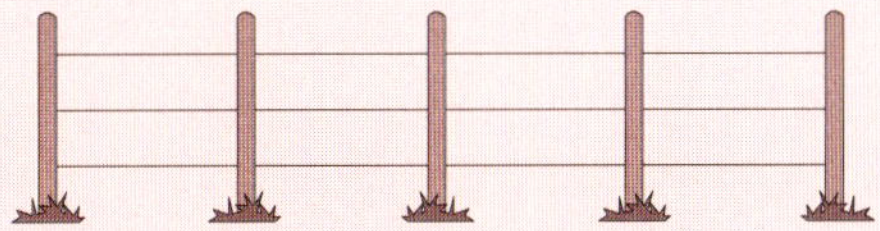

How far apart would the posts be ?
(Assume that he measures to the centre of each post then it does not matter how wide they are.)
What calculation would he do on his calculator ?
What is the answer ?
I got 4.5. What does .5 mean ?
So the distance between the posts was 4.5 m. This seemed rather a large gap so Mr Briden decided to have 9 posts. He did the calculation again and got 2.25.
What does .2 mean ? What does .25 mean ?
How long are the spaces between the posts, in metres ?
How long are the spaces between the posts, in centimetres ?
When he went to buy the posts he could only get 8 of them. So to calculate how far apart to put them he did 18 ÷ 7.
The answer was 2.5714285.
What does .5 mean ? How many cm is 0.5 m ?
What does .57 mean ? How many cm is 0.57 m ?
What does .571 mean ? How many cm is 0.571 m ?
Is it any use to know that the answer was 2.5714285 ?
How far apart will he put his posts ?

5 Decimals

Decimals are fractions which have denominators of 10, or of powers of 10 such as 100, 1000, 10 000, . . .
The decimal point is used to separate the whole number part from the decimal part of a number.

251.37

↙ ↘

whole number part
251

decimal part
3 tenths and 7 hundredths
(which is the same as 37 hundredths)

251.374
↓
4 thousandths

This number is read as two hundred and fifty-one point three seven four.

If there is no whole number part it is usual to write a 0 before the point. Write 0.3 rather than .3 because the 0 helps to draw attention to the decimal point. This number can be read as point three. On your calculator it is sufficient to press .3

In the number 1.26, the 2 represents 2 tenths and the 6 represents 6 hundredths.
6 hundredths are smaller than 1 tenth.

Here are units, represented by squares, divided into tenths and hundredths.

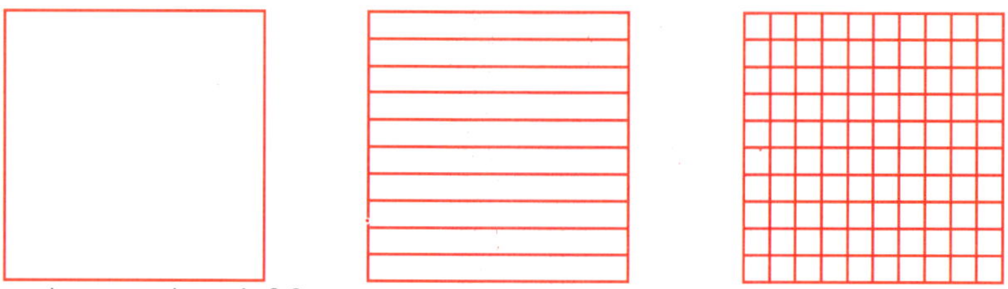

This represents the number 1.26

1 unit **2 tenths** **6 hundredths**

Multiplying by 10, 100, 1000, . . .

You can already multiply whole numbers by 10.

e.g.
$3 \times 10 = 30$
$53 \times 10 = 530$
$600 \times 10 = 6000$

The figures 3 units, 5 tens, 6 hundreds have all become ten times bigger by moving up one place to become 3 tens, 5 hundreds, 6 thousands. 0's are used to fill in the empty spaces.

The same thing happens with decimals.

$0.2 \times 10 = 2$
$0.24 \times 10 = 2.4$
$0.007 \times 10 = 0.07$
$3.007 \times 10 = 30.07$

The figures 2 tenths, 4 hundredths, 7 thousandths, have all become ten times bigger by moving up one place to become 2 units, 4 tenths, 7 hundredths. The 0's which were filling in empty spaces have disappeared if they are no longer needed.

To multiply by 100 is simply the same as multiplying by 10, and then by 10 again.
To multiply by 1000 is the same as multiplying by 10, by 10 again and by 10 again.
Here are the rules:

> To multiply by 10, 100, 1000, . . ., the numbers grow larger, so the figures move upwards (to the left) 1, 2, 3, . . . places, assuming that the decimal point is fixed. Add 0's to fill any empty places between the figures and the decimal point.

Examples

$1.2 \times 10 = 12$
$0.76 \times 10 = 7.6$
$0.2 \times 100 = 20$
$1.84 \times 100 = 184$
$0.003 \times 100 = 0.3$
$0.61 \times 1000 = 610$

Dividing by 10, 100, 1000, . . .

> The numbers become smaller, so the figures move downwards (to the right) 1, 2, 3, . . . places, assuming that the decimal point is fixed. Add 0's to fill any empty places between the decimal point and the figures.

Examples

$6 \div 10 = 0.6$
$7.17 \div 100 = 0.0717$
$83.05 \div 1000 = 0.08305$
$0.2 \div 10 = 0.02$
$350 \div 100 = 3.5$
$804 \div 1000 = 0.804$

Exercise 5.1

Do not use your calculator in this exercise.

1. On graph paper, you can represent numbers in this way:

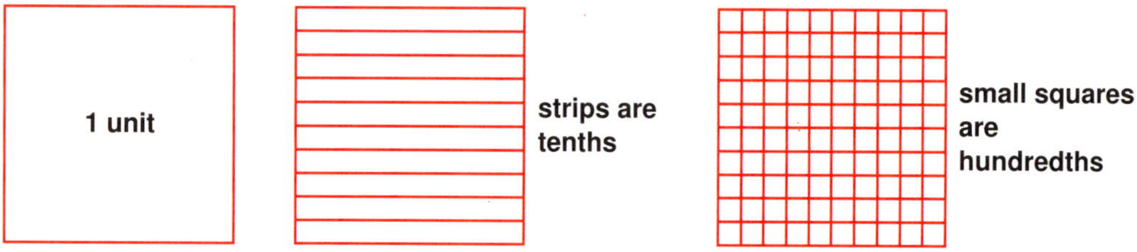

Use graph paper to represent these numbers.

1 1.58 **2** 2.02 **3** 1.46 **4** 3.33 **5** 1.99

2. Find the values of

1 0.9×10
2 8.02×10
3 34.12×10
4 0.061×10
5 0.45×10
6 38.42×10
7 0.154×10
8 4.41×10
9 0.0052×10
10 0.603×10

3. Find the values of

1 3.79×100
2 0.15×100
3 1.25×1000
4 0.0036×1000
5 0.07×1000
6 3.17×1000
7 0.238×100
8 23.42×100
9 0.013×1000
10 80.5×100

4. Find the values of

1 $14.92 \div 10$
2 $47.6 \div 10$
3 $2.08 \div 10$
4 $0.3 \div 10$
5 $0.04 \div 10$
6 $117.3 \div 10$
7 $1.38 \div 10$
8 $0.059 \div 10$
9 $85 \div 10$
10 $20.6 \div 10$

5. Find the values of

1	$29.5 \div 100$	6	$2.54 \div 100$
2	$7.6 \div 100$	7	$389 \div 1000$
3	$0.5 \div 100$	8	$7.98 \div 1000$
4	$35.8 \div 1000$	9	$140.2 \div 1000$
5	$19 \div 1000$	10	$0.25 \div 100$

6. What is the total height of a pile of 10 books if the thickness of each book is 3.4 cm ?

7. If a litre of sea-water weighs 1.026 kg, what do 100 litres weigh ?

8. If 10 parcels together weigh 56.5 kg, what is the average weight of 1 parcel ?

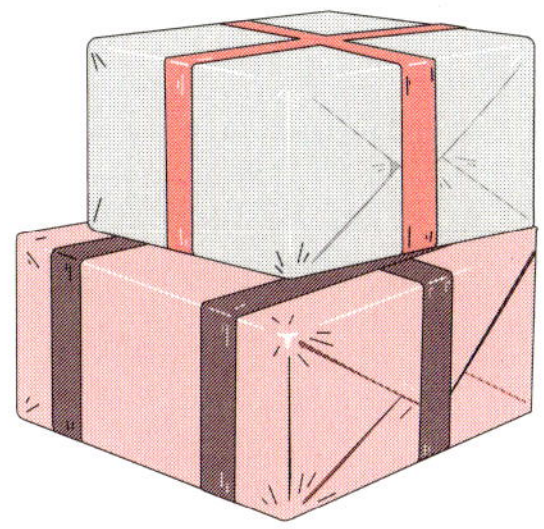

9. If 1000 m is equivalent to 3281 feet, how many feet are equivalent to 1 metre ?

Adding, subtracting, and multiplying and dividing by small whole numbers

You can do these questions without using your calculator.
Just keep the figures in their correct positions relative to the decimal point.

Examples

1 $12.3 + 3.85$

$$\begin{array}{r} 12.3 \\ +\ \underline{3.85} \\ \underline{16.15} \end{array}$$

2 $14.5 - 1.83$

$$\begin{array}{r} 14.50 \\ -\ \underline{1.83} \\ \underline{12.67} \end{array}$$

3 27.5×3

$$\begin{array}{r} 27.5 \\ \times\ \underline{\quad 3} \\ \underline{82.5} \end{array}$$

4 $216.81 \div 9$

$$\begin{array}{r} 24.09 \\ 9\overline{)216.81} \end{array}$$

Exercise 5.2

Do not use your calculator in this exercise.

1.
1 $1.12 + 2.8 + 3.25$
2 $0.9 + 8.02 + 6.98$
3 $6.49 + 1.26 + 0.47$
4 $0.04 + 0.82 + 0.17$
5 $23.93 + 0.03 + 8.07$
6 $1.25 + 0.75$
7 $2.75 + 3.3 + 15.82$
8 $2.76 + 3.5 + 5.14$
9 $16.82 + 0.53$
10 $9.93 + 0.78$

2.
1 $4.07 - 1.99$
2 $9.67 - 8.6$
3 $8.3 - 1.09$
4 $2 - 0.37$
5 $3.5 - 0.02$
6 $4.37 - 2.09$
7 $6 - 0.03$
8 $1.92 - 0.06$
9 $100 - 81.62$
10 $7.62 - 6.86$

3.
1 8.02×7
2 1.5×8
3 0.72×4
4 6.02×5
5 0.03×6
6 1.9×4
7 6.15×2
8 0.29×6
9 8.05×9
10 29.3×3

4.
1 $9.42 \div 3$
2 $9.6 \div 5$
3 $5.04 \div 8$
4 $0.6 \div 4$
5 $0.056 \div 7$
6 $1.72 \div 4$
7 $33.6 \div 6$
8 $15.1 \div 5$
9 $18.72 \div 9$
10 $0.564 \div 2$

5. The weight of a jar is 78.8 g. When it was filled with jam it weighed 121.3 g. What was the weight of the jam ?

6. 6 parcels had an average weight of 3.22 kg. Find the total weight of the parcels.

7. The lengths of 3 planks are 4.32 m, 3.07 m and 2.56 m. What is the total length if the planks are laid end-to-end ?

8. If 66.33 francs are worth £9, how many francs are equivalent to £1 ?

9. **1** The rainfall for 3 days was 2.8 cm, 3.3 cm and 2.6 cm. What was the total rainfall ?

2 If 11.6 cm of rain fell in 4 days, what was the average rainfall per day ?

Numbers to the nearest whole number

If you need an answer correct to the nearest whole number, continue the division to 1 decimal place.

e.g. For numbers between 14 and 15.
Any number less than 14.5 is given as 14 to the nearest whole number.
Any number from 14.5 upwards is given as 15 to the nearest whole number.
(Actually, 14.5 is exactly halfway between 14 and 15 but it is usual to correct it **up** to 15.)
So, if the figure in the 1st decimal place is 5 or more, correct up to the next whole number.

Examples

2.3 = 2, to the nearest whole number.
15.9 = 16, to the nearest whole number.
16.1 = 16, to the nearest whole number.
19.6 = 20, to the nearest whole number.
20.48 = 20, to the nearest whole number.

Sometimes when doing division the answer is not exact and it will be necessary to stop after a suitable number of decimal places. The method for this is similar to that used to correct numbers to the nearest whole number.

Look at the figure to the right of the last figure you need. If this extra figure is 5 or more, add 1 to the final figure of your answer.

1 Find the value of $29 \div 7$, correct to 3 decimal places.

We want 3 decimal places, so find the figures in the first 4 decimal places, that is one more place than we need.

$$\begin{array}{r} 4.1428 \\ 7\overline{)29.0000} \end{array}$$

Since the figure in the 4th decimal place (8) is 5 or more, the figure in the 3rd decimal place must be corrected up from 2 to 3.

$29 \div 7 = 4.143$, correct to 3 decimal places.

If you had used your calculator the answer given would be 4.1428571.
Since you want the answer to 3 decimal places you look at the figure in the 4th decimal place, which is 8, as we had before. The answer to 3 decimal places is 4.143. You do not need to consider the rest of the figures on the calculator (571).

2 Find the value of $36.86 \div 6$, correct to 2 decimal places.

$$\begin{array}{r} 6.143 \\ 6\overline{)36.860} \end{array}$$

Since the figure in the 3rd decimal place (3) is less than 5, the figure in the 2nd decimal place is not changed.

$36.86 \div 6 = 6.14$, correct to 2 decimal places.

Here are some other examples:

3.2976 = 3.298 to 3 decimal places
0.8692 = 0.869 to 3 decimal places
0.0827 = 0.083 to 3 decimal places
0.00426 = 0.004 to 3 decimal places

0.849 = 0.85 to 2 decimal places
3.297 = 3.30 to 2 decimal places
1.0347 = 1.03 to 2 decimal places

0.849 = 0.8 to 1 decimal place
3.297 = 3.3 to 1 decimal place
1.0347 = 1.0 to 1 decimal place
1.0747 = 1.1 to 1 decimal place

Multiplication and division by decimal numbers

Use your calculator to do multiplication and division by decimal numbers.

e.g. $38.7 \times 7.9 = 305.73$ (If you need this answer correct to 1 decimal place, it is 305.7)

$0.009 \times 1.2 = 0.0108$
$0.048 \div 1.6 = 0.03$
$270 \div 0.12 = 2250$

If a division question does not work out exactly, you will have to decide how many decimal places to leave in the answer. Usually 1, 2 or 3 will be sufficient.
e.g. $128 \div 0.63 = 203.1746$

If you want the answer correct to the nearest whole number it is 203, if to 1 decimal place it is 203.2, to 2 decimal places it is 203.17 or to 3 decimal places it is 203.175.

$2.13 \div 5.62 = 0.3790035$
To 2 decimal places this is 0.38, to 3 decimal places it is 0.379.

Exercise 5.3

1. Write these numbers correct to the nearest whole number.

1 12.3 **2** 7.9 **3** 10.3 **4** 29.72 **5** 93.88

2. Write these numbers correct to 1 decimal place.

1 5.31 **2** 5.493 **3** 0.39 **4** 1.08 **5** 2.062

3. Write these numbers correct to 2 decimal places.

1 3.578 **2** 5.806 **3** 0.704 **4** 6.589 **5** 0.008

4. Find the answers to these questions correct to 1 decimal place. Do not use your calculator, and show your working.

1 $4.45 \div 3$
2 $3.7 \div 6$
3 $25.89 \div 7$
4 $12.34 \div 5$
5 $109 \div 9$
6 $6.35 \div 4$
7 $0.17 \div 3$
8 $18.1 \div 8$
9 $28.76 \div 2$
10 $51.23 \div 5$

5. Use your calculator to work out the exact answers to these questions.

1 13.06 × 26.1
2 463 × 0.17
3 0.0625 × 1.74
4 16.2 × 0.07
5 0.049 × 3.4

6. Use your calculator to work out the answers to these questions. Give each answer correct to 2 decimal places.

1 0.46 ÷ 2.9
2 0.11 ÷ 0.015
3 5.4 ÷ 0.73
4 26.7 ÷ 9.3
5 362 ÷ 5.4

7. In a staircase there are 12 steps. The height of each rise is 19.4 cm. What is the total height from bottom to top of the staircase ?

8. If a roll of ribbon of total length 828 cm is cut into 16 equal pieces, how long is each piece ?

9. Write down any number between 1 and 10. Add 2.45 and multiply the total by 2.8. Now subtract 3.5 and then divide by 5.6. Add 4.4 and double the result. Subtract the number you started with. What is your answer ?

Money

Since there are 100 pence in £1, our money calculations use the decimal system.
£3 and 67 pence is written as £3.67
£4 and 8 pence is written as £4.08
£4 and 80 pence is £4.80. On a calculator this may be recorded as 4.8
This means £4.80, not £4.08.

Examples, working in £'s.

Addition £2.36 + £4.54

$$\begin{array}{r} 2.36 \\ +\underline{4.54} \\ \underline{6.90} \end{array}$$

Answer £6.90

(On a calculator this will be recorded as 6.9)

Subtraction £10 − £3.96

$$\begin{array}{r} 10.00 \\ -\ \underline{3.96} \\ \underline{6.04} \end{array}$$ Answer £6.04

(On a calculator there is no need to enter 10.00 for £10.00. 10 will do.)

Multiplication £6.25 × 8

$$\begin{array}{r} 6.25 \\ \times\ \underline{\quad 8} \\ \underline{50.00} \end{array}$$

Answer £50 or £50.00, whichever is more appropriate.
(A calculator will just show 50)

Division £45 ÷ 6

$$6\overline{)45.0} = 7.5$$ Answer £7.50

(A calculator will just show 7.5)

Division How many books costing £6.40 each can be bought for £60 ?

This is £60 ÷ £6.40.
Using your calculator work out 60 ÷ 6.4.
The answer is 9.375, showing that 9 books can be bought and there is some money left over.

To find how much is left, multiply £6.40 by 9 and subtract the total from £60.
60 − (9 × 6.4) = 2.4, so there is £2.40 left.

Amounts to the nearest penny

If you are working in pence:
29.3 pence = 29p, to the nearest penny.
12.62 pence = 13p, to the nearest penny.
(If the figure in the 1st decimal place is 5 or more, round up to the next penny.)

If you are working in £'s:
£3.776 = £3.78, to the nearest penny.
£2.494 = £2.49, to the nearest penny.
(The figures in the first two decimal places give the number of pence. If the figure in the 3rd decimal place is 5 or more, round the pence up to the next penny.)

Multiplying pence by 100

Since 100 × 1p = £1, multiplying by 100 changes pence into £'s.
If a packet of sweets cost 12p, then 100 packets cost £12.
If the coach fare per child is 75p, then for 100 children it is £75.
If 1 pencil costs 6p, then 100 cost £6, so 200 cost £12.

Articles costing 99p, £1.99, £2.99, etc.

To find the cost of 7 articles at 99p each, this is 7 at £1 less 7 × 1p = £7 − 7p = £6.93.
To find the cost of 4 articles at £5.99 each, this is 4 at £6 less 4 × 1p
= £24 − 4p = £23.96.

Approximations and estimations

When you go shopping, it is useful to make an approximate calculation of any bill so that you can see if you have enough money, and you can check that you do not get the wrong change.
For example, in a shop suppose you select 3 articles at £1.99 each, 2 at £2.95 each and 1 at £4.90. Before you go to the cash desk you could do an approximate calculation to see if you had enough money to pay for them. It is nearly 3 at £2, 2 at £3 and 1 at £5 so you would need nearly £17. You also expect to get just over £3 in change if you pay with a £20 note.
(When the exact amount is shown on the till you can check your exact change.)

Subtraction, by the method of adding on.

This is useful when subtracting from an exact amount such as £1, £5, £10.
e.g. £5 − £1.83.
£1.83 and <u>7p</u> makes £1.90, and <u>10p</u> makes £2, and <u>£3</u> makes £5.
The answer is 7p + 10p + £3 = £3.17.
This is the way a shopkeeper would count out the change as you are given it.

Exercise 5.4

1. **1** If 1 article costs 3p, what do 100 cost ?
   2 If 1 article costs 14p, what do 300 cost ?

2. **1** Find the cost of 8 articles at 99p each.
   2 Find the cost of 7 articles at £2.99 each.

3. Find the change from £5 if I spend:
   48p, £3.61, £4.11, £2.30, £1.73.

4. Mrs Fraser spent £7.84 on meat and £2.36 on vegetables. How much was this altogether ? What change did she get from a £20 note ?

5. Mrs Harris buys 8 m of curtain material at £5.45 per metre. What is the total cost ?

6. Mrs Desai makes 200 soft toys. The material for each toy costs £2.66. Other expenses amount to £75. She sells the toys for £4.99 each. What profit does she make ?

7. Mr Grant spends £9 on petrol for his car and this takes him 120 miles. What is the cost per mile ?

8. 12 people win a competition and share the prize money of £500 equally. How much do they each get, to the nearest penny ?

9. How many 17p packets of sweets can be bought for £10, and how much change is there ?

10. Two books together cost £5.70, one being £1.80 more than the other. What did each one cost ?

11. Equal numbers of 25p and 30p stamps were bought for £17.60. How many of each kind were there ?

12. The electricity bill for a certain householder was worked out as follows:–
a standing charge of £10.80 per quarter plus a cost of 6.6p per unit used. The meter reading was 49616, and the previous reading was 48516.
How many units had been used, and what was the total cost for that quarter ?

13. Mrs Wilson wants to buy 2 curtains size 54 × 46, and 4 curtains size 72 × 66.
   1 Show how she can find a quick estimate of the cost, and give the estimated total.
   2 Use your calculator, or another method, to find the exact cost.

Very good value! Price per pair			
54 × 46	£29.99	54 × 66	£49.99
72 × 46	£42.99	72 × 66	£59.99
90 × 46	£49.99	90 × 66	£74.99
108 × 46	£59.99	108 × 66	£89.99
54 × 90	£68.99	90 × 90	£99.99
72 × 90	£86.99	108 × 90	£124.99

Reading numbers on scales

Example

What reading is shown by the arrow on this scale ?

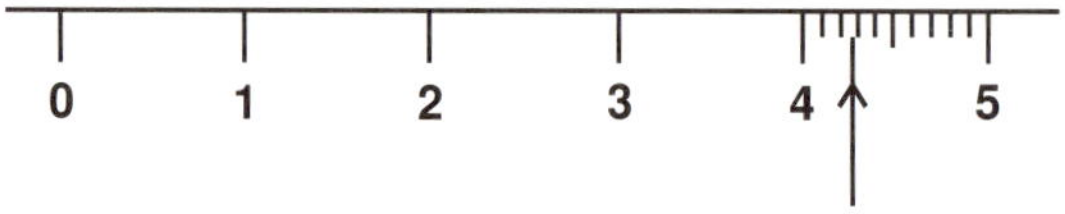

Decide between which two whole numbers the reading lies.

This one lies between 4 and 5, so it starts 4.

Here is an enlargement of the part of the scale between 4 and 5.

Decide between which two tenths the reading lies.

This one lies between 2 and 3, so it is 4.2.
If you have to answer correct to 1 decimal place decide whether it is nearer 2 or 3.
This one is nearer 3 so give the answer as 4.3.

If you have to estimate the answer to 2 decimal places, imagine an enlargement of the part of the scale between 4.2 and 4.3.

The reading is nearer to 4.3 than to 4.2, so it is bigger than 4.25. It is approximately 4.27.

Exercise 5.5

1. Read the numbers marked at A, B, C, D, E correct to 1 decimal place.

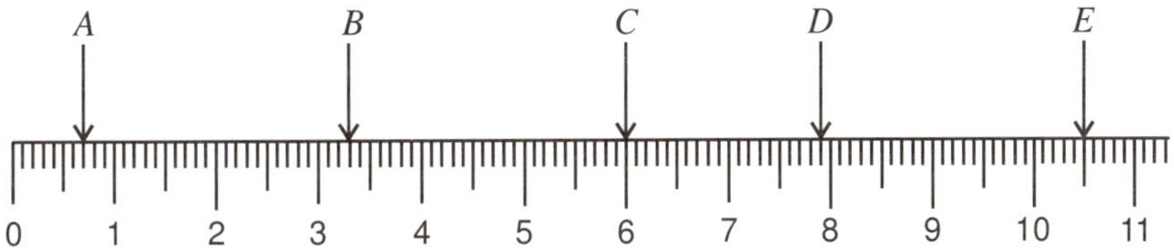

2. Read off the numbers marked at F, G, H, J, K, correct to 1 decimal place.

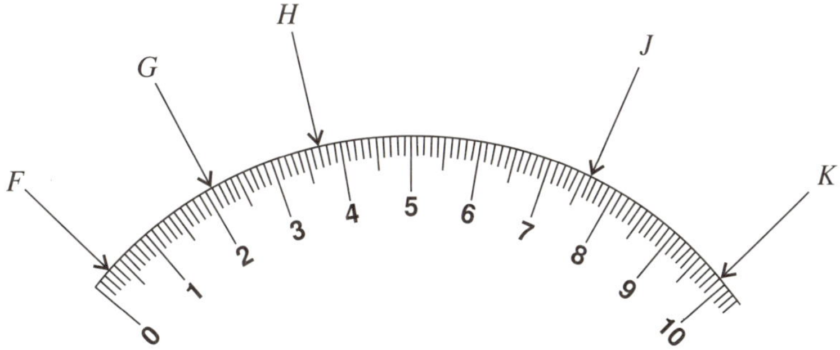

3. Use a strip of graph paper to make a number-scale as shown.

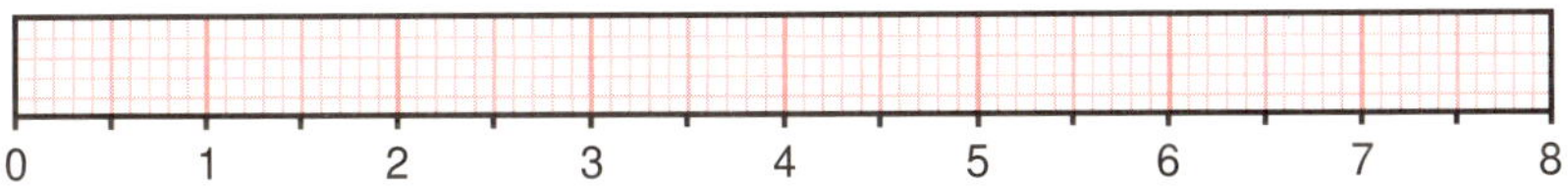

Mark on your strip the readings for the numbers A 2.5, B 5.9, C 0.2, D 7.7, E 3.1.

4. Use a strip of graph paper to make a number-scale as shown. Mark on your strip the readings for numbers *A* 0.67, *B* 0.51, *C* 0.07, *D* 0.75, *E* 0.99.

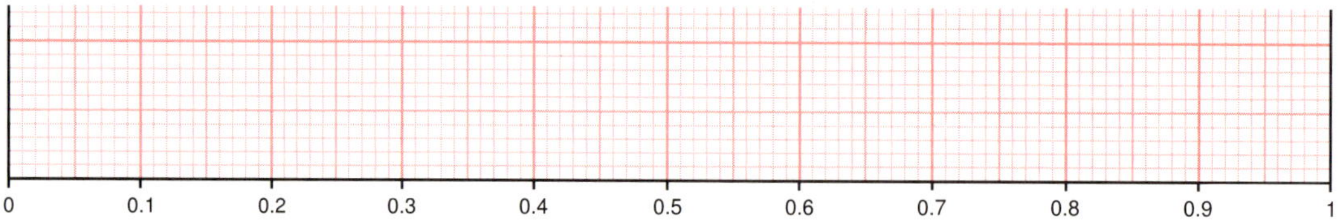

Exercise 5.6 Applications and Activities

1. **Missing numbers**

Use your calculator to find the numbers represented by □ in these statements. Then repeat each calculation in its normal order to check the answer.

1 $\square + 2.45 = 19.27$

2 $4.96 - \square = 2.93$

3 $\square \times 0.52 = 1.6328$

4 $3.74 - (1.93 + \square) = 1.14$

5 $54.6 \div \square = 182$

6 $\square \div 0.34 = 7.78$

7 $\square - 92.58 = 7.42$

8 $\square \times (3.7 + 8.5) = 85.4$

9 $\square + (25.8 \times 1.4) = 39.96$

10 $5.6 \div (2.31 - \square) = 4.375$

2. **Correcting mistakes**

In each of these calculations a mistake has been made. Find the correct answers. Can you also discover what mistake was made, in each case ?

1 $10 - 0.726 = 2.74$

2 $1.23 + 2.4 + 3.13 = 6.082$

3 $13.93 \div 0.07 = 19.9$

4 $4.78 \times 8.543 = 39.913$

5 $(15.6 + 2.8) \times 4.3 = 27.64$

3. **A curious sum**

Write down any sum of money less than £100 which includes £'s and pence.
Write it down again, interchanging £'s and pence, e.g. £63.47 becomes £47.63.
You may have to put in or lose a 0, £9.26 becomes £26.09 and £18.03 becomes £3.18.
Subtract the smaller amount from the larger one and write down your answer
Write down the answer again with the £'s and pence interchanged.
Find the sum of the last two amounts you have written down.
What is your final answer ?

4. **Square roots**

number	square root
1	1
4	2
9	3
16	4
25	5
36	6
49	7
64	8
81	9
100	10

The numbers 1, 4, 9, ... have exact square roots. Other numbers have square roots which can be found approximately.

Numbers between 1 and 4 have square roots between 1 and 2.
Using your calculator you will find that, correct to 2 decimal places,

$$\sqrt{2} = 1.41$$

$$\sqrt{2.5} = 1.58$$

$$\sqrt{3} = 1.73$$

Numbers between 4 and 9 have square roots between 2 and 3.
Use your calculator to find the square roots of 5, 6, 7 and 8, correct to 2 decimal places.

Similar rules work for other numbers.
e.g. 45 is between 36 and 49 so its square root is between 6 and 7, so you know it begins with 6.
Find its value correct to 2 decimal places, using your calculator.

Find the square roots of 10, 20, 30, 40, 50 and 60, correct to 1 decimal place.

Use a strip of graph paper to make a number scale as shown.

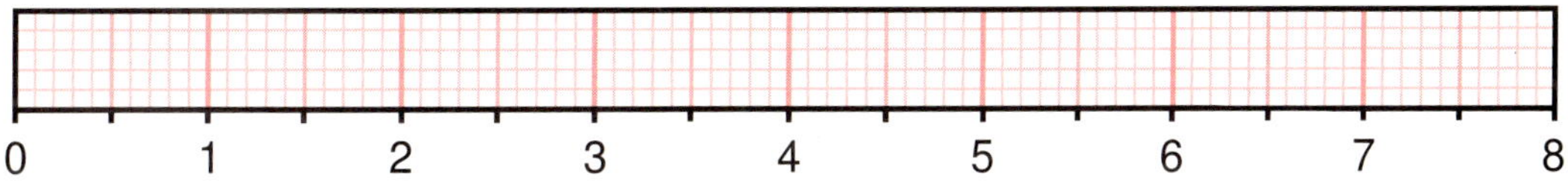

Mark on your strip the readings for these square roots. Label them $\sqrt{10}$, $\sqrt{20}$, etc.

Investigate the connection between the square roots of a number and the number which is 100 times bigger or smaller.

5. **Dividing by 9 and 11**

Investigate the decimal patterns resulting from these division questions. Record all the decimals as shown on your calculator. (Note that if the end figure does not match the pattern it may have been corrected up.)
Comment on the patterns, and on any connection between the two lists.

$1 \div 9 =$
$2 \div 9 =$
$3 \div 9 =$
$4 \div 9 =$
$5 \div 9 =$
$6 \div 9 =$
$7 \div 9 =$
$8 \div 9 =$

$1 \div 11 =$
$2 \div 11 =$
$3 \div 11 =$
$4 \div 11 =$
$5 \div 11 =$
$6 \div 11 =$
$7 \div 11 =$
$8 \div 11 =$
$9 \div 11 =$
$10 \div 11 =$

6. **A calculator investigation**

On your calculator the numbers from 1 to 9 are arranged in a 3 by 3 square. From this square, write down 3 figures which lie in order in a straight line (from a row, a column or a diagonal line starting at either end), followed by the same 3 figures in reverse order, making a 6-figure number, e.g. 258852.

Multiply the first figure by 8.1 and add the second figure to the result.
e.g. $2 \times 8.1 + 5 = 21.2$

Divide the 6-figure number by 110, and then divide the answer by the number found above.
What is your final answer ?

Investigate by starting with different figures and comment on the results.

Chapter 5 test

Do not use your calculator in questions 1, 2 or 3.

1. Find the values of

1 117.4×100
2 $3.58 \div 10$
3 15.72×4
4 $26.6 \div 7$
5 $3.71 + 8.23 - 4.57$

2. The four sides of a field have lengths 55.4 m, 38.3 m, 62.9 m and 23.8 m. What is the total length of fencing needed to enclose the field ?

3. **1** If 1 km is equivalent to 0.62137 miles, what distance in miles is equivalent to 100 km, to the nearest mile ?

   2 If 1000 kg is equivalent to 2204.6 lb, what weight in pounds is equivalent to 1 kg, to the nearest 0.1 lb ?

4. Use your calculator to find the values of the following, correct to 2 decimal places.

   1 501×0.638
   2 26.9×1.82
   3 0.037×263
   4 $280 \div 13.9$
   5 $0.083 \div 0.036$

5. A glass weighs 265.8 g when empty and 451.3 g when full of water. What is the weight of the water ?
   Glycerine is 1.26 times as heavy as water. What would the glass weigh if it was full of glycerine ?

6. On a holiday, the total distance travelled by a car was 919 miles and the car used 24 gallons of petrol. How far, on average, did the car run on a gallon of petrol ?

7. Read the numbers marked at *A, B, C, D, E* correct to 2 decimal places.

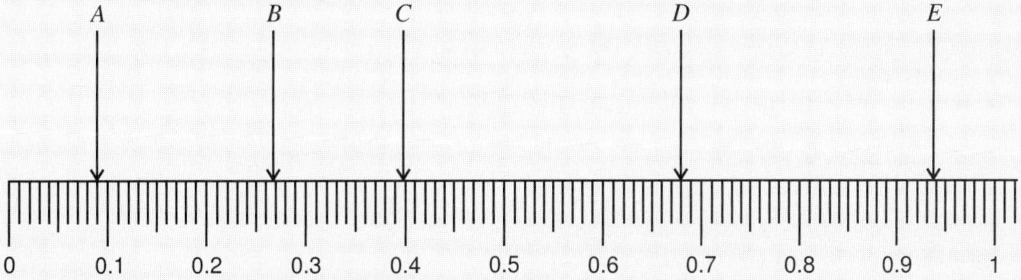

8. Find the total cost of 3 bottles of milk at 31p per bottle, 2 packets of tea at 58p per packet, and $\frac{1}{2}$ dozen eggs at £1.18 per dozen.

9. From a mail order catalogue Caroline orders 3 items at £2.99 each and 2 items at £9.99 each. What is the total cost ?

10. Mr Douglas has a £20 voucher to spend at the garden centre. He decides to buy 3 bushes for £2.35 each and spend the rest on bulbs at 35p each. How many bulbs can he buy ?

6 Thinking about probability

What is probability ?

'The family next door will probably go to Spain for their holidays.'

Think of some sentences which include the word 'probably'.

I'll probably go ...
I'll probably buy ...
The bus will probably be late again.
My mother will probably let me come.

These are predictions for the future, but they are not definite predictions.

Consider these statements:
'The family next door are going to Spain for their holidays.'
Unless something unforeseen happens, it is certain that they will go.
'The family next door may go to Spain for their holidays.'
There is nothing certain here, it is not even as likely as 'probably'.
Perhaps you can tell from the tone of voice of the speaker, or you know from past experience, how likely the event is to happen.

Which of these events are more likely to happen ? Put the statements in order, with the more likely ones last.

You will have chips for tea tonight.
It will rain today.
Someone in your family will have a large win on the lottery.
It will go dark tonight.
If you toss a coin, it will come down heads.
You will be involved in a road accident within the next month.
You will travel abroad within the next year.

You are making a judgement about the likelihood or the probability of the event happening
In Mathematics we give this a numerical value varying from 0, (completely unlikely to happen), to 1, (absolutely certain to happen). Try to give a numerical value to your previous answers. If not 0, or 1, give them as decimals, to 1 or 2 decimal places.

Sometimes you can alter the probability by taking certain actions. What action could you take to lessen the probability that you will be late for school ?
Suggest some actions that you could take to lessen the probability that you will be involved in a road accident.

Investing money in stocks and shares means judging how well a company will do.

Will a by-pass be needed in the future ?

Some people gamble on horse racing.

Using probability

Probability is often associated with gambling. A professional gambler will work out how likely he is to win a game or a bet. And for you to learn about probability, the simple questions are often based on the probabilities of the results of tossing coins, throwing dice or picking cards out of a pack. But, in real life, probability has many, more important, uses.

Government departments, business firms, industrialists, scientists, medical researchers and many other people and organisations use the figures from past events to predict what is likely to happen in the future, and so they can plan ahead. For example, insurance companies use their knowledge of past claims to predict future ones, and they can then decide what premiums they must charge.

The insurance company may decide that there are likely to be fewer burglaries.

6 Probability Experiments

Probability or chance is the likelihood of an event happening, for example, a tossed coin showing heads. It is measured on a numerical scale from 0 to 1 and can be given as a fraction, a decimal or a percentage.
For example, the probability of a tossed coin showing heads can be given as $\frac{1}{2}$, 0.5 or 50%.

We can show the chances of success on a probability line.

0		$\frac{1}{2}$		1
No chance of success	**Success is less likely to happen than not**	**Success will happen in about $\frac{1}{2}$ of the outcomes**	**Success is more likely to happen than not**	**Certain chance of success**

An experiment

A simple experiment is carried out using coloured beads in a bag. Some beads are red and some are blue, but otherwise they are identical. Without knowing how many of each colour there are, we want to find the probability of picking a red bead if a bead is picked out of the bag at random.
The experiment consists of trials.
One trial involves picking out a bead at random, recording its colour, replacing it in the bag and giving the bag a good shake to mix up the beads again.
After a few trials we can work out the **relative frequency** of a red bead.

$$\text{Relative frequency} = \frac{\text{number of trials giving a red bead}}{\text{total number of trials}}$$

These are the results from one such experiment when the bag contained fewer red beads than blue ones.

Number of trials (n)	Number of red beads (r)	Fraction $\frac{r}{n}$	$\frac{r}{n}$ to 2 decimal places
10	3	$\frac{3}{10}$	0.30
25	9	$\frac{9}{25}$	0.36
50	16	$\frac{16}{50}$	0.32
100	31	$\frac{31}{100}$	0.31
200	56	$\frac{56}{200}$	0.28
300	93	$\frac{93}{300}$	0.31
500	143	$\frac{143}{500}$	0.29
1000	302	$\frac{302}{1000}$	0.30

This graphs shows the first 100 results, worked out after every 10 trials, plotted on a graph.

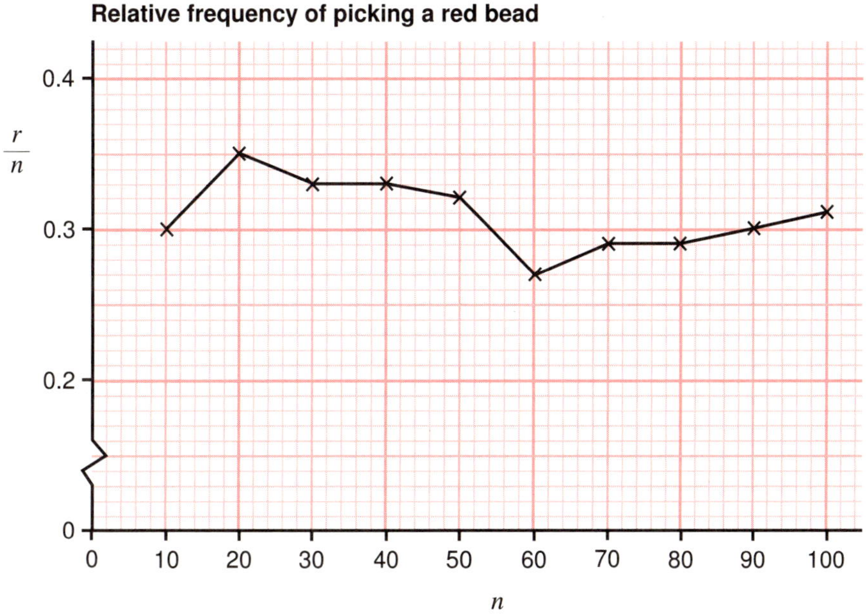

This graph shows the results for 1000 trials, worked out after every 100 trials.

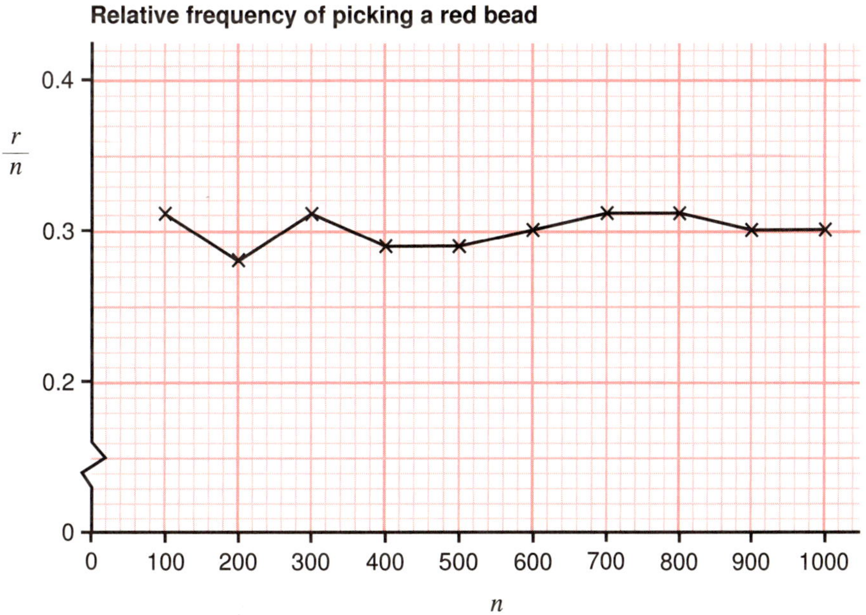

Although the results are erratic after only a few trials, they then settle down around 0.3 so that in the long run red appears in 0.3 of the trials.

$$\text{The relative frequency of a red bead} = \frac{\text{number of red beads drawn out}}{\text{total number of beads drawn out}} = 0.3$$

The relative frequency gives an estimate of the probability of a red bead being drawn out.
The estimated probability of a red bead = 0.3.

We can only use this method for estimating probability if we do enough trials to show that the fraction is settling down to a steady value. If the event was unpredictable the fraction would not settle down and we could not find a value for the probability.

When we know the probability of an event happening we can use its value to predict the likelihood of a future result.

In many cases we can **calculate** probabilities (see Chapter 12). For instance, if we had known that the bag of beads contained 30 red and 70 blue beads, we could calculate that the probability of a red bead $= \frac{30}{100} = 0.3$, without doing the experiment.

In other cases it is not possible to do a calculation. If you are entering for a race, the probability that you will win cannot be calculated by a mathematical formula. It will depend on how well you can run, compared with the speeds of the other runners, and this may be affected by such things as the length of the race, the weather, how comfortable your shoes are, etc. Perhaps someone will estimate that the chance of you winning is 75%. This means that according to them, you are more likely to win than not, but not certain to win. In similar races, they think that you would win in 75% or $\frac{3}{4}$ of them.

Experiments to try

In Exercise 6.1 there are some suggestions for experiments. We have chosen simple equipment such as coins, dice and playing cards. If you have not got proper equipment it is often possible to think of a substitute.
All the trials should be done randomly and fairly. Toss a coin properly. Give a die (dice) a good shake before rolling it out onto a flat surface. With a pack of cards, take out the jokers first so that the pack contains the 52 cards of the 4 suits, and then shuffle them properly.
If you can combine other people's results with yours to give more trials, then do so. Keep a proper record of all your results because you may be able to use them again later.

Using random numbers to simulate results

Instead of actually doing the experiments, you may prefer to use a graphics calculator or a computer to produce random numbers.
To simulate the throwing of a die, on the graphics calculator, press

[Int] [(] [Ran#] [×] 6 [+] 1 [)] [EXE] [EXE] [EXE] . . .

and you will get a sequence of random numbers between 1 and 6.
By changing 6 into 2 in the instructions, you will get a sequence of 1's or 2's which you can use as the results of tossing coins, with 1 for heads and 2 for tails.

You can produce similar results on a computer using a simple basic program.
However, you may have commercial computer programs available which will do these and other simulated experiments.

Exercise 6.1

1. **Tossing coins**

There are several experiments you can do using the results of tossing coins, so instead of continually having to toss coins again, start off by tossing a coin 200 times. Record your results in order, in a grid of 10 columns by 20 rows. Put H for head and T for tail.
The grid could start like this:

H	H	T	H	T	T	H			

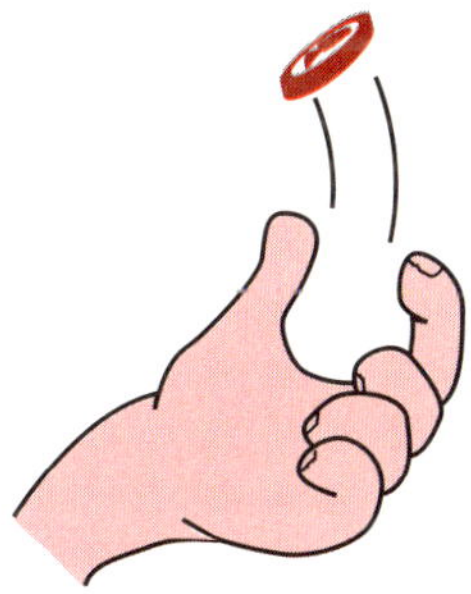

1 What is the probability of a toss showing a head ?

Guess how many heads you are likely to get if you toss a coin 200 times.
Using the results you have recorded, make a table similar to the one on the next page and fill it in.

Number of tosses (n)	Number of heads (h)	Fraction $\frac{h}{n}$	$\frac{h}{n}$ to 2 decimal places
1			
2			
3			
4			
5			
10			
20			
50			
100			
150			
200			

Was your guess a good one ?

From your results, what is the estimated probability of a toss showing a head ?

Often a coin is tossed at the beginning of a game, such as in football or cricket matches. Why is tossing a coin chosen at such times ?

2 If two coins are tossed, what is the probability that both of them will show heads ?

Guess how many times you are likely to get two heads if two coins are tossed 100 times.

Now use the results in your grid in pairs. You could write down in a tally chart the number of heads in each pair of tosses.

e.g. If your table begins

	H H	T H	T T	H H	T T	. . .
Number of heads in two tosses	2	1	0	2	0	

Tally chart

Number of heads in two tosses	Tally	f
0	I I . .	
1	I . . .	
2	I I . .	
		100

Was your guess a good one ?

The estimated probability of getting two heads

$$= \frac{\text{number of trials giving two heads}}{\text{total number of trials}} = \frac{\dots}{100} = \dots$$

In a similar way find the estimated probability of getting two tails, and of getting one head and one tail.

You can investigate in a similar way taking coins 3 at a time, or 4 at a time.

2. **Throwing a die**

(Although you probably talk about playing with a **dice**, the correct word is a **die**. Two or more are called **dice**.)

Instead of throwing a die for every different experiment, start off by recording your throws (the numbers which land on the top face) when you throw a die 400 times.
Make a grid of 20 columns by 20 rows.

1 What is the probability of a die showing a six ?

Guess how many sixes you are likely to get if you throw a die 400 times.

Using the results you have recorded, make a table similar to this and fill it in.

Number of throws (n)	Number of 6's (s)	Fraction $\frac{s}{n}$	$\frac{s}{n}$ to 2 decimal places
10			
20			
50			
100			
200			
300			
400			

From your results, what value would you give for the estimated probability of a throw showing a six ?

2. **2** If you throw two dice and add the two numbers together, what is the most likely total, and what is the probability of getting that total ?

Guess the most likely total, and also guess how many times that total will occur if you throw two dice 200 times.

Now use the results in your grid in twos. Make a new grid to show the totals.

e.g. If your table begins	6 4	1 2	3 5	1 4	. . .
Totals for the pair	10	3	8	5	

You could also record the totals in a tally chart.

Copy and complete the following.

According to these results, the most likely total is . . .
The estimated probability of getting this total

$$= \frac{\text{number of trials giving this total}}{\text{total number of trials}} = \frac{\dots}{200} = \dots$$

(200 trials is not really enough to give a reliable answer, so your most likely total may not be the correct one. Do not feel annoyed at this. The important thing is that it is correct according to your experiment. Not all dice are fair ones. Maybe the one you used is not perfect, and favours some numbers more than others. You could investigate this. You could also combine someone else's results with yours, to see if this affects the answers. The more trials there are, the closer the results should be to the theoretical ones.)

3 Is it true that, if you throw a die 6 times, you **must** get at least one six ?

What is the probability of getting at least one six if you throw a die 6 times ? Guess how many times this will happen out of 66 sets of results.

Use the results in your first grid in groups of 6 at a time. Record ✓ (a tick) if the group of 6 contains at least one six and ✕ (a cross) if it does not. From the 400 results you will have 66 groups of 6 (with 4 left over). Count how many ticks you have. Compare the results with your guess, and work out the estimated probability.
Again, you may get answers which are closer to the theoretical ones if you combine your results with those of other people to give you more trials.

Exercise 6.2 Applications and Activities

1. **Drawing-pins**

Put 10 similar drawing-pins into a cup and holding it approximately 20 cm above a table, gently tip the drawing-pins out so that they land on the table. They come to rest point upwards, like this  or on their side, like this  .
Count and record how many land point upwards. Repeat the experiment 50 times. Find the total number of drawing-pins landing point upwards after 1, 5, 10, 20, 30, 40 and 50 repetitions of the experiment.

Make a table similar to this and fill it in.

Total number tipped out (n)	Number landing point upwards (s)	Fraction $\frac{s}{n}$	$\frac{s}{n}$ to 2 decimal places
10			
50			
100			
200			
300			
400			
500			

If the results are settling down to a certain value this gives the value of the estimated probability that a drawing-pin in this type of experiment will land point upwards.
(There is no theoretical way of checking this result.)

The height through which the drawing-pins fall may affect the result. You could investigate this by repeating the experiment from different heights. Different makes of drawing-pins may also give different results.

2. **Marbles in a circle**

You need 7 marbles, 2 of which are coloured differently from the others. (We will call these the red ones.) You also need two polythene cups. The marbles should fit in the bottom of a cup like this. If they don't all touch the bottom of the cup, give it a gentle shake.

If you put the 7 marbles in at random, what is the probability that the 2 red marbles are next to each other ?

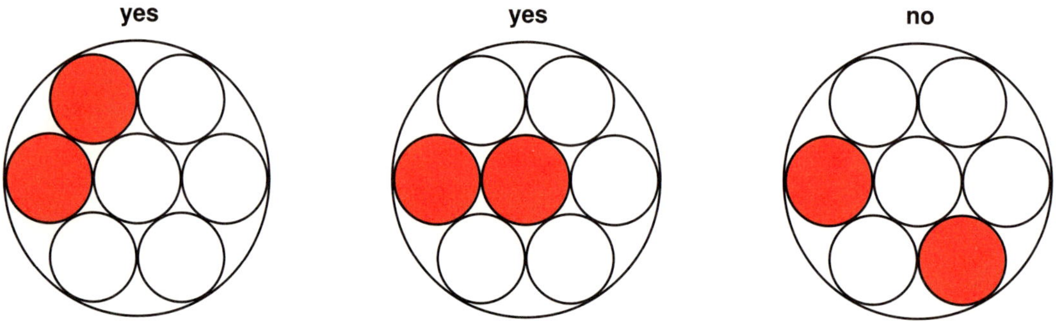

Make a guess first.

When you have carried out one trial, record the results as a tick (✓) or a cross (✗). Then pour the marbles into the other cup for the next trial. Repeat until you have collected at least 100 results.

Estimated probability of the 2 red marbles being next to each other

$$= \frac{\text{number of successful results}}{\text{total number of results}}$$

Was your guess a good one ?

3. **High cards**

If you are playing a card game using the 52 cards in an ordinary pack, where you begin with 3 cards, what is the probability that they include at least one which is an Ace, King, Queen or Jack ?

Make a guess first.

Shuffle a pack of cards and pick out 3 cards.
Record with a tick if they contain at least one of those cards and with a cross if they do not.
Replace the cards, shuffle the pack and repeat until you have 100 results.

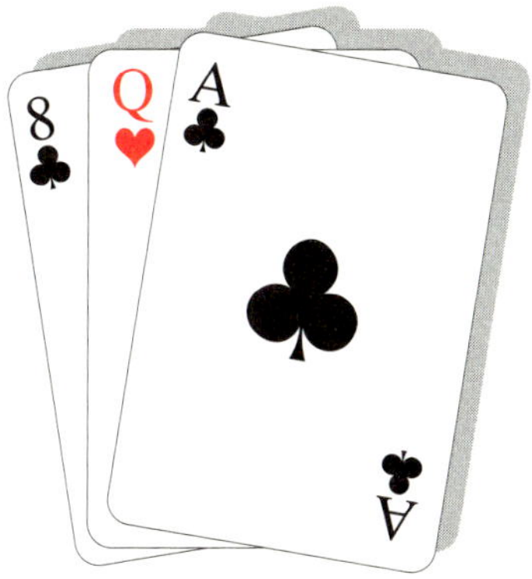

$$\text{Estimated probability} = \frac{\text{number of successful results}}{\text{total number of results}}$$

Was your guess a good one ?

4. **Starting a game**

Archie, Bertie and Charlie were playing a game where they had to throw a six with a die to begin. They argued about wanting to go first, because they thought that the first player had a better chance of throwing a six before the others.
Is this correct ?

What is the probability of the first player to begin being the first to throw a six ?

Use the beginning of your dice grid as the scores of the 3 boys in turn, starting with A (Archie), then B, then C, then A again, etc. When you reach a six, record which boy has thrown it. Then begin again, starting with the next throw on your grid as belonging to A. When you have used all your results, borrow someone else's grid to use as well. Try to get 100 results. Then you can estimate the probability of A getting a six first.

$$\text{Probability} = \frac{\text{number of results in which A threw a six}}{\text{total number of results}}$$

You can also estimate the probability of B and C getting a six first.

Suggest a fair way for the boys to decide who shall go first.

5. **Dominoes**

You can do probability experiments with dominoes.

If you have a set going up to double six then the numbers on them are

0-0 0-1 0-2 ... up to 0-6,
1-1 1-2 1-3 ... up to 1-6,
2-2 2-3 and so on, up to 6-6.

How many dominoes are there altogether ?
Put the dominoes in a bag and draw them out without looking.

If you pick out 2 dominoes at random, what is the probability that they will match ?

They match if they have one number the same.
e.g.

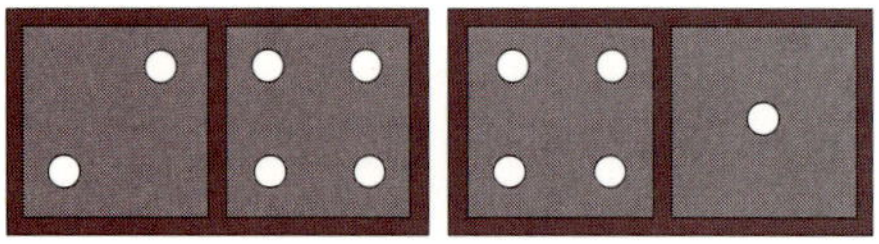

Match

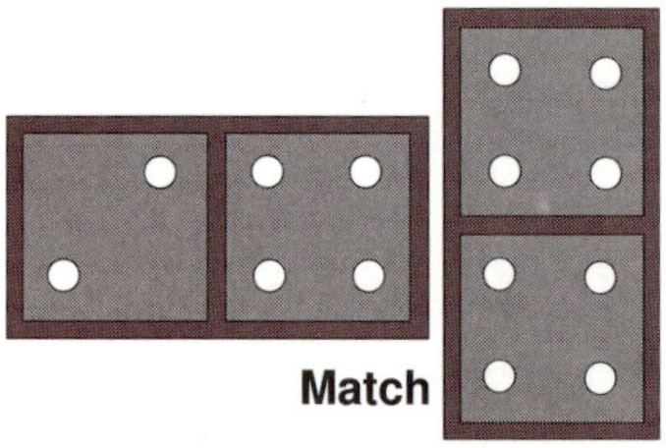

Match

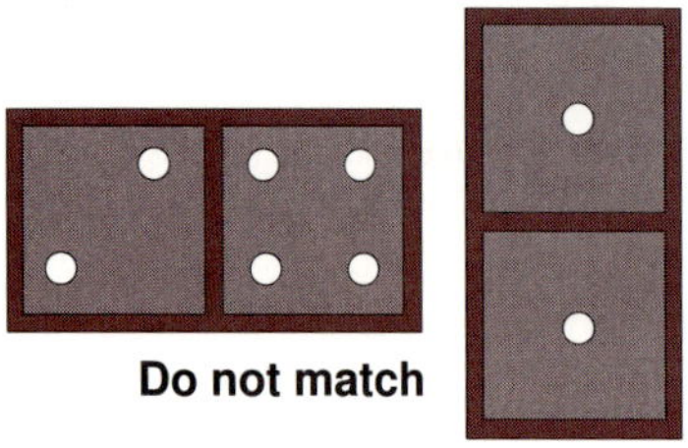

Do not match

Make a guess first.

You can estimate the probability by drawing out 2 dominoes. Record a tick if they match and a cross if they do not. Put the two dominoes back, give the bag a good shake and repeat until you have collected at least 100 results.

$$\text{Probability of 2 dominoes matching} = \frac{\text{number of results which match}}{\text{total number of results}}$$

Was your guess a good one ?

Chapter 6 test

1. In a game at a summer fair, competitors had to roll three balls down a slope into spaces at the far end. Each space was numbered and the total score recorded. Here are the total scores of the first 100 people who played the game.

9	7	12	12	13	13	9	13	17	11	14	5	8	10	14
10	5	12	12	11	13	14	8	6	11	10	8	9	11	13
8	18	14	7	8	5	13	13	13	12	6	15	10	9	10
9	7	7	11	16	15	11	12	15	9	11	9	4	12	11
7	12	12	15	16	12	10	6	8	17	13	9	13	14	10
11	12	8	13	12	10	13	10	8	9	15	14	8	6	9
8	11	14	17	8	11	12	18	10	10					

Use these results as experimental evidence in the questions.

1 There is a prize for totals of 5, 10 or 15. What is the probability that the next player will win a prize ?

2 Later on, the rules were changed so that a prize was given for a total score of 3, 4, 17 or 18. What was the probability that the next player would win a prize ?

2. Henry did an experiment of throwing three dice. He counted the number of sixes showing.
After 200 throws the results were:

0 sixes	1 six	2 sixes	3 sixes	Total throws
114	66	14	6	200

Using these results as experimental evidence, when these three dice are thrown, what is the probability of getting

1 no sixes,
2 1 six,
3 2 sixes,
4 at least 2 sixes ?

PUZZLE

5. If a chiming clock takes 2 seconds to strike 2 o'clock, how long does it take to strike 3 o'clock ?

Miscellaneous Section A

Aural Practice

Often in life you will need to do quick calculations without using pencil and paper or calculator. Sometimes you will **see** the numbers written down, and sometimes you will just **hear** the questions. These aural exercises will give you some practice in **listening** to questions.
These aural exercises, A1 and A2, should be read to you, probably by your teacher or a friend, and you should write down the answers only, doing any working out in your head. You should do the 15 questions within 10 minutes.

Exercise A1

1. What is the value of 9 squared ?
2. What is 60×20 ?
3. What is the greatest number which is a factor of both 32 and 56 ?
4. Write correct to 1 decimal place the number 68.87.
5. Mr Robinson buys a saw costing £8.95. How much change should he get from a £10 note ?
6. These numbers follow a pattern. What are the next 2 numbers in the sequence ? 3, 7, 11, 15, 19.
7. 360 marbles are shared out among some children. They get 40 each. How many children are there ?
8. What is 1.4 multiplied by 100 ?
9. A piece of wood is one hundred and twenty-four centimetres in length. What is this length to the nearest 10 cm ?
10. How many axes of symmetry has a printed capital letter H ?
11. 5 similar pairs of socks cost £4. How much does one pair cost ?

12. In the number 5.842, what is the value of the figure 4 ?

13. In dropping a drawing-pin onto a table, it came to rest point upwards 60 times out of 100. What is an estimate of the probability that the next time it is dropped it will land point upwards ?

14. Write down an approximate value for the product of 29 and 31.

15. Sheila has to take 2 spoonfuls of medicine 4 times each day. How much does she take daily, if a spoonful is 5 ml ?

Exercise A2

1. What is the cost of 100 lollies at 12p each ?

2. A milkman started out with 400 pints of milk and returned with 54 pints. How many pints had he delivered ?

3. Write down the cube root of 8.

4. One lap on a race course is 3.54 miles. Write down this distance correct to 1 decimal place.

5. What is the lowest number into which 2, 3 and 5 all divide exactly ?

6. What is the order of rotational symmetry of a square ?

7. What is 52.4 divided by 10 ?

8. What are the next two numbers in the sequence 100, 96, 92, 88, 84 ?

9. Kiri buys 4 cans of drink for 21 pence each. What change should she get from a £1 coin ?

10. Write down an estimated whole number answer to the question 6.9×5.1.

11. What is the cost of a turkey of weight 9 lb if the price is 80 pence per pound ?

12. What is the value of 3^3 ?

13. A box of pencils was labelled 'Contents one dozen'. How many pencils would there be in 8 boxes ?

14. In an experiment, throwing a disc at random to land on a surface of square tiles, the disc landed completely within a square 70 times out of 100 throws. What is an estimate of the probability that the next time it is thrown it will land completely within a square ?

15. The admission charges for a museum were 80 pence for father, 60 pence for granny and 50 pence each for the 2 children. How much is this altogether ?

Exercise A3 Revision

1. Which of these numbers are prime numbers ? 31, 33, 35, 37, 39.

2. This is the fares table for a local bus service.

Fares in pence

Town centre				
45	Pollard Street			
65	60	Victoria Road		
80	70	45	Addison Road	
95	90	80	65	Long Lane

1 What is the total cost for Mr and Mrs Lambert to travel from Addison Road to the town centre ?

2 What is the total cost for 3 children to travel from Pollard Street to Long Lane ? (Children pay half-fare.)

3. Write these numbers correct to 2 decimal places.

1 7.182 **2** 6.2845 **3** 2029.157 **4** 46.789 **5** 0.03527

4. When boxes are stacked in piles of 5 there are 2 left over, but they can be stacked exactly in piles of 6 or 8. How many are there, if there are less than 100 ?

5. For each of these diagrams, state how many axes of symmetry there are, and whether or not there is rotational symmetry.

1 **2** **3** **4** **5**

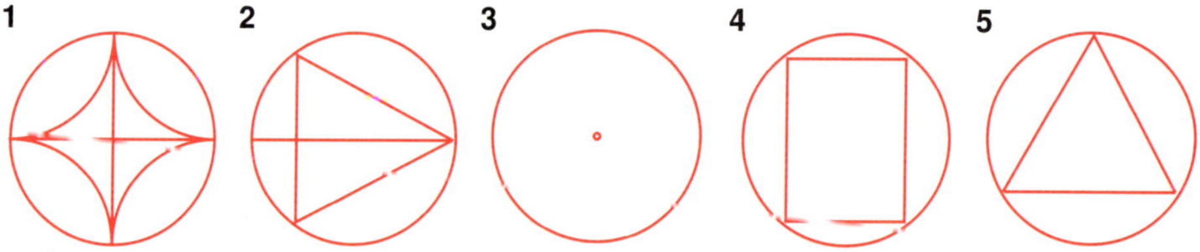

6. The number of insects in a colony doubles each week. If there were 10 insects at first, after how many weeks would there be more than 10 000 ?

7. If 600 cups which should cost 95 p each are bought at a reduced price of 65 p each, what is the total saving ?

8. Find the values of the following, without using your calculator.

1 $8 - 0.4$
2 8×0.4
3 $0.8 \div 4$
4 $0.8 + 0.4$
5 $8000 \div 40$

9. Simon made a wooden die, and he tested it to see if it was a fair one.
In 500 throws, here are the results.

Number	1	2	3	4	5	6
Frequency	80	120	64	27	99	110

Based on these experimental results,

1 what is the probability of scoring a 1 or 2,
2 what is the probability of scoring an even number ?
3 If Simon threw the die another 200 times, how many times approximately could he expect to get the number 6 ?

10. Copy and complete this number pattern to the line beginning $9 \times 9 + 9$.

$1 \times 9 + 1 = 1 \times 7 + 3 = 1 \times 5 + 5 = 1 \times 3 + 7 = 1 \times 1 + 9 = 10$
$3 \times 9 + 3 = 3 \times 7 + 9 = 3 \times 5 + 15 = \ldots$
$5 \times 9 + 5 = 5 \times 7 + 15 = \ldots$
$\ldots$

Exercise A4 Revision

1. If oranges are packed 80 to a box, 30 boxes are needed. How many boxes are needed if they are packed 200 to a box ?

2. A village hall can seat 160 people. Tickets for a charity concert are to be sold at 75 p for adults and 30 p for children. If 50 tickets are to be sold to children and the rest to adults, what will be the total amount raised ?

3. Write these numbers correct to the nearest 100.

1 10 365 **2** 7495 **3** 43 310 **4** 3649 **5** 4962

4. State the order of rotational symmetry of these shapes.

1

2

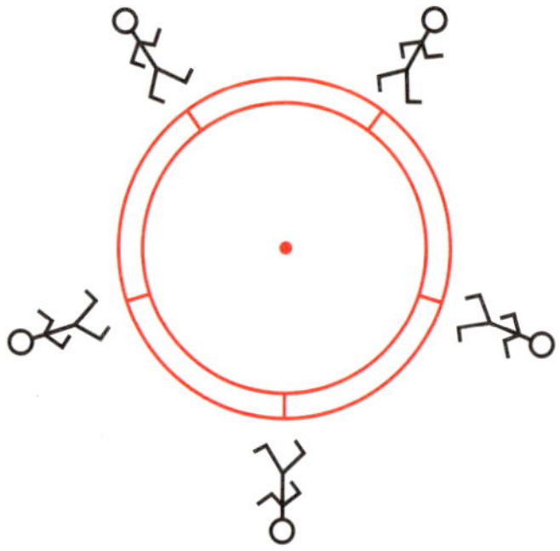

5. Use your calculator to find the value of $(7964 \div 181) - (589 \div 31)$.

6. Bronze model airplanes weigh 5.5 kg. 0.76 of this weight is copper and the rest is tin. How much copper is needed to make 10 such models ?

7. (Try to answer this question without using your calculator.)
The total cost of 35 packets of sweets was £9.80. What was the cost of 1 packet ? If 22 packets of these sweets were bought, what would they cost ?

8. Find the values of

1 2^5 **2** 4^3 **3** $\sqrt{81}$ **4** $\sqrt[3]{125}$ **5** 10^6

9. Lucy had a bag which contained a large number of discs, each with a number from 1 to 5 written on. She did not know how many of each number there were. She took a disc out at random, recorded its number, and then replaced it. Her results after 500 goes shows a disc with a number 3 on coming out 200 times. What is an estimate of the probability that the next disc taken out will have a number 3 on it ?

10. Copy and complete the 1st 9 rows of this pattern.

$$\begin{aligned} 1 &= \frac{1 \times 2}{2} = 1 \\ 1+2 &= \frac{2 \times 3}{2} = 3 \\ 1+2+3 &= \frac{3 \times 4}{2} = 6 \\ 1+2+3+4 &= \qquad = \\ \ldots \end{aligned}$$

Now using the method of this pattern, work out the sum of the numbers from 1 to 40.

Exercise A5 Activities

1. **Planning a party** or an adventure afternoon for younger children.
This can be in your own home, for a younger brother or sister, or it may be for members of a children's club, held in the clubroom. It can be for a birthday, for Christmas, or for some other festival time or celebration.

First, decide on what sort of afternoon you are planning, how many children there will be, the ages of the children involved and when and where it will be held. You could have a theme for the afternoon, such as 'pirates' or 'clowns'. Design an invitation card.

Find out how much you can spend, perhaps as an over-all total or as 'so much a head'.

Plan a menu and decide how much of each item must be bought. Do not forget to include soft drinks.

Plan a timetable for the afternoon with the time of beginning and the time it will end, times for various activities such as games and entertainment, and time for eating.

Decide what other things must be bought, other than food, e.g. balloons, decorations, small prizes. Are there any other expenses such as the hire of an entertainer or the hire of a room ? Find the total cost of everything.

Write all these details in a booklet and illustrate it with pictures.

2. **A number pattern**

Make a pattern involving 4 consecutive numbers. Multiply them all together and add 1. Investigate the results.

Numbers	Product	Add 1
1, 2, 3, 4	24	25
2, 3, 4, 5	120	121
3, 4, 5, 6	...	
...		

3. **Multiplication**

This is a multiplication table chart using the numbers 3, 6, 9 only.

×	3	6	9
3	9	18	27
6	18	36	54
9	27	54	81

Now copy the table, but change all the 2-figure numbers, such as 18, to 1-figure numbers, by adding the 2 figures together.
e.g. for 18, $1 + 8 = 9$, so write down 9.
Comment on the table.

Now make a similar multiplication table, with 2-figure numbers changed to 1-figure numbers, using the numbers 1, 2, 4, 5, 7, 8.
For a result such as 56, change 56 to $5 + 6 = 11$, then change 11 to $1 + 1 = 2$.
Look for patterns in the table and comment on them.

4. **Cube numbers and multiples of three**

1 Write down a list of the cubes of numbers from 0 to 9.

2 Here is a rule for a number chain.
For a 1-figure number, cube the number. For other numbers, cube each figure of the number and find the sum of these cubes.
Repeat this rule as long as you get to a different number.
e.g. for $126 \rightarrow 1^3 + 2^3 + 6^3 = 1 + 8 + 216 = 225$
then $225 \rightarrow 2^3 + 2^3 + 5^3 = \ldots$, and so on.
Investigate this number chain, but only start with any numbers which are multiples of 3.

3 There is a slight connection with triangular numbers. Can you say what it is ?

4 If you have a Bible, you may be interested to look at St. John, chapter 21, verse 11.

5. **Roman Numerals**

These are still in use as numbers, although not for calculations. Find the numbers from one to twelve on a clock or watch. There the number four will be shown as IIII, but the more usual way is IV. Note that number one is the capital letter I, not figure 1.

In old books you will find the chapters labelled in Roman numerals. Larger numbers can be found as dates on foundation stones, old gravestones or memorial tablets. Parts of questions in some textbooks are numbered using small-lettered numbers in the Roman numeral system, e.g. (i), (ii), etc.

Look for examples of Roman numerals and make a list of those you find.
From these you can discover how the system works.
What are the letters used for 1, 10, 100, 1000 ?
What are the letters used for 5, 50, 500 ?
Note the connections between

1	10	100	1000
2	20	200	2000
3	30	300	3000
4	40	400	
5	50	500	
6	60	600	
etc.			

To change a number such as 1946 into Roman numerals you deal with each figure in turn. Change 1000, then 900, then 40, then 6.

Change these numbers into Roman numerals:

1 27 **2** 84 **3** 1990 **4** 475 **5** 1839

Change these Roman numerals into ordinary numbers:

6 MMCMII **7** XLIII **8** CDIV **9** MCMXCV **10** CCLIX

7 Thinking about the metric system

The metric system — a new beginning

In order to trade, we need a standard system of weights and measures. Most systems develop from ancient uses in a haphazard way, and values given to the various weights and measures could differ in different areas.

The metric system was planned to make a new beginning, with well-defined units, the metre, the gram and the litre, and it was based on a scale of ten, as that is the basis for our numbering system. Although it was developed about 200 years ago, it was only made legal in Britain in 1864, and even then it could not be used in trade until 1897. One hundred years later, we are still not fully committed to using the metric system although we are gradually using it more and more.

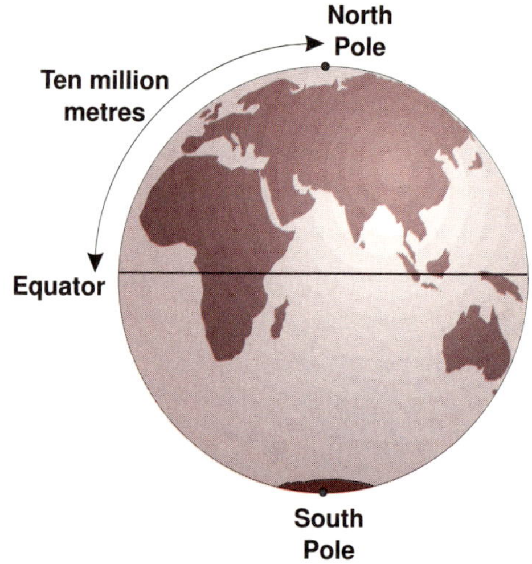

1 metre was to be measured as $\frac{1}{10\,000\,000}$ of the distance from the North Pole to the equator.

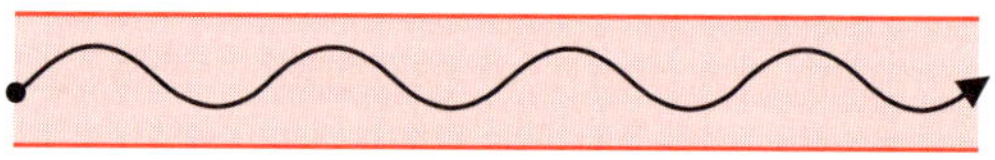

A metre is the length of the path travelled by light in a vacuum during a time interval of $\frac{1}{299\,792\,458}$ of a second.
This is how a metre is defined today.

Selling in metric measures

Name some items, bought by weight, which will be weighed in kilograms or grams.
Name some items, bought by length, which will be measured in metres or centimetres.
Name some liquids which are sold in litres, centilitres or millilitres.

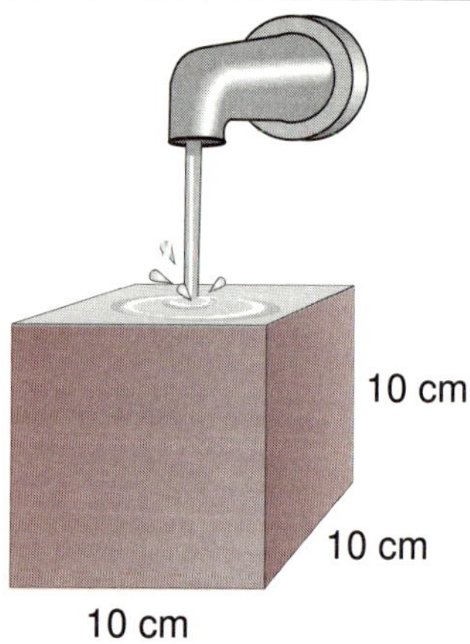

This cube will hold 1 litre.
The water to fill it will weigh 1 kilogram.

Capacity in litres or ml

Weights in kg or g. Notice that the bag of potatoes holds 5 lb but the weight is also shown in kilograms.

Metric activities

Mark out on the floor a length of 1 metre.

Find an object which weighs 1 kilogram.

Find a container which will hold 1 litre.

A road sign in Australia

Using metric measures

Name some advantages which the metric system has over the British system of weights and measures.
Why is it used so much in scientific work ?

Name some situations where these people would use metric measures, and say what units are involved:

A motorist
A person baking a cake
A surveyor
A child at school
A health visitor
A person on holiday in Europe
A builder
A greengrocer
An athlete or a swimmer
A person knitting a sweater

Think of some other people who use metric weights and measures in their jobs or leisure activities, and say what units are involved.

7 The metric system

Length

The main unit is called the **metre** (m).
One-thousandth part of a metre is a millimetre (mm).
One-hundredth part of a metre is a centimetre (cm).
One thousand metres is a kilometre (km).

i.e.

1000 mm = 1 m
100 cm = 1 m (so 10 mm = 1 cm)
1000 m = 1 km

Weight

The main unit is the **gram** (g).
One-thousandth part of a gram is a milligram (mg).
One-hundredth part of a gram is a centigram (cg).
One thousand grams is a kilogram (kg).
Since a kilogram is rather a small weight, a larger unit is often needed.
One thousand kilograms is a tonne, sometimes called a metric ton.

i.e.

1000 mg = 1 g
100 cg = 1 g
1000 g = 1 kg
100 kg = 1 tonne

Capacity

The main unit is the **litre** (ℓ).
One-thousandth part of a litre is a millilitre (ml).
One-hundredth part of a litre is a centilitre (cl).
One thousand litres is a kilolitre (kl).

i.e.

1000 ml = 1 ℓ
100 cl = 1 ℓ
1000 ℓ = 1 kl

It is useful to know that

1 millilitre of water weighs 1 gram,
1 litre of water weighs 1 kilogram.

To change from one unit to another

centimetres into millimetres

1 cm = 10 mm, so to change cm into mm multiply by 10.
5 cm = 50 mm
6.2 cm = 62 mm

mm into cm

10 mm = 1 cm, so to change mm into cm divide by 10.
30 mm = 3 cm
24 mm = 2.4 cm

metres into cm

1 m = 100 cm, so to change metres into cm multiply by 100.
3.2 m = 320 cm
5.61 m = 561 cm

cm into metres

100 cm = 1 m, so to change cm into metres divide by 100.
62 cm = 0.62 m
560 cm = 5.6 m

metres into mm

1 m = 1000 mm, so to change metres into mm multiply by 1000.
2 m = 2000 mm
1.5 m = 1500 mm
0.07 m = 70 mm

mm into metres

1000 mm = 1 m, so to change mm into metres divide by 1000.
2500 mm = 2.5 m
6 mm = 0.006 m

The methods are similar for changing units of weight and capacity.
e.g. To change grams into kg, divide by 1000.
To change litres into ml, multiply by 1000.

Exercise 7.1

1. How many

1	mm in 8 cm	**5**	mg in 3 g	**8**	ml in $1\frac{1}{2}$ litres
2	g in 4 kg	**6**	mm in 5 m	**9**	cm in 60 mm
3	cm in $\frac{1}{2}$m	**7**	kg in 10 tonnes	**10**	kg in 2000 g ?
4	m in 2 km				

2. Write

1	2560 g in kg	**5**	2.3 m in cm	**8**	800 cl in ℓ
2	25 cm in m	**6**	3.5 kg in g	**9**	356 cm in m
3	4 ℓ in ml	**7**	36 mm in cm	**10**	0.75 kg in g
4	9 cm in mm				

3. If 1 washer weighs 7 g, what do 1000 washers weigh, in kg ?

4. An urn contains 8 ℓ of tea. A cup holds 160 ml of tea. How many cups can be filled from the urn ?

5. A roll of cloth contains 75 m of the cloth. A pattern for a dress uses 4.5 m of the cloth. How many of these dresses can be made from 3 rolls of cloth ?

6. Helen has 4 packets of seeds.
She wants to plant the seeds in rows 6 m long.
How many rows can she plant ?

7. A charity collected 60.5 kg of knitting wool. They plan to use this to knit baby garments, which each take 110 g of wool. How many garments will it make ?

8. A chemist has 5 cartons of bottles of cough medicine. How many litres of medicine are there altogether ?

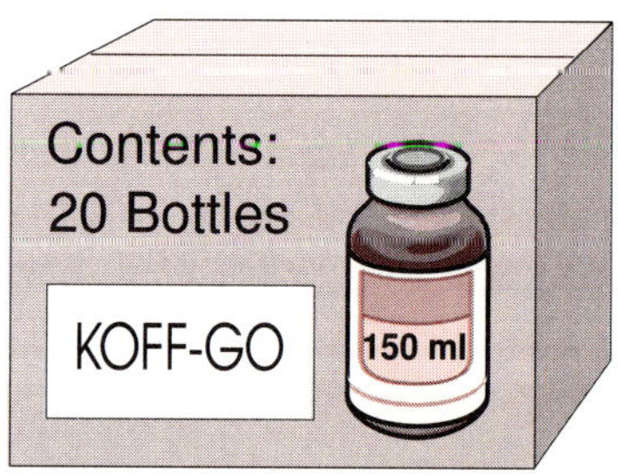

9. 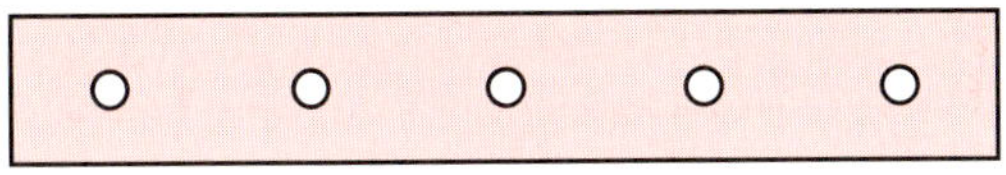

The diagram shows a piece of wood with 5 screw holes marked. The distance between each pair of holes is 11.5 cm and the distance between the end holes and the edge of the wood is 4.2 cm. (The measurements are taken to the centres of the holes.) How long is the piece of wood ?

10. A grocer buys tea in bulk, blends it, and then sells it in 120 g packets. How many packets can he make from 54 kg of tea ?

11. A surveyor used a chain marked as 20 m long to measure out the line for a fence of length 300 m. The chain was actually 20.1 m long. How long was the fence likely to be ?

12. Party glasses hold 160 ml. How many glasses can be filled from a 3-litre bottle of lemonade ?
A 2-litre bottle of orange squash is diluted with four times as much water. How many glasses can be filled from this diluted squash ?

Accuracy of measurements

If you had to measure the width of a field then your first problem would be to decide where the exact boundaries were. It would probably be sufficient for your purpose to measure it in metres, and if this was not accurate enough you could measure it to the nearest 0.1 m. It is easier to measure the floor of a room, because it is clearer to see where to begin and end the measurement. You could measure this to the nearest 0.1 m (10 cm). If you needed a more accurate measurement, for example, to buy a fitted carpet, you could measure it to the nearest centimetre. When measuring lines in geometry, we usually measure to the nearest millimetre.
Therefore, the accuracy that you must choose depends on what you are measuring, for what purpose you need the measurement, and how accurate your measuring instruments are.

Similar ideas apply to weighing. With many heavy objects it might be sufficient to weigh in kg, but lighter objects need to be measured correct to 100 g, 25 g or 10 g. You would need to measure more accurately for scientific experiments.

Shopkeepers and others who sell goods by weight, length or capacity have to have accurate weighing and measuring instruments. However, many goods are supplied pre-packed nowadays, so that the quantity is stated on the package and the shopkeeper does not need to weigh or measure anything.

Measuring a length

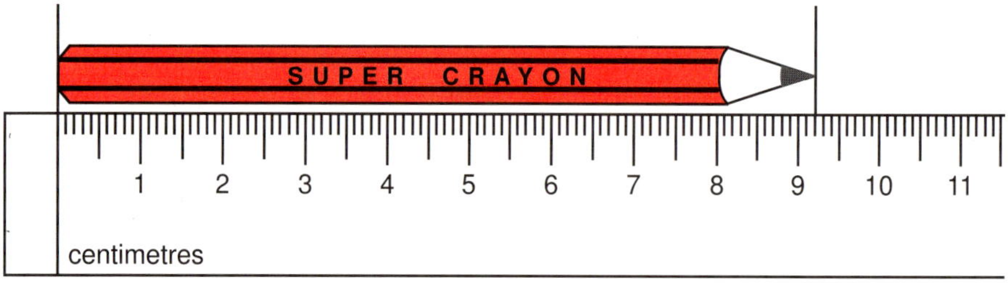

To measure the length of the crayon, first decide how many whole centimetres there are (9), and then count how many millimetres to the nearest millimetre mark (2).
So the measurement is 9 cm 2 mm.
This would be written as 9.2 cm or 92 mm.

Readings on a weighing scale

This is a weighing scale which weighs in kilograms from 0 to 3 kg. The half-kilogram marks are marked 500 for 500 g. Between 0 and 500 there are 4 larger marks. These represent 100, 200, 300 and 400 g. The smaller marks between each of these represent 50 g.

The measurement shown is between 2 kg and 3 kg. Counting the longer marks it is between 200 g and 300 g. It is halfway between them, making it 250 g. So the weight is 2 kg 250 g.
This would be written in grams as 2250 g, or in kilograms as 2.25 kg.

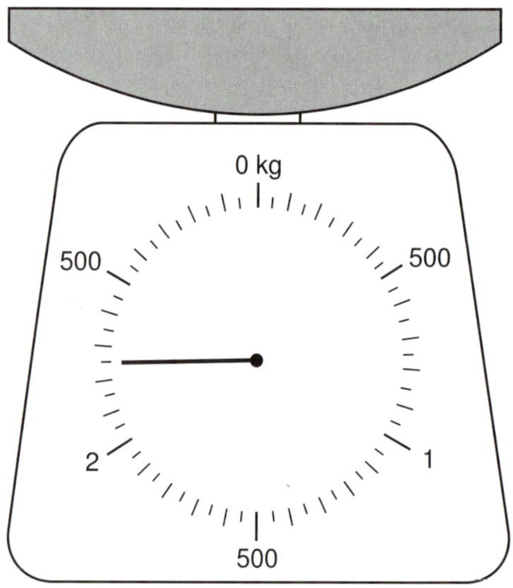

Exercise 7.2

1. Give the readings shown on these instruments.

1 Weight in kg.

2 Weighing scale in kg and g.

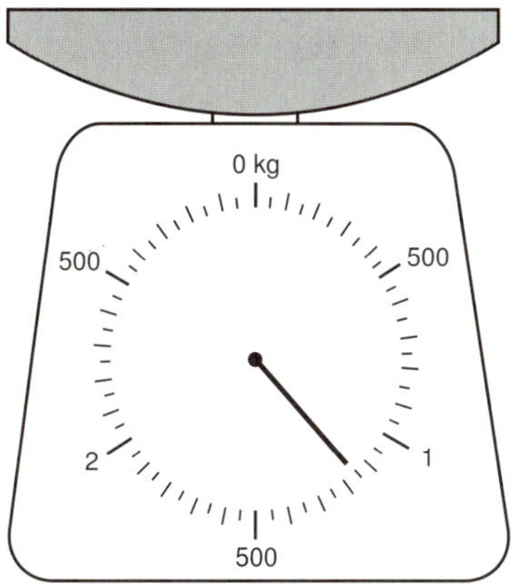

3 Measuring jug.

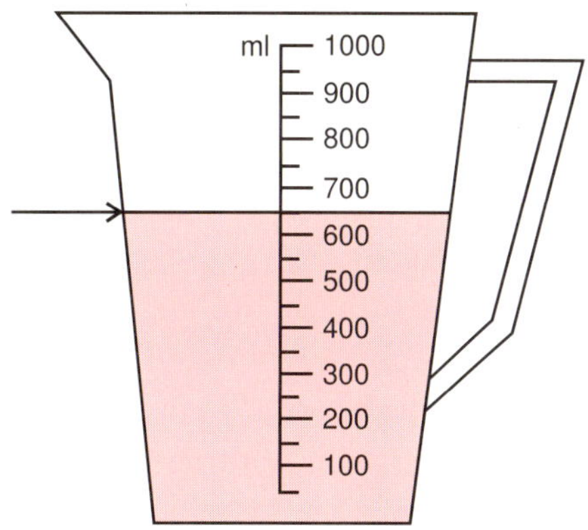

2. Using the ruler shown in the diagram.

1 what is the reading shown at A,

2 what is the reading shown at B,

3 what is the length of the elephant, in cm ?

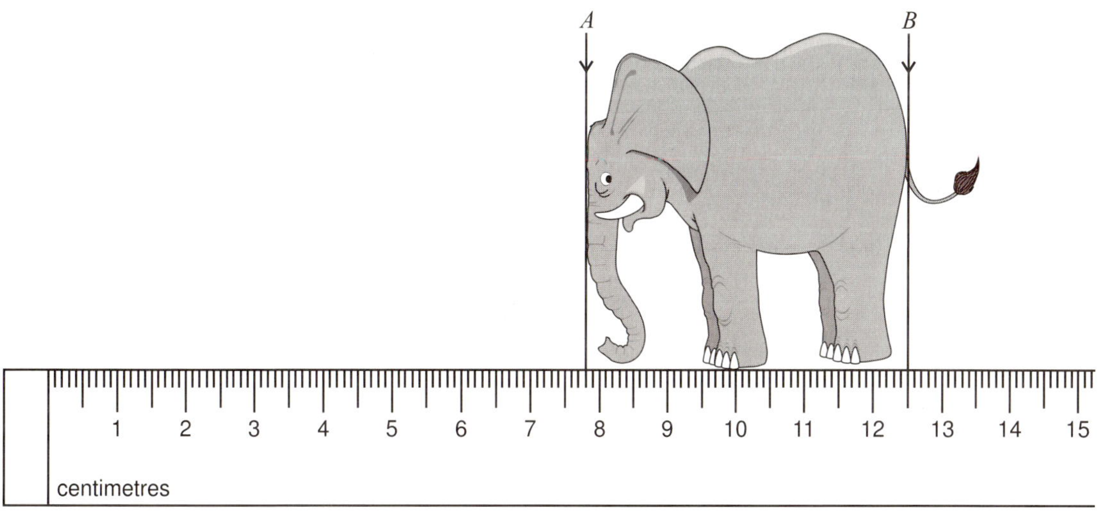

Estimation

It is useful to be able to make good estimates of weights and measurements. Here are some suggestions to improve your skill. You should think of others.

Length

Find out the measurements of your thumb as far as the knuckle, the width of your hand across four fingers, the length of your hand-span, the length of your foot with a shoe on, your height, the distance you can reach with arms stretched out, the height you can reach on tiptoe, and so on. Use a measured distance of 100 m to find the length of your pace when you walk normally, and how long your stride is. Practise estimating distances by comparing them with these lengths.

You could make your own measuring instruments by getting a length of rope and marking it off every metre. Then get a length of wood 1 metre long and mark it off every 10 cm or 5 cm. Use your ruler as well, and you should be able to measure lengths quite accurately.

Weight

Get used to the weight of 1 kg (a bag of sugar) and 2.5 kg (a bag of potatoes). For smaller weights, a 20 p coin weighs 5 g, so 20 of them weigh 100 g. Find your own weight in kg and the weight of a small child. Estimate other weights by comparing them with these known weights.

Capacity

Estimate how much water various containers hold and check by using a measuring jug or a litre bottle. A bucket or a watering can may have measuring lines marked on it. It is useful to remember that 1 litre of water weighs 1 kg.

Exercise 7.3

1. Estimate the following and then check as many as possible by making accurate measurements or weighings.

   1 The width of the doorway.
   2 The weight of your calculator.
   3 The height of the step on the nearest staircase.
   4 The amount of water to fill a washbasin.
   5 The length of a piece of string which will just go round your waist.
   6 The weight of a chair.
   7 The weight of a pencil.
   8 The amount of liquid to fill a small glass.
   9 The height of the ceiling.
   10 The width of your house frontage.

2. For these statements, 4 alternatives are given in brackets. Which one makes the most sensible statement ?

   1 Marion's 20-year-old brother is (1.2) (1.8) (2.4) (6) metres tall.

   2 Alan's baby sister weighs (35 g) (350 g) ($3\frac{1}{2}$ kg) (35 kg). His other young sister weighs (35 g) (350 g) ($3\frac{1}{2}$ kg) (35 kg).

   3 The height of the oak tree in the field is (1.5) (20) (50) (75) metres.

   4 The amount of water in a full garden watering can is (100 ml) (500 ml) (1 ℓ) (10 ℓ).

   5 To knit a child's jumper you need about (250 g) (2 kg) (5 kg) (10 kg) of wool.

3. The photograph shows two people standing by a megolithic monument in Minorca. Estimate the height of the monument. (You can assume the people are about 1.7 m tall.)

Exercise 7.4 Applications and Activities

1. **Capacity**

   Look in your home for containers which have the capacity marked on them.
   Then make a list, from the smallest to the largest.

e.g.	Bottle of Tipp-Ex	20 ml
	Antiseptic liquid	200 ml
	Washing-up liquid	500 ml
	Tin of motor oil	5 ℓ
	Watering can	8 ℓ

2. **Weights**

Look in your home for items which weigh 5 g, 10 g, 50 g, 100 g, 200 g, 500 g, 1 kg, 2 kg, etc.
Display the items in order, from the lightest to the heaviest, and label them with their weights.
If possible, take a photograph of the items on display.

3. **The metric system**

Find out as much as you can about this and design a poster about it.
Here are some of the things you can consider:
When was it introduced ? In which country ?
What was the original definition of a metre ? What is the present definition of a metre ?
Although we usually use the prefixes milli-, centi-, kilo-, there are others, e.g. deci-. Find out about these. Why were these words chosen for the prefixes ?

4. **Estimating**

Arrange to hold a competition involving estimation. There could be several parts, involving length, height, weight (heavy and light), and capacity (large and small). Judge the entries and decide which one is the winner.

Chapter 7 test

1. A cupboard is placed along a wall of a room, as shown. The wall is 3.7 m long. How wide is the cupboard ?

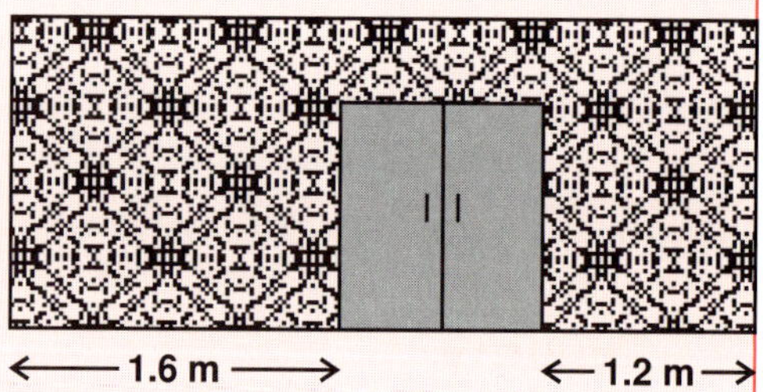

2. A bag of damp sand weighed 5.5 kg. After it dried out it weighed 4.7 kg. What was the loss of weight, in grams ?

3. A box of sweets weighed 550 g. The box weighed 70 g and there were 80 sweets inside. What was the average weight of 1 sweet ?

4. A tin of powdered food contains a plastic measuring scoop, which holds 9 ml of the powder. The tin contains 0.45 litres of powder. How many scoopfuls can be taken out ?

5. A piece of ribbon is 5 m long. 5 pieces of length 85 cm are cut from it. How long is the piece that is left, in cm ?

6. A fence is made by placing 12 posts, 2.6 m between each pair, and joining them with 4 strands of wire. How long is the fence, and how much wire is needed ? (Ignore the thickness of the posts.)

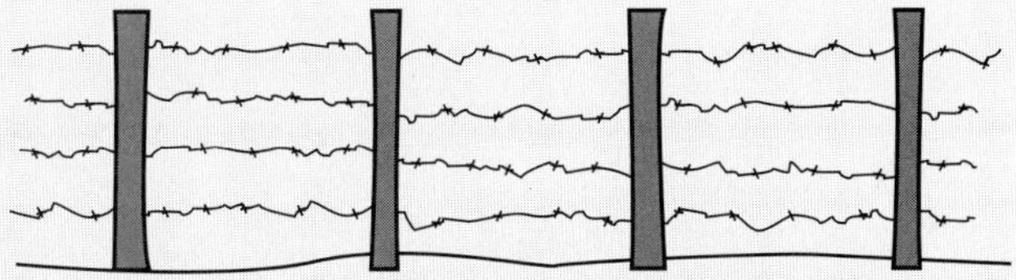

7. Give the readings shown on these instruments.

1 Weighing scale in kg and g. **2** Measuring jug.

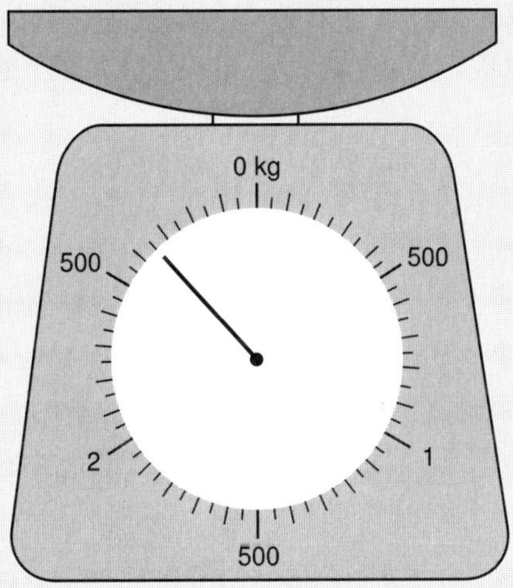

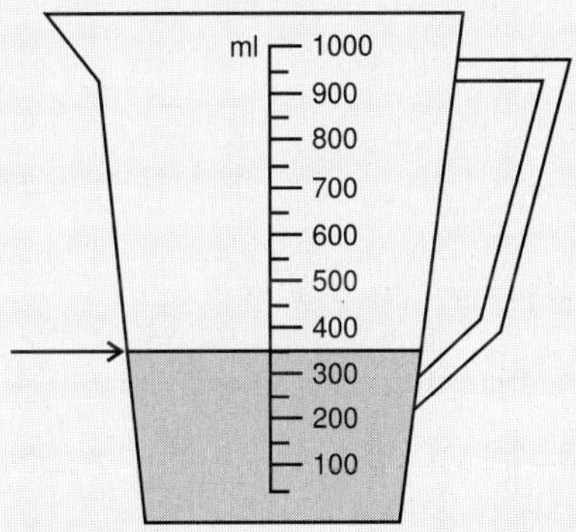

8. For these statements, 4 alternatives are given in brackets. Which one makes the most sensible statement ?

1 If 50 new pencils were placed end-to-end to make a long straight line, the line would stretch for
(80 cm) (1.5 m) (2 m) (8 m).

2 The rise of each step of a staircase in a house is
(2 cm) (5 cm) (20 cm) (50 cm).

3 The weight of a bucket full of sand is
(1 kg) (10 kg) (50 kg) (100 kg).

4 The amount of liquid in a small bottle of shampoo is
(3 ml) (10 ml) (300 ml) (2 ℓ).

8 Thinking about lines and angles

Geometry instruments

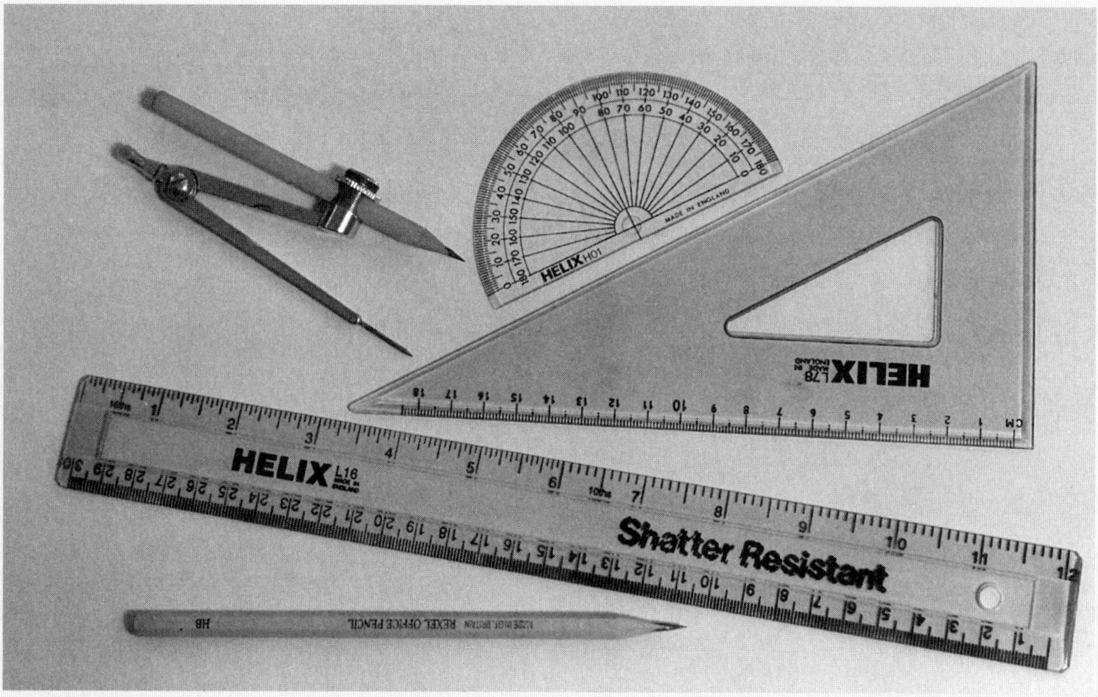

We draw and measure lines using a ruler.
A set-square is used to draw parallel lines.
It can also be used to draw right angles and perpendicular lines.
A protractor is used to draw and measure angles.
Compasses are used to draw circles or arcs of circles.
For accurate drawing, use a sharp pencil which is not too hard or too soft.

Which line is longer ?

Measure the lines AB and CD in centimetres, to the nearest millimetre.

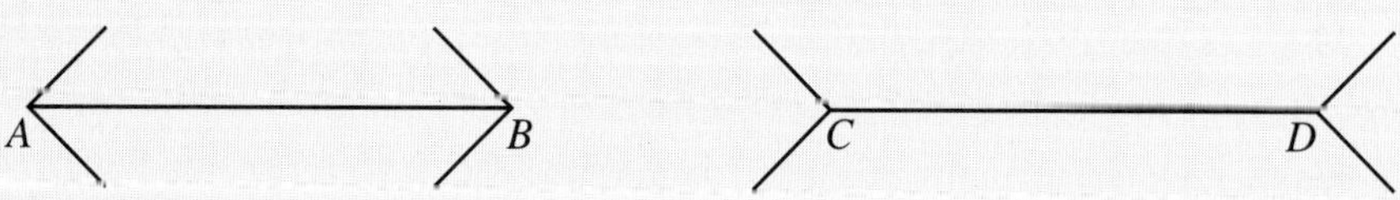

Angles and their measurement

What is an angle ?
Look for different-sized angles in objects seen in daily life.
What kind of angle do we see most often ?

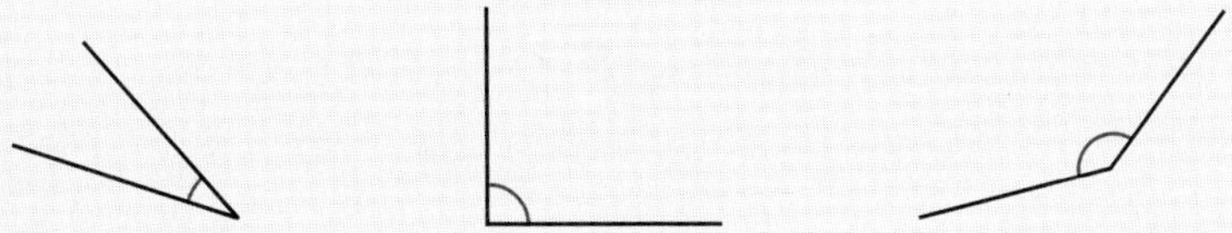

(sharp angle) (a quarter-turn) (blunt angle)

What are the proper names given to these sorts of angles ? Look up the meanings of the words in a dictionary and you will see why these names were chosen.

What do we call an angle making a complete turn ?
What smaller units do we use to measure angles ?
What instrument do we use to measure angles ? There are also instruments used to measure complete turns, especially in machines. What are these called ?
We do not split a complete turn into 100 (or 10) smaller units because we are not using a metric system for angle measurement. How many units do we split it into ?
The units were established in Ancient Babylon. Where is Babylon ? Why was such a number of units chosen for a complete turn ?

What is a reflex angle ?

What other facts concerning angles do you know ?

Angles and turning

Give some examples of things which **turn**.
Open your desk lid, the classroom door, or your textbook, to make various angles with its closed position. Guess the sizes of the angles turned through.
Estimate the sizes of the angles involved when you turn on a tap, screw in a screw, turn a key to unlock a door, turn a handle to open a door, open a door to enter a room, or put your arm out to signal for the bus to stop. You can think of other examples for yourself.

How big is the angle of the fan ?

8 Lines and angles

Drawing and measuring lines

This is the line *AB*.

A and *B* are the points at the ends of the line.

If a line has to be drawn **to an accurate length** it is useful to draw the line slightly longer than needed and then mark the accurate length by small marks crossing the line.

Example

Draw a line *CD*, 6.2 cm long.
This is 6 cm 2 mm.

Draw a line longer than needed, and put a cross-mark for *C* near one end.
First count along 6 cm and then another 2 mm, and mark *D* there.
The part of the line between the cross-marks for *C* and *D* should be 6.2 cm long.

Exercise 8.1

1. Measure these lines, in centimetres to the nearest millimetre.

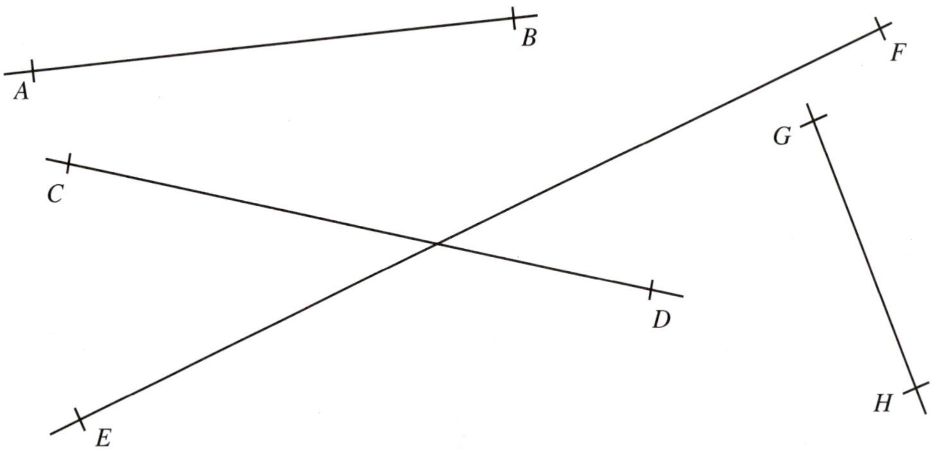

2. Draw these lines accurately.
$AB = 7.3$ cm, $CD = 5.8$ cm, $EF = 11.7$ cm, $GH = 2.6$ cm, $JK = 14.1$ cm.

Angles

An **angle** measures the amount of turning or the change of direction between two lines.

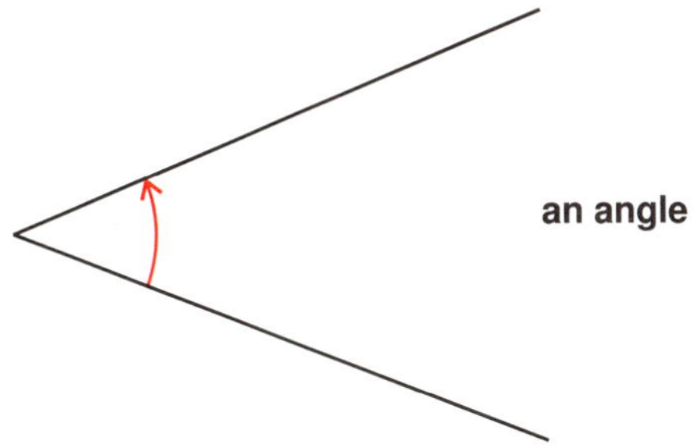

The size of an angle

Imagine that you are standing at the point O and you are facing A.
You now turn and face B.
To do this you turn through the angle shown.

The size of an angle is measured in **degrees**.

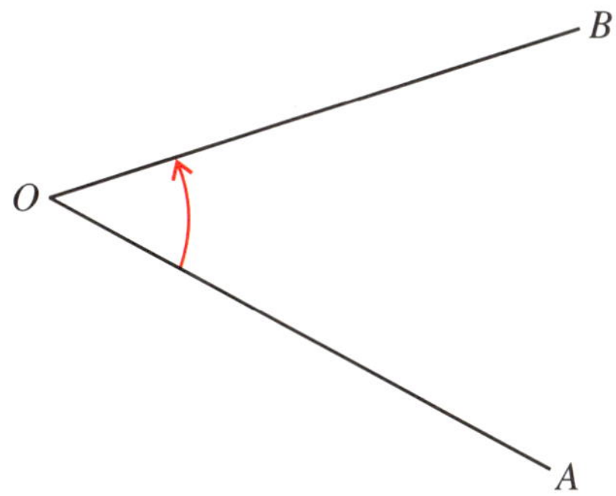

Types of angle

1 complete turn is called a revolution.
It is divided into 360° (360 degrees).

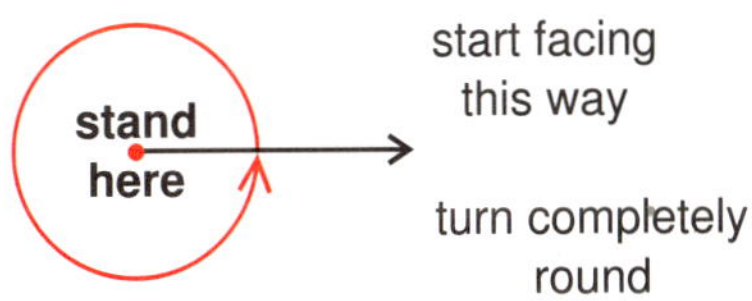

1 half-turn is 180°.

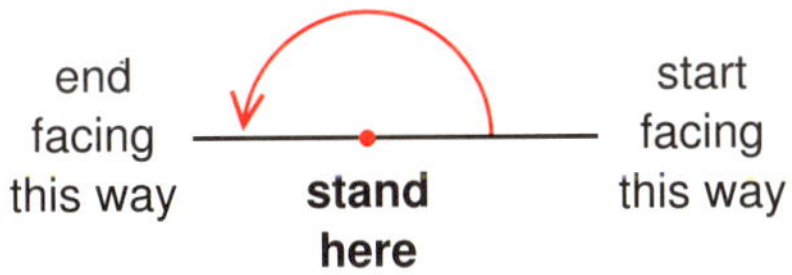

Right angle

1 quarter-turn is 90°. This is also called a **right angle**.

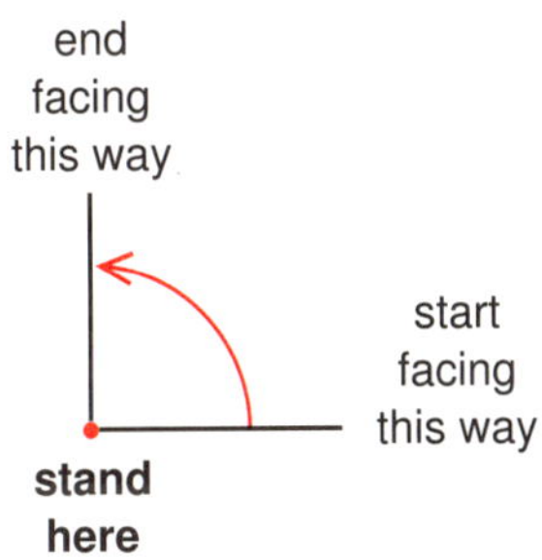

The sign for a right angle is a mark in the corner of the angle making a small square.

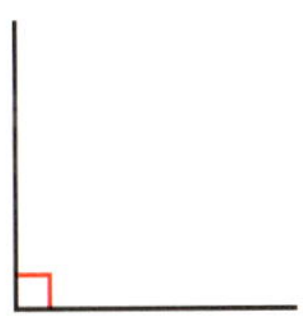

Acute angle

An angle less than 90° is called an **acute** angle.

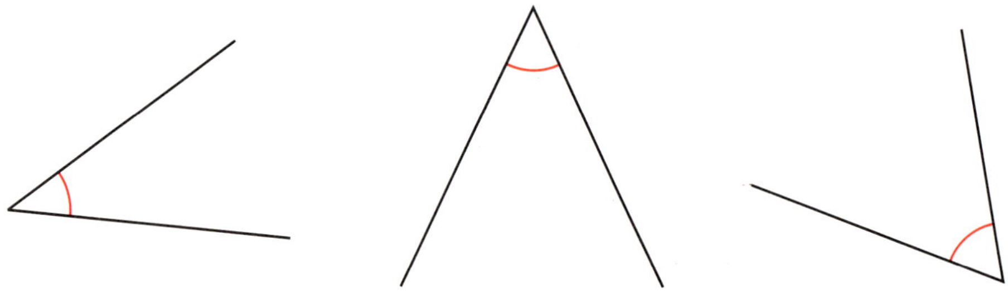

acute angles

Obtuse angle

An angle between 90° and 180° is called an **obtuse** angle.

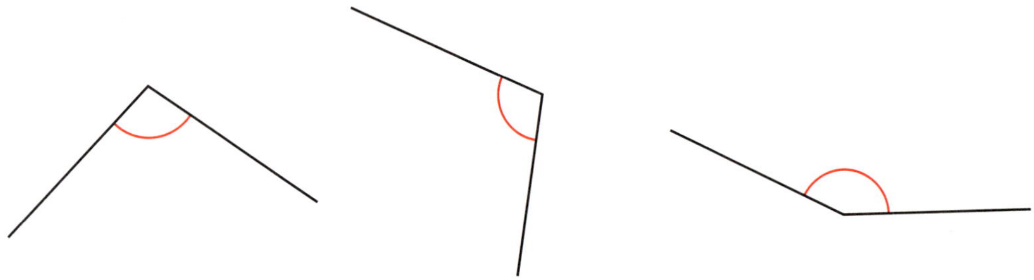

obtuse angles

Reflex angle

An angle between 180° and 360° is called a **reflex** angle.

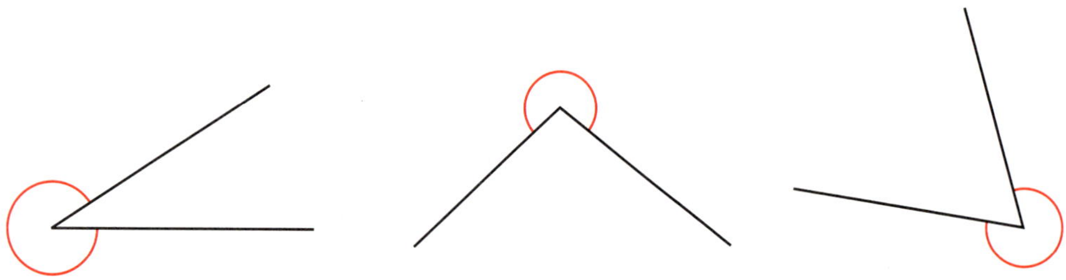

reflex angles

Exercise 8.2

Say whether these angles are acute, obtuse or reflex angles.

1.
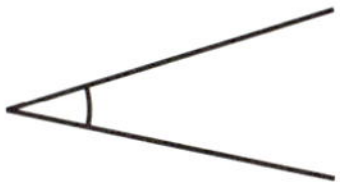

2.

3.

4.
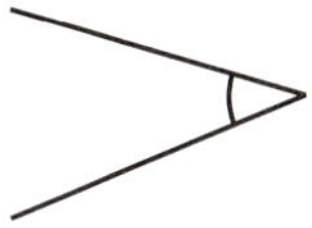

5.

6.
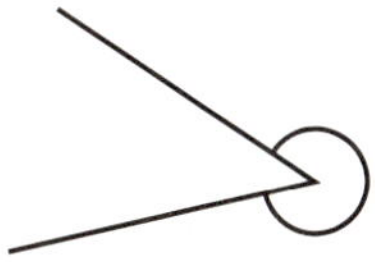

7.

8.

9.
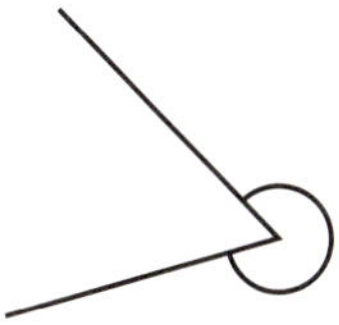

10.
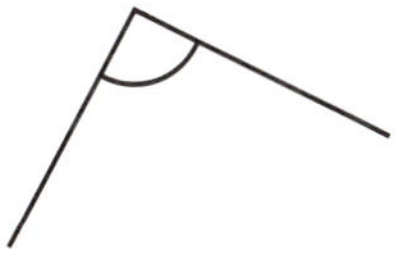

Use of a protractor

There are two types of protractor, one is semi-circular in shape and the other is circular. Both of these can be used to measure an angle, or to draw an angle of a particular size.

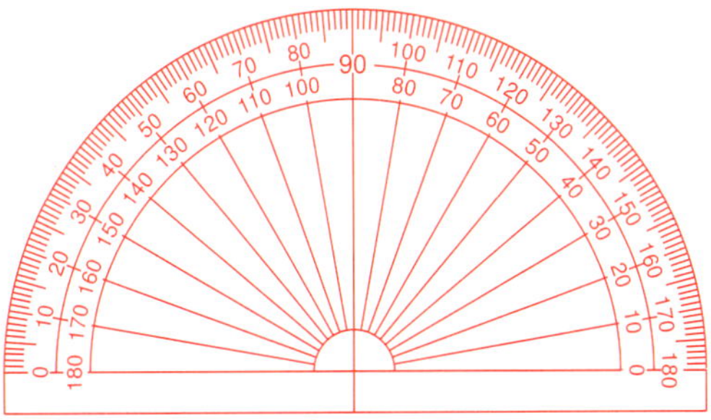

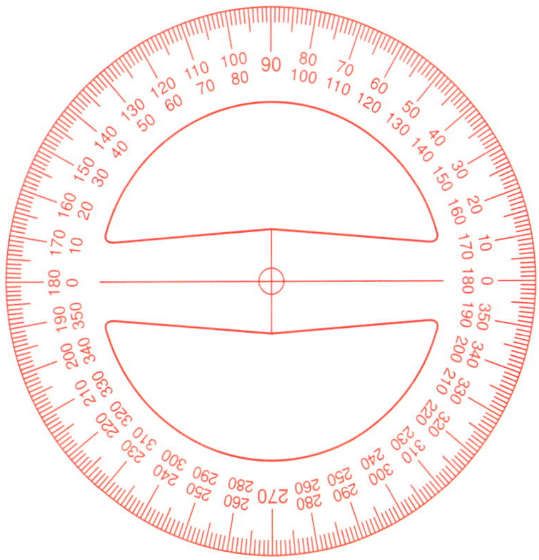

To measure an angle

1 Put the centre point of the protractor on the point of the angle.
2 Put the 0° line of the protractor on one of the lines of the angle.
3 Count round from 0° to read the size of the angle.
If the 0° you are using is on the **outside** set of figures, use those figures, counting past 10°, 20°, 30°, etc.
If the 0° you are using is on the **inside** set of figures, then you will use those figures.
(Not all circular protractors are marked in the same way so yours may not be numbered like the one shown below.)

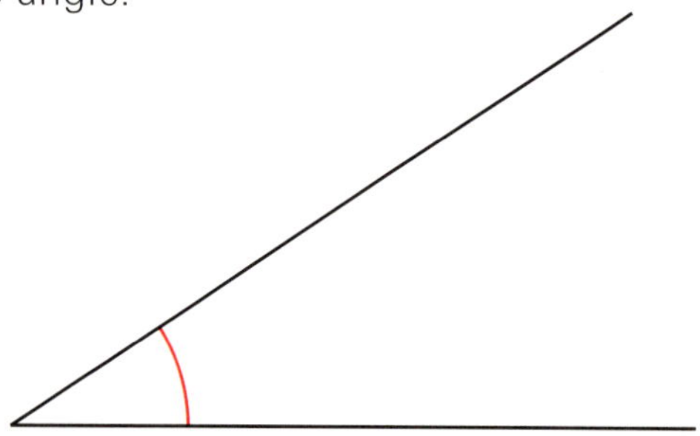

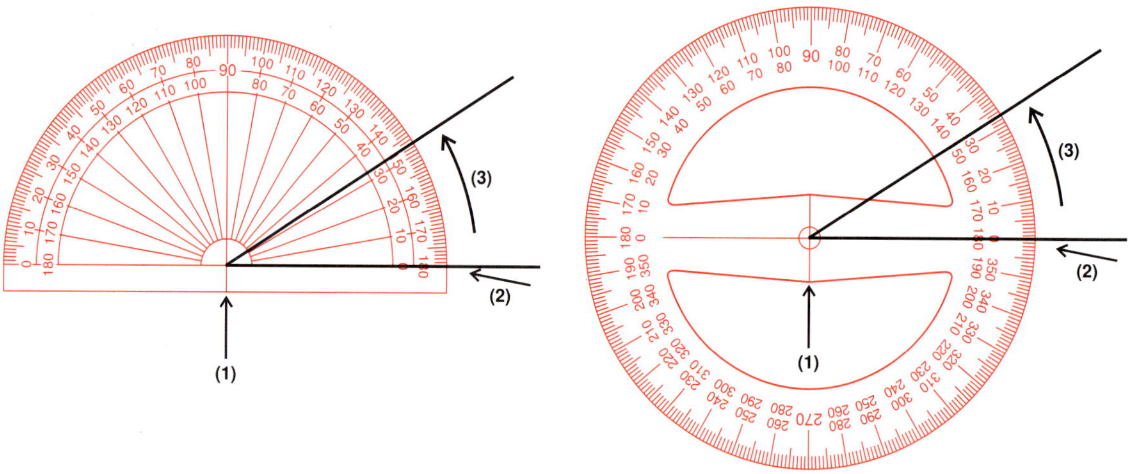

These protractors show an angle of 33° being measured.

Use your protractor to measure this angle.

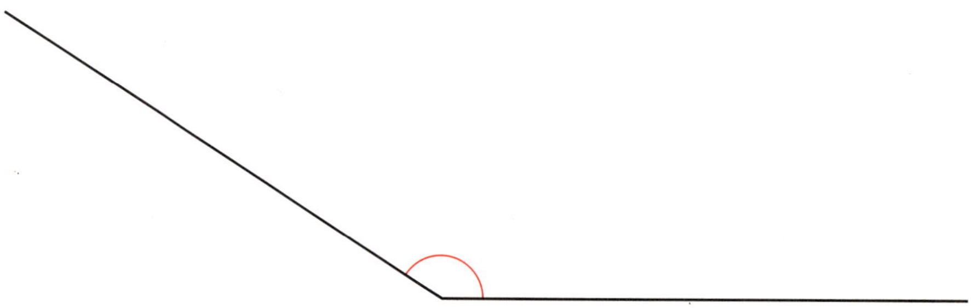

Use the other 0° line if it is more convenient.

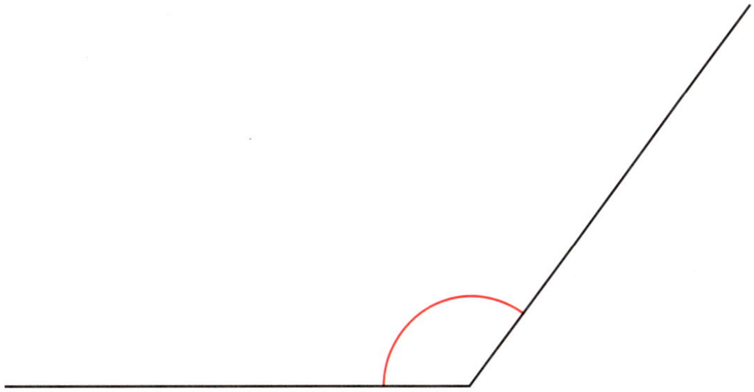

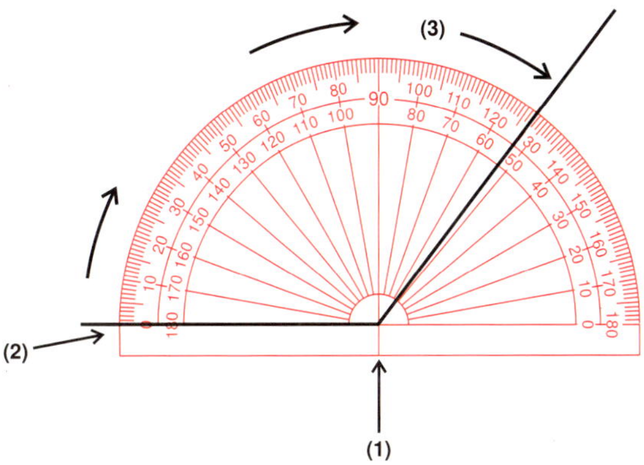

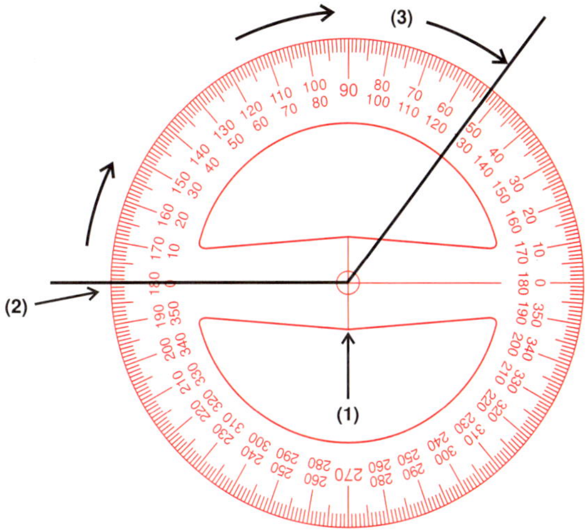

These protractors show an angle of 127° being measured.

Use your protractor to measure this angle.

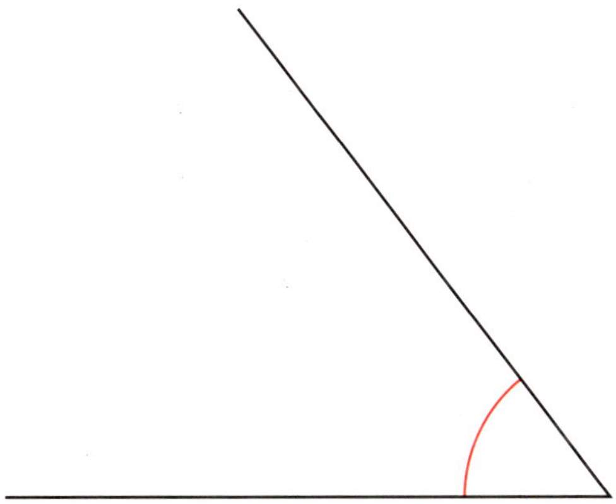

To draw an angle

Mark a point P on a line PQ, as shown.
At point P, using the line PQ, make an angle of 28°.

1 Put the centre point of the protractor on the point P.
2 Put the 0° line of the protractor on the line PQ.
3 Count round from 0° to 28°. Put a dot at 28°.
(Decide from where 0° is, whether you are using the inside or the outside set of figures.)

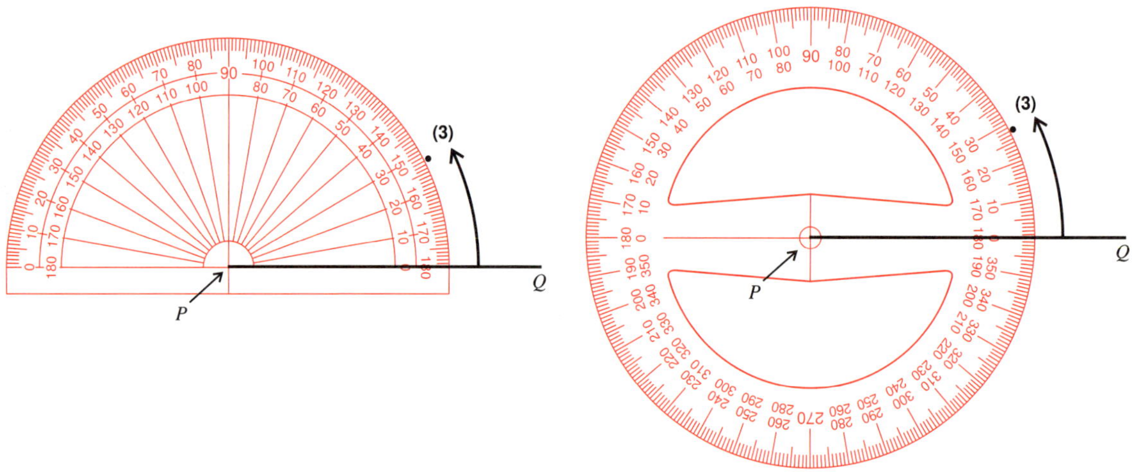

4 When you have removed the protractor, join the dot to point P.

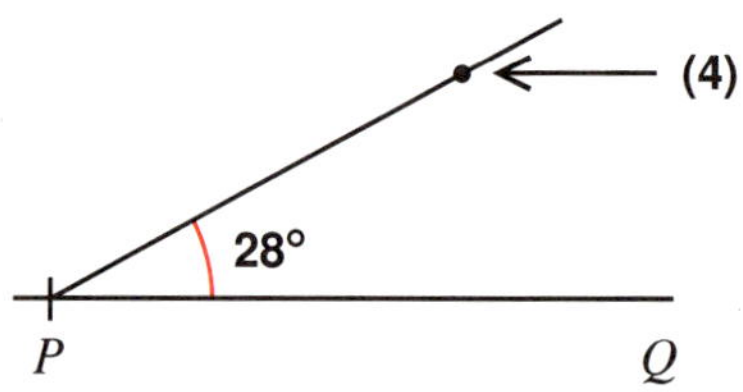

Mark a point P on a line PR, as shown.
At point P, using the line PR, make an angle of 105°.

1 Put the centre point of the protractor on the point P.
2 Put the 0° line of the protractor on the line PR.
3 Count round from 0° to 105°. Put a dot at 105°.

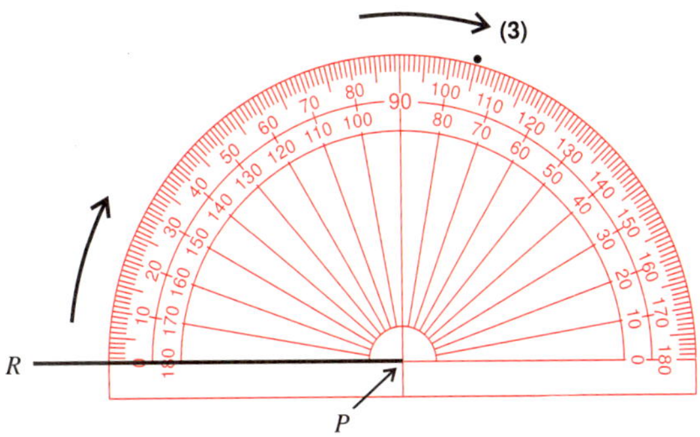

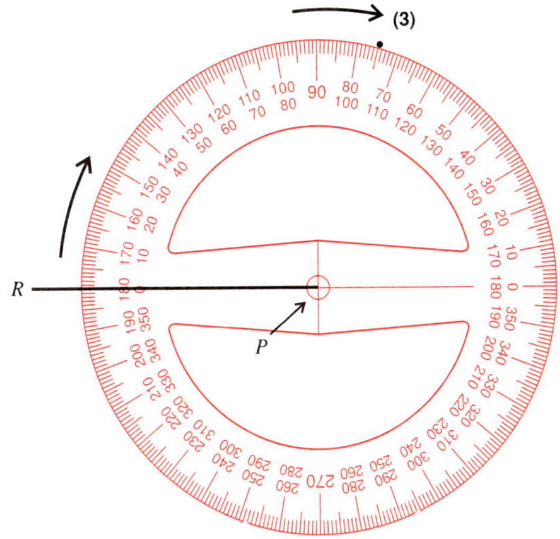

4 When you have removed the protractor, join the dot to point P.

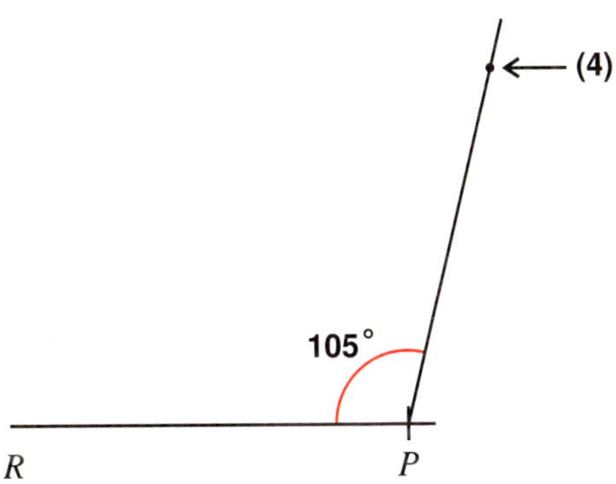

Exercise 8.3

1. First, look at these angles and say whether they are acute angles, right angles or obtuse angles.
   Then measure them with your protractor and write down their sizes in degrees.

1

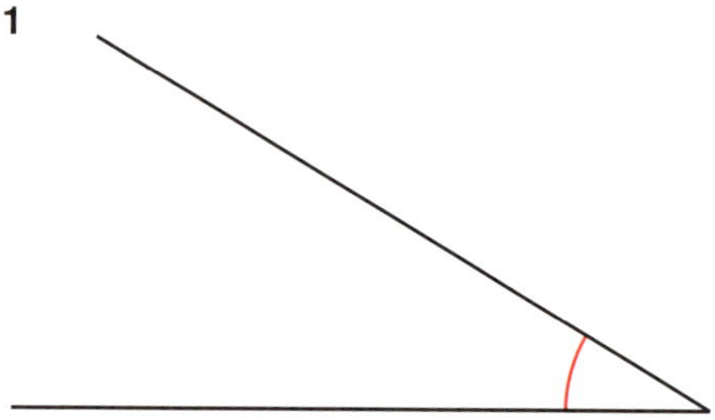

2

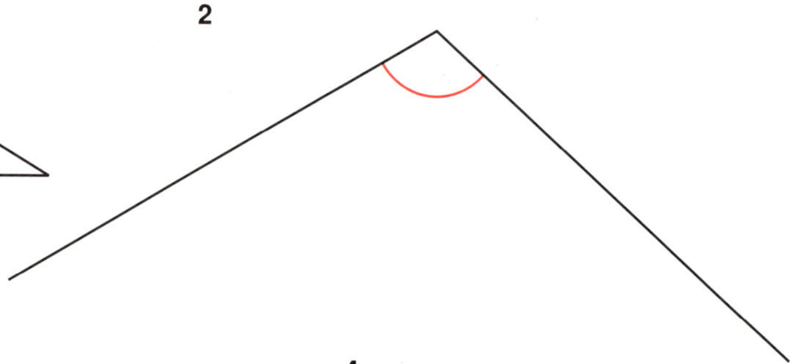

3

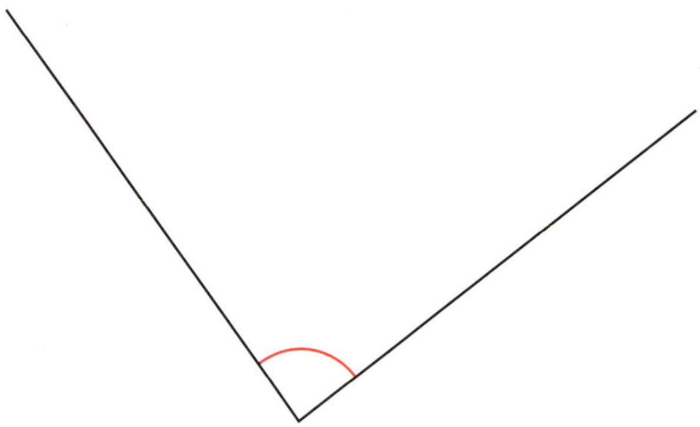

4

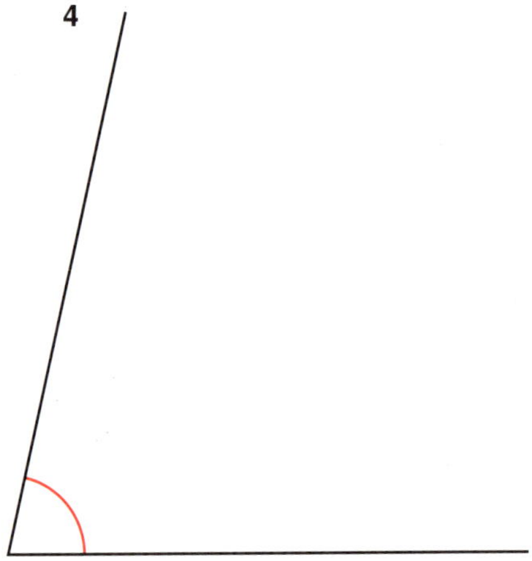

5

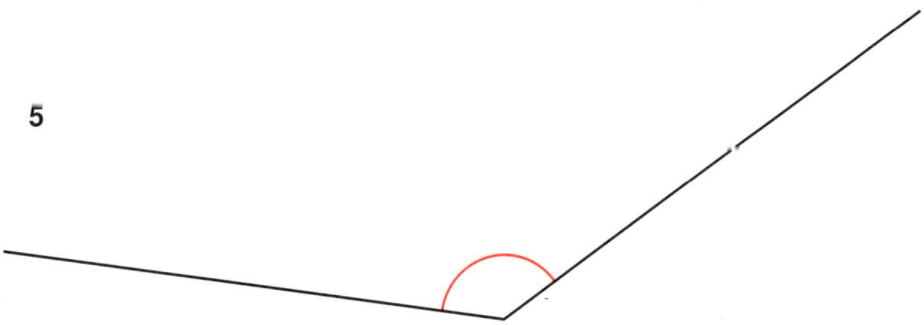

2. Start with a line and a point A. Using the 0° mark on the right side of your protractor, draw these angles at the point A, using a separate diagram for each one.

1 100° **2** 67° **3** 45° **4** 143° **5** 85°

3. Start with a line and a point B. Using the 0° mark on the left side of your protractor, draw these angles at the point B, using a separate diagram for each one.

1 20° **2** 75° **3** 108° **4** 90° **5** 152°

4. Copy these figures with the angles drawn accurately.

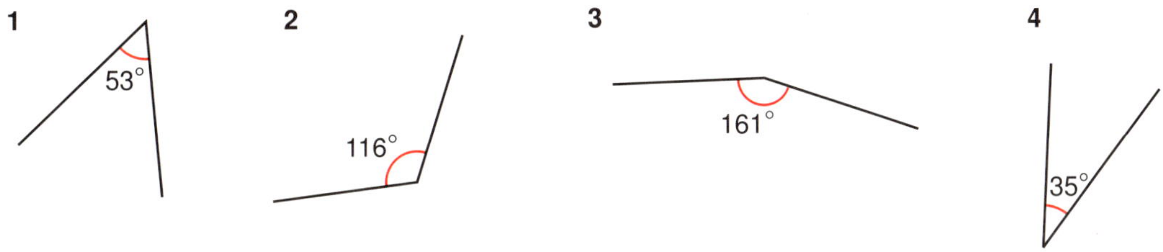

Perpendicular lines

Lines which are at right angles to each other are called **perpendicular lines**.

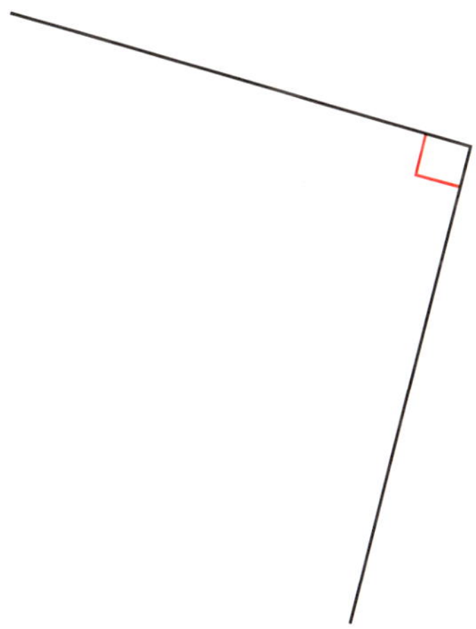

Naming of angles

In this chapter, we are going to identify angles by labelling them with small letters, (not capital letters, which we will use to label points).

This angle is b.

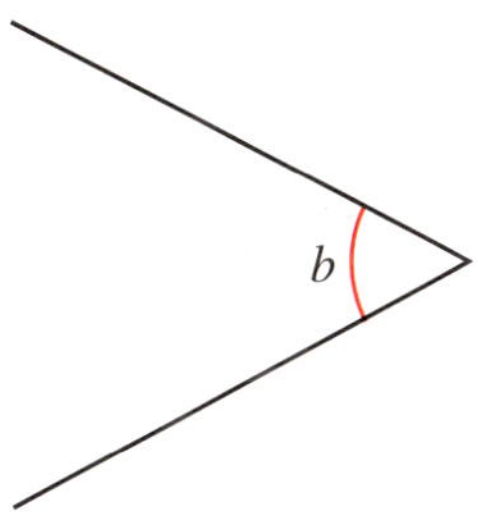

Exercise 8.4

1. Check with your protractor that these lines are perpendicular lines.

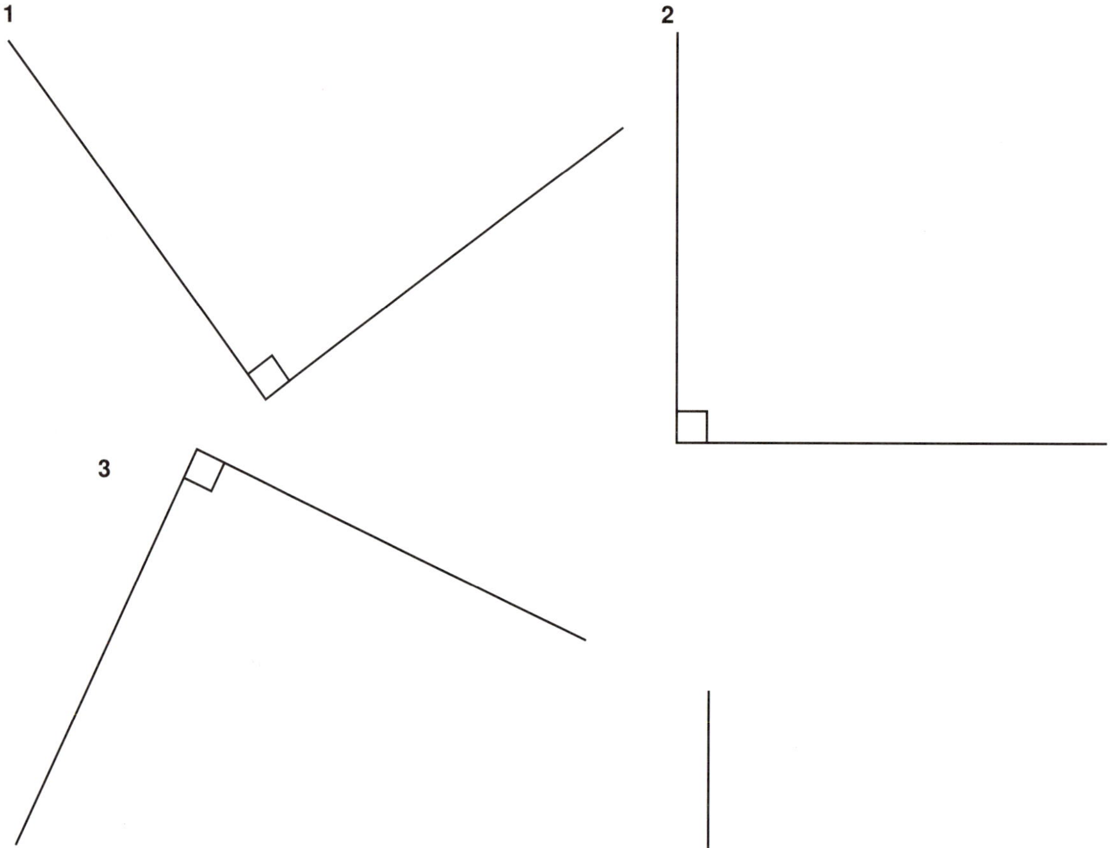

2. Here there are 4 lines meeting at a point making 4 angles a, b, c and d.
Can you decide what the **sum** of the 4 angles will equal ?
Measure the angles a, b, c and d with your protractor.
Find $a+b+c+d$ and see whether your previous decision was correct.
(It may not agree exactly due to having to measure to the nearest degree.)

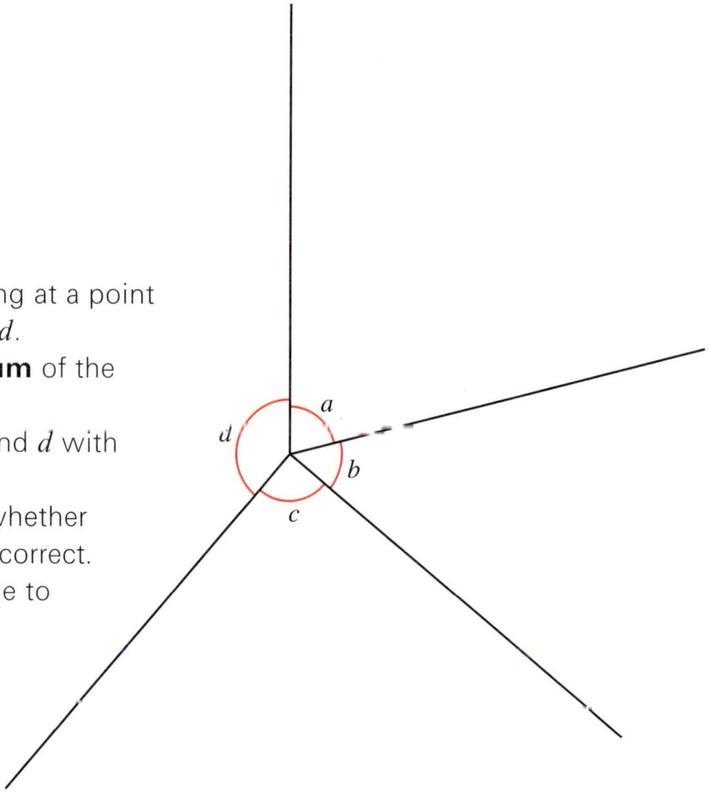

3. Can you decide what the sum of the 5 angles p, q, r, s, t will equal ? Measure the angles and find $p+q+r+s+t$. Was your decision correct ? Angles in a diagram like this are called **angles at a point**.

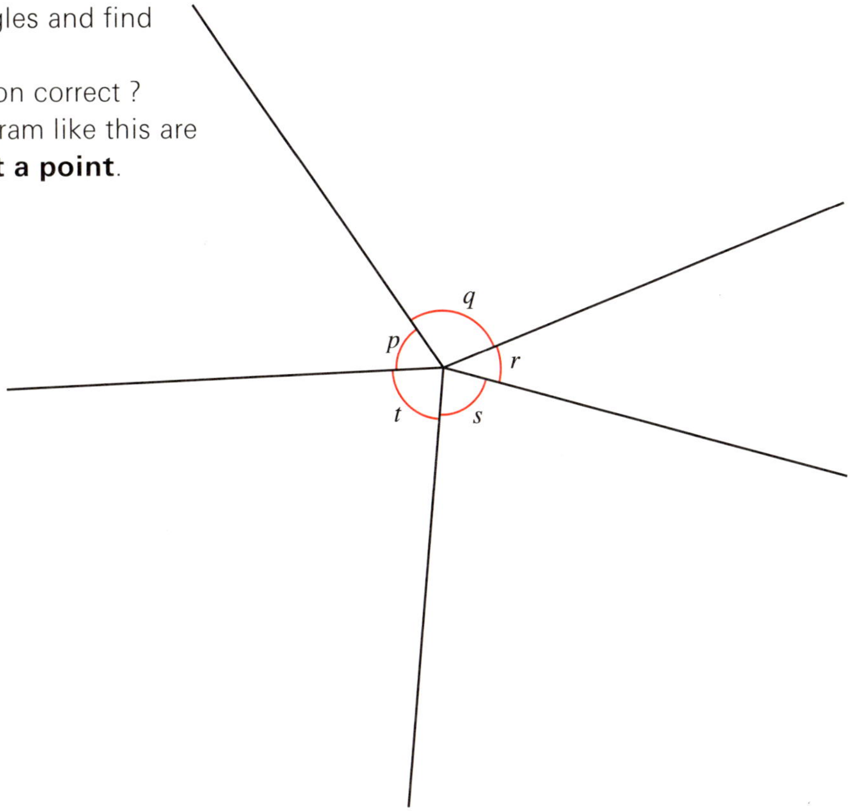

4. These angles are called **adjacent angles on a straight line.** (Adjacent means 'next to each other'.) Can you decide what the sum of the angles a and b will equal ? Measure your angles and find $a+b$. Was your decision correct ?

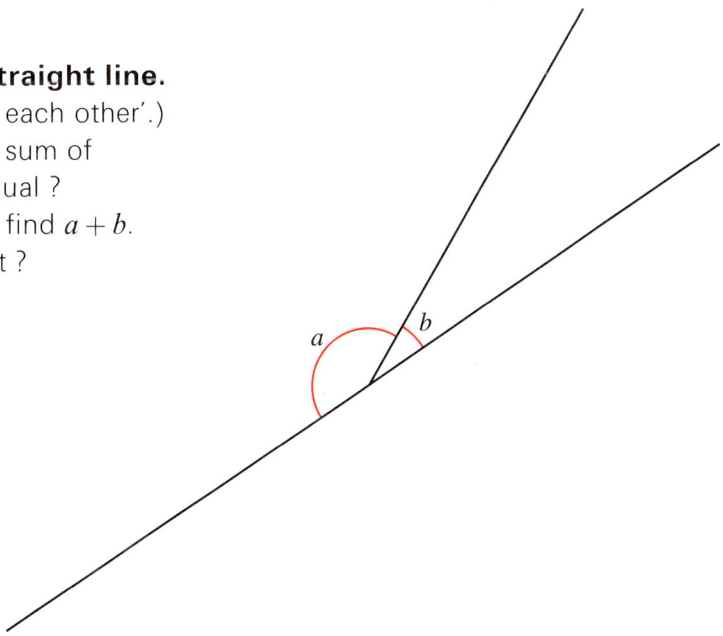

5. Repeat question 4 using angles c and d.

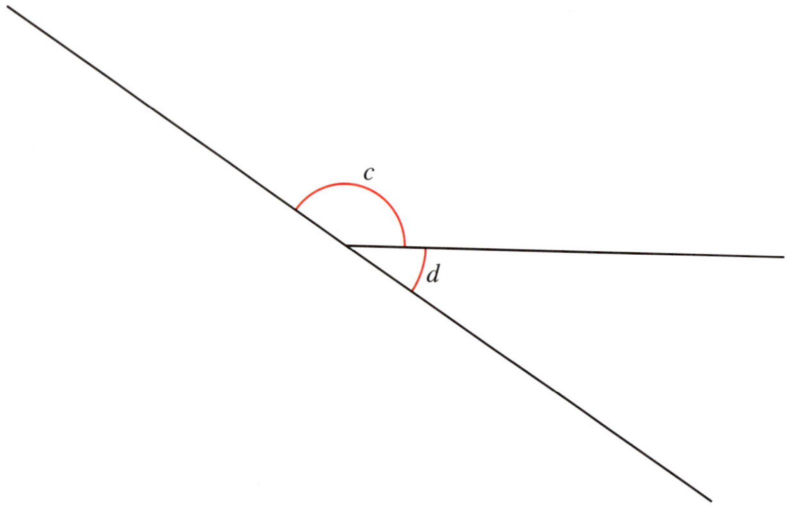

6. These angles are made by two straight lines crossing each other.
g and j are called **vertically opposite angles**, so are h and k.
(Here, vertically means having the same vertex, that is, they are at the same point. It does not mean that any of the lines are vertical.)
Can you decide anything about the sizes of g and j, or of h and k ?
Measure the angles to see if your decision is correct.

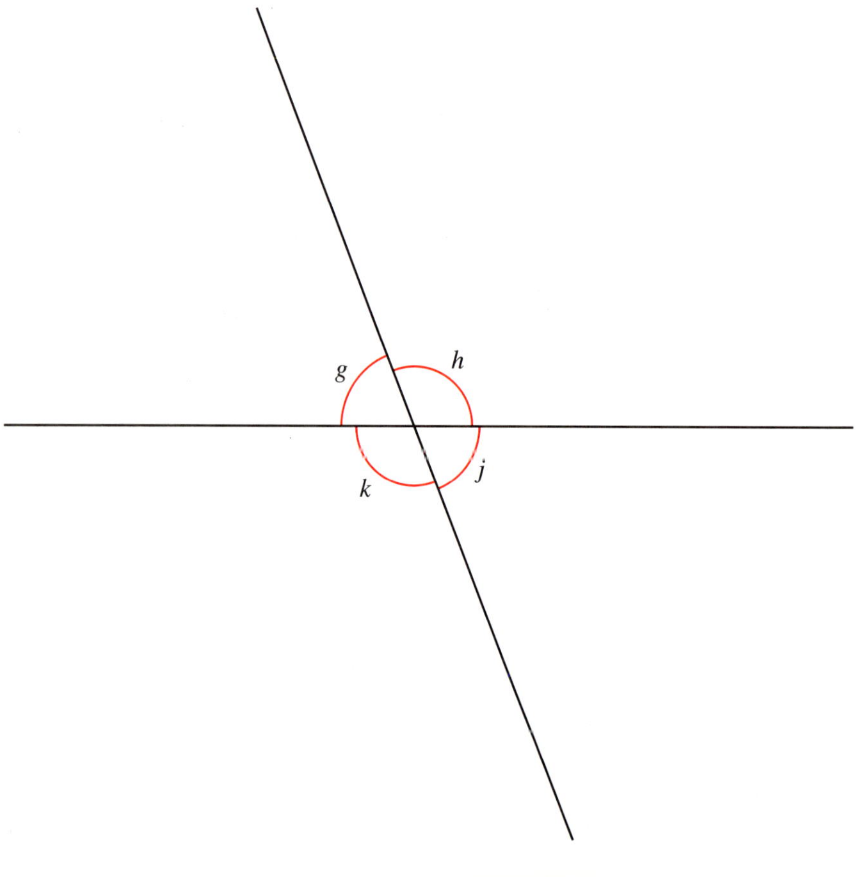

7. Repeat question 6 using vertically opposite angles p and r, and q and s.

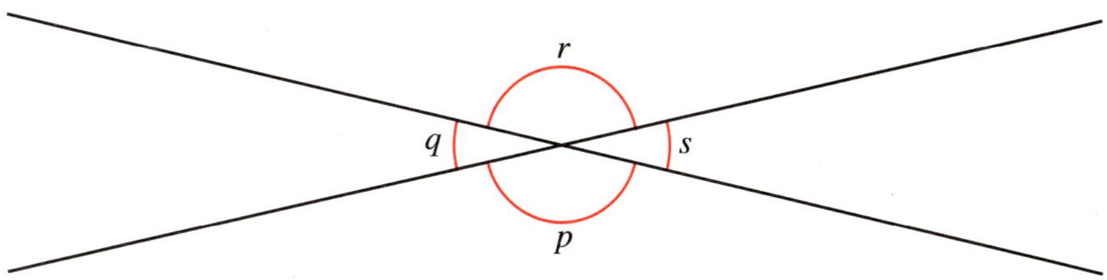

Parallel lines

Parallel lines are lines with the same direction. They remain the same distance apart, so never meet each other.
The sign for parallel lines is similar arrows on the lines.

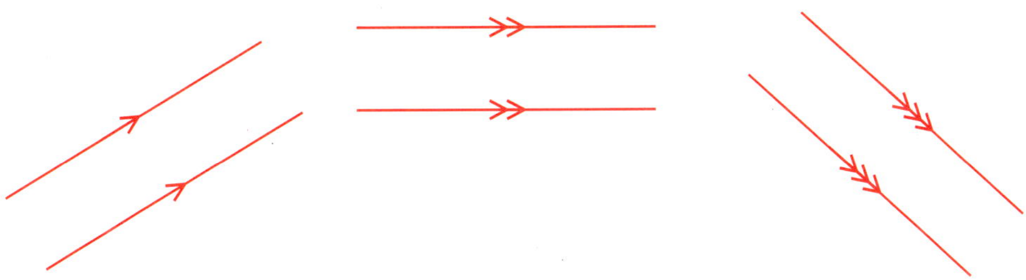

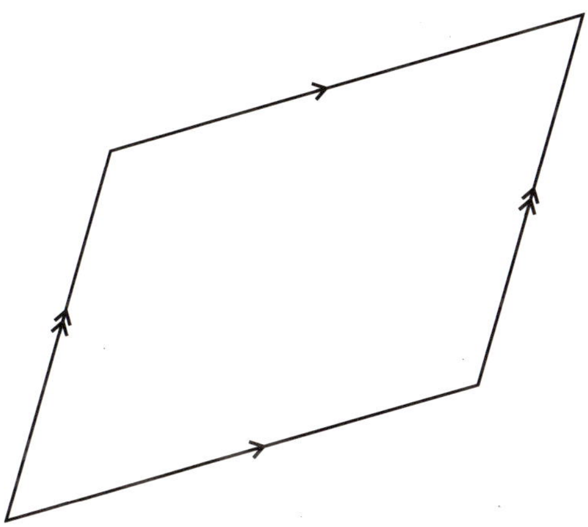

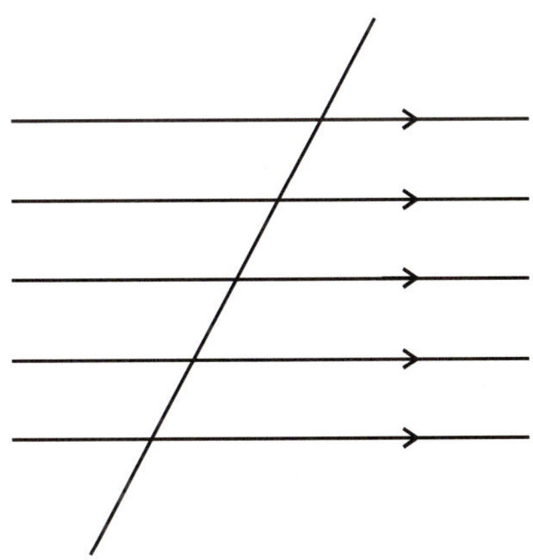

To draw parallel lines with a set-square

Example

Draw a line through C, parallel to AB.

Place the longest side of the set-square on AB so that, if possible, the set-square is placed over C.
Place a ruler along one of the other sides of the set-square.

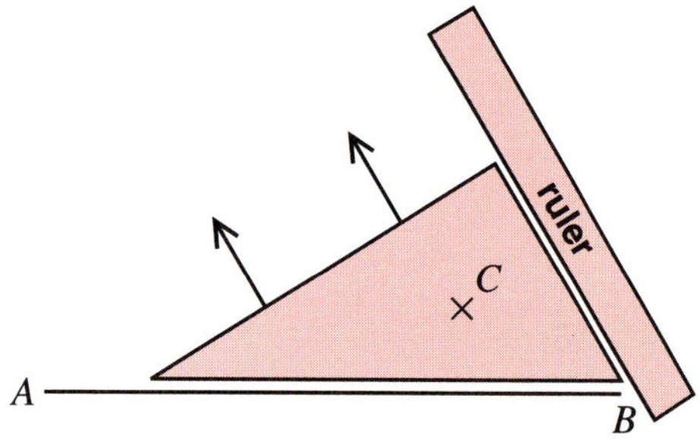

Keeping the ruler fixed, slide the set-square along the ruler until its longest side passes through C. Draw a line along this edge.

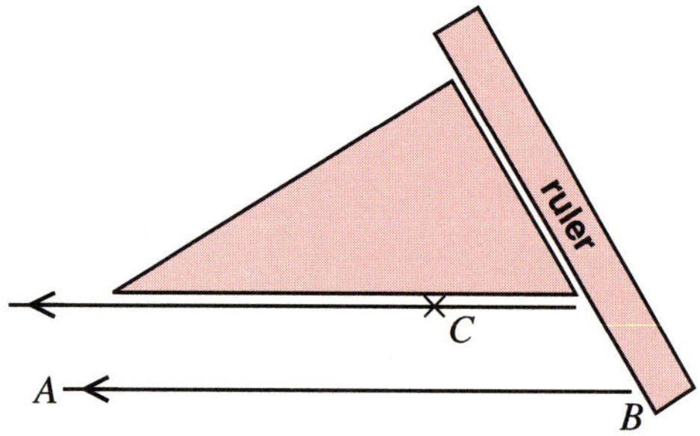

Practise drawing different parallel lines until you are sure that you can draw them correctly.

Exercise 8.5

1. These parallel lines have been drawn accurately. Measure the marked angles and comment on your answers.

1

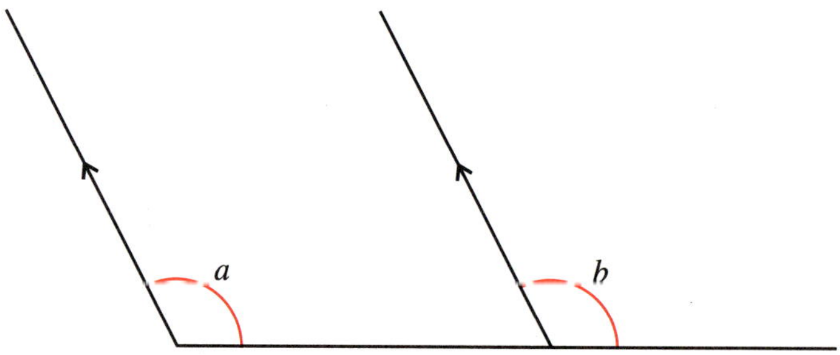

2

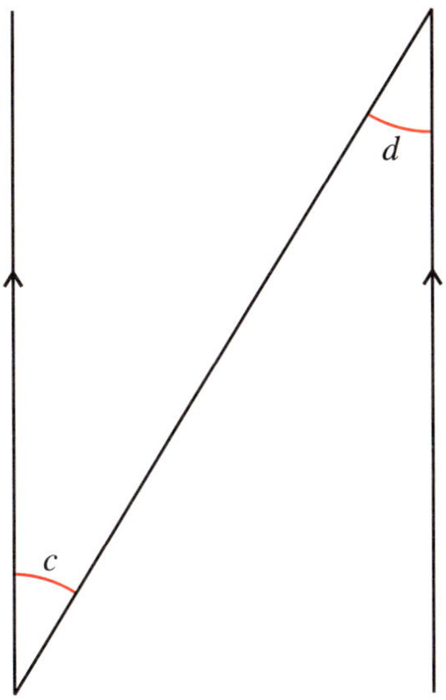

3

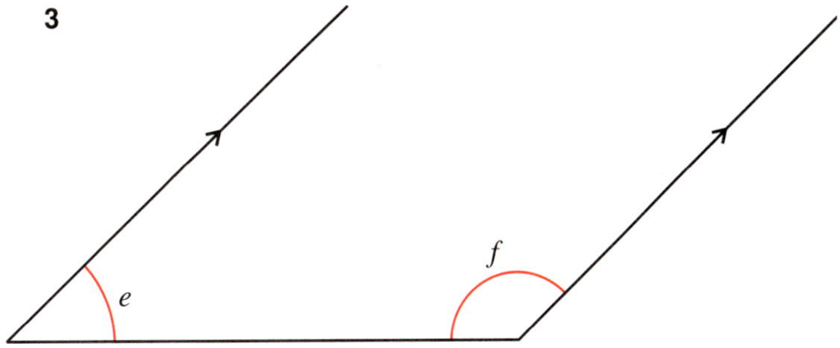

2. **Practice in drawing parallel lines**

1 Draw two lines AB and AE making an obtuse angle at A.
Mark the point C about halfway along AE.
Use your ruler and set-square to draw a line through C parallel to AB.

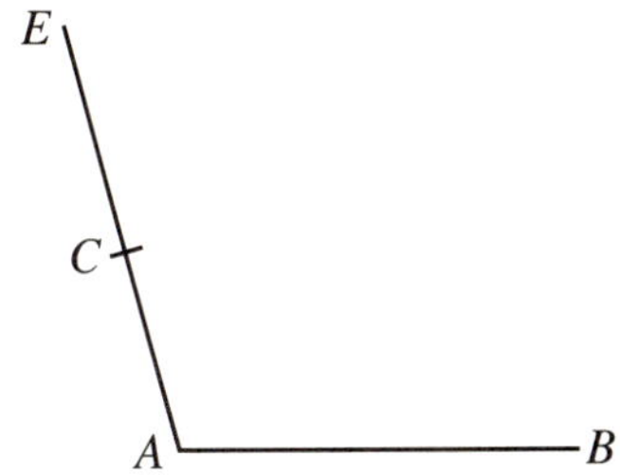

Measure the angles a and c. They will be equal if your lines are really parallel.

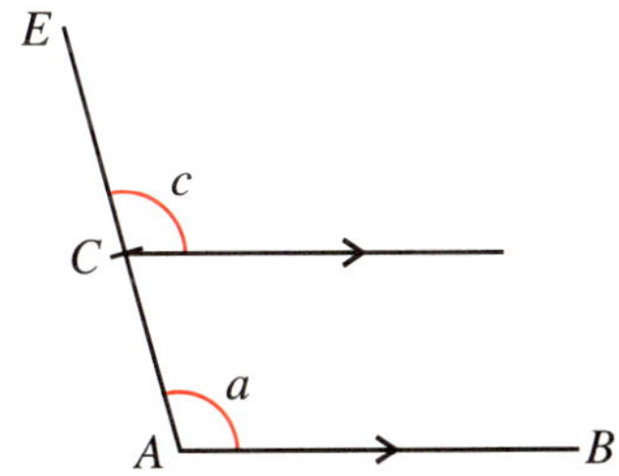

2 Draw two lines AB and BC making an acute angle at B. Mark the point C clearly. Use your ruler and set-square to draw a line through C parallel to AB.

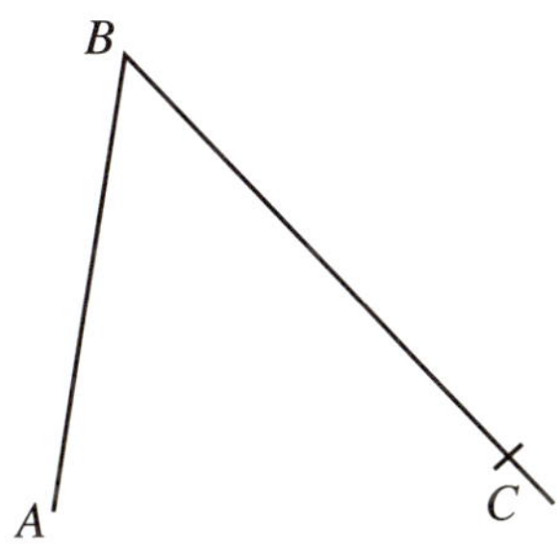

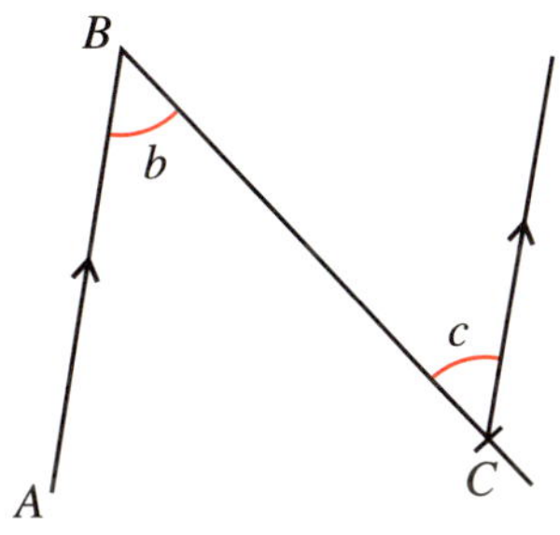

Measure the angles b and c. They will be equal if your lines are really parallel.

Exercise 8.6 Applications and Activities

1. Use the measurements shown on the diagram.
   1 Draw the line AB accurately.
   2 Make accurate angles at A and at B.
   3 Find point D so that AD is the length shown.
   4 Find point C so that BC is the length shown.
   5 Join DC.
   6 Measure the length of DC.
   7 Measure the sizes of the angles d and c.
   8 Comment on your answers.

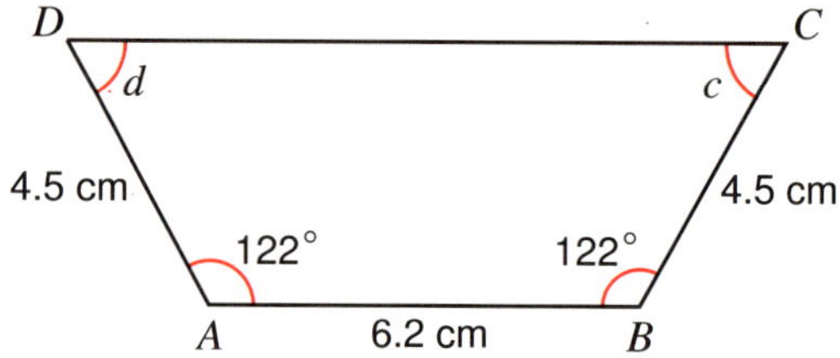

Questions 2, 3 and 4.

Repeat the instructions of question 1, using these diagrams.

2.
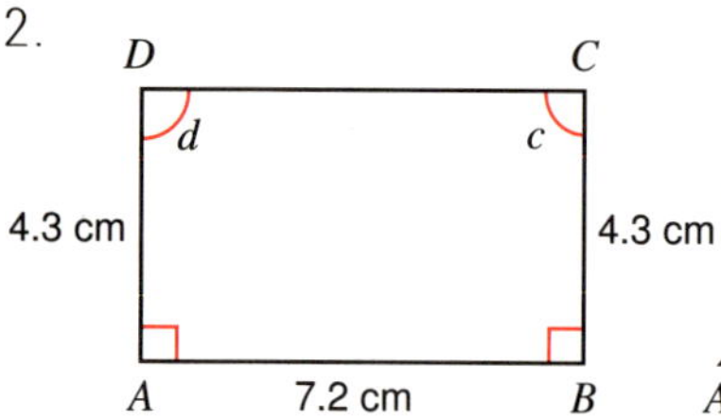

3.
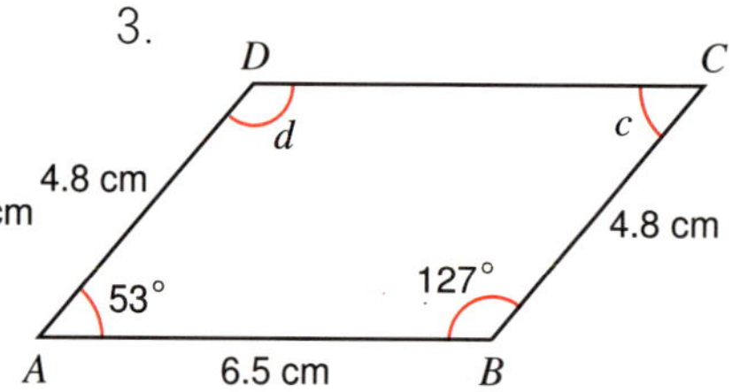

4.
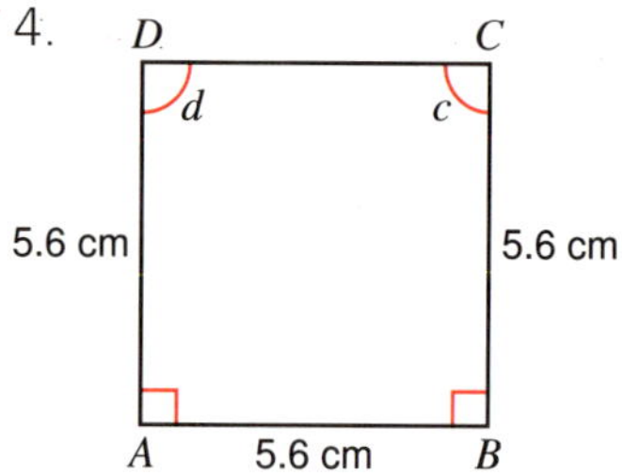

5. Use the measurements shown on the diagram.
   1 Draw the line AP accurately.
   2 Make accurate angles at A and at P.
   3 Mark points B, C, D and E on AE such that $AB = BC = CD = DE = 1.5$ cm.
   4 Draw a line parallel to AP through B, and let it meet PZ at point Q.
   5 Draw a line parallel to AP through C, and let it meet PZ at point R.
   6 Draw a line parallel to AP through D, and let it meet PZ at point S.
   7 Draw a line parallel to AP through E, and let it meet PZ at point T.
   8 Measure the lengths PQ, QR, RS and ST. They will be equal if your lines are really parallel.

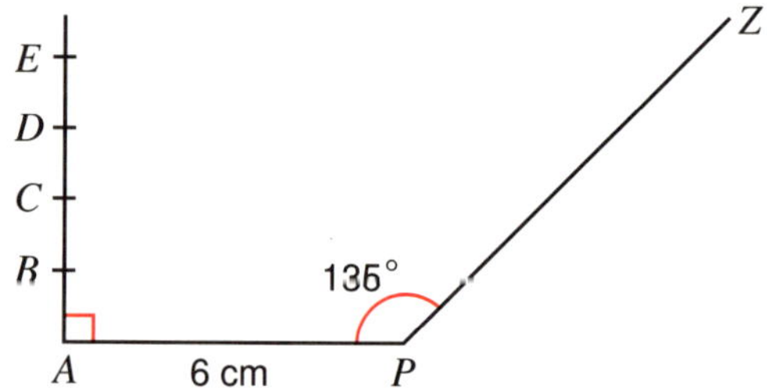

6. **Triangles**

1 Measure the angles of these triangles.

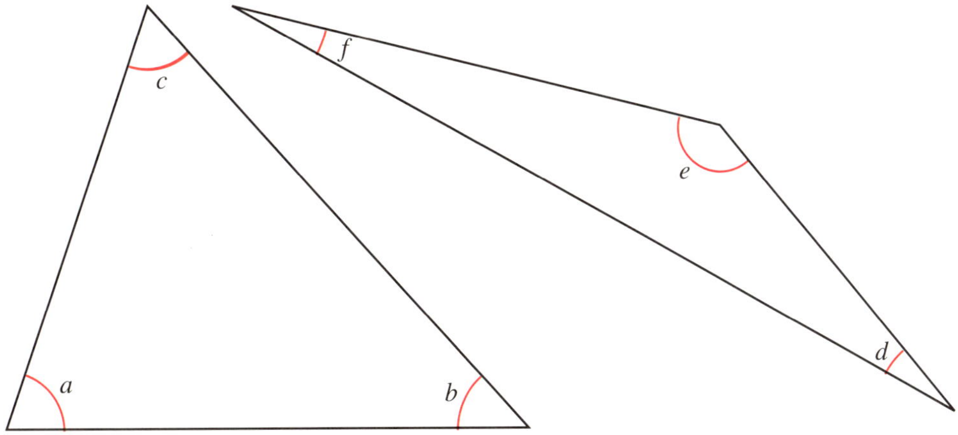

Find the sum of the three angles in each triangle.
Can you deduce anything about the sum ? If so, check your result by drawing other different-shaped triangles.

2 Draw a triangle on paper and cut it out. Colour the 3 angles and mark the corner of each, then tear them off. Arrange them together with points and edges touching. Which diagram shows the result ? What does this demonstrate ?

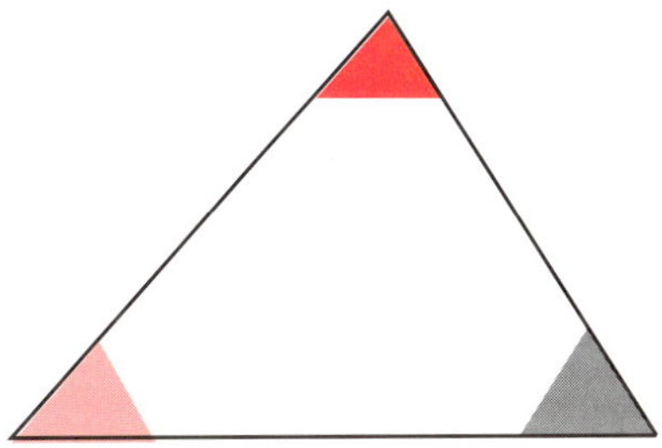

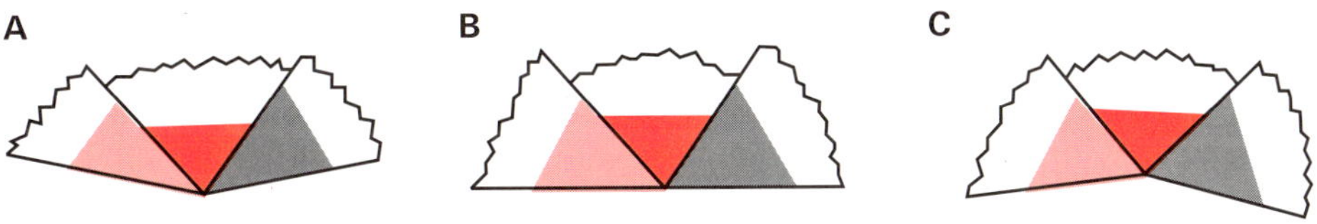

6. **3** Draw a triangle on paper and cut it out.
Colour the 3 angles on both sides of the paper.
Find the mid-points of 2 sides and make a crease joining them.
The crease is shown by the dotted line.

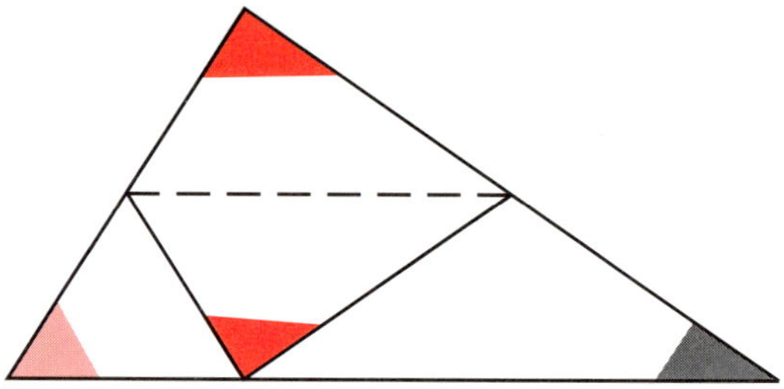

Fold along the crease so that it looks like this.

Make 2 more creases at right angles to the first one.
Fold along them.

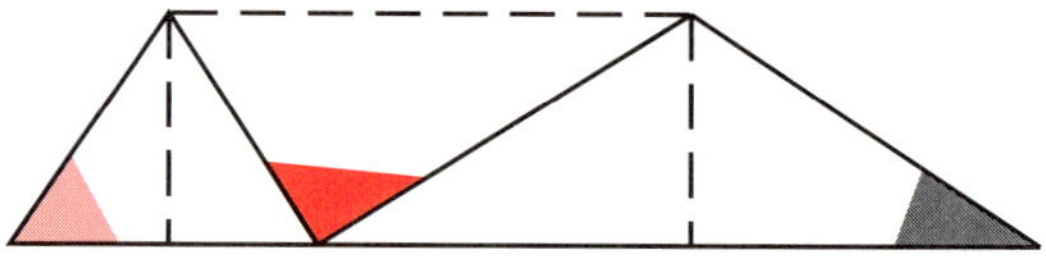

Where are the 3 angles of the original triangle ?
What does this demonstrate ?

7. Starting from a point O, draw lines OA, OB, OC, OD, OE, OF, OG and OH, all 5 cm long, with each line making an angle of 45° with the next one, as shown in the diagram.
Join AB, BC, CD, DE, EF, FG, GH and HA.

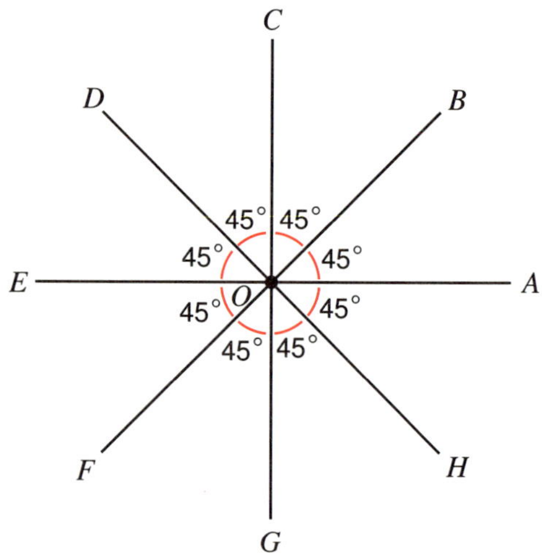

$ABCDEFGH$ is a **regular octagon**.
Measure the lengths of its sides, which should all be equal.
Measure the angles a, b, c, d, e, f, g and h. They should all be equal.

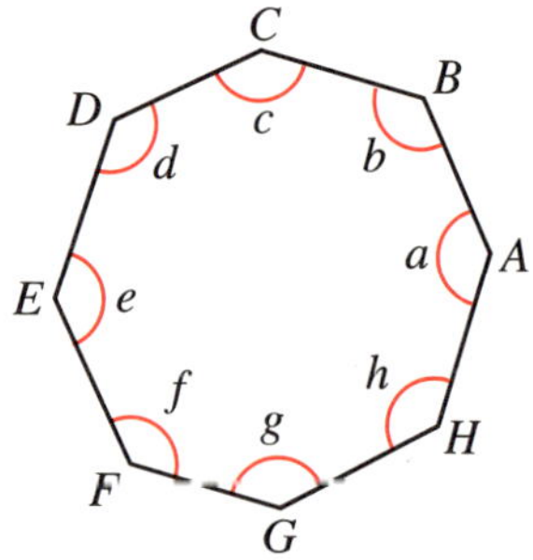

Chapter 8 test

1. Look at the angles in these diagrams.

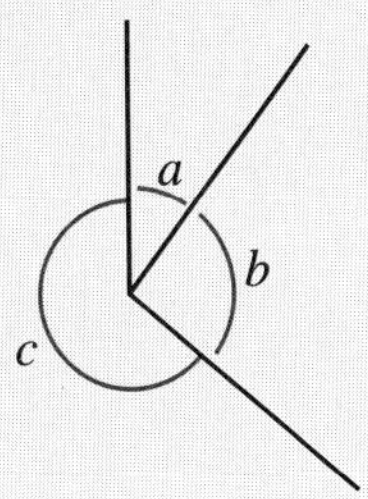

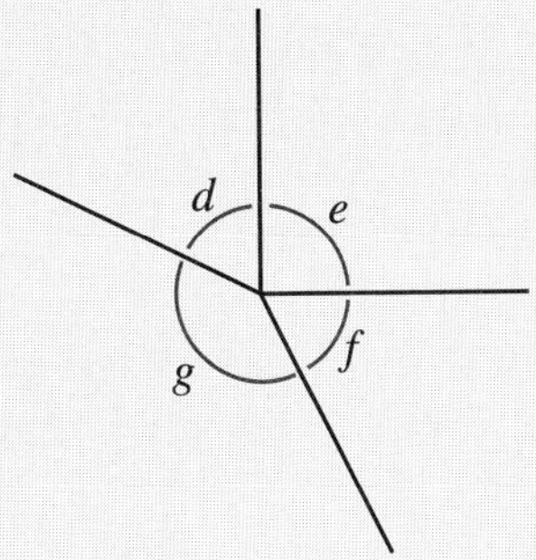

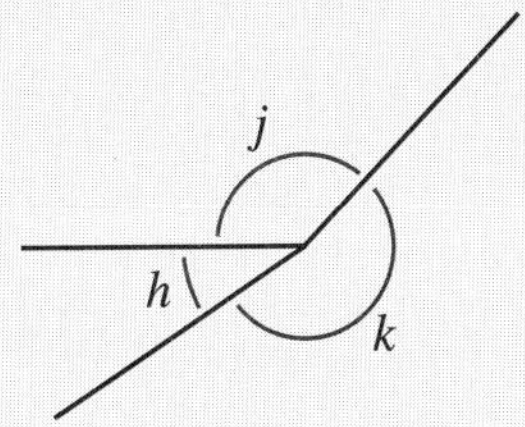

List
1 the acute angles,
2 the right angles,
3 the obtuse angles,
4 the reflex angles.

2. **1** Draw the line AC 13 cm long with a point B such that $AB = 6.3$ cm and $BC = 6.7$ cm.
2 Make angles at B of 42° and 38°, as shown.
3 Measure angle b.

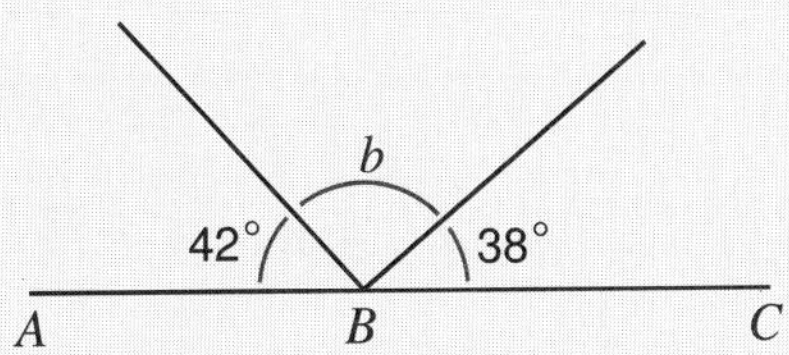

3. **1** Draw a line AB of length 8.2 cm.
2 Make an angle of 116° at A, as shown.
3 Find point C such that $AC = 5.8$ cm.
4 Through point C draw a line parallel to AB.
5 Through point B draw a line parallel to AC, to meet the previous line at D.
6 Measure the lengths of CD and DB.
7 Measure the angles b, c and d.
8 Comment on your answers.

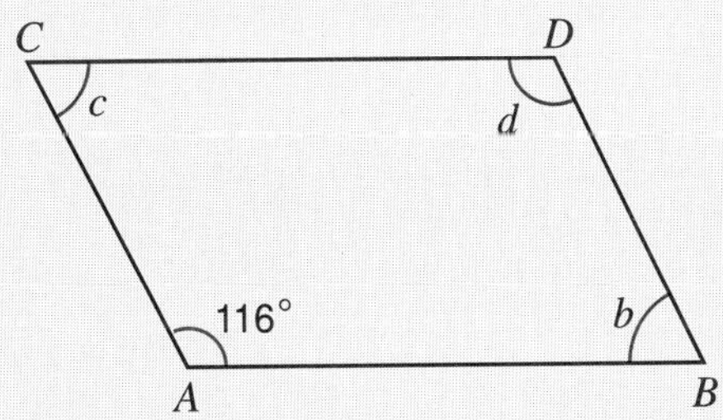

PUZZLE

6. Sakina is given 15 coins for her birthday, all 10p, 20p or 50p coins. She got £5.10 altogether. How many of each coin were there ?

9 Thinking about fractions and

Using fractions

You are already familiar with simple fractions such as $\frac{1}{2}$, $\frac{1}{4}$, $\frac{3}{4}$. Other fractions such as $\frac{1}{3}$, $\frac{2}{3}$, $\frac{1}{5}$, $\frac{1}{6}$ are not used in practical situations quite so often.
Think of situations where you have used fractions, or seen fractions used.

Name some situations where these people would use fractions.

A shoe retailer
A grocer selling cooked meats
A child learning to tell the time
A musician
A mother dividing a cake among 5 children
A milkman supplying milk to school for the children to drink
A publican selling beer, and spirits
A mechanic using spanners
A photographer

A fractions problem

Sam was trying to reduce the fraction $\frac{16}{64}$ to its lowest terms but instead of doing it the correct way he carelessly cancelled the 6's, $\frac{1\not{6}}{\not{6}4}$ and he got the answer $\frac{1}{4}$. When he found out that was the correct answer he thought he had discovered a good way to do such questions. But unfortunately for him, it does not usually work out right.

Can you find the three other fractions with denominators less than 100 for which this wrong method would work ? (In one of them the fraction is still not in its lowest terms.)

For distances less than a mile, fractions are used.
What is odd about the way the fractions are written ?

What is the difference in size between each bit and the next larger ?

percentages

Which of these two notices do you think is better ?

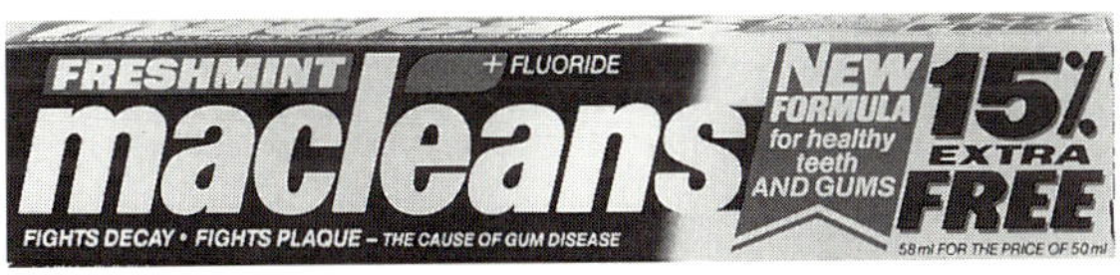

Special offers on goods are a way to persuade you to buy.

Using percentages

Percentages are simply fractions, with the % sign meaning 'out of 100'. They are used extensively nowadays in a variety of situations, but especially where finance is involved. One advantage of using percentages is that it is easier to compare them with each other, than it is to compare fractions with different denominators. For instance, which is the larger, $\frac{2}{3}$ or $\frac{3}{5}$?

Which is the larger, $66\frac{2}{3}$% or 60% ?

What is 1% of £1 ? What is 1% of £100 ?

A shop has a sale and reduces all its prices by 25%. Why will a shopkeeper do this ? How will he work out the new prices ?

Why do manufacturers make some products whose containers have such labels as '10% extra free' ? What fraction are you getting extra ?

What does 'She gives 100% effort' mean ?

For what purpose are percentages often used in schools ?

Percentage of households with videos

1982	7%	1988	53%
1983	14%	1989	60%
1984	24%	1990	64%
1985	30%	1991	68%
1986	37%	1992	72%
1987	44%	1993	73%

9 Fractions and percentages

Fractions

Fractions are numbers such as $\frac{1}{4}$ (one-quarter), $\frac{1}{3}$ (one-third), $\frac{2}{5}$ (two-fifths), $\frac{5}{9}$ (five-ninths).

The number underneath is called the **denominator**. It tells us how many smaller equal parts the whole unit is divided into.
The number on top is called the **numerator**. It tells how many of the smaller parts are counted.

Divide a whole unit into 9 equal parts and shade 5 of these parts.

The shaded region is $\frac{5}{9}$ of the whole square.

The unshaded region is $\frac{4}{9}$ of the whole square.

The shaded part represents $\frac{1}{4}$ (one-quarter) of the circle.
(The whole circle is divided into 4 equal parts and 1 part is shaded.)
The unshaded part represents $\frac{3}{4}$ (three-quarters) of the circle.

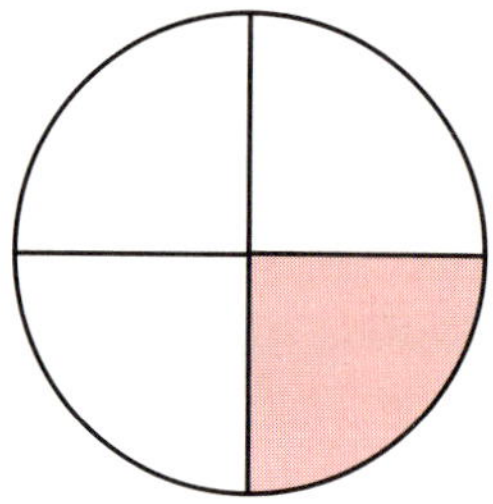

Equivalent fractions

The shaded part represents $\frac{2}{5}$ (two-fifths) of the rectangle.
(The whole rectangle is divided into 5 equal parts and 2 parts are shaded.)
The unshaded part represents $\frac{3}{5}$ of the rectangle.

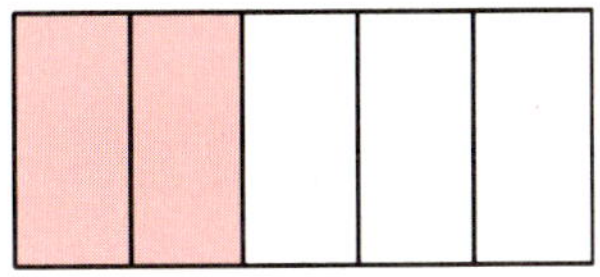

This diagram shows that $\frac{2}{5}$ is equivalent to $\frac{4}{10}$.

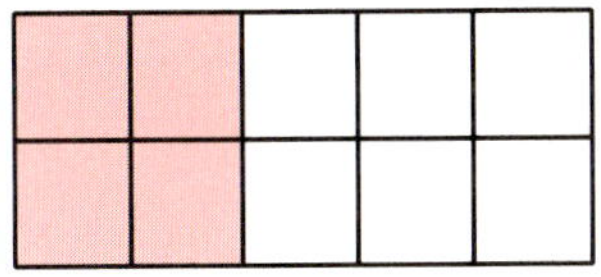

This diagram shows that $\frac{2}{5}+\frac{1}{10}=\frac{4}{10}+\frac{1}{10}=\frac{5}{10}=\frac{1}{2}$.

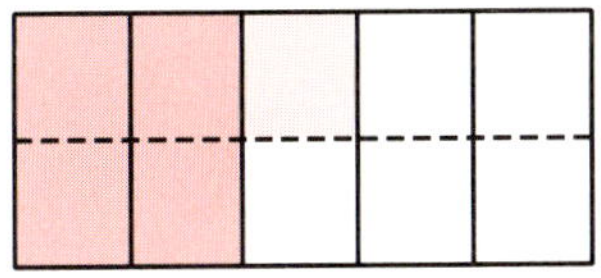

Improper fractions and mixed numbers

Improper fractions are numbers with a greater numerator than denominator, such as $\frac{6}{5}$ and $\frac{5}{2}$.

Mixed numbers are numbers with a whole number part and a fraction part, such as $1\frac{1}{5}$ and $2\frac{1}{2}$.

This diagram shows that $\frac{6}{5}=1\frac{1}{5}$.

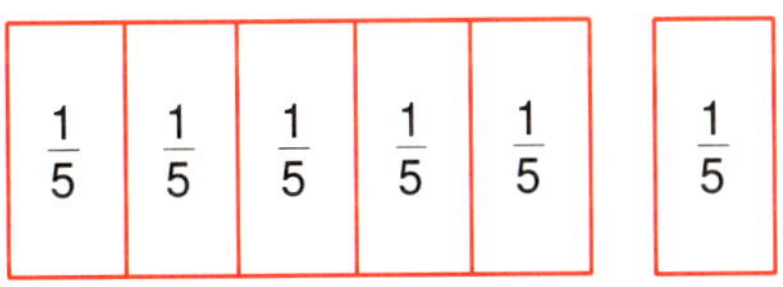

This diagram shows that $\frac{5}{2}=2\frac{1}{2}$.

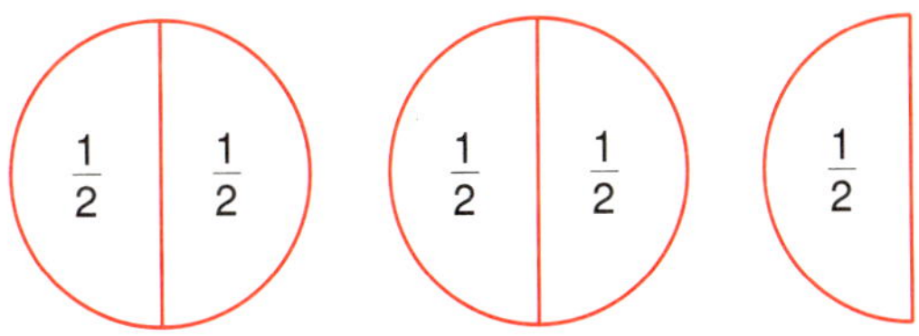

Using fractions

Examples

1 Change $3\frac{7}{8}$ into an improper fraction.

(Multiply the whole number 3 by 8 to change it into eighths. This is 24 eighths and another 7 eighths make 31 eighths.)

$3\frac{7}{8} = \frac{24}{8} + \frac{7}{8} = \frac{31}{8}$

2 Change $\frac{45}{7}$ into a mixed number.

(Divide 7 into 45. It goes 6 times so there are 6 whole ones. $6 \times 7 = 42$ and the remainder is 3, so there is also $\frac{3}{7}$.)

$\frac{45}{7} = \frac{42+3}{7} = \frac{42}{7} + \frac{3}{7} = 6 + \frac{3}{7} = 6\frac{3}{7}$

3 Reduce $\frac{60}{75}$ to its lowest terms.

60 and 75 both divide by 5 so reduce the fraction by dividing both the numerator and the denominator by 5. This process can be called **cancelling**.

$\frac{\overset{12}{\cancel{60}}}{\underset{15}{\cancel{75}}}$ This gives the fraction $\frac{12}{15}$ but this is still not in its lowest terms because 12 and 15 both divide by 3. So divide both the numerator and the denominator by 3.

$\frac{\overset{\overset{4}{\cancel{12}}}{\cancel{60}}}{\underset{\underset{5}{\cancel{15}}}{\cancel{75}}} = \frac{4}{5}$ This is the fraction in its lowest terms.

4 Change $\frac{5}{6}$ into a fraction with denominator 18.

6 becomes 18 when multiplied by 3, so multiply the numerator and the denominator by 3.

$\frac{5}{6} = \frac{5 \times 3}{6 \times 3} = \frac{15}{18}$

Exercise 9.1

1. What fraction of the shape is shaded ?

1

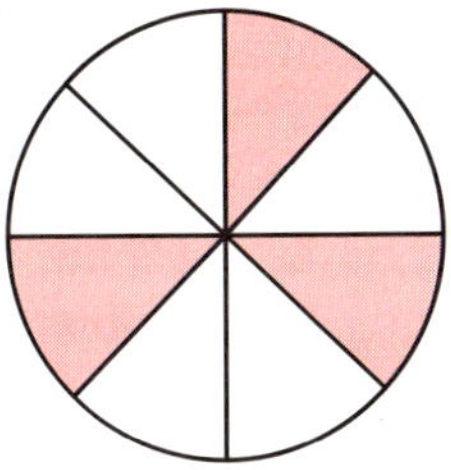

2

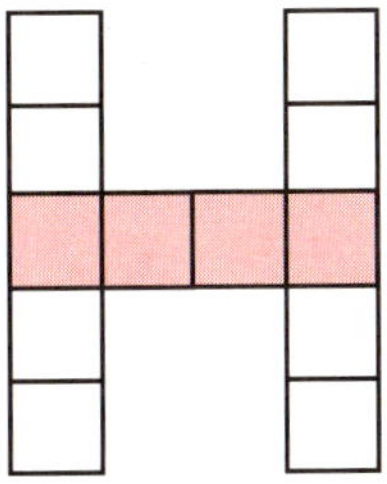

3

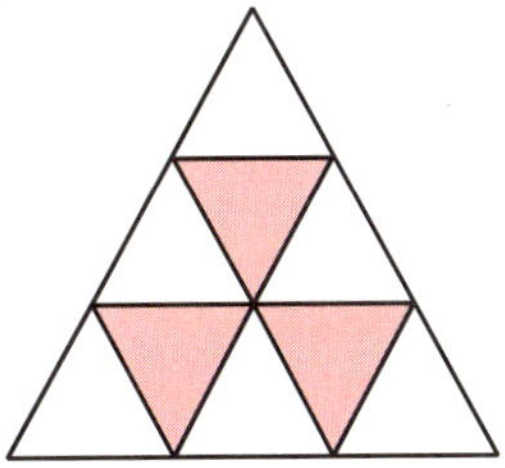

4

5

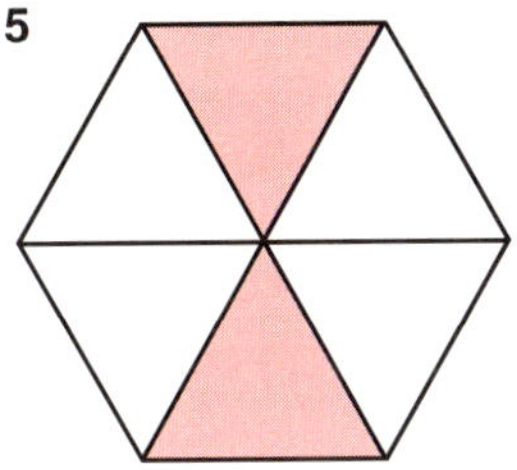

6

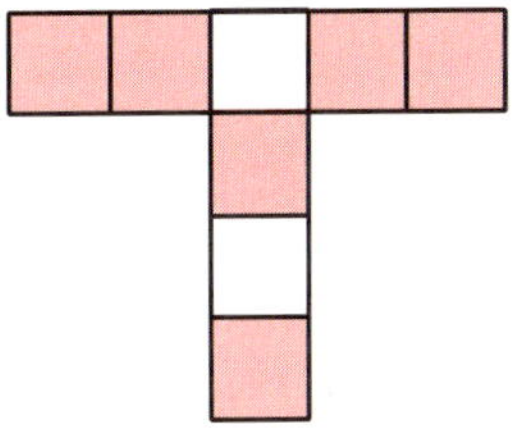

2. Copy the diagrams and shade the fraction stated.

1 $\frac{2}{5}$

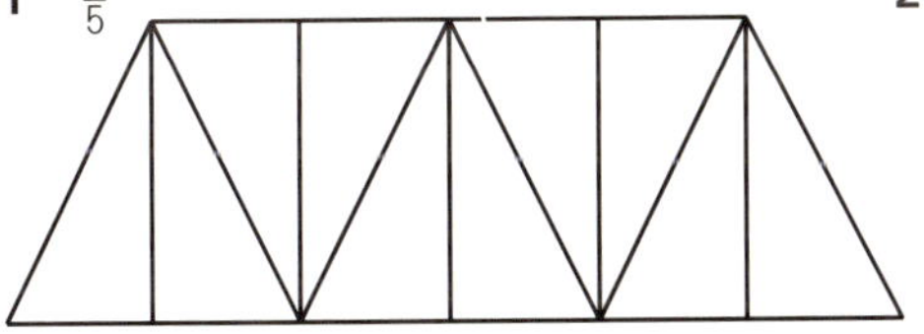

2 $\frac{4}{7}$

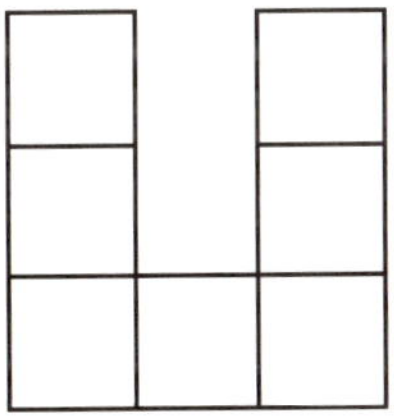

3 $\frac{5}{8}$

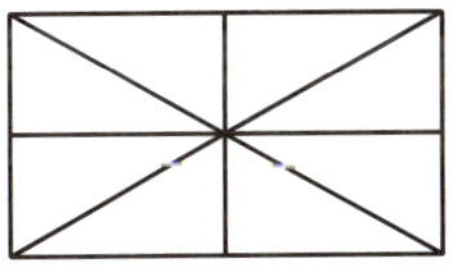

4 $\frac{5}{6}$

5 $\frac{3}{8}$

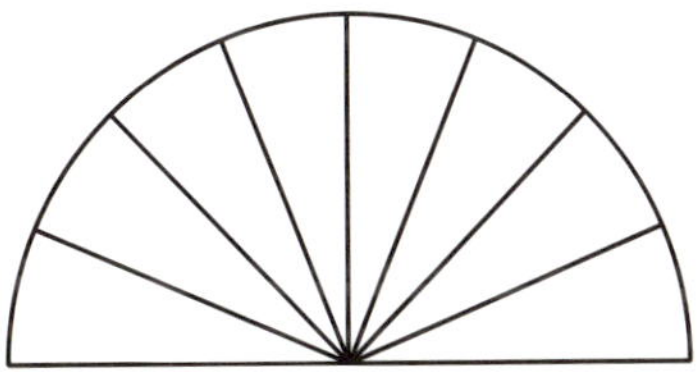

6 $\frac{3}{4}$

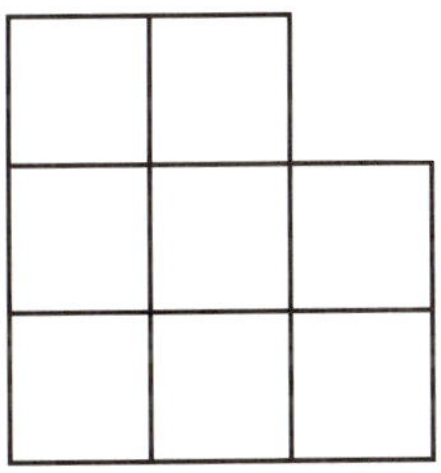

3. Reduce these fractions to their lowest terms.

1	$\frac{3}{9}$	**2**	$\frac{24}{36}$	**3**	$\frac{9}{12}$	**4**	$\frac{27}{54}$	**5**	$\frac{12}{30}$
6	$\frac{5}{20}$	**7**	$\frac{70}{100}$	**8**	$\frac{21}{56}$	**9**	$\frac{60}{80}$	**10**	$\frac{35}{45}$

4. **1** Change $\frac{3}{8}$ into a fraction with denominator 24.
2 Change $\frac{5}{6}$ into a fraction with denominator 12.
3 Change $\frac{2}{3}$ into a fraction with denominator 15.
4 Change $\frac{3}{4}$ into a fraction with denominator 36.
5 Change $\frac{3}{10}$ into a fraction with denominator 50.
6 Change $\frac{1}{2}$ into a fraction with denominator 6.
7 Change $\frac{2}{5}$ into a fraction with denominator 20.
8 Change $\frac{7}{8}$ into a fraction with denominator 48.
9 Change $\frac{2}{9}$ into a fraction with denominator 27.
10 Change $\frac{1}{4}$ into a fraction with denominator 32.

5. Change these mixed numbers to improper fractions.

1	$4\frac{2}{5}$	**2**	$2\frac{5}{6}$	**3**	$2\frac{1}{10}$	**4**	$3\frac{3}{4}$	**5**	$6\frac{2}{3}$
6	$2\frac{3}{5}$	**7**	$4\frac{1}{4}$	**8**	$8\frac{1}{3}$	**9**	$3\frac{1}{7}$	**10**	$1\frac{9}{10}$

6. Change these improper fractions to mixed numbers.

1	$\frac{7}{4}$	**2**	$\frac{7}{3}$	**3**	$\frac{17}{12}$	**4**	$\frac{37}{10}$	**5**	$\frac{29}{6}$
6	$\frac{100}{9}$	**7**	$\frac{42}{5}$	**8**	$\frac{25}{8}$	**9**	$\frac{11}{2}$	**10**	$\frac{20}{3}$

To find a fraction of a quantity

Examples

1 Find $\frac{2}{3}$ of £3.90.

$\frac{1}{3}$ of £3.90 is £3.90 ÷ 3 = £1.30.
So $\frac{2}{3}$ of £3.90 is £1.30 × 2 = £2.60.

2 Find $\frac{3}{5}$ of 1 hr 20 min

1 hr 20 min is 80 min.
$\frac{1}{5}$ of 80 min = 16 min.
So $\frac{3}{5}$ of 80 min = 16 × 3 min = 48 min.

Using your calculator:
$\frac{3}{5} = \frac{6}{10} = 0.6$ so you need 0.6 × 80 = 48.

Fractions with denominators 3, 6, 9 or 7 do not have exact decimal equivalents. You can still use your calculator to work out fractional parts, but because the fractions are not exact decimals it is better to do the multiplication first and division last.

3 Find $\frac{5}{6}$ of £6.50, to the nearest penny.

You must find $\frac{5}{6} \times 650$ pence.
Do it in this order:– $5 \times 650 \div 6$ rather than $5 \div 6 \times 650$.
The answer is 541.666...
This is £5.42, to the nearest penny.
(You could have worked in £'s, using 6.5 instead of 650.)

4 Find $1\frac{3}{4}$ times 25 m.

$\frac{1}{4}$ of 25m = 6.25 m.
$\frac{3}{4}$ of 25 m = 6.25 × 3 m = 18.75 m.
$1\frac{3}{4}$ of 25 m = (25 + 18.75) m = 43.75 m.

Or do it this way:
$1\frac{3}{4}$ is the same as $\frac{7}{4}$.
$\frac{1}{4}$ of 25 m = 6.25 m.
$\frac{7}{4}$ of 25 m = 6.25 × 7 m = 43.75 m.
Using your calculator, $1\frac{3}{4} = 1.75$ so you need $1.75 \times 25 = 43.75$.

Exercise 9.2

1. **1** Find one-half of each of these numbers.

60	20	44	10	80	16	34	70	56	200

2 Find one-third of each of these numbers.

6	15	24	66	33	48	18	90	9	36

3 Find one-quarter of each of these numbers.

88	16	8	24	84	48	32	52	120	200

4 Find two-thirds of each of these numbers.

3	21	75	18	99	60	12	45	27	30

5 Find three-quarters of each of these numbers.

4	20	160	36	12	28	80	100	44	60

2. Find the values of the following.

1 $\frac{1}{2}$ of £5.70
2 $\frac{2}{3}$ of 3.75 km
3 $\frac{3}{4}$ of 180°
4 $\frac{2}{5}$ of 1 m
5 $\frac{7}{10}$ of 200 g
6 $\frac{1}{3}$ of £2.91
7 $\frac{3}{5}$ of 6 ℓ
8 $\frac{1}{4}$ of 2 kg
9 $\frac{3}{8}$ of 4 hours
10 $\frac{4}{5}$ of £125
11 $\frac{3}{10}$ of £5.20
12 $\frac{1}{11}$ of 660 g
13 $\frac{2}{9}$ of 360°
14 $\frac{1}{20}$ of 3 m
15 $\frac{7}{8}$ of £12

3. Use your calculator to find these amounts to the nearest penny.

1 $\frac{5}{6}$ of £5
2 $\frac{2}{7}$ of £10.30
3 $\frac{3}{8}$ of £1.05
4 $\frac{1}{6}$ of £11.49
5 $\frac{7}{9}$ of £23

4. Find the values of the following.

1 $1\frac{3}{4}$ times 5 m
2 $1\frac{2}{3}$ times 300 g
3 $3\frac{1}{3}$ times 12 min
4 $4\frac{1}{2}$ times £10.60
5 $2\frac{2}{5}$ times 7.5 ℓ

5. A water tank held 720 ℓ of water. The gardener used $\frac{1}{4}$ of the water on Monday, $\frac{1}{3}$ of the remainder on Tuesday and on Wednesday he used $\frac{2}{3}$ of what was left. How much water remained ?

6. June and her mum went to pick mushrooms. June found 18 and her mum found $2\frac{1}{2}$ times as many. How many did they find altogether ?

7. A farmer decided to check and repair a wall which was 240 m long. On the first day he did a length of 96 m, the second day he did $\frac{3}{4}$ of that distance and on the third day he did $\frac{2}{3}$ of the distance of the second day. What fraction of the total length remained to be done ?

8. At a football match one-third of the spectators were seated. The other 16 800 stood up. How many spectators were there altogether ?

9. In an election there were 3 candidates, A, B and C.
3150 people voted and A got $\frac{1}{5}$ of the votes.
How many votes did A get ?
B got $\frac{4}{9}$ of the votes. How many did he get ?
C got the rest of the votes. How many did he get ?
Who won the election ?
How many more votes did the winner get, than the runner-up ?

10. A joint of meat weighed $3\frac{1}{4}$ kg. The cooking time was recommended as 40 minutes per kg plus an extra 20 minutes.
What total cooking time was needed ?
It was planned to have lunch at 1 pm. At what time should the joint have been put in the oven ?

Percentages

The symbol % stands for 'per cent', which means 'out of 100'.
So, 7% means 7 out of 100.
As a fraction this is $\frac{7}{100}$.
As a decimal it is 0.07.

If in an election 61% of the voters have voted for a certain candidate, this means that out of the total number of voters, 61 out of every 100 voted for that candidate.
If in an examination you got 77 marks out of a total of 100 marks, this can be stated as a mark of 77%.

To find a percentage of a sum of money

Change the percentage into a fraction, if it is a simple fraction such as $\frac{1}{2}$, $\frac{1}{4}$, $\frac{1}{5}$, $\frac{1}{10}$, $\frac{1}{20}$, or change it into a decimal and use your calculator.

Example

1 Find 20% of £360.

$20\% = \frac{20}{100} = \frac{1}{5}$, so find $\frac{1}{5}$ of £360.

$\frac{1}{5}$ of £360 = £72.

To find a percentage of a sum of money, using your calculator.

Examples

2 Find 24% of £35.

To do this if there is no [%] key on your calculator:
24% as a decimal is 0.24, so find 0.24 × 35. Your calculator gives 8.4 so 24% of £35 is £8.40.

If there is a [%] key on your calculator then press 24 [×] 35 [%].
(The order of the two numbers does not matter, but press [%] last, instead of [=].)
You should get 8.4. If you do not, then perhaps your calculator works in a different way. Look at its instruction booklet, or try to find out how it works. Perhaps, on your calculator, you have to press [=] also.

3 Find 70% of £216.

70% as a decimal is 0.7 so find 0.7 × 216. Your calculator gives 151.2 so 70% of £216 is £151.20.
Using the [%] key you can press 70 [×] 216 [%].

4 Find 4% of £52.40.

4% as a decimal is 0.04 so find 0.04×52.4 (or 0.04×52.40).
Your calculator gives 2.096. To 2 decimal places this is 2.10, so 4% of £52.40 is £2.10, correct to the nearest penny.
Using the [%] key you can press 4 [×] 52.4 [%].

To find a percentage of a quantity

Example

5 Find 44% of 250 kg.

44% as a decimal is 0.44 so find 0.44×250. Your calculator gives 110, so 44% of 250 kg is 110 kg.
Using the [%] key you can press 44 [×] 250 [%].

Exercise 9.3

1. Express these percentages as fractions in their simplest forms.

1 30% **2** 75% **3** 15% **4** 24% **5** 40%

2. Express these percentages as decimals.

1 18% **2** 95% **3** 6% **4** 11% **5** 60%

3. Find the values of the following.

1 48% of £5.50
2 5% of £12
3 25% of £13.20
4 12% of £95
5 80% of £23.40
6 60% of £8
7 8% of £3.50
8 15% of £72
9 3% of £16
10 20% of £28.30

4. Find the values of the following.

1 4% of 3 m
2 15% of 2 kg
3 60% of $\frac{1}{2}$ hour
4 9% of 50 cm
5 21% of 5 ℓ
6 40% of 5 m
7 2% of 3 ℓ
8 80% of 1 min
9 6% of 50 cm
10 25% of 2 kg

5. In a school of 625 pupils, on one day 8% of the pupils were absent.
1 How many pupils were absent ?
2 How many pupils were present ?

6. A holiday company has decided to improve its accommodation and services and to do this it raises its prices by 9%.

   1 What is the increase in price of a holiday previously costing £260 ?

   2 What is the new cost of the holiday ?

7. A length of curtain material was 1.5 m long, but after being washed it shrunk and lost 6% of its length.

   1 By how much did it shrink ?

   2 What was the new length ?

8. This seed packet contains 250 seeds. At least how many seeds can you expect to germinate ?

9. A couple stay in a hotel for 3 nights at a cost of £36 per person per night. A service charge of 10% is added to the bill.

   1 What is the service charge, per person per night ?

   2 What is the total service charge for the couple ?

   3 What is the total cost of the bill for the couple ?

10. A group of 5 boys do a job for which they earn £60. The organiser takes 25% of this and the rest of the money is shared equally among the other four. How much does each boy receive ?

11. During a storm 18% of the trees in a forest were destroyed. If there were 450 trees at first,

   1 how many were destroyed,

   2 how many trees remained ?

12. The insurance premium for a car is £240. It is reduced by 60% for 'no claim discount'.

   1 What percentage of the premium must be paid ?

   2 How much does the motorist have to pay ?

   3 He pays this in 12 monthly instalments. How much does he pay each month ?

13. A furniture store had a dressing table for sale at £120. Since it was slightly damaged the price was then reduced by 15%.

    1 By how much was it reduced ?
    2 How much was it sold for ?

14. It is estimated that some gravel will lose 12% of its weight when drying. A load weighed 350 kg.

    1 How much weight will it lose when drying ?
    2 What will it weigh when dry ?

15. A brass bar weighing 40 kg is made of copper and zinc. Copper forms 55% of the weight of the bar and the rest is zinc.

    1 What percentage of the weight of the bar is zinc ?
    2 How many kg of zinc does it contain ?

Exercise 9.4 Applications and Activities

1. **Percentages in daily life**

Get a copy of a daily newspaper and cut out all the references to percentage that you can find. You should find quite a few, in the articles themselves, in the financial pages and in the advertisements. Arrange these cut-outs on a poster.

2. **A fraction fountain**

On a sheet of graph paper make a rectangle 12 cm wide (60 small squares) and 11 cm long, using the thick lines as edges. Then draw lines across to make 11 strips, each 12 cm across and 1 cm in depth. Divide the top strip in half with a vertical line, as shown. Label this middle line $\frac{1}{2}$.

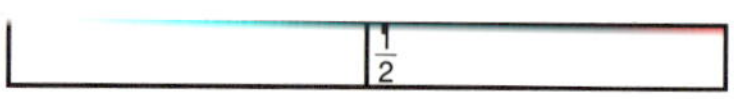

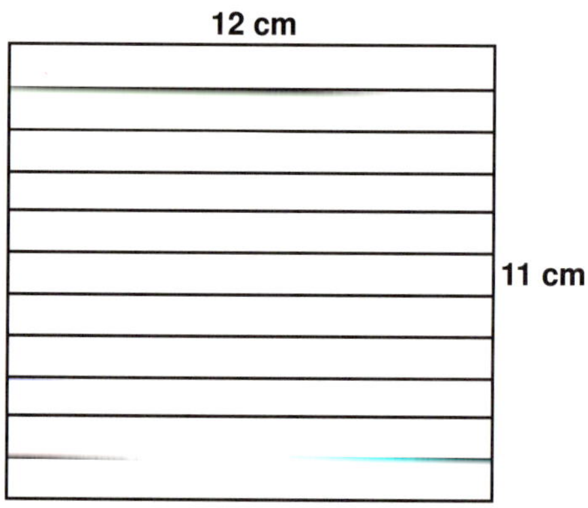

Divide the next strip into 3 equal parts.

Divide the next strip into 4 equal parts and label the lines $\frac{1}{4}$, $\frac{2}{4}$ and $\frac{3}{4}$.

Continue in this way, until the last strip is divided into 12 equal parts.

Be very careful with 7ths, 9ths and 11ths.
Using your calculator, $\frac{1}{7}$ of $60 = 60 \div 7 = 8.57\ldots$ so the 1st vertical line is just over $8\frac{1}{2}$ small squares from the edge. For the next one you want $\frac{2}{7}$ of 60 which is $60 \times 2 \div 7 = 17.14\ldots$, just over 17 small squares from the edge, and so on.

When the diagram is complete, put your ruler along the left-hand edge and then move it along towards the right edge, keeping it parallel to the edges.
The first fraction bar you come to is $\frac{1}{12}$. This is the smallest fraction on the diagram. Then the next two in order are $\frac{1}{11}$ and $\frac{1}{10}$. Write down the next few. $\frac{2}{12}$ and $\frac{1}{6}$ are in the same vertical position. They have equal value. The higher one, $\frac{1}{6}$, is the fraction in its simplest form.

Use your diagram to answer these questions.
Which is larger, $\frac{3}{7}$ or $\frac{4}{9}$?
Which fractions have the same value as $\frac{1}{3}$?
What is $\frac{8}{12}$ in its simplest form ?
What is half of $\frac{6}{7}$?
What is $\frac{7}{10} - \frac{3}{10}$, in its simplest form ?

To draw the 'fountain'

Use crayons or felt tips. Choose a colour, e.g. red.
Put a red blob on the top of the vertical bar of each fraction with numerator 1, i.e. $\frac{1}{2}$, $\frac{1}{3}$, $\frac{1}{4}$, etc., and join these blobs with a smooth red curve, drawn freehand.
To match this curve, keep to the same colour and put a blob on top of the vertical bar of each fraction where the numerator is 1 less than the denominator, i.e. $\frac{1}{2}$ (again), $\frac{2}{3}$, $\frac{3}{4}$,..., and draw another curve through these points.
Change to another colour and draw another 2 curves, one with blobs where the fraction has numerator 2, beginning with $\frac{2}{3}$, and the other where the numerator is 2 less than the denominator, beginning with $\frac{1}{3}$.
Continue in a similar way, until the last 2 curves will go through $\frac{10}{11}$, $\frac{10}{12}$ and $\frac{1}{11}$, $\frac{2}{12}$.

3. **Fractions in order of size**

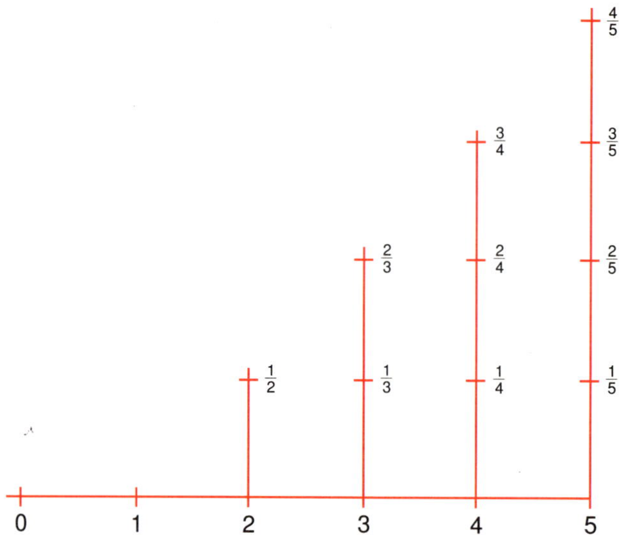

Look at this diagram. The points 0 and 5 are marked off along a horizontal line. Vertical lines are drawn upwards and the fractions have been marked off, those with numerator 1 on level 1, those with numerator 2 on level 2, and so on.

To write these fractions in order of size, put your ruler on the base line. Keeping the ruler passing through 0, turn it gradually until it also passes through one of the fraction points. The first fraction it comes to is $\frac{1}{5}$, because $\frac{1}{5}$ is the smallest fraction of the ten shown on the diagram, and so its line is the least steep. As you continue to turn the ruler more, still keeping it passing through 0, it will pass through all the other fractions, in order of size.

Two of the fractions are equivalent, that is, the same size, and the ruler passes through both together. Which are they ?

Write down all the fractions in order of size. For the equivalent fractions, write down the one which is in its lowest terms.
This kind of sequence is called a **Farey sequence**.

Using squared paper or graph paper, make your own diagram, but drawing the horizontal line as far as point 10. Write down all your fractions in order of size.

You can make discoveries about these fractions.
If two consecutive fractions in the list are $\frac{a}{b}$ and $\frac{c}{d}$, investigate $b \times c$ and $a \times d$.
e.g. If two consecutive fractions are $\frac{2}{5}$ and $\frac{3}{7}$, find 5×3 and 2×7.
Repeat for other consecutive fractions and see if there is a pattern.

If three consecutive fractions in the list are $\frac{a}{b}$, $\frac{c}{d}$ and $\frac{e}{f}$, investigate $a + e$ and $b + f$.

4. Using a calculator with a fractions key

This key is labelled $\boxed{a^{b}/_{c}}$.
The second function on the key is labelled $\boxed{^{d}/_{c}}$.

To enter a fraction

e.g. To enter $\frac{5}{8}$, press 5 $\boxed{a^{b}/_{c}}$ 8. The display will show 5 ⌋ 8.

To enter $\frac{13}{8}$, press 13 $\boxed{a^{b}/_{c}}$ 8.

To enter a mixed number

e.g. To enter $2\frac{5}{8}$ press 2 $\boxed{a^{b}/_{c}}$ 5 $\boxed{a^{b}/_{c}}$ 8. The display will show 2 ⌋ 5 ⌋ 8.

To change a fraction to a decimal

Enter the fraction then press $\boxed{=}$ $\boxed{a^{b}/_{c}}$.
e.g. enter $2\frac{5}{8}$ then press $\boxed{=}$ $\boxed{a^{b}/_{c}}$ and the display will show 2.625.
Press $\boxed{a^{b}/_{c}}$ again to change the number back to a mixed number.

To reduce a fraction to its lowest terms

Enter the fraction and then press $\boxed{=}$ or $\boxed{+}$, $\boxed{-}$, $\boxed{\times}$ or $\boxed{\div}$.

To change a mixed number to an improper fraction

Enter the mixed number then press the second function key then $\boxed{^{d}/_{c}}$.
To change it back, press $\boxed{=}$.
To change it to a decimal, press $\boxed{a^{b}/_{c}}$.

To change an improper fraction to a mixed number

Enter the improper fraction and then press $\boxed{=}$.

To find a fraction of a number

Press fraction $\boxed{\times}$ number $\boxed{=}$.
e.g. To find $\frac{2}{3}$ of $4\frac{1}{2}$kg press 2 $\boxed{a^{b}/_{c}}$ 3 $\boxed{\times}$ 4 $\boxed{a^{b}/_{c}}$ 1 $\boxed{a^{b}/_{c}}$ 2 $\boxed{=}$ and you will get the answer 3 (kg).

Use the fractions key on your calculator to do some of the questions of Exercises 9.1 and 9.2, checking that you get the same answers as before.

Do not rely on your calculator entirely. You still need to know the methods for working out fractions.

Chapter 9 test

1. Reduce these fractions to their lowest terms.

   1 $\frac{15}{25}$ **2** $\frac{12}{21}$ **3** $\frac{8}{24}$ **4** $\frac{25}{35}$ **5** $\frac{48}{80}$

2. Change these mixed numbers to improper fractions.

   1 $6\frac{3}{8}$ **2** $4\frac{2}{3}$ **3** $2\frac{3}{4}$ **4** $3\frac{2}{5}$ **5** $1\frac{7}{8}$

3. Change these improper fractions to mixed numbers.

   1 $\frac{11}{6}$ **2** $\frac{17}{4}$ **3** $\frac{41}{8}$ **4** $\frac{14}{3}$ **5** $\frac{19}{12}$

4. Find the values of the following.

   1 $\frac{2}{3}$ of £2.16
   2 $\frac{4}{7}$ of 3.5 m
   3 $\frac{3}{5}$ of 550 g
   4 $\frac{5}{6}$ of 1.2 ℓ
   5 $\frac{7}{10}$ of 1 hour

5. On a farm there were 280 animals. $\frac{5}{8}$ of them were sheep, $\frac{1}{10}$ of them were pigs, there were 2 ponies, 4 dogs, 3 cats, 5 rabbits and the rest were cows. How many cows were there ? What fraction of the total number of animals were cows ?

6. Mrs Evans won £450 in a competition. She gave $\frac{1}{3}$ of it to her husband and $\frac{2}{5}$ of the remainder to her daughter. She kept the remaining money for herself. How much did she keep ?

7. Express 35% as a fraction in its simplest form, and also as a decimal.

8. Find the values of

   1 5% of £2.40
   2 45% of 1 kg
   3 22% of 3 ℓ
   4 6% of 200 m
   5 15% of £18

9. A house was bought for £36 000. It is estimated that since that time house values have risen by 40%.

   1 What is 40% of £36 000 ?
   2 What is the house worth now ?

10. The foreman put in a report that 12% of the machines in the workshop needed repairing. If there were 225 machines altogether, how many were working properly ?

PUZZLES

7. A secretary typed 4 letters to 4 different people and addressed the 4 envelopes. Then she told the office junior to put them in the envelopes. If the junior inserts the letters at random, what is the probability that exactly 3 letters will go into the right envelopes ?

8. Put the numbers 1 to 7 in the circles so that each row of three connected circles adds up to 12.

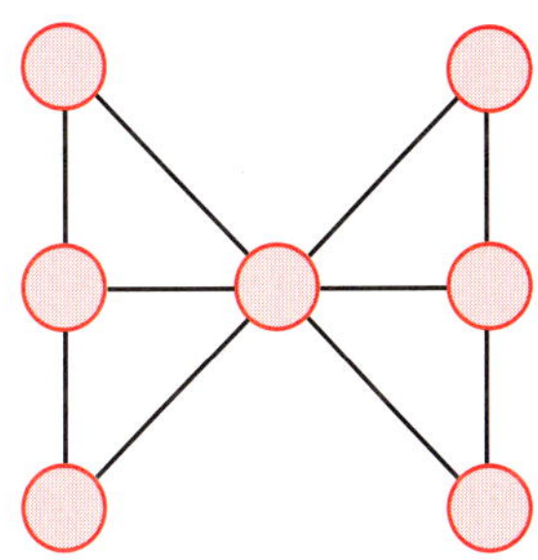

9. How many times, between 1 am and 1 pm, are the hands of a clock pointing in the same direction ?

10. Agnes Thompson was born in the 19th century, in a year that reads the same when turned upside down. She died in a year with the same property. What are the dates of her birth and death, and how old was she when she died, if she had had a birthday that year ?

11. A man filled two buckets with water. One was left in the garage all night, where the temperature was 15°C. The other was left in the garden where the temperature was 15°F.
The man's small son came along and dropped a penny into each bucket. Which penny reached the bottom of its bucket more quickly ?

10 Thinking about statistics

Statistics through the ages

We know that in the Old Roman Empire, 2000 years ago, a count was made of the population. We read in the Bible that Mary and Joseph had to go to Bethlehem to be counted. In England, 900 years ago, the king, William the Conqueror, sent out commissioners to survey his new kingdom, and they collected information about the people and their land holdings. This record survives today in the Domesday Book. So statistics, the collecting and analysing of data, is not a new subject. What use can a Government make of the figures when it has counted the population ? Today, this is called taking a census. In Britain it has been taken every 10 years from 1801. When do you think the next one will be ? (There was no census taken in 1941. Why do you think that one was left out ?) As well as counting the population, what other information about the population will the government find useful, and for what purposes ?
With the use of computers, it is much easier and quicker to process the data than it used to be, so that much more use is being made of statistical data now than even a few years ago.

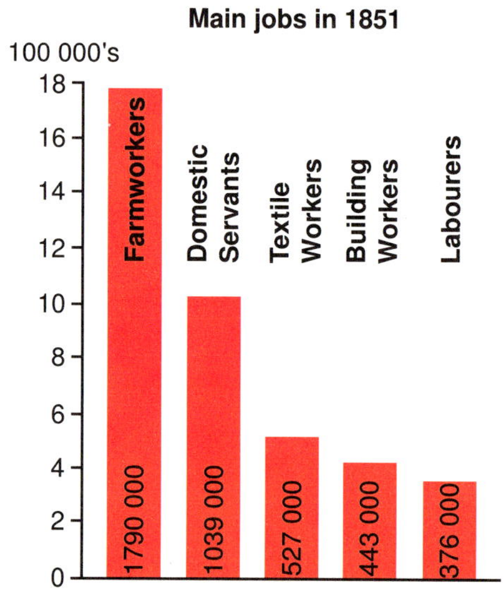

A Lancashire farm family from the last century

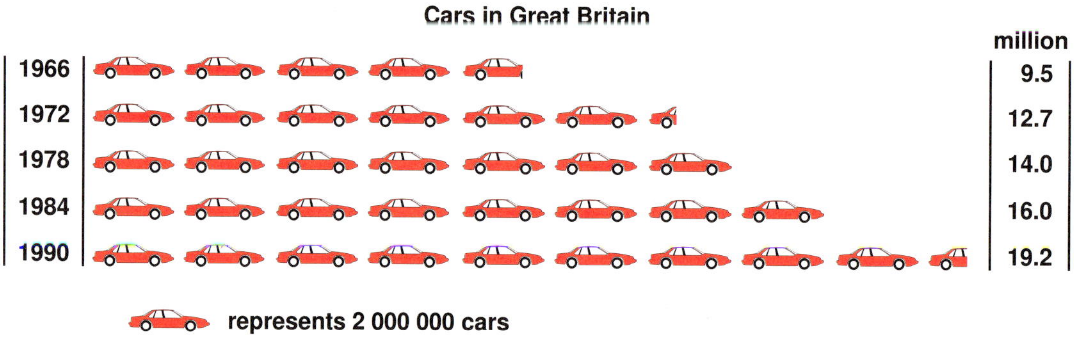

A pie chart

Why do you think the name pie chart was chosen ?
Here is a pie chart showing how the price you pay for a compact disc is divided among the people who are involved in its manufacture and sale.

Costs of a Compact Disc

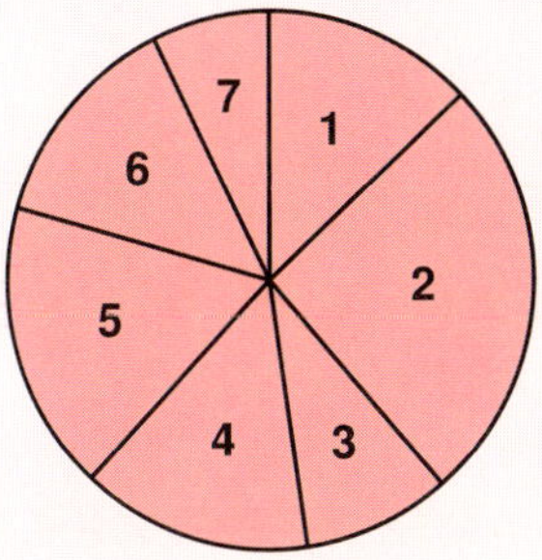

1 VAT £1.68
2 Shop profit £2.82
3 Dealer profit £1.02
4 Royalty and copyright £1.59
5 Design, manufacturing, promotion £1.89
6 Record company costs £1.47
7 Record company profit 78p
Total cost £11.25

Using statistics

Name some sorts of numerical data which these people might find useful:

A shoe manufacturer
An athletics coach
A farmer
A football manager
Someone new to the district, who wanted to choose which school to send their children to
A scientist doing medical research
An insurance company, for car insurance
A person wishing to buy a new washing machine

Think of some other people who make use of statistics, and say what sort of data they use.

Average house prices in 1994

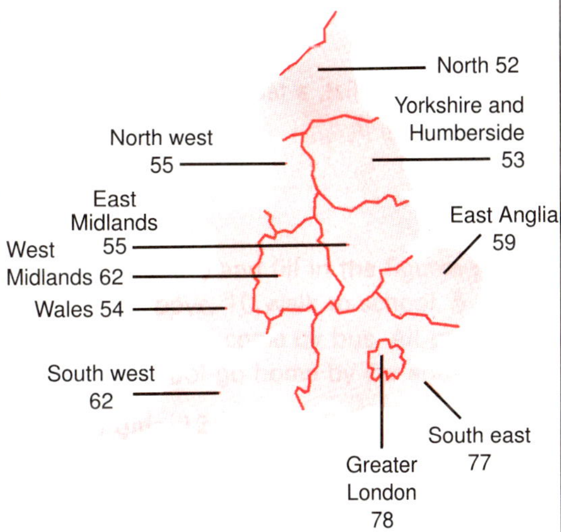

Figures in £1000's to nearest £1000

10 Statistics

We often need to collect and use numerical facts.
Your teacher needs to know the number of children in your class, how many boys and how many girls, and the range of ages. He/she needs this information to plan ahead. Are there enough desks or tables ? How can the class best be split into suitable groups for group work ? Is the work which has been planned suitable for the age range ?
At home, you know how many children there are in your family and their ages, and how much pocket money you get.
Your parents need to know the family earnings, and the plan for using this money, so much for rent or mortgage payments, fuel bills, food, clothing, etc.

The branch of Mathematics concerned with collecting numerical data and then using it, often to make decisions for future action, is called **Statistics**.
The word **statistics** is also used for the actual numbers collected, i.e. the data.

Statistics is a subject which has a wide variety of uses. The Government collects many kinds of statistics which are published in journals. Scientists use statistics in their research. Industry uses statistics to plan future action. Insurance companies use statistics to fix the premiums they must charge. Sports' associations keep statistical records.

After data is collected, it is often displayed in the form of a list, a table or a graph. Then it can be studied, in order to make conclusions from it.

Tally tables

Example

1 Workers in an office were asked which method of transport they used to get to work that morning. Their replies were as follows:

Walk, bus, car, walk, walk, walk, car, walk, bus, bus, walk, car, car, motorbike, car, car, bus, car, car, walk, car, walk, car, car, walk, car, motorbike, walk, walk, car, motorbike, car, bus, motorbike, walk, car, bus, car.

The items are entered in a tally chart as they occur.

	Tally	Total
Car	~~IIII~~ ~~IIII~~ ~~IIII~~ I	16
Motorbike	IIII	4
Bus	~~IIII~~ I	6
Walk	~~IIII~~ ~~IIII~~ II	12
		38

Notice that the tally marks are grouped in fives, the fifth tally mark going through the first four.
The groups of 5 are kept in neat columns. This makes the totals easy to compare.

Presenting the data in a table

Example

2 **Method of transport to and from school**

	Morning			Afternoon		
	Boys	Girls	Total	Boys	Girls	Total
Walk						
Cycle						
Motorbike						
Car						
Bus						
Total						

Copy this table and fill in the figures to satisfy this information.
Of the 50 boys, 10 walk to school, 5 cycle, 3 come on their motorbikes and 8 come by car. The rest come by bus. All go home by the same method except that 2 who walk to school go home by car and 3 who come by car go home by bus.

Of the girls, 12 walk to school, 8 cycle, 1 comes on her motorbike, 3 come by car and 16 come by bus. 4 of the girls who come by bus walk home and 2 others go home by car instead of by bus.

How many pupils come to school by bus ?
How many pupils go home by bus ?

Statistical diagrams

You will already have drawn simple diagrams. These diagrams of the data of example **1** will remind you about pictograms and bar charts.

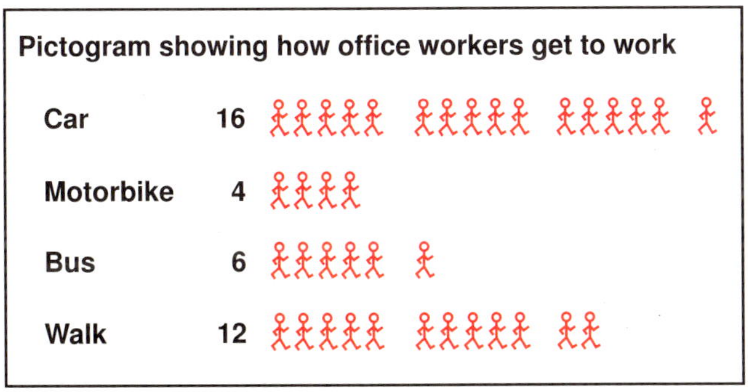

Pictogram showing how office workers get to work

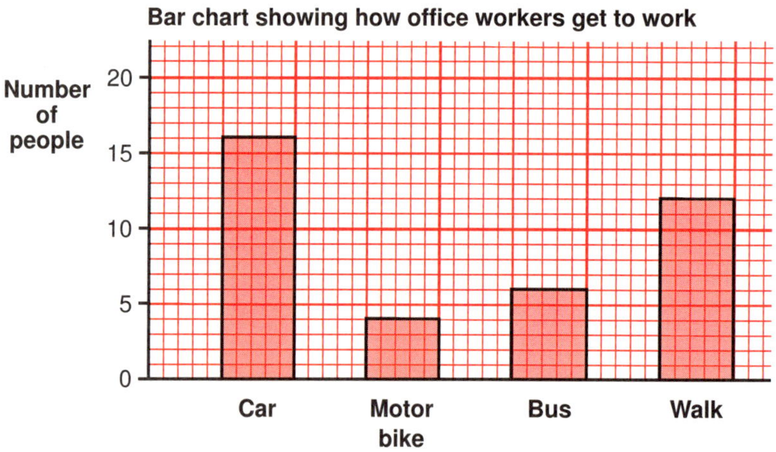

A line-graph (time-series graph)

These graphs always have time on the horizontal axis and the quantity which is being recorded on the vertical axis.

They are useful to show if there is any **trend**, that is a gradual increase or decrease as time goes on, or if there are any patterns such as seasonal patterns, and they also show any irregular variations.

Example

3

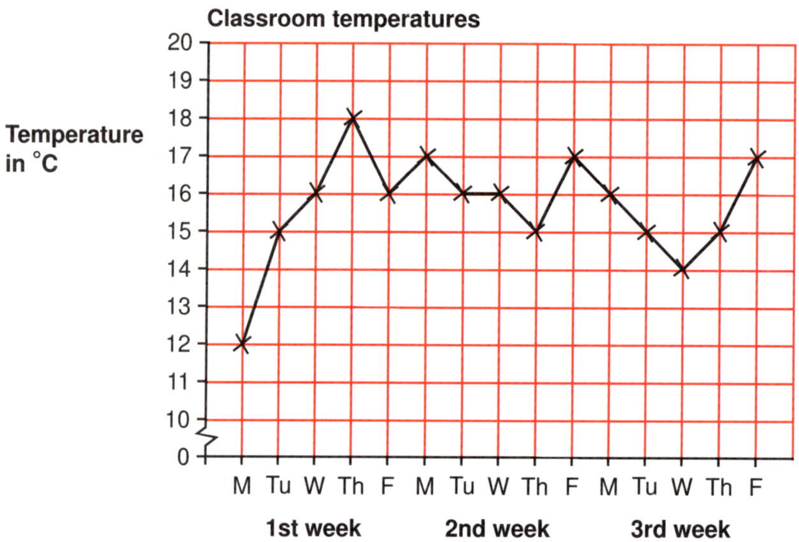

On which day was it very cold in the classroom ? Give a possible reason for this.

The points are joined from one to the next by straight lines, because this shows increases and decreases more easily, but in this graph the lines have no other meaning. We cannot use the graph to find temperatures at in-between times.

Exercise 10.1

1. This list shows the number of cats in five European countries.

Italy	69
France	65
U.K.	65
West Germany	39
Netherlands	21

Figures are in 100 000's.

Show this information in a pictogram or bar chart.

2. The land surface of the Earth is divided as follows:

Europe	11
Asia	44
Africa	30
North and Central America	24
South America	18
Oceania	9
Antarctica	14

The numbers are in 1 000 000's of km^2, to the nearest 1 000 000.

Show this information on a bar chart.

3. Some families were asked to say what was the main method of transport for their holiday this summer. Their replies were:

Canal barge, plane, coach, train, car, plane, car and ferry, plane, plane, plane, car and ferry, car, car, car, plane, car, car, cruise ship, car, coach, car, car, plane, car, car, car, car and ferry, car and ferry, plane, plane, car, car and ferry, car, train, car, car, car.

Show this information in a list and on a suitable diagram.

Can you use this information to estimate how many of these families went abroad for their holiday ?

4. The UK population figures are given in this table. (Figures are in millions to the nearest million.)

Year	1901	1911	1921	1931	1941	1951	1961	1971	1981
Population	38	42	44	46	48	51	53	56	56

Draw a line-graph to represent the data.
Comment on the trend shown.

Pie charts

One way of showing how a whole item is split up into several parts, is to draw the whole as a circle and divide it into sectors for the different parts.
This kind of diagram is called a **pie chart**.

Example

In a survey, 180 people were asked to name their favourite leisure pursuit chosen from these five categories. The results are as shown:

Watching television	70
Reading	50
Taking part in sports	25
DIY and car maintenance	15
Entertaining and visiting friends	20
	180

Pie chart to show leisure pursuits

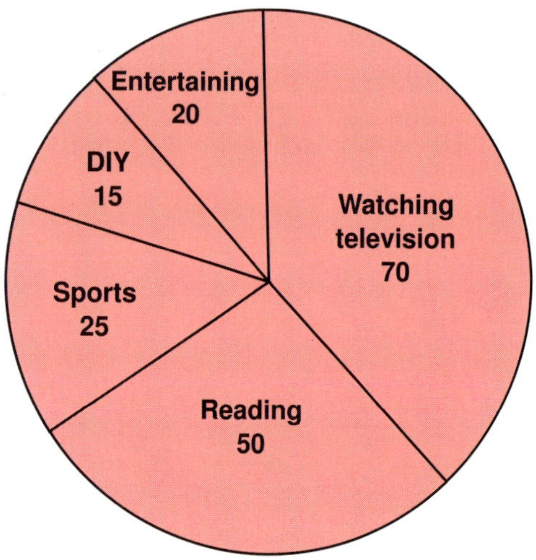

The working for the pie chart

Since 180 people are represented by 360°,
1 person is represented by 2°.

Television	$70 \times 2° = 140°$
Reading	$50 \times 2° = 100°$
Sports	$25 \times 2° = 50°$
DIY, etc.	$15 \times 2° = 30°$
Entertaining	$20 \times 2° = 40°$
	$360°$

One advantage of a pie chart is that it is easy to see approximately what fraction of the whole is involved. Here, the largest part is 'watching television', and this, together with 'entertaining', makes half. Reading is just bigger than $\frac{1}{4}$, and sports and DIY together are just less than $\frac{1}{4}$.

Exercise 10.2

1. The pie chart shows the time Marie spends on different subjects in each week.

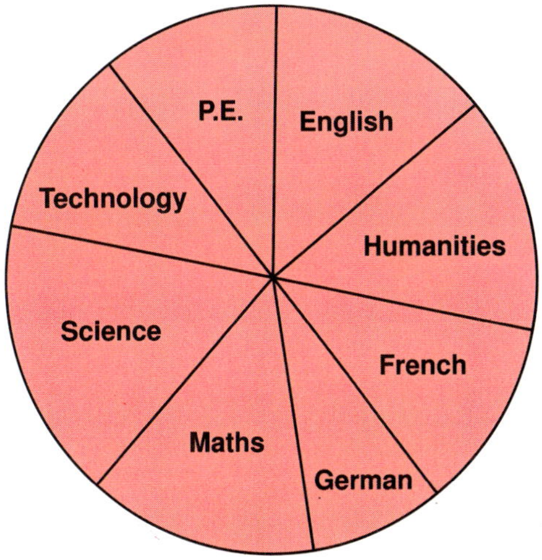

1 There are 7 lessons on 4 days and 8 lessons on the 5th day. How many lessons are there in a week ?
2 What size of angle represents 1 lesson ?
3 Which subject has most lessons ?
4 How many lessons are there for Maths ?
5 How many lessons are there for P.E. ?
6 How many lessons are there for foreign languages ?

2. The 30 children in a class were asked how they came to school. The results were represented on a pie chart and the angles of the sectors were:

Bus	132°
Car	48°
Cycle	24°

1 The remaining sector represented the children who walked to school. What was the angle in this sector ?
2 What size of angle represents 1 child ?
3 How many children were there in each category ?

3. The results of a survey on the types of soft drinks sold are shown in this pie chart.

What fractions of the total sales are spent on
1 fizzy drinks,
2 squash,
3 fruit juice ?

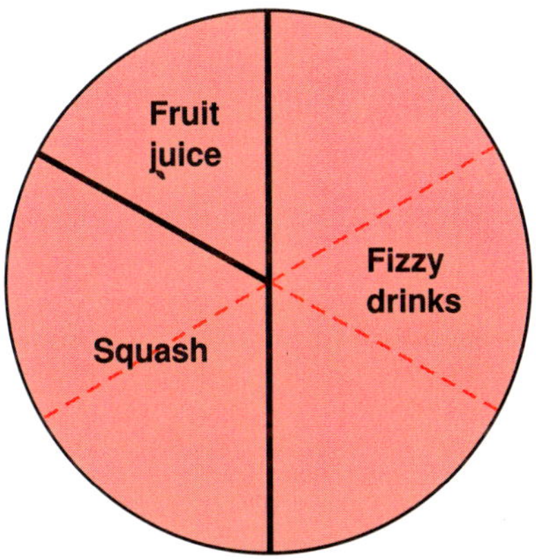

4. This list shows the vehicles used by a 'typical' police force. Show this information on a pie chart.

Large cars	80
Small cars	160
Vans	55
Motorcycles	35
Coaches	25
Lorries, etc.	5
	360

5. According to a survey, an 'average' family spends £30 a week on transport. This shows how the money is spent, (amounts to nearest 50p).

Cost of buying a car	£11.50
Cost of running a car	£13.50
Bus fares	£1.50
Other fares	£3.50

('Other fares' includes train fares, air fares, taxis, ferries and cycles.)

What size of angle on a pie chart would represent £1 ?

Show the information on a pie chart.

6. 36 girls were asked to name their favourite colour. Here are their replies:

Blue, blue, blue, pink, green, white, pink, black, pink, pink, yellow, red, pink, black, black, black, yellow, green, black, yellow, pink, blue, blue, red, black, blue, red, blue, red, blue, pink, blue, blue, red, yellow, pink.

Make a list of these replies and draw a pie chart to show the information.

7. The cost of running a car for a year was split up into the following amounts:

Petrol	£1220
Oil, tyres, servicing	£265
Licence and insurance	£315

What is the total cost ?

On a pie chart, what amount would be represented by an angle of 1° ?

Draw a pie chart to show the information.

Averages

Mean, median and mode

Example

1 This list shows the number of people attending a weekly meeting, for the first 10 weeks.
What is the average attendance ?

1st week	20
2nd week	19
3rd week	24
4th week	22
5th week	20
6th week	23
7th week	20
8th week	28
9th week	24
10th week	20

The mean

The usual average is found by adding up the numbers.
This gives a total of 220, over 10 weeks.
So the average attendance is 220 ÷ 10, which is 22.

This kind of average is called the **arithmetic mean**, or simply the **mean**.

The symbol we use for the mean is x with a bar on top, $\bar{x}$, called x-bar.

$$\bar{x} = \frac{\text{sum of the items}}{\text{number of items}} = \frac{S}{n}$$

In the example, $\bar{x} = \frac{S}{n} = \frac{220}{10} = 22.$

There are two other kinds of average which we can use.

The median

When the items are arranged in order of size, the **median** is the value of the middle item, or the value halfway between the middle two if there is an even number of items.

(Arrange the items in order of size.)

19 20 20 20 20 ↑ middle 22 23 24 24 28

The median is halfway between 20 and 22, i.e. 21.
(Half the values are less than 21 and half are greater than 21.)

The mode

The **mode** is the value which occurs most often. (Sometimes a set of values will not have a mode, as there may not be any value which occurs more often than any of the others.)

The value which occurs most often is 20 (as there were 4 weeks when 20 members were present), so the mode is 20.

Summary:– Mean = 22, median = 21, mode = 20.

Which average to use ?

All these averages can be used in different circumstances, although the most usual one is the mean, as this is the one which involves all the values. If one of the values is very high or low compared to the others, this will affect the mean and in this case the median might be a better average to use. The mode is the simplest average to find, but generally it is not as useful as the other two.

Example

2 In a class test, the marks were:

5 10 25 25 25 30 30 30 30 35

The mean mark is 24.5, the median mark is 27.5 and the mode mark is 30.
Comment about the averages.

The fairest average to quote here is the median. Half the students have less than 27.5 and half have more.
The mean has been distorted by the two low values, and only two students have marks less than the mean.
The mode is not a representative average, as only 1 student has a better mark.

If the word 'average' is used without specifying which one in an arithmetical question, it refers to the mean.

Using a statistical calculator to find the mean

Example

3 To find the mean of 23, 24, 28, 29, 31.

Set the calculator to work in statistical mode, then press

23 [DATA] 24 [DATA] 28 [DATA] 29 [DATA] 31 [DATA]

When you have entered all the data, pressing
[n] will tell you the number of items entered, 5,
[Σx] will tell you the sum of the items entered, $S = 135$,
[$\bar{x}$] will tell you the mean of the items entered, 27.

Range

The average (mean, median or mode) gives us a general idea of the data, but two sets of numbers can have the same average but be very different in other ways. We can compare them by finding the range.

Range = highest value − lowest value

In example **1**,
Range $= 28 - 19 = 9$.

In example **2**,
Range $= 35 - 5 = 30$.

In example **3**,
Range $= 31 - 23 = 8$.

Example

4 Here are the weights of 9 boys, in kg.
53, 48, 41, 55, 42, 57, 52, 47, 51.
Find the mean, median and range of the weights.

Mean weight $\bar{x} = \frac{S}{n} = \frac{446}{9}$ kg $= 49.6$ kg, correct to 1 decimal place.

To find the median weight, first put the weights in order of size.
41 42 47 48 51 52 53 55 57
↑ middle

The median weight is 51 kg.

Range of weights $= (57 - 41)$ kg $= 16$ kg.

1 Remember to give the units of measurement, e.g. cm, kg, in your answers.
2 Check that your answers seem to be reasonable.
3 Do not give too many decimal places. If the data is accurate to the nearest whole number then it is reasonable to give the averages to 1 decimal place.

Exercise 10.3

1. Find the mean, median and range in the following cases.

   1 The numbers of matches in a sample of 12 boxes were
   36 35 38 41 43 39 33 41 39 37 35 42

   2 The distances, in km, travelled each day by a group of people on a week's walking holiday were
   21 22 24 23 19 20 18

   3 The times taken, in seconds, for 10 children to complete a simple puzzle were
   57 52 65 54 68 60 53 51 61 48

   4 The weekly wages for 8 workers were
   £109, £133, £141, £126, £119, £138, £150, £124.

   5 The weights of 6 parcels are, in kg,
   3.5, 4.4, 3.9, 2.7, 5.0, 3.3.

2. Find the median, mode and range of these sets of numbers.

   1 7 8 8 8 8 10 11 11 12 13 13 15 15 16

   2 2 8 7 3 8 2 1 4 10 6 8 9

   3 6 4 8 2 7 4 5 1 8 4 7 4 2 7 8 4 5 6 3
   0 5 8 3 2 7

3. The weights, in kg, of 10 children are 49, 36, 46, 33, 38, 43, 31, 44, 34, 36. Find the mean, the median and the range of the weights.

4. The lengths of 5 javelin throws, in metres, are
   42.4, 39.0, 41.8, 44.2, 37.3.
   Find the mean, the median and the range of these distances.

Statistical investigations

Here are some examples of statistical investigations and the purpose of each.

1 To see how much pocket money children of various ages get, and what they spend it on.
Suppliers of sweets, snacks, soft drinks, magazines, etc. find this information useful. It should also be useful if you are running a school tuck shop.

2 To ask for pupils' opinions about school dinners, to see whether they are satisfactory or not.
This information might be useful to the school authorities and of benefit to the pupils. The quality of the meals is largely determined by the price charged and by certain local rules, but it may be possible to make changes which lead to improvement.

3 If you want to persuade the Council that a pedestrian crossing is needed on a road in your area, you should get some data about the amount of traffic using the road (preferably at different times of day) and the numbers of pedestrians at different times of day (possibly grouped into children, adults and elderly people).

4 A small shopkeeper will keep a record of the sales of different items, to see if sales are rising, steady or falling. He must also take account of seasonal variations. Some things sell better in summer, or warm weather, and many things sell well at Christmas.

To carry out a statistical investigation

1 **The aim of the investigation**

Decide what you are trying to find out. This is the **aim** of the investigation, and you should write it down as a heading.

2. **Collecting information**

Decide how you are going to collect the information. Sometimes you will make your own observations, such as counting cars in a traffic survey. Sometimes you will ask other people questions, and sometimes you can find the data in newspapers or reference books.

3. **Recording data**

If you are making your own observations, decide what you are going to observe. Design an observation sheet on which to record your data. This could be in the form of a tally table.
Afterwards you can make a summary of the results.

4. **Who to ask ?**

If you are going to ask people questions, decide who you are going to ask. If it is a survey of your class you may want to ask everyone in the class, but if it is a school matter you will probably want to ask just a **sample** of pupils. You will have to decide how many people to have in your sample, and how to select them. The sample should be a random sample, chosen fairly, so that each person has an equal chance of being selected. The sample should be large enough to represent fairly the different categories or views of all the people involved. For example, in a survey about views on school uniform (in a mixed school) the sample should include all age groups and both girls and boys.

5. **Questionnaires**

If you are going to ask people questions you must decide what you are going to ask them. You want to ask everyone the same questions, so write them down in a list which is called a **questionnaire**. You can either give people the questionnaire to fill in themselves or you can ask the questions and write down the answers.

6. **Analysing the data**

When you have collected all the data, you can make a summary of it, using lists or tables. You should then study it. It is often clearer if you draw statistical diagrams. You may want to do some calculations, such as finding averages and ranges of the data.

7. **Conclusion**

You should study your results and write down any conclusions you can make from them.

Note

If you are doing an observation out of doors, for example doing a traffic survey on a busy road, then do be careful to keep well away from the road. Accidents can happen ! It is also sensible to be with friends, not alone. In school hours, your teacher should be in charge of you. Out of school hours you should have your parents' permission.

If you are getting information by asking people, decide who you are going to ask. This could be the pupils in your class and possibly other pupils or teachers in your school. At home you could ask parents and friends. You should not approach strangers unless your teacher is supervising you. You should decide what questions you are going to ask. Some people may not wish to give you answers which they regard as personal or private information. For example, if you asked people how much money they earned they might not want you to know.
So choose your investigation carefully and plan to ask questions which people will be willing to answer. Then check with your teacher before you go ahead.

Exercise 10.4 Applications and Activities

1. A firm sold two models of a product, standard and de-luxe, and they made them in three colours, red, green and blue.
   A salesman took the orders shown below.
   R (red), G (green), B (blue), S (standard), D (de-luxe).

GS	BS	BS	RS	GD	RS	BS	RD	RD	GD	RS	RS
RD	BS	GD	GD	BS	GS	RD	BS	RS	RD	RS	RD
RD	BS	BD	RS	RD	RD	GD	RD	BD	RS	RS	BD
RS	GS	BS	RD	RS	RD	GD	RS	GD	GS	GS	RD
BD	GD	RS	RD	RD	RS	BD	BD	BD	RD	BS	RS

   Design a table for him to use to record the orders by tally marks, and fill it in.
   Make another table showing the number of orders for each item, and also showing the totals for standard models and de-luxe models, and the totals for red, green and blue models, with a final total of all the orders.

2. Here is a table to show the number of staff employed by a firm.

   Employees on 1st January each year

	Men	Women	Total
1993			
1994			
1995			

   Copy and fill in the table, using this information.
   On 1 Jan 1993 the company had 500 employees of which 320 were male.
   During the year, 80 employees left, 60 of these being men, but there were 60 new employees of which 48 were men.
   During 1994, 40 men and 20 women left, and the only new employees were 8 men and 12 women.
   Find the decrease in the total number of employees from 1 Jan 93 to 1 Jan 95.

3. The attendance figures for spectators at football matches in the top 4 English Divisions are as shown.
(Figures in millions, to the nearest 0.1 million.)

Season	Attendance
82–83	18.8
83–84	18.3
84–85	17.8
85–86	16.5
86–87	17.4
87–88	18.0
88–89	18.5
89–90	19.4
90–91	19.5
91–92	20.5
92–93	20.7
93–94	21.7

Draw a line-graph to represent the data.
Comment on the trend shown.

4. The sales of gas to domestic users (not industry) over 3 years are shown in this table. The figures are in 100 000 000 therms.

1st year				2nd year				3rd year			
Quarters 1	2	3	4	1	2	3	4	1	2	3	4
20	10	7	17	23	11	6	18	24	11	7	19

Draw a line-graph to represent the data.
Comment on the seasonal variations.

5. The pie chart represents the houses built by 3 builders, A, B, C.

1 Measure the angles of each sector, to the nearest 5°

2 If builder A built 30 houses, what was the total number of houses built ?

3 What angle on the pie chart would represent 1 house ?

4 How many houses were built by B, and by C ?

5 Represent this information in a pictogram.

Houses built

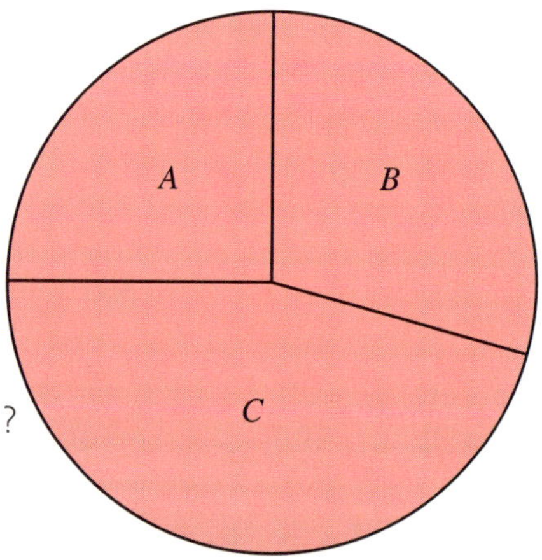

6. The weekly spending in a small business firm was listed, and represented on a pie chart.

	Amount in £	Sector angle in degrees
Wages	600	b
Materials	400	c
Transport	d	60
Other expenses	e	f
Total	1800	a

Find the missing numbers represented by letters a, b, c, d, e, f, working in that order. Draw the pie chart.

7. A survey of 15 year-old girls and boys showed that the most popular part-time jobs were:

Girls

Shopwork	49%
Hotel or cafe work	17%
Paper rounds	11%
Other jobs	23%

Boys

Paper rounds	36%
Shopwork	27%
Manual work	16%
Other jobs	21%

Draw two bar charts showing this information.

Comment on the results of the survey.

8. In a survey about television viewing, people were asked how long they spent watching TV or videos in a normal week. Here are the results, each in hours.

Men under 30:
40 22 8 10 40 10 35 21 10 11

Women under 30:
16 4 20 30 21 8 35 15 28 30

Men over 60 who do not go to work:
16 4 40 12 30 40

Women over 60 who do not go to work:
28 7 28 30 35 35 50 22 18

Analyse these results by finding the mean, median and range of times for each group.
Comment on the results.

(This is only a very small sample of people. A larger sample might have produced more reliable results.)

Maybe you can do your own survey, and compare your results with these.

9. Here are some ideas for statistical investigations. You may decide on different ones which are topical or more relevant to your school or area. For instance, if at your school it is planned to change the school uniform then you could gather opinions by asking pupils and parents for their views.

1 Methods of travelling to school.

2 Arrangements at lunch time:– school dinner, bring own lunch, go home, etc.

3 Choice of favourite sports, if playing and if watching.

4 Kinds of pets at home.

5 From the TV timetables in the newspaper or magazines, choose an evening from 5 pm to 11 pm and find how much time is devoted to news, sport, drama, music, etc. on one of the channels. You can compare the results for the different channels.

6 Do a traffic survey at a safe place. Classify the traffic into categories, such as cars, buses, heavy goods vehicles, etc.

7 You may decide to find out how you and your friends spend your time on an average weekday, and on Saturdays and Sundays.
Design a table to record the times spent sleeping, eating, at school, on homework, watching TV, etc.
Summarise the information.
Analyse the data by drawing diagrams, and finding average times.
Comment on the data. Do you think the times are satisfactory ? Is there any way you can improve your lifestyles ?

8 You may decide to find out how you and your friends spend (or save) your pocket money. (Your friends must be willing to do this with you.)
Find the average amounts per week for each person.
Analyse the data by drawing diagrams.
You will have to decide how to cope with the fact that you do not all have equal pocket money. Perhaps you might work out the percentages spent on each item.
Complete the investigation and comment on the data. Are you satisfied with how you spend your money, or could you make better use of it ?

9 Make a weather survey, which could include the kind of weather, temperatures and the amounts of sunshine or rainfall.

Chapter 10 test

1. The number of times lifeboats of the RNLI were launched for rescue work in recent years are shown in this table.
(Figures are to the nearest 100.)

Year	Launches
1981	3000
1982	3300
1983	3700
1984	3600
1985	3900
1986	3700
1987	3800
1988	4300
1989	4600
1990	4900

Draw a line-graph to represent the data.
Comment on the trend shown.

2. The lifeboat launches in 1990 were to assist the following:

sail pleasure craft	1430
power pleasure craft	960
manual pleasure craft	280
fishing vessels	810
swimmers and people cut off by tide	780
other	640
	4900

Show the data in a bar chart.

3. The temperatures in a seaside town on each day of a summer week were (in °C),
25°, 25°, 28°, 29°, 28°, 27°, 27°.
Find the mean temperature and the range of temperatures.

4. The pie chart shows how the money spent on a camping holiday was used.

1 Which item needed most money ?
2 Which item needed least money ?
3 What fraction of the total cost went on transport ?
4 Which two items together needed $\frac{1}{2}$ of the money ?
5 Which two items together needed $\frac{1}{4}$ of the money ?

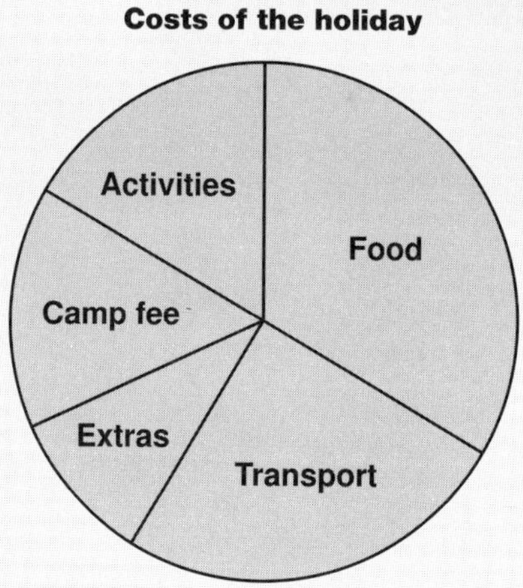

5. The bar chart illustrates the weekly budget of a family.

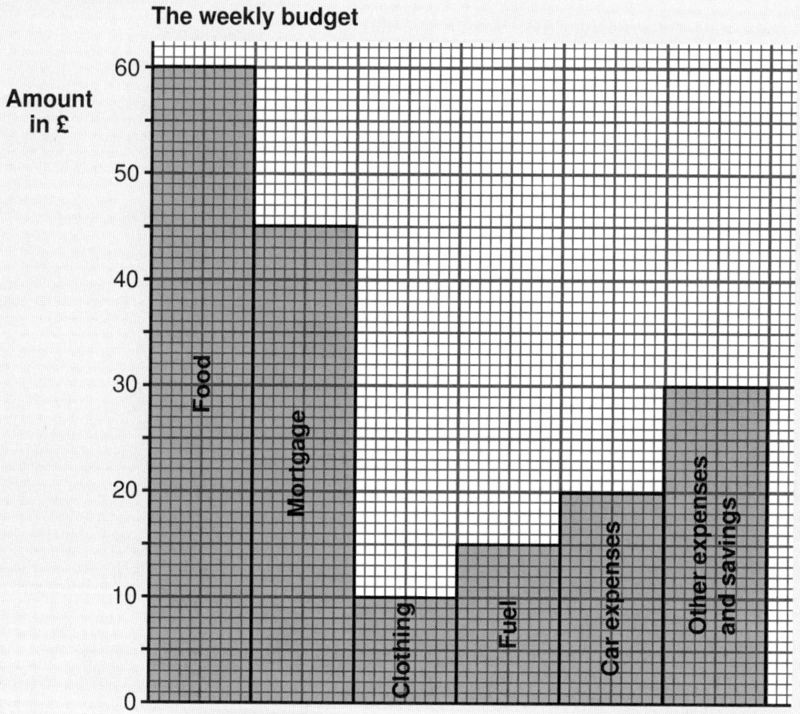

Use the chart to calculate the family's weekly income, and the fraction of the weekly income used on each item.
Draw a pie chart to show the same information.

6. From a survey, the heights of 10 men and 9 women, aged between 20 and 30 years old, are shown. (The heights are in centimetres, to the nearest cm.) Find the mean, median and range of heights for the men and for the women.

Men:
183 173 183 170 163 175 178 187 170 173

Women:
163 163 158 165 152 157 168 151 155

Comment on the results.

PUZZLES

12. There were 200 runners in a road race. A trainer was asked who would come 1st, 2nd and 3rd, and he replied:

'If x is the number worn by the winner,
x does not divide by 2, 3, 4, 5, 6 or 8,
x is not a prime number,
x is 2 less than a square number.

If y is the number worn by the second runner,
the sum of y's digits is 9,
when y is divided by 11 there is a remainder of 1,
y is the product of 2 square numbers.

If z is the number worn by the runner coming third,
z is a cube number,
z is the sum of 2 square numbers, and also the sum of 2 other square numbers.'

The trainer's predictions turned out to be correct. What numbers were worn by the first three in the race ?

13. The scrap-metal dealer decided to make a set of weights from scrap metal, to use for weighing up to 40 kg. His assistant told him that he needed weights of 1, 2, 4, 8, 16 and 32 kg.
'No, that will take 63 kg of metal and I can do it with less, by making weights of 1, 3, 9 and 27 kg. That way I only have to make 4 weights and only use 40 kg of metal altogether.'
Show how the dealer can use his weights on his balance scales to weigh any whole number of kilograms from 1 kg to 40 kg.

11 Thinking about algebra

Using algebra

Algebra is a very useful branch of mathematics. Many of the problems to be solved in our world today need the use of algebraic expressions, formulae and equations, so it is a vital subject for a very wide range of users, such as Government departments, financial businesses, industrialists, researchers, and especially for all kinds of scientific work. You are not so likely to need it in day-to-day living, although you may find some uses, but you are benefiting from the use made by others.

For example, consider the production of a motor car. Algebra is used in the designing of the car taking into account the engine performance, the costs of production and the safety aspects, and in the marketing of the car, the fixing of a price which will persuade people to buy it yet leave a profit for the producers, the spending on advertising, the planning of a distribution chain which will get the cars into the showrooms where they are needed, and so on.
Similarly, we take electricity for granted, but think of all the planning which has been necessary to bring electricity, at the right voltage and at a reasonable price, into our homes, and into the factories which make the goods we buy and use.

At present, you are just beginning to learn all about algebra, so you are going to start with easy work, but who knows where it might lead you in the future. So, enjoy learning the basic work.

Consider the algebra involved in the production of a motor car.

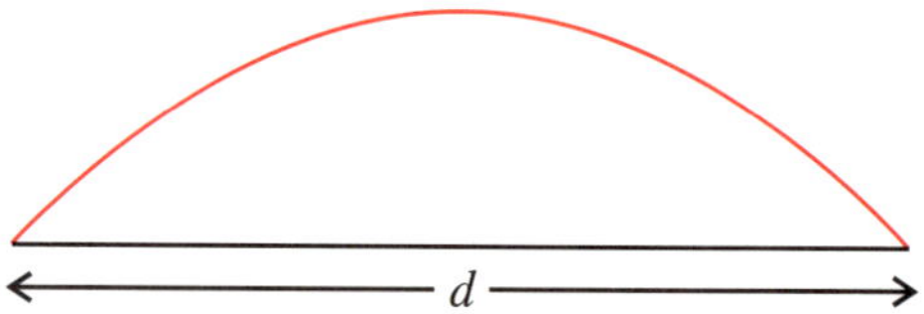

The greatest horizontal distance a projectile will travel, in metres, is given by the formula

$$d = \frac{v^2}{9.8}$$

where v is the speed of projection in m/s.

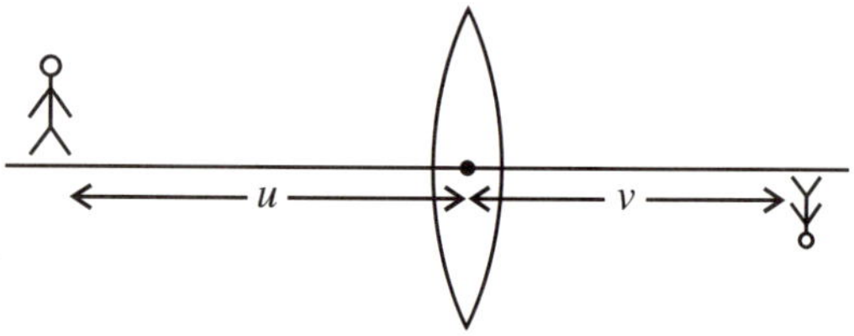

The formula giving the connection between u, the object length, v, the image length and f, the focal length of the lens is

$$\frac{1}{u} + \frac{1}{v} = \frac{1}{f}$$

An algebraic expression

Here is a simple use of an algebraic expression:
Try this question with a group of friends, all starting with different numbers.

Write down any number.
Add 12 and multiply the total by 8.
Now subtract 20 and then divide by 4.
Add 5 and halve the result.
Subtract the number you started with. What is your answer ?
What do you notice about your answers ?

Now you can follow the steps with algebraic expressions.
Since we start with any number, we can let this be x.
Adding 12 gives $x + 12$.
Multiplying the total by 8 gives $8x + 96$. ($8x$ means $8 \times x$. We must multiply both **terms** by 8.)
Subtracting 20 gives $8x + 76$.
Dividing by 4 gives $2x + 19$. (We must divide both terms by 4.)
Continue with this until you get to a final answer. What is it ?
Since the final answer does not involve x, it does not matter which number you begin with. (It does not even need to be a whole number. Try it again starting with a decimal.)

An algebraic formula

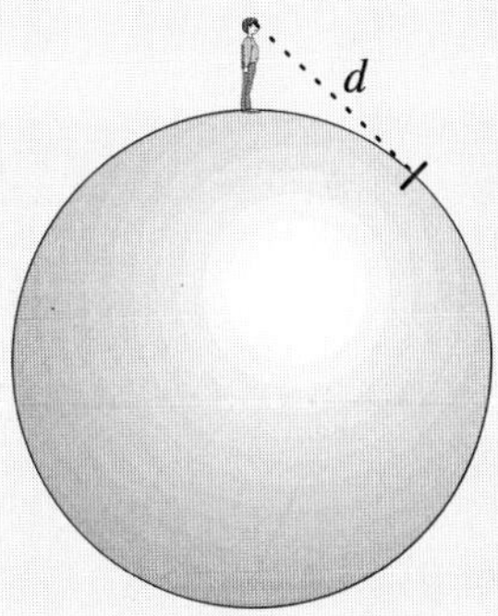

Here is a use of a formula:
We cannot see very far because the earth is round, not flat, and the curvature of the earth blocks our view.
If we stand higher up we can see further.
Here is a formula showing how far we can see.

$d = \sqrt{\frac{3h}{2}}$, where d = the distance in miles, and
h = height of eye-level in feet.

A tall man walking over level ground can see for a distance which used to be called a league. How far is this ?

Assume the man's eye-level is 6 feet from the ground, so that $h = 6$. Find the value of $3 \times h \div 2$ and then take the square root. What is d ? This is the distance in miles.

Castles were often built on high ground. There are various reasons for this. Can you think of some ? Suppose the battlements on a castle are 96 feet above a level plain.
How far could the occupants see on a clear day ?

11 Algebra

Algebra is a branch of Mathematics which uses letters to represent numbers.
e.g. $3x + 2y$ is an algebraic expression. It means three times number x plus twice number y. The expression cannot be simplified but if we know particular values for x and y then we can find the value of the expression.
If $x = 4$ and $y = 7$, $3x + 2y = (3 \times 4) + (2 \times 7) = 12 + 14 = 26$.
If $x = 6$ and $y = \frac{1}{2}$, $3x + 2y = (3 \times 6) + (2 \times \frac{1}{2}) = 18 + 1 = 19$.

Small letters $a, b, c, \ldots$ are usually used to represent numbers although occasionally capital letters may be used instead. In any question, use the sort of letter which is given, do not change from small letters to capital letters or vice versa.
x and y are often used for numbers whose values have to be found. We also use them on graphs.

Write the letters carefully, otherwise your work will be difficult to read and understand. Make b different from number 6. Make ℓ different from number 1. Make x different from $\times$ (a multiplication sign). Make z different from a 2 or a 3.
o and O are not normally used as letters in Algebra as it is too easy to confuse them with number 0.

Making expressions

Examples

1 If apples cost a pence per lb, what is the cost, in pence, of 3 lb of apples ?

Suppose the apples cost 15 pence per lb, then to find the cost of 3 lb you would multiply 15 by 3.
So if they cost a pence per lb, you multiply a by 3.
This is written as $3a$.
So 3 lb of apples cost $3a$ pence.

2 If I have £10 and spend £b, how much have I left ?

Suppose I spent £2, then to find how much I had left I would find 10 – 2.
So if I spend £b then I have £$(10 - b)$ left.

3 What is the total cost, in pence, of c stamps costing 25 pence each and d stamps costing 30 pence each ?

The cost of c stamps costing 25 pence each is $25c$ pence.
The cost of d stamps costing 30 pence each is $30d$ pence.
The total cost is $(25c + 30d)$ pence.

Exercise 11.1

1. If Emma is 8 years old and her younger sister Lisa is b years old, how much older is Emma than Lisa ?

2. What is the total weight of 5 parcels weighing w kg each ?

3. Crisps cost c pence per packet and lemonade costs 20 pence per bottle. What is the total cost of a packet of crisps and 2 bottles of lemonade ?

4. Two towns are 60 miles apart. When a motorist has already driven m miles from one town towards the other, how much further has he to go ?

5. Alan gets £m pocket money and spends £2 of it. How much has he left ?

6. A rectangle is l cm long and b cm wide. What is the total length of the 4 edges ?
(This is called the **perimeter** of the rectangle.)

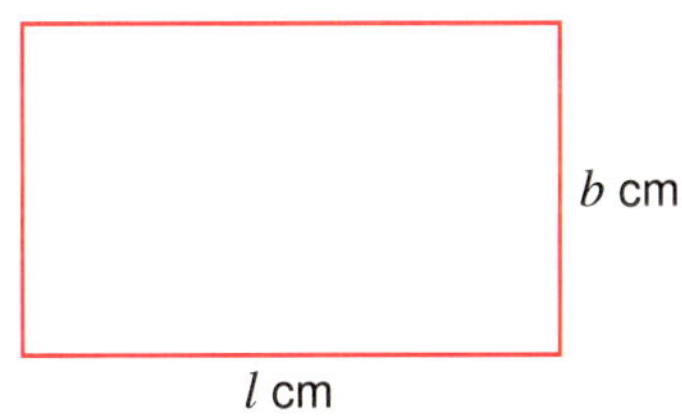

7. A plank is p metres long. Two lengths, each of q metres, are sawn off. What length remains ?

8. Find the total cost of 5 kg of potatoes at g pence per kg, and 2 kg of carrots at h pence per kg.

9. Tara has £1 to spend. She buys p pencils at q pence each. What is the total cost ? How much change, in pence, will she have ?

10. How many minutes are there from 6 minutes to 1 o'clock to m minutes past 1 o'clock ?

Some rules in Algebra

Multiplication

$1 \times a$ or $a \times 1$ is written as a.
$2 \times a$ or $a \times 2$ is written as $2a$.
(The number is always written in front of the letter. $a \times 2$ would not be written as $a2$.)

$0 \times a$ or $a \times 0$ equals 0. (Anything multiplied by zero equals zero.)
$a \times b$ or $b \times a$ is written as ab (or ba).

$a \times a = a^2$
$a \times a \times a = a^3$
$2 \times a \times a = 2a^2$
$2a \times 3b = 2 \times a \times 3 \times b = 6ab$

Addition and subtraction

$a + a = 2a$
$2b + 4b = 6b$
$8c - 5c = 3c$
$4d - 3d = d$
$7e - 7e = 0$
$f^2 + f^2 = 2 \times f^2 = 2f^2$
Expressions such as $a + b$, $3a + 4b$, $5a - b$ cannot be simplified.

Removing brackets

$4(x + 3) = 4x + 12$
$2(a + 5b) = 2a + 10b$
$3(2c - d) = 6c - 3d$

Collecting terms

$3a - 2b - 3b + a = 4a - 5b$
$2c - 5d + 4c + 6d = 6c + d$

$4(2e + 1) + 3(e - 2) = 8e + 4 + 3e - 6 = 11e - 2$
$5(f + 3g) + 2(2f - 5g) = 5f + 15g + 4f - 10g = 9f + 5g$
$7(h - j) + 4(h + j) = 7h - 7j + 4h + 4j = 11h - 3j$

Exercise 11.2

1. Simplify the following.

1	$a \times 1$	**6**	$h \times h \times h$	**11**	$5q \times 0$
2	$0 \times b$	**7**	$3 \times j \times j$	**12**	$2r \times 3s$
3	$c \times d$	**8**	$k \times 0$	**13**	$1 \times 7t$
4	$e \times e$	**9**	$m \times n \times 3$	**14**	$u \times u^2$
5	$2 \times f \times g$	**10**	$p \times 4 \times p$	**15**	$4v \times 3v$

2. Simplify the following.

1	$a + a$	**6**	$9f + 3f$	**11**	$4m - m - 3m$
2	$5b - 3b$	**7**	$9g - 3g$	**12**	$5n - 4n + 3n$
3	$4c - 4c$	**8**	$5h + 2h - 7h$	**13**	$p + 9p - 4p$
4	$d + 4d$	**9**	$6j - 4j + j$	**14**	$2q + 7q - 8q$
5	$6e - 5e$	**10**	$7k - k - 5k$	**15**	$5r - r - 3r$

3. Remove the brackets.

1	$2(a + 2b)$	**6**	$6(3k + 4)$
2	$4(c - d)$	**7**	$2(m - 3n)$
3	$3(e - 2f + 3g)$	**8**	$8(2p + 1)$
4	$5(h + 8)$	**9**	$7(q + 2r)$
5	$2(j - 4k)$	**10**	$3(3s - 5)$

4. Simplify the following.

1	$2a - b + 3a + 2b$	**4**	$4h - 5j - h + 5j$
2	$3c - 2d + c + d$	**5**	$k - 2m - k + 2m$
3	$e - f + 2e + 3f$		

5. Remove the brackets and simplify.

1	$5(l + 4) + 2(l - 5)$	**4**	$6(s + t) + 2(2s - t)$
2	$4(m + 3) + 2(2m - 9)$	**5**	$5(x - 2y - z) + 3(x + y + 2z)$
3	$2(3p - q) + (p + 2q)$		

6. Find an expression for the perimeter of this T-shaped figure, which is composed of two rectangular pieces.

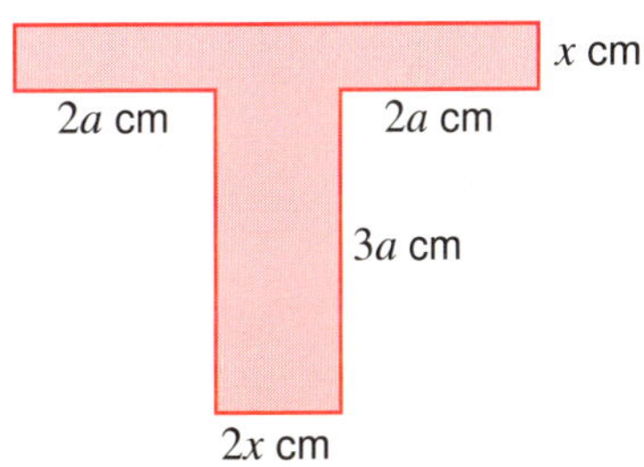

7. A square pyramid is made using 8 strips of wire. The strips on the base are each x cm long, and the other strips are each 4 cm longer.
Find an expression for the total length of wire used, and simplify it.

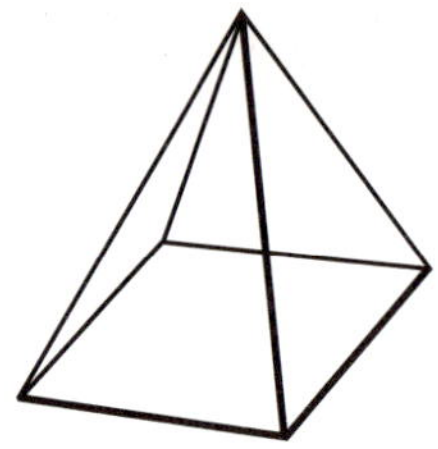

Division

$a \div 1 = a$ (Anything divided by 1 stays the same.)
$a \div a = 1$ (Anything divided by itself equals 1.)

$a \div 2$ is written as $\frac{a}{2}$ or $\frac{1}{2}a$.

$2a \div 3$ is written as $\frac{2a}{3}$ or $\frac{2}{3}a$.

$4a \div 3$ is written as $\frac{4a}{3}$ or $\frac{4}{3}a$.

$2 \div a$ is written as $\frac{2}{a}$.

$b \div a$ is written as $\frac{b}{a}$.

$0 \div a = 0$ (Zero divided by any other number equals zero.)

In the examples above where numbers are divided by a, a cannot be 0 since we cannot divide by 0.

Example

How many minutes are there in s seconds ?

If you wanted to find how many minutes there were in 240 seconds, you would divide 240 by 60.
So to find how many minutes there are in s seconds, you should divide s by 60.
This is written as $\frac{s}{60}$ or $\frac{1}{60}s$.
Therefore, in s seconds there are $\frac{s}{60}$ minutes.

Exercise 11.3

1. Simplify the following.

1	$a \div 1$	**6**	$2f \div 5$	**11**	$4 \div q$
2	$b \div b$	**7**	$5g \div 3$	**12**	$2r \div s$
3	$0 \div c$	**8**	$3 \div j$	**13**	$6t \div 5$
4	$d \div 2$	**9**	$m \div n$	**14**	$4u \div 8$
5	$e \div 3$	**10**	$0 \div 3p$	**15**	$0 \div v$

2. A roll of ribbon, d metres long, is to be cut into 20 equal pieces. How long is each piece ?

3. If a gardener has 3000 grams of fertilizer and it is to be spread over a lawn using f grams per square metre of lawn, how many square metres will it cover ?

4. How many metres are there in c cm ?

5. If b bags of crisps cost 90 pence, how much does 1 bag of crisps cost ?

6. Sylvia bought p kg of plums for a cost of q pence. What was the cost per kg ?

Making formulae

Examples

1 The area of a rectangle, in cm^2, is found by multiplying the length, in cm, by the breadth, in cm.

If A cm^2 is the area of a rectangle with length l cm and breadth b cm then we can write a formula, $A = lb$.

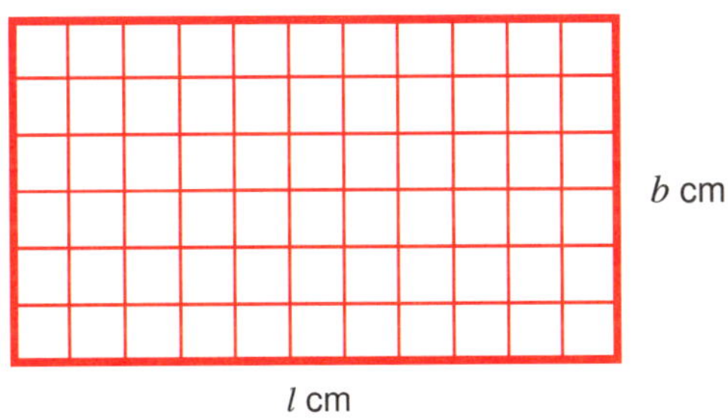

2 A rule for finding a suitable rise, in cm, on a staircase, is to subtract the length of the tread, in cm, from 60 and then divide by 2.

If the rise is r cm and the tread is t cm then the formula is $r = \frac{1}{2}(60 - t)$.

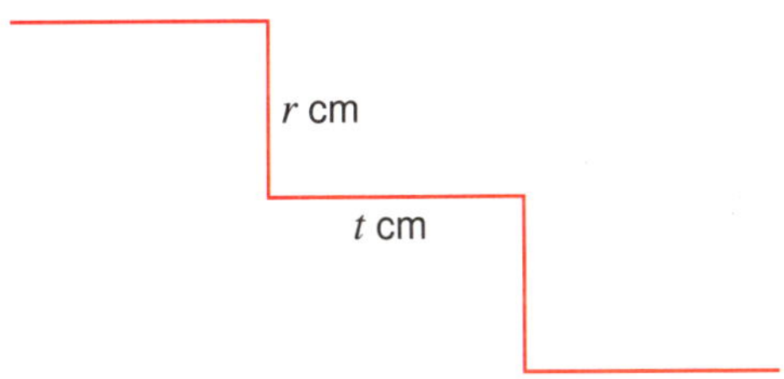

Exercise 11.4

1. The rule for finding the number of edges on a certain type of solid figure is to add the number of faces to the number of vertices and subtract 2.
   If the number of faces is F and the number of vertices is V, find the formula for E, the number of edges.

2. To find a batsman's average for several innings, divide the total of the runs scored by the number of completed innings.
   If in 5 completed innings the batsman scored, in turn, a, b, c, d and e runs, find a formula for R, the average number of runs per innings.

3. The amount for the monthly payment on an interest-free credit sale is found by subtracting the deposit from the total price and dividing the result by the number of months of the loan.
   If the total price is £T, the deposit is £D and the loan is to run for 24 months, find a formula for M where £M is the monthly payment.

4. A ferry charges £50 for each car plus driver and £7 for each car's passenger.
   If there were n people with c cars on a crossing, find a formula for T, where £T is the total cost.

5. If a stone is dropped (e.g. from the edge of a cliff) the distance in metres it will fall in a certain time can be calculated by squaring the time in seconds and multiplying by 5.
   If the time is t seconds find a formula for d, where d metres is the distance it falls.

Substitution

If $a = 3$, $b = 5$ and $c = 0$, then

$3a + 2b = (3 \times 3) + (2 \times 5) = 9 + 10 = 19$
$4a - b + 2c = (4 \times 3) - 5 + (2 \times 0) = 12 - 5 + 0 = 7$
$abc = 3 \times 5 \times 0 = 0$
$2a^2 = 2 \times 3 \times 3 = 18$

Using expressions and formulae

Examples

1 An expression for the profit, if n items costing a pence each are sold for b pence each, is £$\frac{n(b-a)}{100}$.

Find the profit if 150 items are bought for 85p each and sold for £1.09 each.

Here, $n = 150$, $a = 85$ and $b = 109$.

$$\text{Profit} = £\,\frac{150 \times (109 - 85)}{100} = £\,\frac{150 \times 24}{100} = £36.$$

2 A formula to find the perimeter of a rectangle is $P = 2l + 2b$.
If $l = 12$ and $b = 8$, find P.

$P = (2 \times 12) + (2 \times 8) = 24 + 16 = 40$

3 A formula to find the cost of making some toys is $C = F + 5n$.
Find C when $F = 60$ and $n = 100$.

$C = 60 + (5 \times 100) = 60 + 500 = 560$

Exercise 11.5

1. If $a = 1$, $b = 5$ and $c = 7$, find the values of the following.

1 $a + b$
2 $c - b$
3 $3b$
4 $4c - 2b$
5 $2a + 3b + c$
6 ab
7 c^2
8 $a^2 + b^2$
9 $2a + b^2$
10 $b^2 - a - c$

2. If $p = 3$, $q = 2$ and $r = 0$, find the values of the following.

1 $2p + q$
2 pq
3 pqr
4 $2p + 3q + r$
5 $p^2 + q^2$
6 $5pq - qr$
7 $\frac{p+q}{p-q}$
8 $\frac{10p + 5q}{8}$
9 $3q^2$
10 $p(q + r + 9)$

3. An expression for the weight which can be lifted by a certain pulley is $(7p - 3q)$ kg. Find the weight which can be lifted if $p = 50$ and $q = 30$.

4. A formula for finding the area of the walls of a certain room is $A = 6l + 6b$.
Find A when $l = 5$ and $b = 4$.

5. A formula for finding the speed of an object at different times is $v = 20 + 4t$.
Find v when $t = 8$.

6. A formula used to change hours into minutes is $m = 60h$.
Find m when $h = 3$.

7. A formula for the number of people who can be carried by m minibuses and c coaches of a certain firm is $n = 12m + 52c$, where n is the number of people. How many people visited an exhibition if they came in 6 full minibuses and 10 full coaches of that firm ?

Exercise 11.6 Applications and Activities

1. Simplify the following.

1 $a + a$
2 $a - a$
3 $a \times a$
4 $a \div a$
5 $\sqrt{a^2}$

2. Simplify the following.

1 $6b + 2b$
2 $6b - 2b$
3 $6b \times 2b$
4 $6b \div 2b$
5 $0 \div 2b$

3. A formula to find the cost of using an electric fire is given by $C = kpt$, where
k is the power in kilowatts, of the fire,
p is the price of electricity in pence per unit,
t is the number of hours for which the fire is used,
C is the cost, in pence.
What is the cost of using a 2 kilowatt electric fire for 4 hours, if electricity costs 7 pence per unit ?

4. A formula giving the distance travelled, d km, by a vehicle going for t hours at an average speed of v km/hour is $d = vt$.
What is the distance travelled by a lorry in 4 hours, going at an average speed of 70 km/hour ?

5. A formula to find out how much paint is needed to paint a certain area is given by $P = \frac{A}{18}$, where A is the area in square metres and P is the amount of paint in litres.
How much paint is needed to give an area of 45 square metres two coats of the paint ?

6. A formula to find the size of each angle in a regular polygon with n sides is $a = 180 - \frac{360}{n}$, where a is the size of each angle in degrees.
Use this formula to find the size of the angles in a regular polygon with 10 sides.

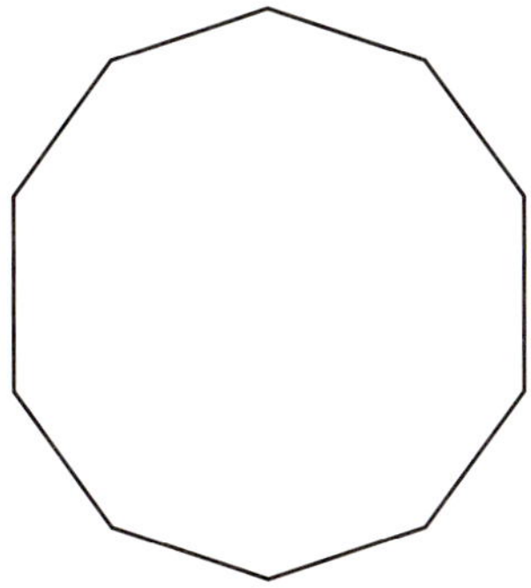

7. Here are the first 4 terms of a number pattern.

$1 \times 2 \times 3, \quad 2 \times 3 \times 4, \quad 3 \times 4 \times 5, \quad 4 \times 5 \times 6, \quad \ldots$

If it continues for n terms the expression for the last term is $n(n+1)(n+2)$.
(This means the value of n multiplied by the value of $n+1$ multiplied by the value of $n+2$.)
Use this expression to work out the value of the 8th term.

A formula to work out the sum s of the numbers in the first n terms is
$s = \frac{1}{4}n(n+1)(n+2)(n+3)$
The sum of the first 3 terms is $6 + 24 + 60 = 90$. Substitute $n = 3$ in the formula for s to check this result.
Use the formula to find the sum of the first 8 terms.

8. This is a magic square.
Find expressions (and simplify them) for
1 the sum of the numbers in each column,
2 the sum of the numbers in each row,
3 the sum of the numbers in the main diagonals.
Check that all these are the same.

$x+3$	$x-4$	$x+1$
$x-2$	x	$x+2$
$x-1$	$x+4$	$x-3$

Substitute $x = 10$ to make a magic square whose rows, columns and diagonals have a sum of 30.

9. Here is a formula for the nth triangular number T.
$T = \frac{1}{2}n(n+1)$.

1 By substituting $n = 10$, find the 10th triangular number.
2 By substituting $n = 288$, find the 288th triangular number, and show that this is also a square number.

10. Find the values of the expression $13x - x^2 + 1$ for values of x from 1 to 12, and say whether the results are prime numbers.

Chapter 11 test

1. The time taken to cook a joint of meat is given as 20 minutes, plus an extra 40 minutes for each kilogram the joint of meat weighs.
How many minutes would it take to cook a joint weighing 3 kg ?
Find an expression for the time needed for a joint weighing m kg.

2. A rectangular table has a perimeter of 6 metres. If it is t metres wide, what is an expression for its length ?
Find its length if its width is 1.2 metres.

3. Simplify the following.

1 $a + 3a$
2 $5b - b$
3 $c \times 5$
4 $0 \div d$
5 $7e - 6e$
6 $f \times f$
7 $4 \times g \times h$
8 $5j + j - 2j$
9 $k \div 3$
10 $6 \times m \times 0$

4. Remove the brackets in the following.

1 $10(a - 2b)$
2 $3(2c + 5d)$
3 $3(e - 1) + 4(3e + 5)$. Simplify this answer.

5. If £x was shared equally among 5 people, how much did each person get ?

6. If $x = 5$, $y = 3$ and $z = 0$, find the values of

1 $5x - z$
2 xyz
3 $\frac{x + y}{4}$
4 $5(x + z) - 8y$
5 $2x^2$
6 $x^2 - y^2$
7 $5x + 2y$
8 $4(x + 2y)$
9 $2x - y + 3z$
10 $\frac{5y}{3x}$

7. A man earns £a each day from Monday to Friday and £b on Saturdays. He does not work on Sundays. Find a formula for W, where £W is his total wage for the week.
Find the total weekly wage if the man earns £42 each day from Monday to Friday and £32 on Saturday.

8. The average speed of a car, in km/h, over a journey is found by dividing the distance travelled, in km, by the time taken, in hours.
If the speed, is v km/h, the distance is s km and the time is t hours, find a formula for v in terms of s and t.
Find the average speed of the car if it goes 192 km in 3 hours.

PUZZLES

14. The sketch map shows the road round the village green, with five houses built round it.
Mrs Baker often walks across the green to see Mrs Cook, and Mr Cook sometimes walks across to see Mr Eaton. The Eaton children mostly play with their neighbours, the Dyer boys, but they travel to school with the Archer children.
Who are the neighbours of the Bakers ?

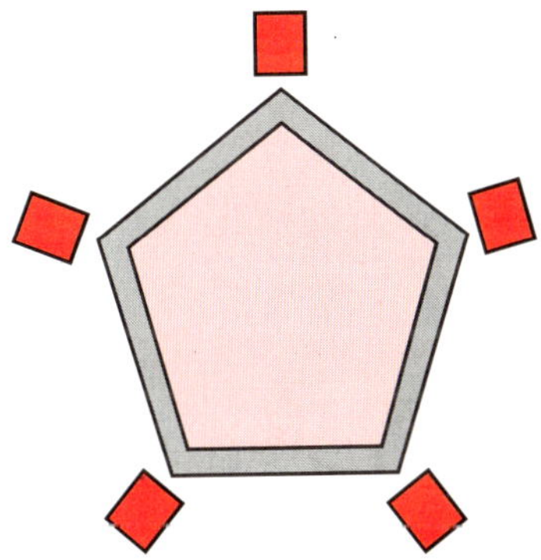

15. In an election one term for the post of football captain, Oliver got 22 votes and Lee got 10. Next term two of the boys who voted for Lee vote for Oliver instead, but several boys who voted for Oliver now vote for Lee. What is the smallest number of boys who must change their minds like this and now vote for Lee if Lee is to be elected captain ?

16. You have 3 flasks which hold exactly 8 litres, 5 litres and 3 litres, and the 8 litre one is filled with an expensive liquid. You want to divide this exactly in half, leaving 4 litres in the big flask and 4 litres in the 5 litre one. By pouring from flask to flask and without wasting any liquid, show how you could do this, in as few pourings as possible.

12 Thinking about probability

Questions about probability

In Chapter 6 you did some probability experiments. In Chapter 12 you are going to calculate probabilities.

Here are some questions to remind you about probability.

What does a probability of 0 mean ? Give an example.

What does a probability of 1 mean ? Give an example.

If we say that someone has a fifty-fifty chance of success, what is the probability of success as a fraction ? Give some examples of events which have a 50–50 chance of success.

If you throw 1 die, what is the probability of scoring a six ?

If you throw 2 dice, what scores are possible for the sum of the two numbers on the dice ? What is the probability of scoring a sum of 12 ? (You have got some results from Exercise 6.1. Does your answer agree with them, and if not, why not ?)

The numbers on a roulette wheel are from 0 to 36. What is the probability of a particular number winning ?

There are various competitions which involve different chances of winning.

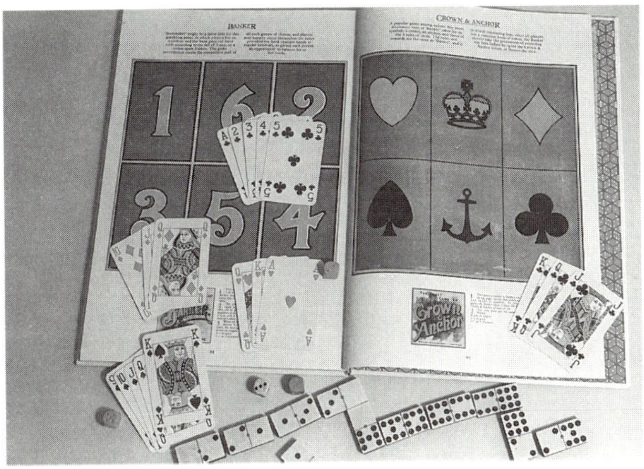

In gambling games, sometimes you can calculate the probability of winning.

Backgammon is played with two dice. Why are games with two dice more interesting than games using one die ?

Random selection

Suppose someone has to be picked at random from your class, to represent you on a committee. What does 'at random' mean ? Think of fair ways of choosing someone. Using these ways, has everyone in the class an equal chance of being chosen ? What is the probability that you will be chosen ? If yours is a class of boys and girls, what is the probability that a boy will be chosen ? What is the probability that a girl will be chosen ? (It is certain that either a boy or a girl will be chosen so what could you say about the last two answers ?) Which is more likely, that a boy will be chosen or a girl will be chosen ?

Using probability

Explain how these people can make use of probability:

A toyshop retailer, ordering stock
A weather forecaster
The education authority
A doctor doing research on a new cure
A firm selling holiday insurance
A person doing the football pools

12 Probability

Probability or chance is the likelihood of an event happening.

We measure probability on a number scale from 0 to 1.

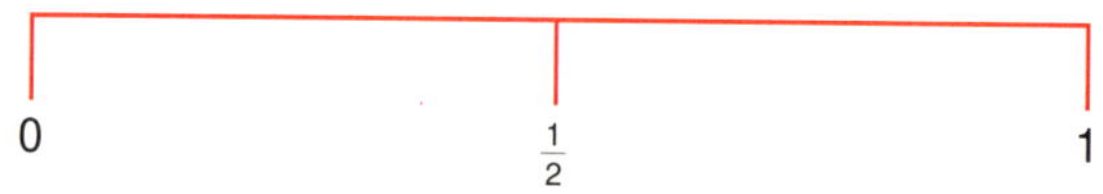

A probability of 0 means that there is no chance of the event happening.
e.g. What is the chance of you visiting the planet Jupiter ?

A probability of 1 means that it is certain that the event will happen.
e.g. If you drop a marble, what is the chance of it falling downwards ?

A probability of $\frac{1}{2}$ means that there is a 50–50 chance (an even chance) of the event happening. In the long run, $\frac{1}{2}$ of the trials will give successful results.
e.g. If you toss a coin properly, the chance of it showing heads is $\frac{1}{2}$.

A probability of $\frac{2}{3}$ means that there is a more than even chance of the event happening. In the long run, $\frac{2}{3}$ of the trials will give successful results.
e.g. If you throw a die properly, the probability of it showing a number less than 5 is $\frac{2}{3}$.

The nearer the value of the probability is to 1, the more chance there is of a successful outcome.

The nearer the value of the probability is to 0, the less chance there is of a successful outcome.

In Chapter 6 you found the value of probability by experiment. In some cases we can find the value by calculation, and that is what we will do in this chapter.

Equally likely outcomes

We can calculate the value of the probability of a certain result in an experiment or trial if there are several outcomes which are equally likely.

For example, in throwing a die, there are six outcomes, the numbers 1, 2, 3, 4, 5, 6; and these are equally likely to occur. If we want to work out the probability of getting a four, then one of the six equally likely outcomes is a successful one, so the probability is 1 out of 6, that is, $\frac{1}{6}$. If we want to work out the probability of getting a number greater than four, then two of the six equally likely outcomes (5 or 6) are successful ones, so the probability is 2 out of 6, that is, $\frac{2}{6}$ or $\frac{1}{3}$.

Formula for probability

Probability of a successful outcome $= \frac{s}{n}$

where n is the **total** number of equally likely outcomes, and s is the number of successful outcomes.

The result can be expressed as a fraction in its lowest terms, as a decimal or as a percentage.

Examples

1 Find the probability of a tossed coin showing heads.

There are 2 equally likely outcomes, heads or tails, and of these 1 outcome, heads, is successful.

Probability of heads $= \frac{s}{n} = \frac{1}{2}$.

2 In a pack of 52 cards one card is drawn at random. What is the probability that it is

(1) a diamond,
(2) a Jack,
(3) a Jack or a diamond,
(4) the Jack of diamonds ?

(1) There are 13 diamonds.

$P(\text{diamond}) = \frac{s}{n} = \frac{13}{52} = \frac{1}{4}$

(We are using the notation P(diamond) to mean 'the probability of a diamond'.)

(2) There are 4 Jacks.

$P(\text{Jack}) = \frac{s}{n} = \frac{4}{52} = \frac{1}{13}$

(3) There are 13 diamonds including the Jack and 3 other Jacks making 16 successful outcomes altogether.

$P(\text{Jack or diamond}) = \frac{s}{n} = \frac{16}{52} = \frac{4}{13}$

(4) There is 1 Jack of diamonds.

$P(\text{Jack of diamonds}) = \frac{s}{n} = \frac{1}{52}$

3 Find the probability of a number picked at random from the numbers 1 to 20 being exactly divisible by 3.

There are twenty equally likely outcomes of which six (3, 6, 9, 12, 15, 18) are successful.

Probability of picking a number exactly divisible by 3 $= \frac{s}{n} = \frac{6}{20} = \frac{3}{10}$

(This means that if you pick a number at random from these numbers, there is a less than even chance that the number is divisible by 3, since $\frac{3}{10}$ is less than $\frac{1}{2}$.
If you do the experiment of picking a number a large number of times, you will get a number which is exactly divisible by 3 in approximately $\frac{3}{10}$ of the trials.)

Exercise 12.1

1. A fair die is thrown once. What is the probability of getting
   1 a six,
   2 an odd number ?
   3 In a game, the die is thrown 300 times. Approximately how many times would a six be thrown ?

2. 12 discs, numbered from 1 to 12, are placed in a bag and one is drawn out without looking at it.

   What is the probability of getting a disc with
   1 a number which divides exactly by 3,
   2 a square number,
   3 a number greater than 9,
   4 a number which includes the figure 1 ?

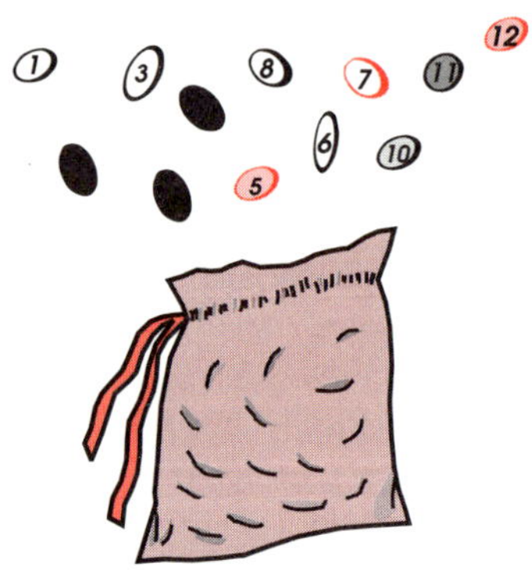

3. In a tombola game, $\frac{9}{10}$ of the counters are blank. The rest have a number on them and they win a prize. If you take a counter out of the drum at random what is the probability that you win a prize ?

4. 30 tickets are sold in a raffle. Anil buys one ticket and Bimla buys two tickets. What is the probability that one of them wins the 1st prize ?

5. In a fairground game a pointer is spun and you win the amount shown in the sector where it stops. Assuming that the pointer is equally likely to come to rest in any sector, what is the probability that

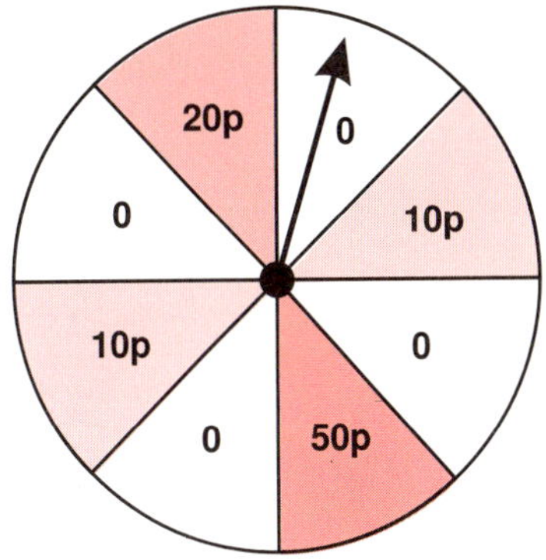

1 you win 50p,
2 you win 10p,
3 you do not win any money ?
4 If the pointer is spun 1000 times during an afternoon, approximately how many times would 50p be won ?

6. The 11 letters of the word PROBABILITY are written on separate cards and the cards are mixed up. One card is drawn at random. What is the probability that on it is
1 the letter T,
2 the letter B,
3 a vowel,
4 a letter from the first half of the alphabet ?

7. A bag contains 8 red beads and 12 blue beads. Julie takes one bead from the bag, without looking. What is the probability that it is red ?

8. In a pencil case there are 3 red crayons, 4 blue ones, 2 green ones and 1 yellow one. If you take a crayon out without looking, what is the probability that it is
1 red, **2** not green ?

9. 5 8 9 12 15 16 17 20 25
These numbers are written on discs which are placed in a bag. One disc is drawn out at random. What is the probability that the number on it is
1 an odd number,
2 a number which divides exactly by 5,
3 a square number,
4 a prime number ?

10. A pack of 52 cards is split into two piles with the Aces, Kings, Queens and Jacks in the first pile and the rest of the cards in the second pile.
1 If a card is drawn at random from the first pile what is the probability that it is the Queen of Hearts ?
2 If a card is drawn at random from the second pile what is the probability that it is a seven ?

Exercise 12.2 Applications and Activities

1. The following numbers were written on pieces of paper, put into a box and drawn out at random.

   6, 9, 17, 23, 25, 29, 37, 39, 41, 48, 49, 64.

   What is the probability that a number drawn out

   1 is even,
   2 is a square number,
   3 is a prime number ?

   4 If an odd number is drawn out and **not** replaced, what is the probability of drawing out a second odd number ?

2. The members of a school club belong to three forms 7R, 7S and 7T.

	7R	7S	7T
Girls	16	14	10
Boys	9	7	14

   The table shows the number of members in each form. If from this club one member is chosen at random, what is the probability that this is

   1 a boy,
   2 a member of 7S,
   3 a girl from 7R ?

   4 If a girl from the club has to be chosen at random, what is the probability that she is from 7T ?

3. What is the probability that if a person is chosen at random, his/her birthday this year is on a Saturday ? If 100 people were chosen, approximately how many would you expect to have a birthday on a Saturday ?

   Ask as many people as you can on what day of the week their birthday falls this year. (Have a calendar available.) Record the results and represent them in a bar chart. Compare these results with the theoretical ones.

4. Seven boys were planning what to do on a half-day's holiday. Their choices were swimming, playing football or going to the fairground.
They wrote these three choices, swim, football, fairground, on slips of paper, put them in a box and drew one out without looking.
What was the probability that 'swim' was the one drawn out ?
In fact, 'fairground' was drawn out, and this led to some argument.

The boys decided to use another method. They all wrote their own choice on a new slip of paper, and again one slip was drawn out.
Their choices were: Hugh, swim; Alec, football; Ken, fairground; Timothy, swim; Peter, football; David, swim; Michael, swim.
What was the probability that going swimming was chosen this time ?

Which do you think was the fairer method of choosing what to do ?

5. In a game played with two dice, the dice are thrown together and the score is the **difference** of the numbers.

Score (**1st die** across, **2nd die** down)

	1	2	3	4	5	6
1			2			
2			1			
3			0			
4			1			
5	4	3	2	1	0	1
6			3			

There are 36 possible outcomes when two dice are thrown.
All these outcomes are equally likely.

Copy and complete the table showing the scores. 1 row and 1 column have already been filled in.

1 How many of the spaces show a score of 0 ?
2 What is the probability of a score of 0 ?
3 What is the highest possible score ?
4 What is the probability of getting this score ?
5 If these dice are thrown 200 times, approximately how many times would you get a score of 1 ?

You could use the previously recorded results of dice throwing, grouped in twos, to get some experimental results, and compare these with your answers.

6. **A coin tossing experiment**

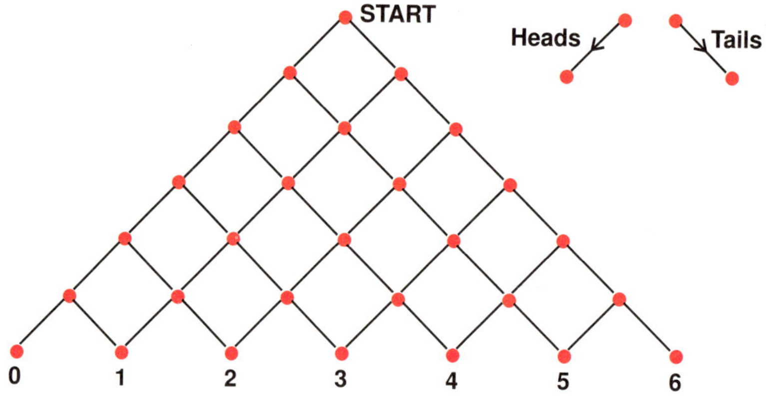

Begin with a counter on START.
Toss a coin. (You can use your previously recorded results of coin tossing.)
If you get a head, move your counter down to the left as far as the next blob.
If you get a tail, move your counter down to the right as far as the next blob.
Toss the coin again, and repeat.
After 6 tosses of the coin your counter will be on one of the 7 destinations labelled 0 to 6. Record which one.
Repeat the experiment about 300 times.
Which destination occurred most often ?

Show your results on a bar-line graph, with the lines numbered from 0 to 6. (An example of a bar-line graph is shown on page 272.)
What shape is the graph ?
Why have the destinations been labelled 0 to 6 ?

Investigate any pattern in your results.
You may want to begin by considering a simpler diagram first, like this.

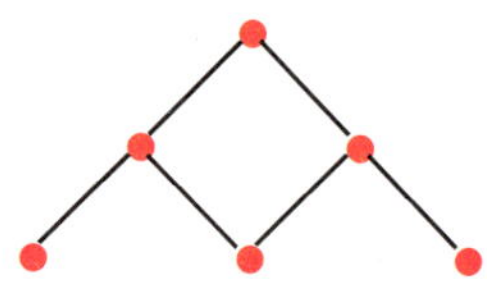

Chapter 12 test

1. A card is drawn from a full pack of 52 playing cards. What is the probability that
   1 it is a seven,
   2 it is a club,
   3 it is the seven of clubs ?

2. Bronya has a bunch of 8 keys of similar type, only one of which will open her front door.

1 What is the probability that the first key she chooses will open the door, if she chooses the key at random ?
2 What is the probability that the first key will not open the door ?
3 If the first key is not the right one, Bronya tries a key from the remaining ones, again at random. What is the probability that this key will open the door ?

3. In a game played with a spinner showing the numbers 1, 2, 3, 4, the spinner is spun twice and the score is the sum of the two numbers.

Score / **1st spin** / **2nd spin**

	1	2	3	4
1	2			
2	3			
3	4			
4	·			

There are 16 possible outcomes when the spinner is spun twice.
All these outcomes are equally likely.

Copy and complete the table showing the scores.

1 How many of the spaces show a score of 5 ?
2 What is the probability of a score of 5 ?
3 What is the highest possible score ?
4 What is the probability of getting this score ?
5 What is the probability of getting a score less than 5 ?

PUZZLE

17. A farmer has five half-sized haystacks in the corner of a field and two three-quarter-sized haystacks in another corner. If he puts them all together, how many haystacks will he have ?

Miscellaneous Section B

Aural Practice

These aural exercises, B1 and B2, should be read to you, probably by your teacher or a friend, and you should write down the answers only, doing any working out in your head. You should do the 15 questions within 10 minutes.

Exercise B1

1. What is the cost of 300 pencils at 20 pence each ?
2. What is the name given to an angle between 0° and 90° ?
3. Write down the fraction 4 hundredths as a decimal.
4. Simplify the expression $11d + d$.
5. Out of a batch of 400 oranges, 20% were bad. How many were fit to sell ?
6. What is the order of rotational symmetry of a rectangle ?
7. In a bag there are 10 discs. 7 are red and 3 are yellow. What is the probability of drawing a yellow one ?
8. Some children held a garden sale and raised £27 for charities. They sent $\frac{2}{3}$ of this to Barnardo's. How much did they send ?
9. In 3 tests Emma got 6, 5 and 10 marks. What was her average mark ?
10. What is the value of $y^2 - 2y$ when $y = 6$?
11. The distance round a running track was 400 m. How many times did Oliver run round it if he ran 2 km ?
12. What is the name given to lines which have the same direction ?
13. What is an expression for the cost of 12 books at £x each ?

14. How many cakes, each using 200 g of flour, can be made from a 3 kg bag of flour ?

15. If the angle at the centre of a sector in a pie chart is 36°, and this represents an amount of £8, what amount is represented by the whole circle ?

Exercise B2

1. £12 is shared between two people, Jack and Jill, so that Jack gets twice as much as Jill. How much does Jack get ?

2. Write down an approximate whole number answer to the question $245 \div 59$.

3. What is 75% of £20 ?

4. What is the name given to an angle between 90° and 180° ?

5. A water tank is $\frac{3}{5}$ full. How much water is in it, if it holds 3000 litres when full ?

6. Write correct to 2 decimal places the number 1.986.

7. Simplify the expression $7b - 6b$.

8. If the angle at the centre of a sector of a pie chart is 60°, what fraction of the whole amount does it represent ?

9. How many axes of symmetry has a square ?

10. Write down an expression for the change in pence if an article costing c pence is paid for with a £1 coin ?

11. For a recipe, Anna needs 200 g of sugar. What fraction of the sugar in a 1 kg bag is this ?

12. What is the probability of throwing a 3 with an ordinary die ?

13. What is the name given to lines which are at right angles to each other ?

14. A formula for area is $A = bh$. What is the value of A if $b = 7$ and $h = 4$?

15. Henry thought of two numbers. When he added the numbers together he got 12, when he multiplied the numbers together he got 27. What were the two numbers he thought of ?

Exercise B3 Revision

1. A man buys a television set which costs £360. He pays an initial payment of $\frac{1}{4}$ of the cost and arranges to pay the rest in 20 equal monthly instalments. How much is the monthly instalment ?

2. Using your calculator, find which is larger $\sqrt{576} + \sqrt{49}$ or $\sqrt{(576 + 49)}$, and by how much.

3. Raffle tickets are numbered from 1 to 50. What is the probability that the winning ticket will include a figure 3 ?

4. A roll of cloth contains 25 m. To make an apron takes 1.8 m of the cloth. How many aprons can be made, and how much cloth is left over ?

5. The items A, B, C are shown in a pie chart. What should be the size of the angle in sector A ?

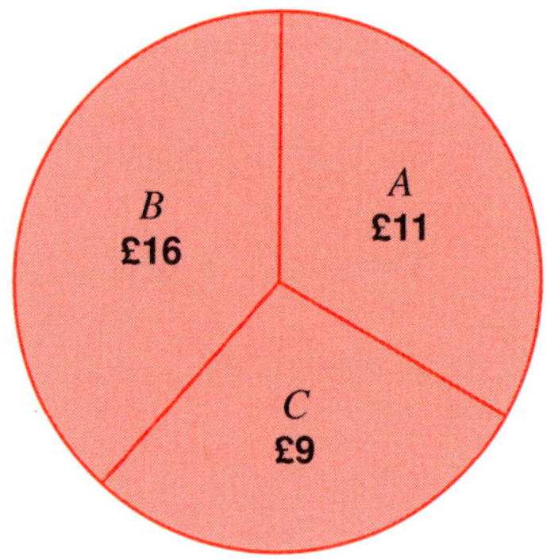

6. In the diagram,
   1 measure the angles a, b, c and d,
   2 measure the lengths AB, BC, CD and DA.

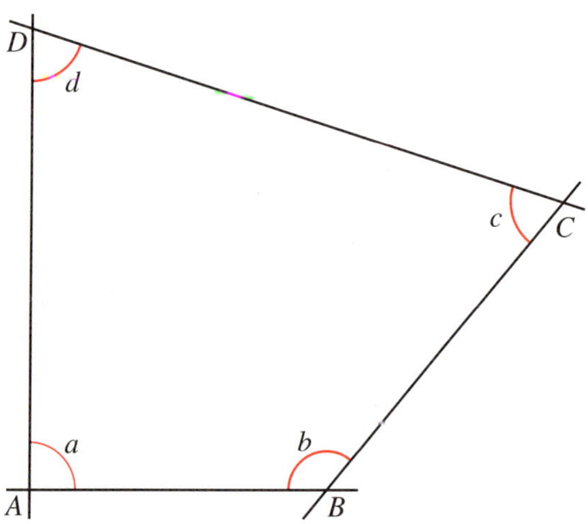

7. Bakula buys 5 packets of biscuits at x pence each, and 3 packets of sweets at y pence each. What is an expression for the total cost ?
If the total cost is c pence, write down a formula for c.

8. A medicine spoon holds 5 ml. How many spoonfuls are there in a bottle containing $\frac{1}{4}$ litre of medicine ?

9. A bush is 2.5 m tall. It is estimated that it will increase its height by 8% in an average year. How tall is it expected to be in a year's time ?

10. The table shows the average daily hours of sunshine over the month for the 12 months of a year, at a weather station.
Plot the data on a line-graph, and comment on it.

Jan	Feb	Mar	Apl	May	Jun	Jly	Aug	Sep	Oct	Nov	Dec
1.6	1.7	3.6	5.4	5.6	8.5	8.3	8.3	3.6	2.2	2.1	1.9

Exercise B4 Revision

1. Write these fractions in their simplest forms.

1 $\frac{32}{48}$ **2** $\frac{60}{84}$ **3** $\frac{27}{45}$ **4** $\frac{49}{77}$ **5** $\frac{30}{54}$

2. Some sugar was taken from a 1 kg bag to bake a cake. 0.7 kg of sugar remained. How many **grams** of sugar had been used ?

3. From the set of numbers 12, 13, 10, 7, 11, 12, 5,
1 what is the mode,
2 what is the median,
3 what is the mean,
4 what is the range ?

4. A salesman is paid a commission of 8% on the value of goods he sells. When he sells goods to the value of £750, how much commission does he get ?

5. (Try to answer this question without using your calculator.)
There were 325 children in a P.E. display. For each child's costume 72 cm of ribbon was needed. What is the total length of ribbon needed ?

6. If $V = x^2h$, what is the value of V when $x = 8$ and $h = 10$?

7. Find
   1 10% of 360°,
   2 30% of 360°,
   3 60% of 360°.

   4 Of the surface of the Earth, 60% is covered by water, 10% by glacial ice and the remaining 30% by land. Show this information on a pie chart.

8. Mrs Barker buys 5 kg of potatoes at x pence per kg and 3 cauliflowers at x pence each. Find an expression for the total cost, and also an expression for the change she should get, in pence, if she pays with a £5 note.

9. There are two discs with numbers on. One has number 1 on one side and 2 on the other side. The other disc has number 3 on one side and 4 on the other side.
   The two discs are pulled out of a bag without looking and placed flat on the table.
   Make a list of the equally likely outcomes.

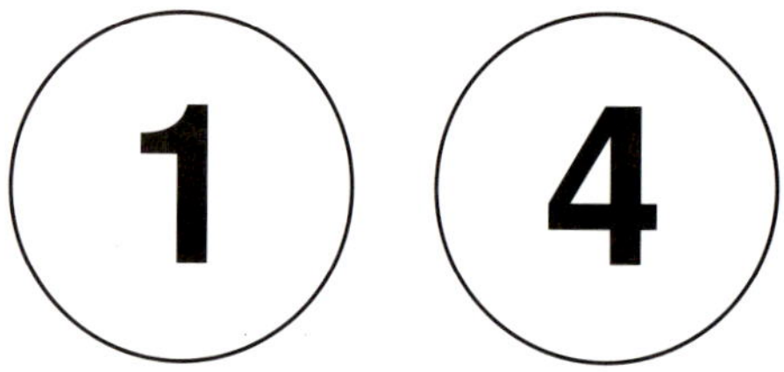

   1 What is the probability that the sum of the two numbers shown is 5 ?
   2 If this procedure was carried out 100 times, approximately how many times would you expect the sum to be 5 ?

10. Draw accurately the line $AB = 8.6$ cm.
    Make angle $a = 36°$.
    Find point C such that $AC = 8.6$ cm.
    Join BC.
    Measure the length of BC.
    Measure the sizes of angles b and c.

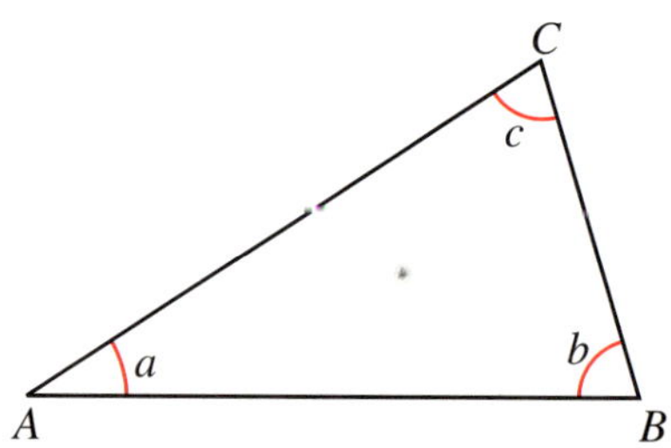

Exercise B5 Activities

1. **The cost of a child**

How much does it cost to keep a child of your age for a year ?
You will not be able to work this out exactly, but you can get an approximate value.
Think of all the expenses. Here are some of them:– Food, clothes, fares to school, school meals, pocket money, money for clubs and leisure activities, holidays, presents. What others can you think of ?
Many parents would say that 'You are worth your weight in gold'. Find the up-to-date price of gold and work out how much you would be worth.

2. **Random numbers**

We often talk about choosing things 'at random'. In Statistics this means that every item in the group has an equal chance of being chosen. You could imagine this as a raffle. Give every item a name or number, and put these into a hat. After mixing them up, pick one out without looking.

What is the probability that a single-figure number (from 0 to 9) picked at random will be a 7 ? If a single-figure number was picked at random, 200 times altogether, approximately how many times would you expect each number to occur ?

One way of getting a collection of random numbers is to use the phone book, using the units figure of each number in turn. (Occasionally a firm may have several consecutive numbers listed. In this case, only use the first one.) Collect 200 single-figure numbers and record them. Represent your results in a bar-line graph. Compare them with the theoretical results.

Can you think of other sources for getting a list of random numbers ? You may prefer to use your own ideas instead of getting the numbers from the phone book.

Is it suitable just to **ask** people for a number, to make a collection of random numbers ?

Ask as many people as you can, but ask them quietly, so that other people you intend to ask do not hear other answers. Try to use the same words each time, such as 'For an experiment, I would like you to tell me any number between 0 and 9.' Do not go into details about being able to include 0 or 9, unless the person asks you. Otherwise you are emphasizing these two numbers by mentioning them specially. Do not comment on the answer, just say 'Thank you'.
Record the answers as before, and represent them in a bar-line graph.
Compare them with the previous results and comment on your findings.

3. **To draw perpendicular lines with a set square**

e.g. Draw a line through P at right angles to PQ.

If you are not drawing accurately, it is sufficient just to put your set-square along the line PQ with the corner at P. However, to make an accurate line going exactly through P you can use this method.

(1)

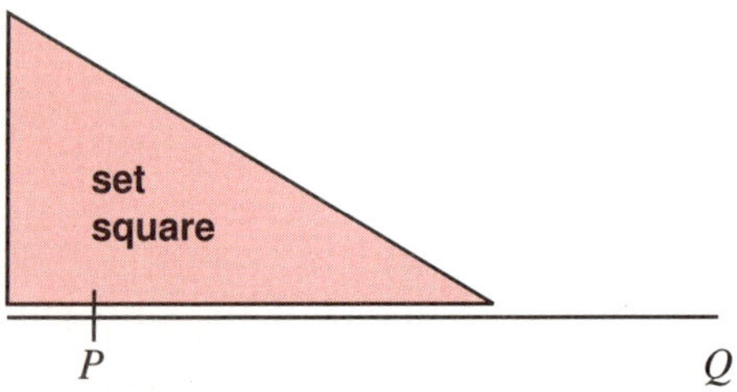

(2)

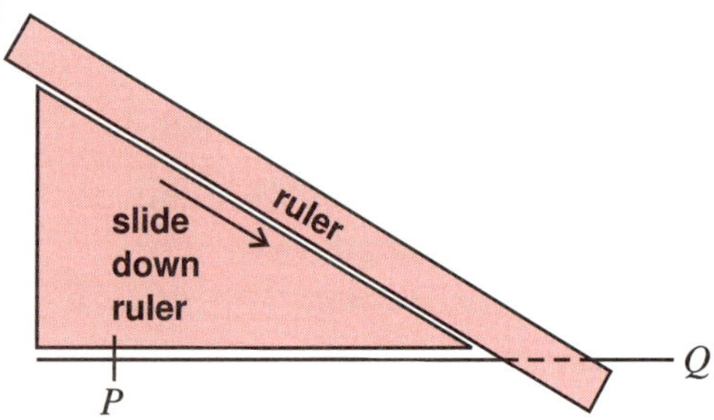

(3)

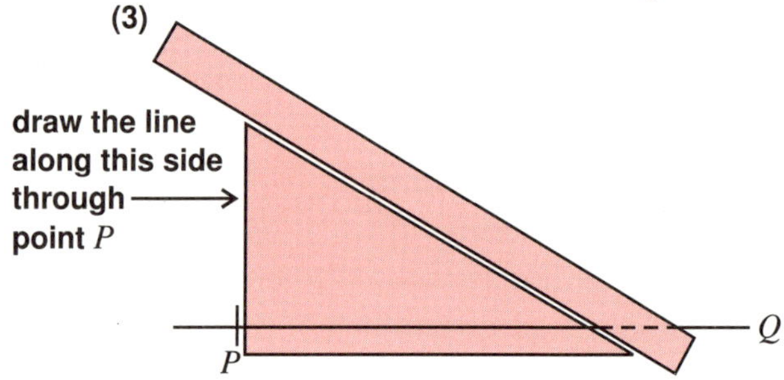

Now you can use your set-square to draw an accurate rectangle.
Begin with a line AB.
Make accurate right angles at A and B, to the line AB.
Choose a point D on the line through A. At D draw a line at right angles to the line AD. Let this meet the line through B at C.
You can check whether your drawing is accurate by measuring the angle at C and the lengths of the 4 sides.

4. **A million**

This is such a big number that it is hard to imagine, so it may help if you find out some facts using this number. Here are some ideas to begin with.
Think of others and add them to your list. Put the facts in a booklet or on a poster, and illustrate them with drawings, pictures or photographs.

Write a million in figures.
Write a million as a power of 10.
How much is a million pence worth ?
How high would a column of a million penny coins be ?
If a million pennies are laid side by side along a line, each one touching the next, how long would the line be ?
How much would a million penny coins weigh ?

What distance is a million mm ?
If you had a million squares of width 1 cm and you put them together to make a large square, how long would a side of the large square be ?

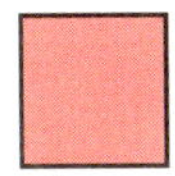

If you had a million cubes of edge 1 cm and you put them together to make a large cube, how long would an edge of the large cube be ?

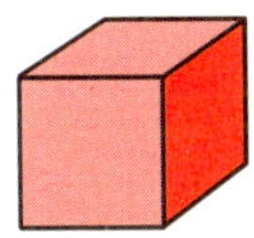

What weight is a million grams ?

How long would it take you to count to a million ?
How long ago was a million seconds ?
How long ago was a million minutes ?
How long ago was a million hours ?
How long ago was a million days ?

How many people live in London, or other large cities ? How many people live in your nearest town ? Wembley Stadium holds 90 000 people. How many such stadiums would be needed to hold a million people ?

Wembley Stadium

If you have the number sequence 1, 3, 9, 27, ... how many terms are there before you get to more than a million ?

5. **Curve stitching and String Art**

Curve stitching is done with embroidery thread onto cardboard. Here is a basic pattern to get you started. Draw any lines and mark points on the wrong side of the cardboard so that only the thread shows on the right side.
Draw 2 lines AB, AC, each 9 cm long, meeting at A at an angle of about 50°.
Mark 8 points along AB 1 cm apart and number them from 1 to 8 starting 1 cm from A. Mark 8 points along CA 1 cm apart and number them from 1′ to 8′ starting 1 cm from C.
3-strand embroidery thread is suitable to use. Choose a colour which shows up against the background of the cardboard.
Begin by making a knot then go through point 1 from the wrong side to the right side. Prick the hole at 1′ so that you can find it from the right side and go through hole 1′ from right side to wrong side. Go on the wrong side to 2′ (because that is nearer than 2), go through 2′ and then through 2. Then go through 3 and 3′, and so on until you have used all the numbers. Fasten off the thread by looping under some on the wrong side, and tying it. On the right side the threads will make the outline of a curve called a parabola.

A design using a square

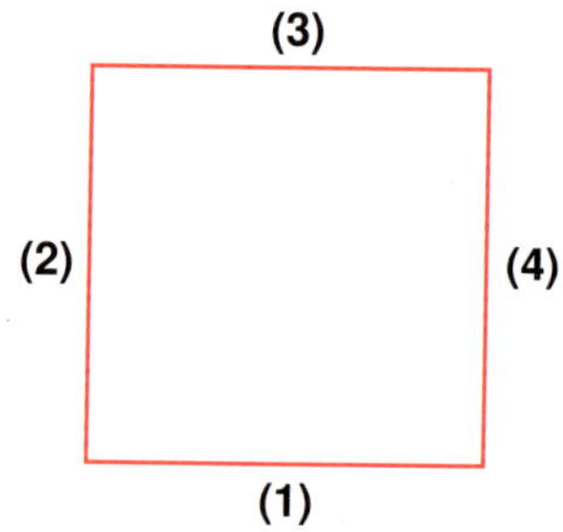

Draw a square, on the wrong side of a piece of cardboard.
Start with the basic pattern on sides (1) and (2).
Then, in the same colour or a different colour, do the pattern again along sides (2) and (3), and then along sides (3) and (4).
Finally use sides (4) and (1). If you are using different colours some of the lines would be better pushed under the previous ones. Think out how to do this.

A design using 2 lines crossing at right angles

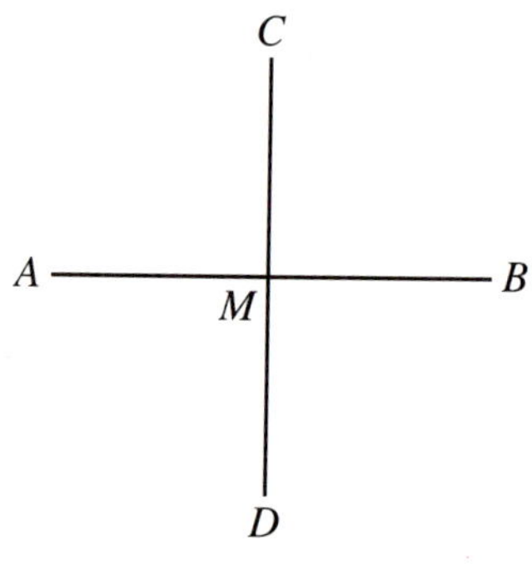

Start with the basic pattern on sides AM and CM.
Then with the same colour repeat the pattern along sides BM and DM.
Now you may like to change colours and fill in the other 2 quarters.

These examples should have given you enough ideas to invent your own patterns.

String Art is based on the same idea but it is done on a board with nails and thread. Paint the board or cover it with cloth, to contrast with the colour of the thread. Use nails 20 mm long, with large heads so that the thread will not slip off. Draw the basic pattern on paper, put it over the board and then knock nails in positions 1 to 8 and 1′ to 8′. Remember which is which and then tear off the paper. Start by knotting the thread round nail 1, leaving a small end to tuck in later.
Take the thread to 1′ and go round the nail, then go to 2′ and round the nail, then to 2, 3, 3′, 4′ and so on. Fasten off round nail 8 and try to tuck the end out of sight.

Now try to use the patterns for a square, and for 2 lines crossing at right angles, and then invent your own patterns.

You could discuss with your teacher the idea of having a competition for curve stitching or string art, perhaps for all the Year 7 classes. You could plan the details of the competition, e.g. the rules for size, and closing date. You could have two sections, one for 'geometrical designs' and one for 'pictures'. When you have got all the entries in, and they have been judged, you could put them on display.

6. **A traffic survey**

Do a survey on a main road to see what sorts of traffic use it, with categories such as car, bus or coach, lorry, light van. Make a table of results and represent them on a pie chart. To make it simpler to calculate the angles in the pie chart you could collect data from 90, 120, 180 or perhaps 360 vehicles. Write down the day and the time when you did your survey.
Perhaps you could repeat your survey at a different time of day, or do it on a weekday and then at a weekend, or do one on a different road, so that you can compare two pie charts to see if they are similar or how they differ. Comment on your results.
(Do not do this survey unless your teacher and your parents approve of your plans, and be careful to stand in a safe place.)

7. A mathematical game

You have probably played games such as snakes and ladders or ludo, where a die is used, or Monopoly or backgammon, where 2 dice are used. There are also games like draughts or chess, played on a board of squares. These do not depend on throws of a die, they are games of skill. You probably know some games you can play with a pack of cards, and there are several games which use cards with instructions on them, such as 'This is your lucky day,—go forward 6 squares'. Noughts and crosses is a quick game, and there are several other pencil and paper games.

Make a list of the games you know, and put them into different categories.

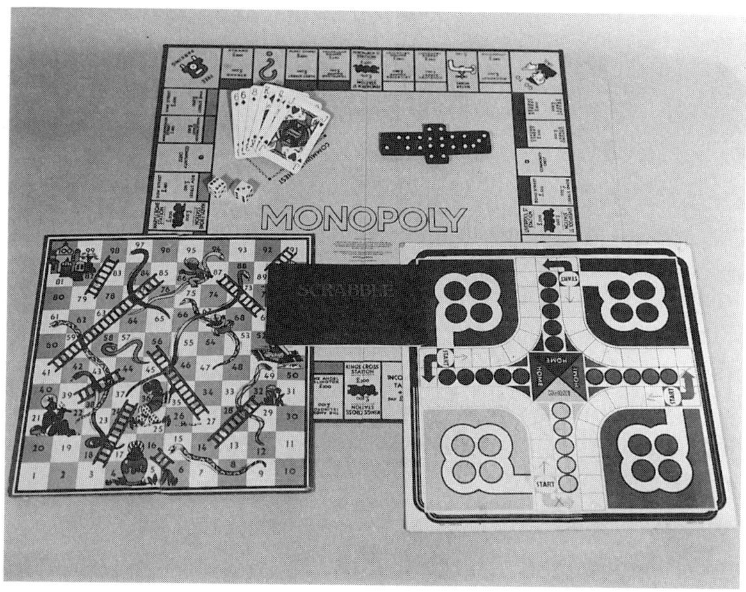

Now design a game yourself, either working alone or with friends. Try to include some Mathematics in it, perhaps negative numbers for going backwards or losing money. It could be based on coordinates. It could include mathematical questions, as in Trivial Pursuit.

Play it several times so that you can make sure that the rules are clear, and improve them where necessary to make the game more fair or more exciting.

When you are satisfied with your game, design attractive equipment for playing it, and lend it to your friends so that they can play it.

8. Using a computer

The use you can make of a computer for Mathematics depends on the make of the computer and the software you have available.

A **spreadsheet program** is a program which is useful for calculations involving columns or rows of numbers. You just enter the figures in it and it will do the calculations for you. It is easy to see how useful such programs are for business purposes.

You can use such a program to investigate the effect of changes. For instance, a small percentage increase on an amount can make a big increase over a few years. The data in a spreadsheet can be represented on a bar chart or pie chart, or if it is suitable, on a histogram. The computer will draw these for you. You can compare the effect of the different types of diagram and decide which is the most suitable for your purpose. The diagrams, too, are helpful in showing the effect of changes in the data.

Drawing symmetrical patterns

If you have a suitable program you can construct and explore symmetrical patterns. You can draw a simple design and reflect it in different axes of symmetry or rotate it about centres of symmetry.

PUZZLES

18. Put the numbers 1 to 8 in these circles so that no number is joined by a line to the next consecutive number.

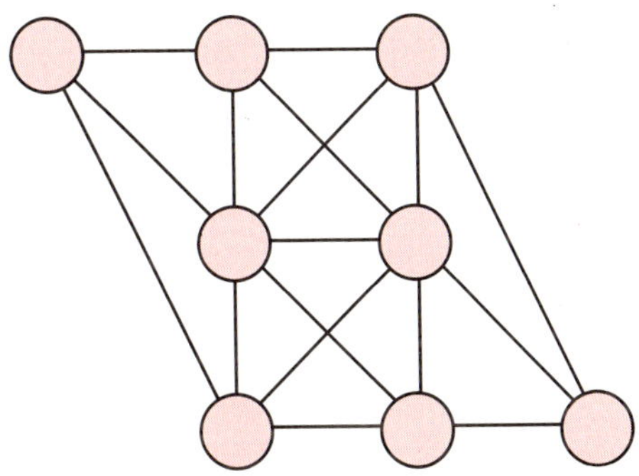

19. If there were 7 crows on a wall and the farmer shot one of them, how many would be left on the wall ?

13 Thinking about British units and time

Using British units

Although we are gradually using the metric measurements more and more, we still use the British measurements in some situations.

Name some items, bought by weight, which will be weighed in British units, and say which units will be used.
In what other situations do we tend to talk of weights in British units ?

Name some liquids which will be measured in British units, and say which units will be used.

Name some lengths which we tend to talk of in British units and say which units will be used.

If you know of any items which are still sold by measures of length in British units, say what they are.

Time for a change ?

Do you think that we should keep using British units or some of them, or should we change over completely to the metric system ?

What length, weight and capacity measures are used here ?

A road sign using British and metric units

Numbers and measures

The metric system is based on a scale of ten, but the British measures were developed in a very unscientific way, so there is a variety of numbers used in converting from one unit to another. For instance, there are 12 inches in a foot.
Can you say where these numbers are used ?

3 4 8 14 16 20 28 112
1760 2240 5280

A sundial on a memorial stone

A traditional clock, in a Swiss village

A modern digital clock

Time

Were you 'on time' for school today ? In a modern country our lives are regulated by time.

Make a timetable for tomorrow, starting with the time you will get up, and the times of the various activities into which the day is divided.

Approximately what fractions of the day will you spend on sleeping, eating, working (at school or elsewhere), leisure activities, and any other activities ?

Approximately how many hours in a week do you spend watching television ? How many hours in a year is this ? Do you think this is making good use of your time ?

Time at work

Most people who go out to work have to put in a certain number of hours at the job. Why is this ?
In some jobs, time is very important. How do these people use time in their jobs or activities, apart from putting in the hours at work ?

A bus driver
A TV producer
A teacher
A mother with a young child
A boxer
An athlete
A farmer
A deep-sea diver

Name some other people whose jobs or activities involve the use of time to a large extent.

13 British units and time

The metric system originated in France at the time of the French Revolution. Since it is based on 10 and powers of 10 it is a very useful system for scientific work.
The British system of units for weights and measures is much older. It is still partly in use although it is not so convenient for use with calculators, not being based on 10.

Length

We use inch, foot, yard, mile.

12 inches	= 1 foot
3 feet	= 1 yard
1760 yards	= 1 mile

The old symbol for inches was ″, and for feet was ′, so 7′6″ means 7 feet 6 inches.
Other units which used to be used are rod, pole, perch (each $5\frac{1}{2}$ yards), chain (22 yards) and furlong (220 yards).

Weight

We use ounces, pounds, stones, hundredweights and tons.

16 ounces	= 1 pound
14 pounds	= 1 stone
112 pounds	= 1 hundredweight
8 stones	= 1 hundredweight
2240 pounds	= 1 ton
20 hundredweights	= 1 ton

The symbol for ounces is oz, for pounds is *lb* (from Latin, libra for pound), for stones st, for hundredweight cwt (from the Roman C for a hundred).
Another unit which used to be used is a quarter ($\frac{1}{4}$ of a hundredweight = 28 pounds).

Capacity

We use pint, gallon.

8 pints	= 1 gallon

Other units which used to be used are a gill ($\frac{1}{4}$ pint), although this unit is sometimes used for $\frac{1}{2}$ pint, e.g. when asking for a gill of beer; also fluid ounces. There are 20 fluid ounces in 1 pint.

It is useful to know that

1 pint of water weighs $1\frac{1}{4}$ lb
1 gallon of water weighs 10 lb

Exercise 13.1

1. Change the following:

1 6′ 3″ into inches
2 8 st 3 lb into lb
3 2 gall 1 pint into pints
4 2 lb 4 oz into oz
5 $\frac{1}{4}$ mile into yards
6 96 inches into feet
7 48 oz into lb
8 20 pints into gallons
9 5280 yards into miles
10 90 feet into yards

2. Read the measurements given on these scales:

1 Weighing scale in stones and lb.

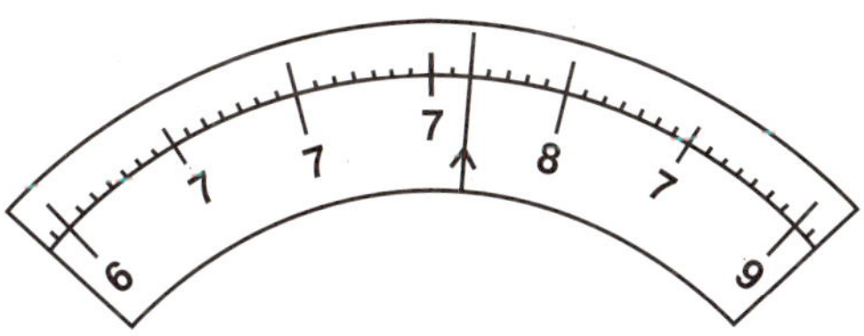

2 Measuring jug in pints.

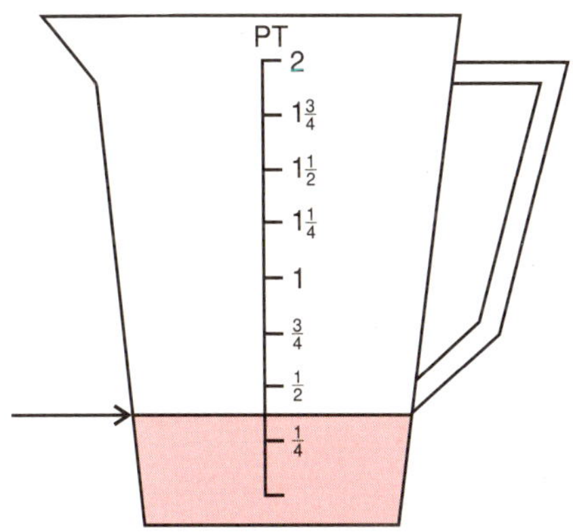

3 Ruler in inches and sixteenths.

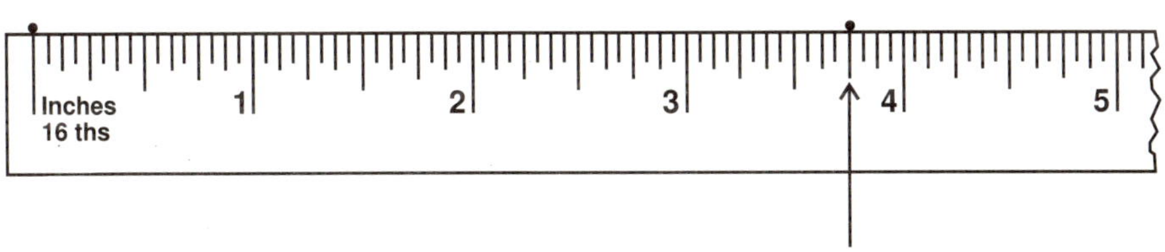

3. **1** Express 9 inches as a fraction of 1 yard.
   2 Express 5 oz as a fraction of 1 lb 9 oz.
   3 Express 3 pints as a fraction of 1 gallon.
   4 Express 880 yards as a fraction of 1 mile.
   5 Express 2′ 3″ as a fraction of 2 yards.

4. Find these quantities.

   1 $\frac{2}{3}$ of 2 ft
   2 $\frac{3}{8}$ of 1 lb 8 oz
   3 $\frac{5}{8}$ of 2 gallons
   4 $\frac{1}{6}$ of 1 yard
   5 $\frac{1}{4}$ of 2 stone

5. A piece of wire 4 ft long is bent to make the outline of a triangle with equal sides. What is the length, in inches, of each side of the triangle ?

6. An empty tank weighs 65 lb. When full the tank holds 18 gallons of water. What is the total weight of the tank when it is half-full of water ? (1 gallon of water weighs 10 lb.)

7. $3\frac{3}{4}$ yards of material are used to make a dress. How much material is left from a 5-yard length ?

8. A car will travel 36 miles on 1 gallon of petrol. How far will the car travel on $3\frac{1}{2}$ gallons ?

Approximate comparisons with the metric system

Length

1 inch ... $2\frac{1}{2}$ cm
1 foot ... 30 cm
1 yard ... 0.9 m
1 mile ... 1.6 km
5 miles ... 8 km

1 cm ... 0.4 inches
1 m ... 40 inches = 4 ins longer than 1 yard
1 km ... $\frac{5}{8}$ mile
8 km ... 5 miles

Weight

1 lb ... 450 g (nearly $\frac{1}{2}$ kg)
1 ton ... 1 tonne

1 kg ... 2.2 lb (just over 2 lb)
1 tonne ... 1 ton

Capacity

1 pint ... just over $\frac{1}{2}$ litre
1 gallon ... $4\frac{1}{2}$ litres

1 litre ... $1\frac{3}{4}$ pints
1 litre ... 0.22 gallon

Exercise 13.2

1. Find approximate metric equivalents for these British weights and measures.

   1 25 miles
   2 6 lb
   3 80 inches
   4 2 gallons
   5 3 tons
   6 60 miles
   7 1 stone
   8 5 feet
   9 5 pints
   10 22 yards

2. Find approximate British equivalents for these metric weights and measures.

   1 20 cm
   2 12 litres
   3 10 kg
   4 80 kg
   5 900 g
   6 $2\frac{1}{2}$ m
   7 5 tonnes
   8 20 litres
   9 250 g
   10 56 km

3. For the British units in these statements, give the approximate metric equivalents, selecting from those given in brackets.

   1 I need some $\frac{1}{2}$-inch nails. (1 cm, 1.2 cm, 1.5 cm)
   2 The tree is 30 feet tall. (9 m, 18 m, 27 m)
   3 Janine weighs 3 stones. (2 kg, 12 kg, 20 kg)
   4 The tank holds 10 gallons. (4.5 ℓ, 45 ℓ, 450 ℓ)
   5 The recipe uses 8 oz of sugar. (8 g, 40 g, 200 g)

4. The luggage allowance when travelling by a certain airline is 15 kg. What is this, approximately, in lbs ?

5. The smallest house in Britain is in Conwy, Wales. It is 72 inches wide, 122 inches high and 100 inches from front to back. Change these measurements into approximate metric units.

6. Paul was told by his trainer to run $7\frac{1}{2}$ miles every morning. What distance is this, approximately, in km ?

More exact comparisons with the metric system

7. This sign shows the price for 4-star petrol. Find the cost of one gallon of petrol. Take 1 gallon = 4.546 litres, and give the answer to the nearest penny.

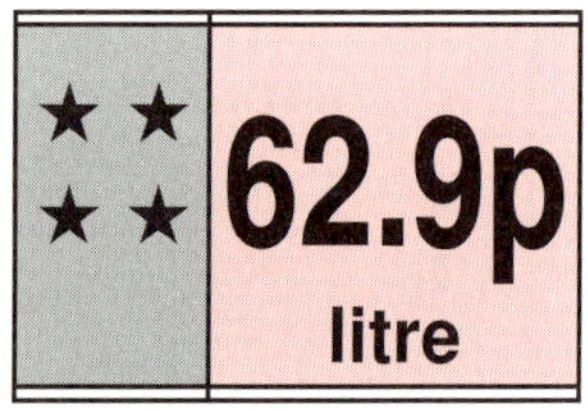

8. Lauren weighs 12 st 5 lb. What is her weight in kg, if 1 lb = 453.6 g (and 1 stone = 14 lb) ?

9. The distance from Liverpool to Panama along a shipping route is 4570 miles. Taking 1 mile as 1.609 km, find this distance in km, to the nearest 10 km.

Time

The units for time are unlikely to be changed in the near future although since they are not based on ten they are not easy to use on a calculator. Perhaps, eventually, things will be changed so that there could be 10 new hours in a day, 10 new minutes in an hour, and even 10 days in a new week. But we cannot change the length of a year because that is the length of time that the Earth takes to go round the Sun, and that is approximately $365\frac{1}{4}$ days.

Here is the present table for time:

60 seconds = 1 minute	52 weeks = 1 year
60 minutes = 1 hour	365 days = 1 year
24 hours = 1 day	366 days = 1 leap year
7 days = 1 week	12 months = 1 year

Recording the time of day can either be by the 12-hour clock, when morning times are denoted by a.m. and afternoon times by p.m., or by the 24-hour clock. To avoid confusion, timetables are often printed with times using the 24-hour clock.

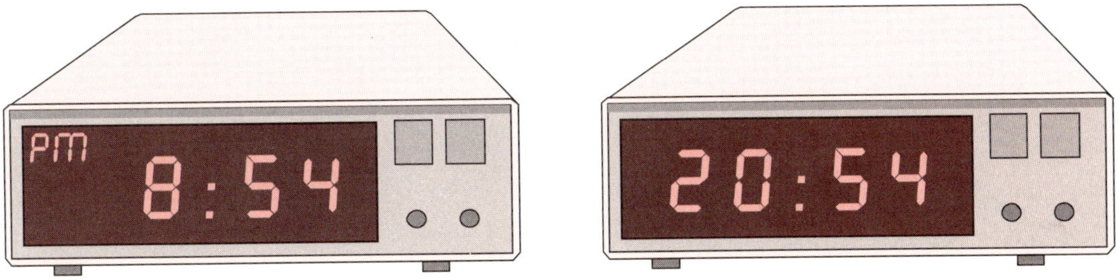

Examples

	12-hour clock	**24-hour clock**
1 o'clock early morning	1.00 am	1.00 or 01.00
5 past 1 early morning	1.05 am	1.05 or 01.05
Noon	12.00 pm	12.00
Quarter-to-1 early afternoon	12.45 pm	12.45
1 o'clock early afternoon	1.00 pm	13.00
Half-past 8 in the evening	8.30 pm	20.30
One minute to midnight	11.59 pm	23.59
Midnight	12.00 am	0.00 or 00.00
One minute past midnight	12.01 am	0.01 or 00.01

(The day changes at the instant of midnight so when the time is shown as 12.00 am or 0.00 the date has changed.)

On a timetable the 24-hour times would be printed as 4-figure numbers. The full stop separating the hours and minutes could be left out.
e.g. 1.23 am would be printed as 0123,
1.23 pm would be printed as 1323.

1323 would be pronounced as thirteen twenty-three or thirteen twenty-three hours. But 1300 would be pronounced as thirteen hundred hours.

Use of a calculator

You cannot use your calculator directly for mixed calculations involving hours and minutes, minutes and seconds, days and weeks, etc. since these are not based on a scale of ten. You will have to do the calculations for the different units separately.

Here are some examples:

1 A plumber does two jobs. The first one takes 1 hour 37 minutes and the second takes 2 hours 46 minutes. What is the total time taken ?

1 hr 37 min
2 hr 46 min
4 hr 23 min

Use your calculator to add 37 and 46. This gives 83. 83 min = 1 hr 23 min so write down 23 min and carry 1 hr forward, making 4 hours altogether.

2 Of a school day of 5 hours, 2 hours 25 minutes was spent on rehearsals for a display. How much time was left for lessons ?

5 hr 0 min
2 hr 25 min
2 hr 35 min

Use your calculator to take 25 from 60, since you cannot take 25 from 0. This gives 35 min. Then adjust for the 1 hour you changed into 60 minutes, so, depending on the way your normally do subtraction, you will have either 5 hr − 3 hr or 4 hr − 2 hr. This gives 2 hours.

3 12 hr 22 min ÷ 7

7)12 hr 22 min
1 hr 46 min

Do the hours part first. 7 into 12 goes 1 remainder 5. Write down 1 hr. Change the remainder, 5 hr, into 5 × 60 min = 300 min, so altogether there are 322 min. 322 ÷ 7 = 46, so the answer is 1 hr 46 min.

4 A train journey takes from 10.52 am to 2.37 pm. How long is this ?

One way to do this is:
From 10.52 am to 11.00 am is 8 minutes,
from 11.00 am to 2.00 pm is 3 hours,
from 2.00 pm to 2.37 pm is 37 minutes.
The total time is 3 hours 45 minutes.

Exercise 13.3

1. Change these times to the 24-hour clock.

   2.10 am, 7.00 pm, 2.15 pm, 4.05 pm, 11.50 pm.

   Change these times to the 12-hour clock.

   0350, 7.30, 12.05, 18.18, 2210.

2. Write down the time shown on this clock when it is in the afternoon.
   1 in the 12-hour system,
   2 in the 24-hour system.

3. Work out the answers to these calculations.
   1 2 min 23 sec + 1 min 48 sec + 4 min 16 sec
   2 12 hr 15 min − 5 hr 40 min
   3 10 hr 18 min × 4
   4 51 min 10 sec ÷ 5
   5 (12 hr 14 min + 1 hr 12 min) × 5

4. A train left London at 11.15 am and arrived at Manchester at 1.58 pm. How long did the journey take ?

5. Sandra works in a local shop from 2.30 pm to 6 pm on five afternoons each week. She is paid £3.20 per hour. How much is her weekly wage ?

6. Andrew set off on a training ride at 10.55 am and cycled for $4\frac{1}{4}$ hours. At what time did he stop ?

7. On a timetable, a plane was due to leave an airport at 2235 and arrive at its destination at 0205 the next day. How long should the journey take ?
It actually arrived 15 minutes early. At what time did it arrive ?

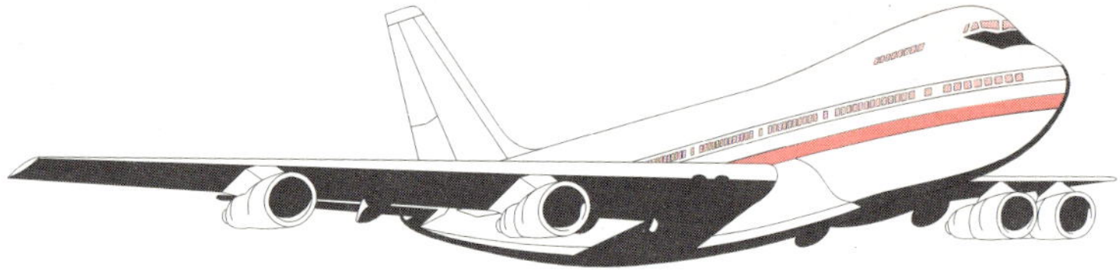

8. This is an evening's programmes on a local TV station.

5.55	Weather
6.00	News
6.25	Sport Today
6.50	Double treble quiz show
7.20	Film: The Silver Arrow
9.35	The Wayfarers
11.05	Local Lives
11.45	Closedown

1 How long did the film last ?

2 If someone switched on at the end of Sport Today and watched TV until closedown, for how long had he been watching ?

3 If The Wayfarers was recorded on a blank 3-hour video tape, how much tape would remain blank ?

9. Here is part of a bus timetable.

Ashmead School	1554	1602	1608	1616	1622	1629
Brook Lane	1604	1612	1618	1626	1632	1639
Carlton Village	1619	1627	–	1641	–	1654
Denham Station	–	–	1640	–	1654	–

1 Saria finishes school at 3.50 pm. What is the time of the first bus she can catch to get to her home in Carlton Village ? How long does the journey take ?
If she just misses the first bus, how long will she then have to wait for the next one ?

2 Her teacher, Mr Bishop, wants to catch the 5 pm train from Denham station. Which bus must he catch at school, and how long does the journey to the station take ?

Exercise 13.4 Applications and Activities

1. On an old weighing scale, the standard weights which were available were 1 oz, 2 oz, 4 oz, 8 oz, 1 lb and 2 lb. There was one of each.
   Which weights would you use to weigh
   1 14 oz, **2** 2 lb 6 oz, **3** 3 lb 9 oz ?

2. A quick way used to measure a yard of string or cloth is to stretch out an arm and measure from the finger and thumb to the tip of the nose.
   Try this with several friends. Measure your results in inches. Ask some adults also.
   Comment on your measurements.

3. **Using British units**

   As with calculations with time, be careful if you are using your calculator when dealing with mixed units not based on 10, such as lb and oz, gallons and pints, feet and inches. You will have to deal with the different units separately.

   Work out the answers to these calculations.

   1 One parcel weighs 14 lb 9 oz and another weighs 10 lb 12 oz. What is the total weight ?

   2 The space between two gateposts is 3 ft 5 in. This space is to be blocked with 6 strands of wire. What total length of wire is needed ?

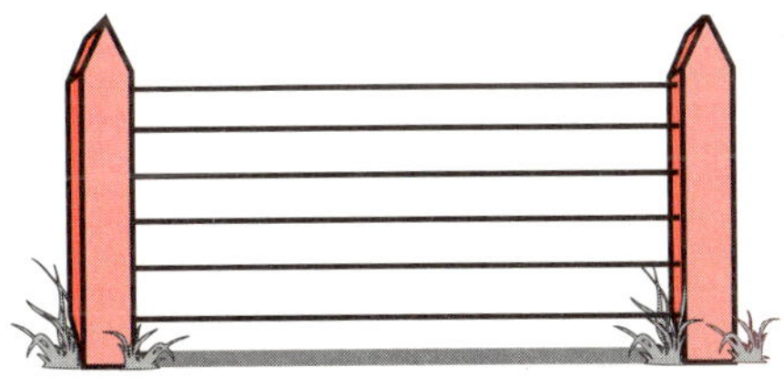

   3 A sackful of apples weighing 23 lb 7 oz is to be divided among 5 people. How much should they each get ?

   4 Paula weighs 6 st 6 lb and Rebecca weighs 4 st 10 lb. How much heavier is Paula than Rebecca ?
   If they stand on the scale together, what weight will be shown ?

   5 How many pieces of wood 1′ 3″ long can be cut from a plank 10′ long ?

   6 A cake weighed 8 lb 3 oz. A man guessed 9 lb 8 oz and his daughter guessed 6 lb 15 oz. Which was the better guess ?

4. **History of British measurement**

It is interesting to find out about the measures which were used long ago in Britain. Did you know that 1 inch was the length of 3 barleycorns placed end to end, and that 1 furlong ($\frac{1}{8}$ of a mile) derives its name from a furrow-length ?
Why was a **foot** so called ?
How is a mile connected with the Romans ?
Why was it necessary to have a standard system of weights and measures ?
Try to find information in reference books, and write about this.

5. **Estimations of time**

Ask your friends, one by one, to estimate 1 minute of time. Use your watch to record their estimates, in seconds. Comment on the results.
You can also choose a task, such as running round the playing field. Ask your friends to estimate how long it will take you, and then do the task and compare the result with the estimates.

6. **Measurement of time**

Make a list of all the instruments or methods you know of for measuring time.

In earlier times these included sundials and water clocks, today we have digital watches, and there are atomic clocks which are accurate to within a millionth of a second.

Try to find more information in reference books and write briefly about the measurement of time.

Chapter 13 test

1. On a road sign in France the distance to the next town was given as 72 km. How many miles, approximately, is this ?

2. A sack of potatoes used to weigh 56 lb. The new sacks weigh 25 kg. How many pounds, approximately, is this ?

3. A bottle holds 2 litres of squash. How many pints is this, approximately ?

4. Wayne is 5 ft 10 in tall. What is this height in cm, if 1 inch = 2.54 cm ?

5. 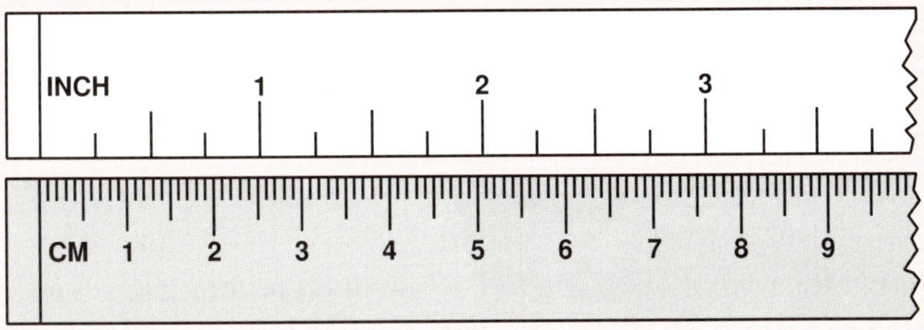

The two rulers show measurements in inches and in centimetres. The top ruler has inches and is divided into quarter inches. The other ruler has centimetres and is divided into millimetres.

1 What measurement in cm is equivalent to $1\frac{3}{4}$ inches ?

2 What measurement in inches is equivalent to 8.9 cm ?

6. A school's lessons begin at 8.50 am and end at 2.50 pm with an hour's break at lunchtime and 20 minutes break mid-morning. If there are 7 lessons of equal length, how long is a lesson ?

7. A candle is 1 ft long. It is lit at 7.30 pm and it burns at the rate of 1 inch every hour. How long will it be at midnight ?

8. A plumber does three repair jobs as follows:– the first from 9.35 am to 11.15 am, the second from 11.45 am to 12.50 pm and the third from 2.05 pm to 4.50 pm. Find the total time taken on the three jobs.

PUZZLES

20. In an enclosure at the Zoo I can see 160 giraffe legs and 80 ostrich legs. How many animals are there in the enclosure ?

21. Find the missing figures in this multiplication sum.

$$\begin{array}{r} 8\cdot\cdot\cdot6 \\ 3\cdot \\ \hline 8\cdot\cdot\cdot6 \\ 2\cdot31\cdot80 \\ \hline 251\cdot\cdot36 \\ \hline \end{array}$$

14 Thinking about negative numbers

What is a negative number ?

I have £35 and I get a bill for £13. If I pay the bill, how much money will be left ? This is an ordinary subtraction sum and you can do it on your calculator by pressing 35 [−] 13 [=]. What is the answer ?
I have £35 and I get a bill for £43. If I pay the bill, how much money will be left ? Now, commonsense tells me that I can't pay the bill. But the calculator does not have any commonsense so I will enter the calculation in the same way as before, pressing 35 [−] 43 [=].
What is the answer ? What does it mean ?
This is a negative number, called 'minus 8' or 'negative 8'.
I tell my mother how hard up I am and she gives me £8. On my calculator there is −8 shown. If I add 8 to this, what do I get ?

Negative numbers need not just be whole numbers, they can be fractions or decimals such as $-\frac{3}{4}$, −3.3, etc.
The ordinary numbers 1, 2, 3, ... as well as the fractions and decimals such as $\frac{2}{3}$, 0.3, can be called positive numbers. If we want to emphasise that they are positive numbers rather than negative numbers we can write +1, +2, +3, $+\frac{2}{3}$, +0.3, etc. There is one number which is neither a positive nor a negative number. Which is it ?
On most calculators minus 8 is shown as −8 and there may be a special key for entering negative numbers. Find out how to use this.

The temperature in Arctic regions can go as low as −90°F.

The lowest point in the Western Hemisphere, 282 feet below sea level, is in Death Valley, California.

In summer 1989, when there had been very low rainfall, the water level in Hafren reservoir in Wales was 60 feet below normal.

Examples of negative numbers

There are many situations where we use negative numbers in our lives. What examples can you think of ? The pictures may give you some ideas.

Nick Faldo with a score of 2 below par, shown on scoreboards as −2.

Apollo 8 lifting off. Times before lift-off are counted down as
10 9 8 7 6 5 4 3 2 1 zero.

14 Negative numbers

Here is a number line where the numbers go below 0.

Numbers get larger as you move up the number line.
e.g. 2 is larger than −5.

Numbers get smaller as you move down the number line.
e.g. −4 is smaller than −3.

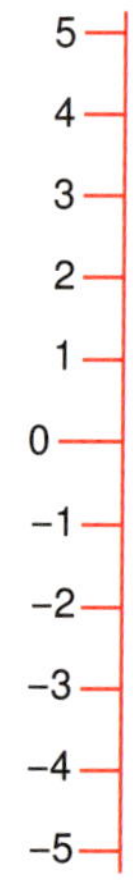

Temperature

This is a thermometer marked in the Celsius scale.
0°C is the temperature at which water freezes, and the temperature can drop below that level, so temperatures below zero are given as −1°, −2°, −3°, etc.
Temperatures above zero are given as ordinary numbers, 1°, 2°, 3°, etc, or they can be given as plus numbers, +1°, +2°, +3°, etc. (+3° is the same as 3°.)

What reading does this thermometer show ?

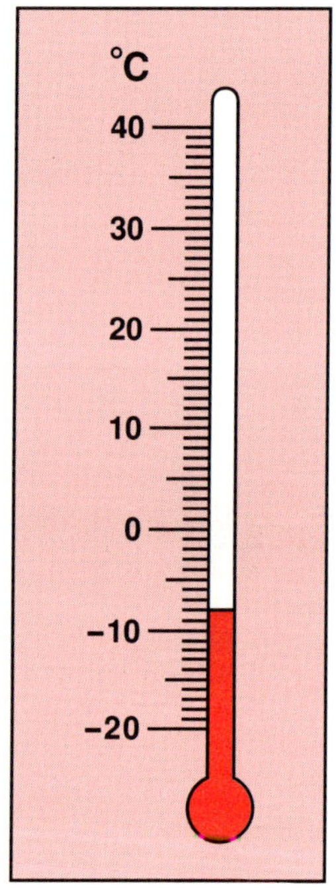

Calculations involving negative numbers

Examples

1 The temperature last night was −4°. It has risen by 10°. What is the temperature now ?

Start on a number line at −4. You are adding 10 so go upwards. Count up 10 steps and you should get to 6. So the temperature now is 6°.

You can write this calculation as (−4) + 10 = 6.

You can do this calculation on your scientific calculator. If you want to enter a negative number on your calculator, use the [+/−] key, e.g. to enter −4, press 4 [+/−].
To calculate (−4) + 10, press 4 [+/−] [+] 10 [=] and you will get the answer 6.

On a simple calculator with no [+/−] key you can get −4 at the beginning of a question by pressing 0 [−] 4 [=].

2 If on a calculator you press 5 [−] 8 [=], what answer should the calculator show ?

Start on a number line at 5. You are taking away 8 so go downwards. Move 8 steps downwards and you should get to −3.
You can write this calculation as $5 - 8 = -3$.
Check this question using your calculator.

3 On the harbour wall there is a line showing the depth of the water in feet.
0 was marked at the average water level. If there is less water negative numbers have to be used.
How much has the water level fallen if it was at 6 feet and later it was at (−3) feet ?

Count down from 6 to −3.
You count down 9 altogether so the water level has fallen by 9 feet.
You could write this calculation as $6 - (-3) = 9$, and do it on your scientific calculator by pressing 6 [−] 3 [+/−] [=].

With a simple calculator you would have to press 0 [−] 3 [=] to get −3, put this into the memory and then press 6 [−] [MR] [=].

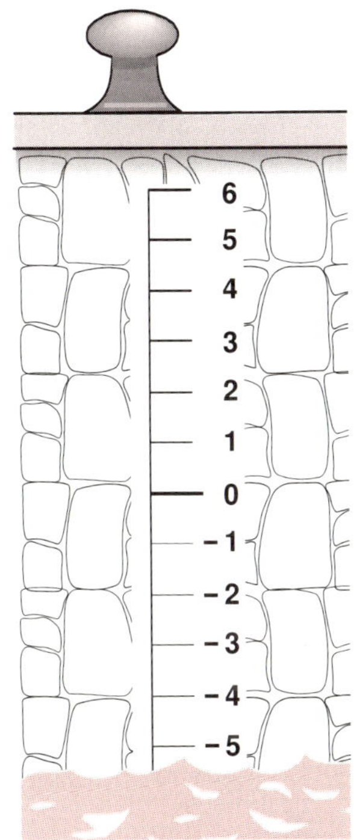

Exercise 14.1

1. Where do you get to on the number scale by following these instructions ?

1 Start at 3 and go down 3.
2 Start at −6 and go up 4.
3 Start at −4 and go down 7.
4 Start at 1 and go up 2.
5 Start at −3 and go down 2.
6 Start at 5 and go down 6.
7 Start at −3 and go up 2.
8 Start at 2 and go down 2.
9 Start at 3 and go down 5.
10 Start at −5 and go up 1.

2. Say whether you should go up or down, and by how many,

1 to get from 5 to 2,
2 to get from −4 to 3,
3 to get from 1 to −4,
4 to get from −2 to −5,
5 to get from −4 to 0,
6 to get from 2 to −4,
7 to get from 3 to 6,
8 to get from −1 to 0,
9 to get from −5 to −1,
10 to get from 7 to −1.

3. Where did you begin in these situations ?

1 If having gone down 3 you get to 6.
2 If having gone up 2 you get to 5.
3 If having gone up 5 you get to 0.
4 If having gone down 2 you get to −3.
5 If having gone up 4 you get to 0.

4. Write these numbers in order of size, smallest first.

1 −2, 5, 4.
2 −3, 0, −5.
3 6, −5, 3.
4 1, −4, −3.
5 −6, −8, −7.

5. Find the new temperature in the following cases.

1 The temperature is +8° and it rises 3°.
2 The temperature is +6° and it falls 9°.
3 The temperature is −4° and it rises 6°.
4 The temperature is −9° and it rises 2°.
5 The temperature is 0° and it falls 6°.
6 The temperature is +10° and it falls 24°.
7 The temperature is −8° and it rises 10°.
8 The temperature is −3° and it rises 3°.
9 The temperature is +5° and it falls 4°.
10 The temperature is −1° and it falls 3°.

6. Say whether the temperature has risen or fallen, and by how many degrees.

1 It was 0° and is now +4°.
2 It was −5° and is now −7°.
3 It was +3° and is now +6°.
4 It was −1° and is now 0°.
5 It was −4° and is now −2°.
6 It was 0° and is now −5°.
7 It was −3° and is now −7°.
8 It was +2° and is now −3°.
9 It was −6° and is now −1°.
10 It was −2° and is now +6°.

7. (In this question give the answer in the form '10 minutes to 1' or '10 minutes past 1'.)

1 If the time is 12 minutes to 1 o'clock, what will be the time in 20 minutes ?
2 If the time is 5 minutes to 2 o'clock, what was the time 5 minutes ago ?
3 If the time is 4 minutes past 3 o'clock, what was the time 2 minutes ago ?
4 If the time is quarter past four, what was the time 20 minutes ago ?
5 If the time is quarter to five, what will be the time in 25 minutes ?

Exercise 14.2 Applications and Activities

1. **A number game**

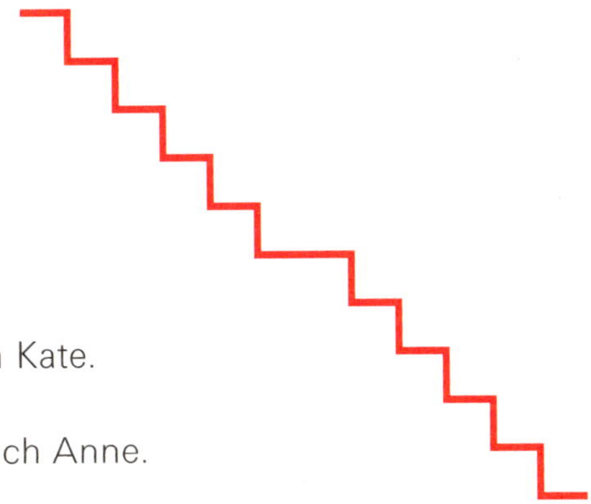

Kate and Anne are playing a number game on this set of steps.
They call the longer step 0, and the steps above 1, 2, 3, . . .
From step 0 they number the steps below as −1, −2, −3, . . .
Kate is on step 3 and Anne on step −1.
Anne would have to go up 4 steps to reach Kate.
This instruction is given as +4.
Kate would have to go down 4 steps to reach Anne.
This instruction is given as −4.
(i.e. To go up, +. To go down, −.)

What is the instruction to get from

1 −3 to 3,
2 0 to −2,
3 1 to −4,
4 −2 to 5,
5 −3 to −1 ?

Where does Anne finish if she was

6 on step 4 and Kate said −3,
7 on step −1 and Kate said +4,
8 on step −2 and Kate said −2,
9 on step 0 and Kate said −1,
10 on step −5 and Kate said +2 ?

2. **A bank account**

Mr Collins has an agreement with his bank to overdraw money, that is, to spend more money than is in his account.

1 If he has £400 in his account and writes a cheque for £650, how much will his account be overdrawn ?
2 If his account is overdrawn by £200 and he puts £80 into the account, how much is he overdrawn now ?
3 If his account is overdrawn by £70 and he puts £130 into the account, how much is his account in credit ?
4 If his account is overdrawn by £150 and he takes out another £30, how much is he overdrawn now ?
5 If he has £250 in his account and writes a cheque for £400, and then puts £80 into the account, is his account overdrawn or in credit, and by how much ?

3. Number patterns

Number patterns can use negative numbers.
e.g. 10, 7, 4, 1, −2, −5, −8, . . . (Taking 3 off each time).

Write down the next three terms in these sequences.

1 20, 15, 10, 5, . . .
2 −10, −8, −6, −4, . . .
3 −3, 0, 3, 6, . . .
4 −22, −17, −12, −7, . . .
5 18, 14, 10, 6, . . .

4. Multiplication

Here is a multiplication number pattern.

4	0	4	8	12	16
3	0	3	6	9	12
2	0	2	4	6	8
1	0	1	2	3	4
0	0	0	0	0	0
	0	1	2	3	4

Here is a similar pattern extended to include negative numbers.

4					0	4	8	12	16
3					0	3	6	9	12
2		−6			0	2	4	6	8
1				−1	0	1	2	3	4
0					0	0	0	0	0
−1									−4
−2					0				
−3									
−4			8						
	−4	−3	−2	−1	0	1	2	3	4

Copy it and use the number patterns in rows and columns to complete it. Some numbers have been filled in, to help you.

The spaces filled in show that $1 \times (-1) = -1$

$$(-2) \times 0 = 0$$
$$2 \times (-3) = -6$$
$$(-1) \times 4 = -4$$
$$(-4) \times (-2) = 8$$

This last result may seem rather strange but it is the true result.

Now you know how to multiply negative numbers.
Here are the rules.

$+ \times + = +$
$+ \times - = -$
$- \times - = +$

Write down the answers to these questions.

1 $0 \times (-6)$
2 $5 \times (-7)$
3 $(-1) \times 10$
4 $(-8) \times 0$
5 $(-5) \times (-6)$
6 $7 \times (-4)$
7 5×4
8 $(-5) \times (-1)$
9 $(-10) \times 8$
10 $0 \times (-5)$
11 $6 \times (-1)$
12 $(-6) \times 10$
13 $(-9) \times (-3)$
14 $(-4) \times 0$
15 $(-8) \times (-6)$

5. **Division**

We can find the rules for division from those for multiplication.

Since $3 \times 7 = 21$, then $21 \div 3 = 7$ and $21 \div 7 = 3$.
Since $(-3) \times 7 = -21$, then $(-21) \div (-3) = 7$ and $(-21) \div 7 = -3$
Since $3 \times (-7) = -21$, then $(-21) \div 3 = -7$ and $(-21) \div (-7) = 3$.
Since $(-3) \times (-7) = 21$, then $21 \div (-3) = -7$ and $21 \div (-7) = -3$.

These give the rules

$+ \div + = +$
$+ \div - = -$
$- \div + = -$
$- \div - = +$

Write down the answers to these questions.

1 $15 \div 5$
2 $49 \div (-7)$
3 $(-45) \div 5$
4 $(-30) \div (-6)$
5 $0 \div 9$
6 $(-32) \div 4$
7 $42 \div 7$
8 $9 \div (-1)$
9 $(-27) \div (-3)$
10 $(-56) \div 8$
11 $0 \div (-6)$
12 $(-77) \div (-11)$
13 $72 \div (-12)$
14 $(-60) \div (-5)$
15 $(-8) \div 1$

Chapter 14 test

1. **1** If the temperature is $+3°$ and it falls by $8°$, what will the new temperature be ?
2 If the temperature is $-4°$, by how many degrees must it rise to become $+7°$?
3 If the temperature was $9°$ and it fell to $-6°$ overnight, through how many degrees did it fall ?
4 After rising 8 degrees the temperature is $+1°$. What was it originally ?
5 After falling 6 degrees the temperature is $-9°$. What was it originally ?

[Turn over]

2. The floors in a building are numbered. The ground floor is number 0. The top floor is number 7.
There are 4 floors below the ground floor and these have negative numbers, −1, −2, −3 and −4 going downwards from the ground floor.

1 How many floors are there altogether ?

2 If Kerry was on floor 5 and went down 6 floors, on which floor was she then ?

3 If Kerry was on floor −3 and went up 3 floors, on which floor was she then ?

4 If Kerry went up 4 floors and she was then on floor 2, where was she originally ?

5 If Kerry was on floor 1 and wanted to get to floor −3, did she go up or down, and for how many floors ?

3. **1** If the time is 12 minutes past 1 o'clock, how many minutes have passed since it was 5 minutes to 1 o'clock ?

2 If the time is 5 minutes to two, in how many minutes will it be 2.15 ?

3 If the time is twenty to three, in how many minutes will it be five to three ?

4 If the time is 6 minutes to four, how many minutes have passed since it was quarter to four ?

5 If the time is ten to five, in how many minutes will it be ten past five ?

4. Vijay and Amul are playing a game with cards marked with + numbers or − numbers. At the end of the game they score according to the numbers on their cards.

e.g. For △+8 △−6 △−3 Vijay scores 8 − 6 − 3 = −1.

What are the scores with these cards ?

1 △−2 △−3 △+5

2 △+1 △−6 △+9

3 △−4 △−2 △−3

4 △+4 △−3 △−3

5 △−1 △−1 △+6

PUZZLES

22. In a hospital ward there is a system of light signals to tell doctors that they are wanted. For example, if the Red only is lit, Dr Snow is wanted. If the Red and Blue are Lit, Dr Corless is needed. How many doctors can be given a signal using all possible combinations of colours ?

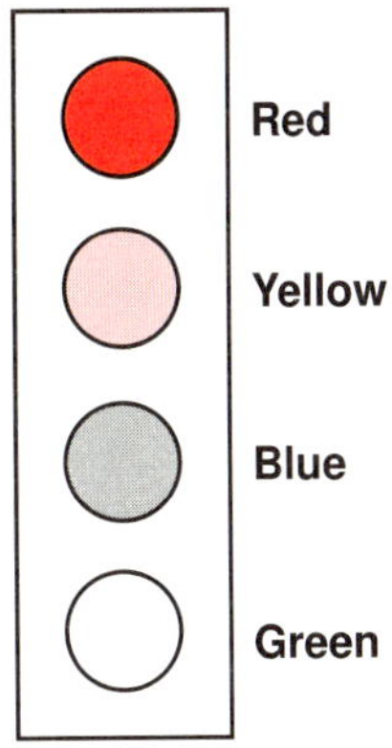

23. If it costs 50p to break a link and £1 to weld it again, what is the least cost of joining these 5 segments of 3 links each together in one long chain ?

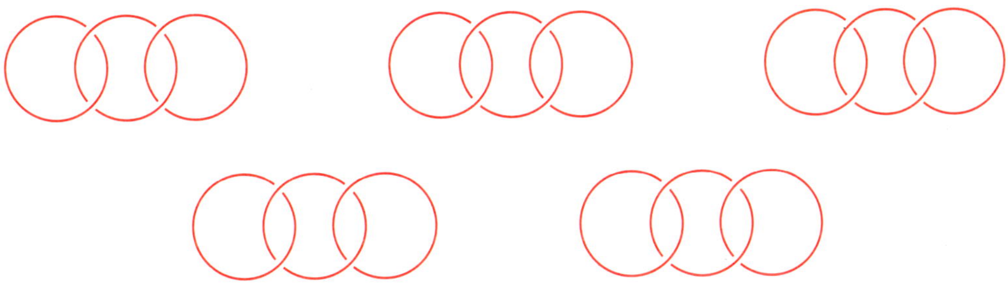

24. If you wrote down all the numbers from 1 to 100, how many times would you write the figure 7 ?

25. This square pattern is made with 24 matches. Remove 8 of the matches to leave two complete squares.

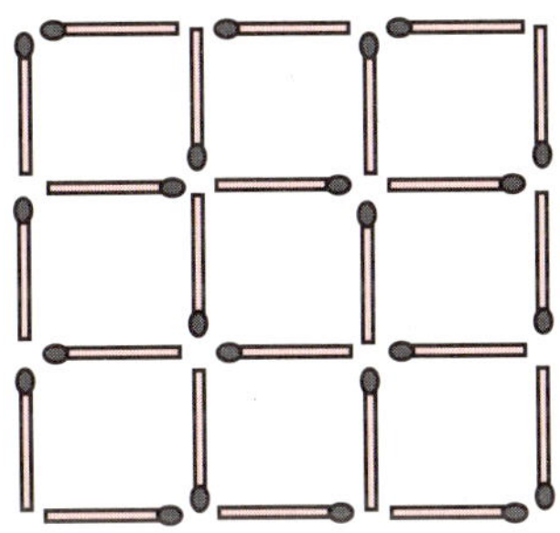

15 Thinking about angles and parallel

Angle facts

You may have made some discoveries about angles in Chapter 8. What facts do you already know about them ?

Adjacent angles

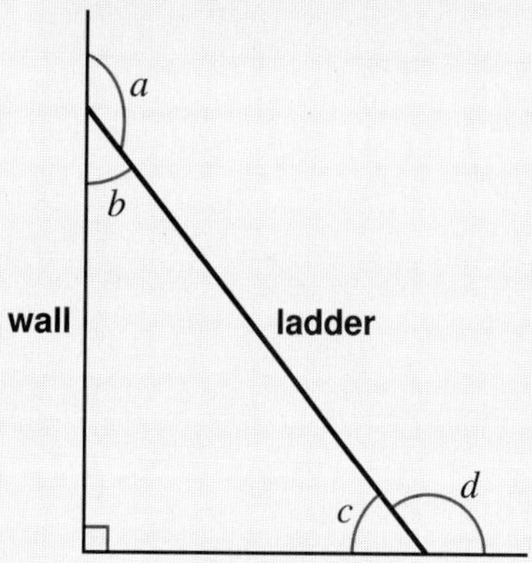

What is the connection between the sizes of angles a and b ?

What is the connection between the sizes of angles c and d ?

You may also notice a connection between the sizes of angles b and c.

Angles at a point

What size is the (hidden) angle at the centre in each sector ?

Vertically opposite angles

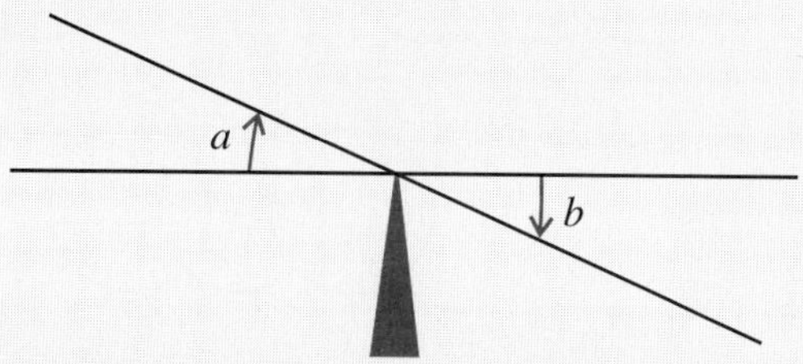

As one end of a seesaw goes up, turning through an angle a, what happens to the angle b at the other end ?

lines

Why are the lines dividing the bowling lanes parallel ?

Why are railway lines parallel ?
Why do they not look parallel ?

Parallel lines

What is meant by **parallel** lines ?
Why are railway lines parallel ?
Look about you in the room. What examples of parallel lines can you see ?

Give examples of parallel lines which we see in daily life.

Angles and parallel lines

Draw two parallel lines with a third line crossing them.

Measure the sizes of angles a, b, c, d, e, f, g and h.

Which angles are equal ?

What do you notice about the pair of angles b and c, or f and g ?

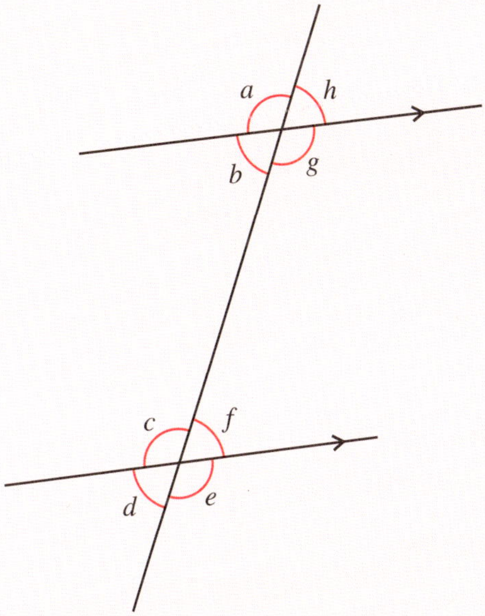

15 Angles and parallel lines

Angles

Calculations with angles

Angles at a point

These add up to 360°.

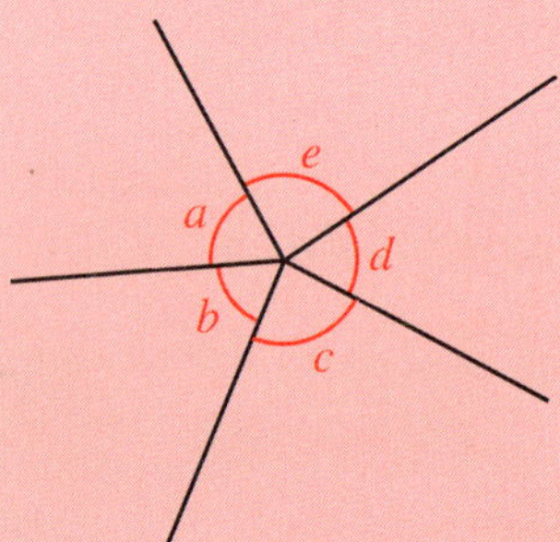

$a + b + c + d + e = 360°$.

Adjacent angles (on a straight line)

These add up to 180°.

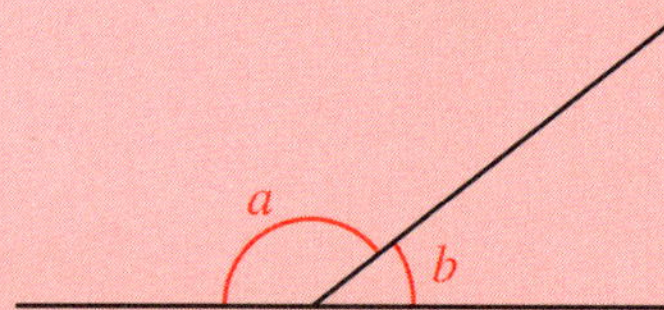

$a + b = 180°$.

Vertically opposite angles

These are equal.

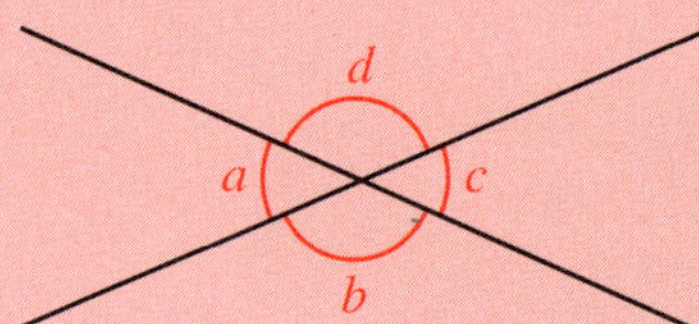

$a = c$
$b = d$

Examples

1 Calculate the size of angle a.

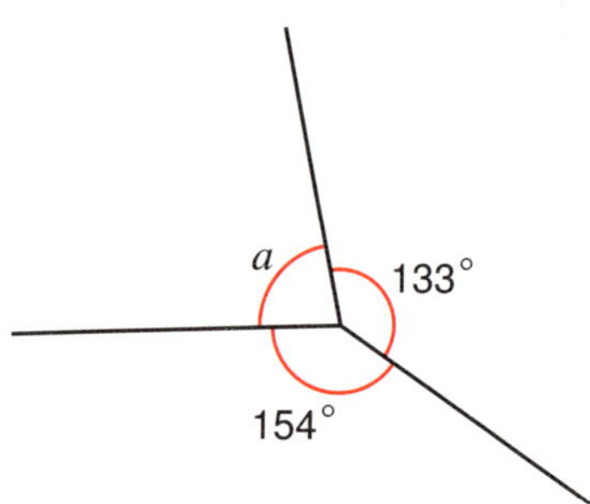

$a + 133° + 154° = 360°$ (angles at a point)

$a = 360° - (133° + 154°)$

$= 360° - 287°$

$= 73°$

2 Calculate the sizes of angles b, c, d.

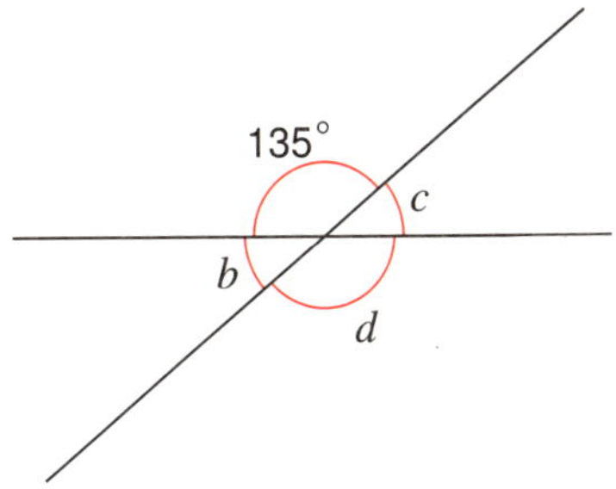

$b + 135° = 180°$ (adjacent angles)

$b = 180° - 135°$

$= 45°$

$c = 45°$ (vertically opposite to b)

$d = 135°$ (vertically opposite to 135°)

Exercise 15.1

Questions 1 to 6.

Find the sizes of the angles marked with small letters, by calculation. The angles are not drawn accurately.

1.

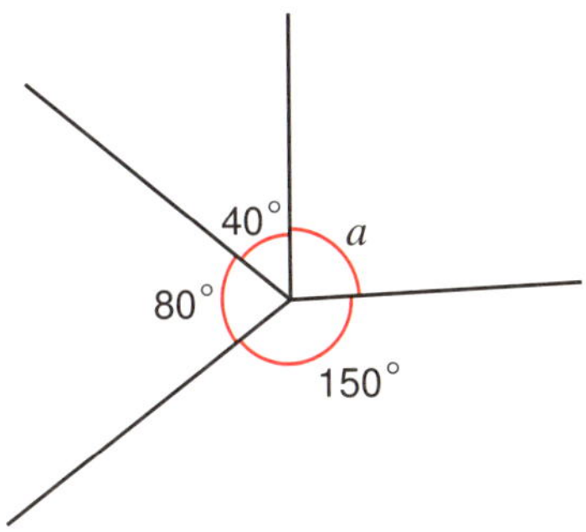

2.

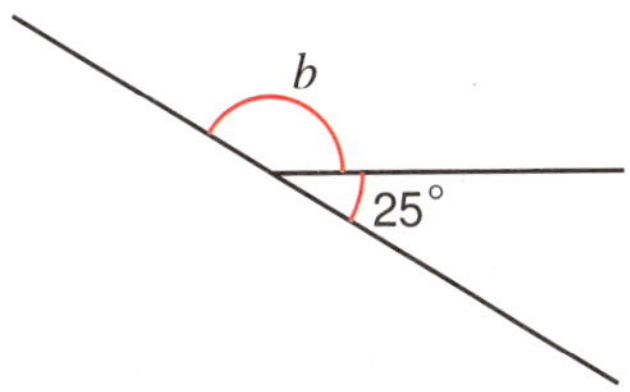

3.

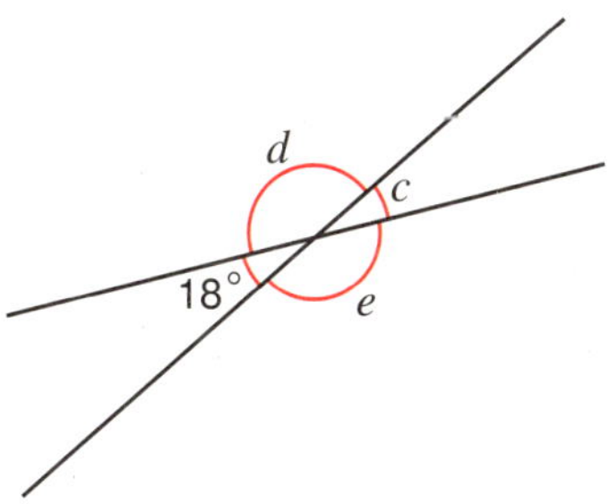

4.

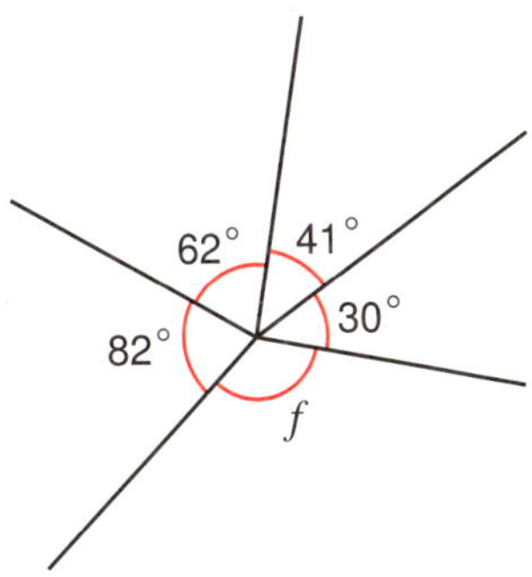

5.

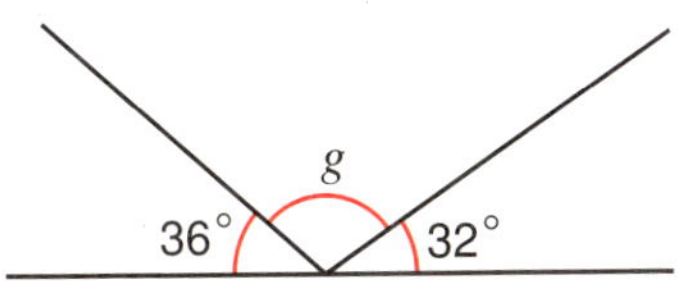

6.

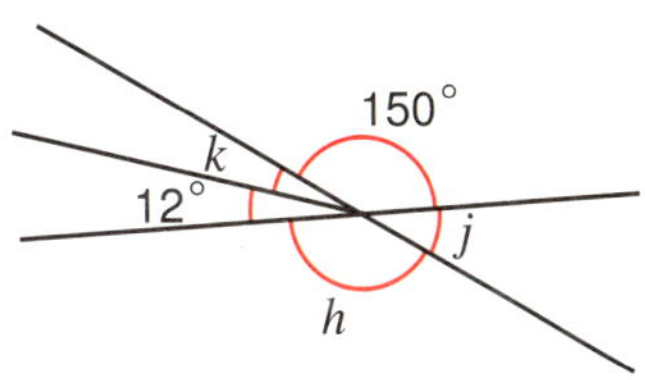

7. The 5 angles in this figure are equal. Find their size.

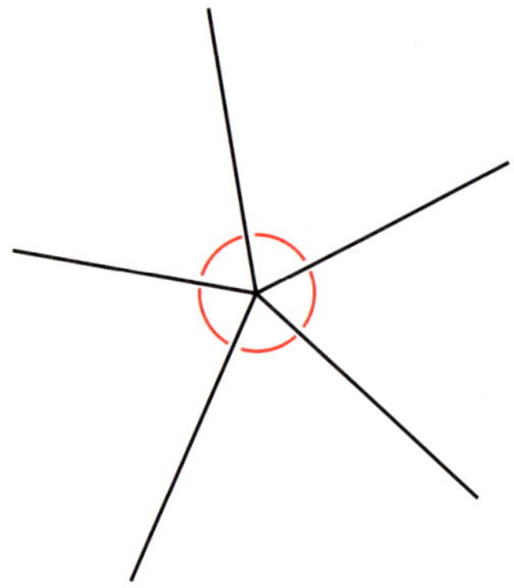

8. The angles k and m are equal. Find their size.

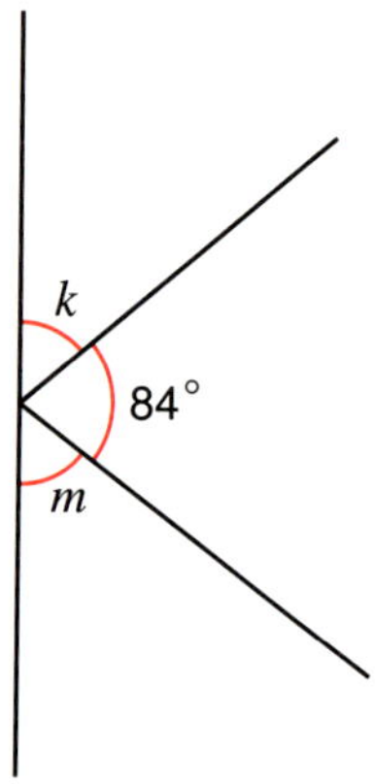

Questions 9 and 10.

In these diagrams measure angle a with your protractor and use your answer to calculate the size of angle b.

9.

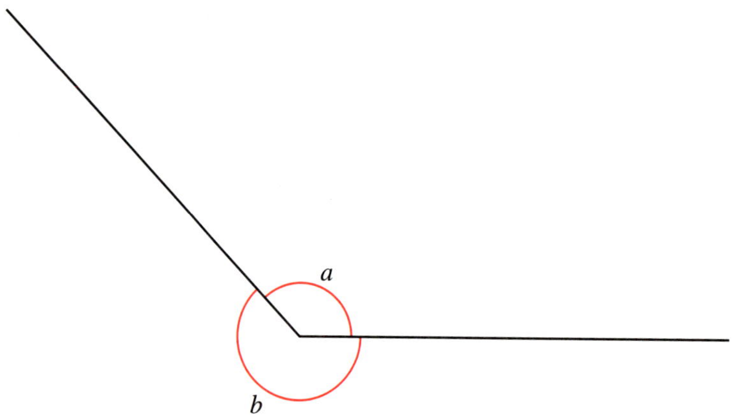

10.

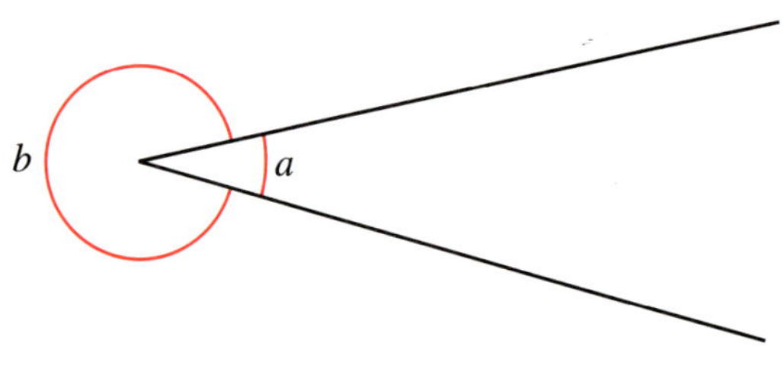

Calculations with angles and parallel lines

Corresponding angles

These are equal.

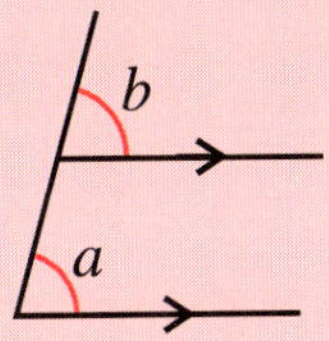

$a = b$

Alternate angles

These are equal.

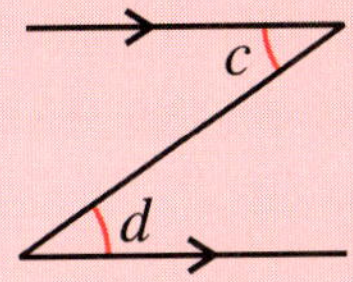

$c = d$

Interior angles

These add up to 180°.

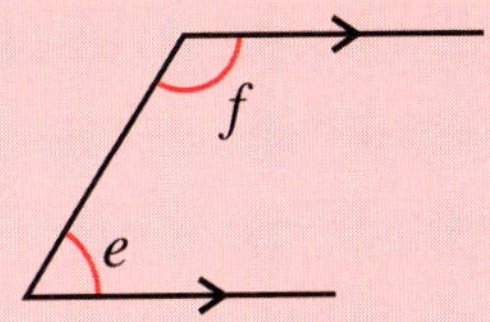

$e + f = 180°$

Example

Calculate the sizes of angles a, b and c.

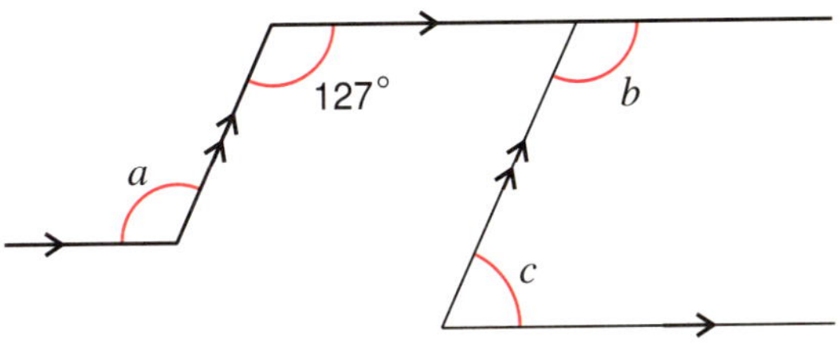

$a = 127°$ (alternate angles)
$b = 127°$ (corresponding angles)
$c = 180° - 127°$ (interior angle to b)
$= 53°$

Exercise 15.2

1. Calculate the sizes of the marked angles.

1

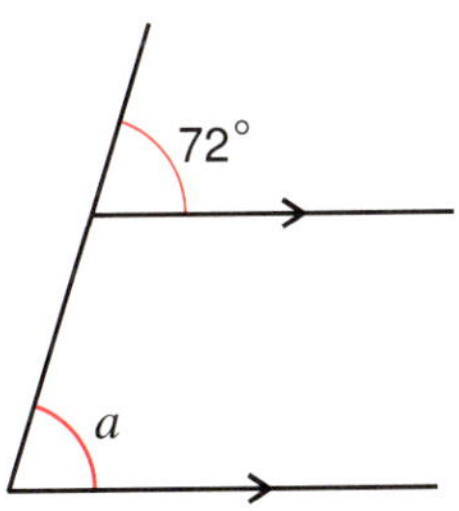

2

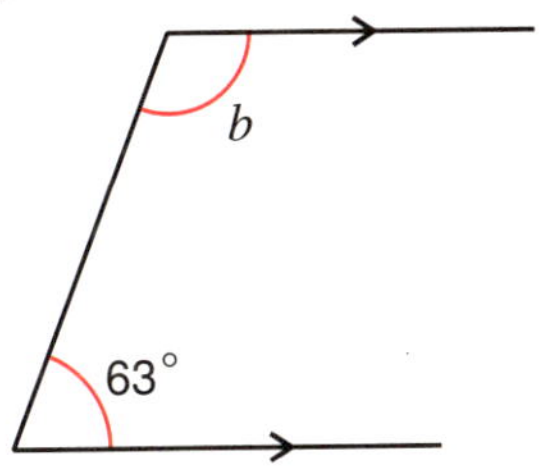

3

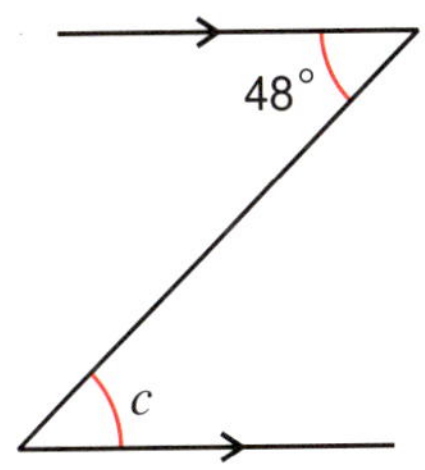

4

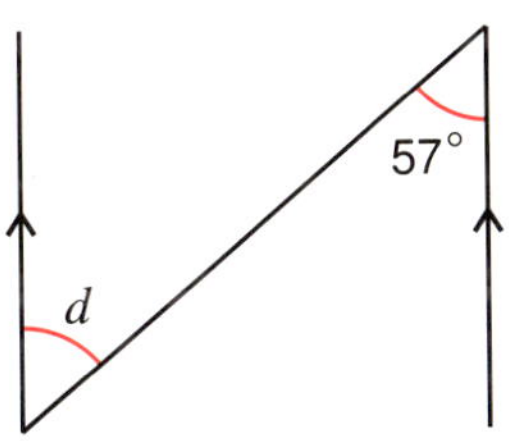

5

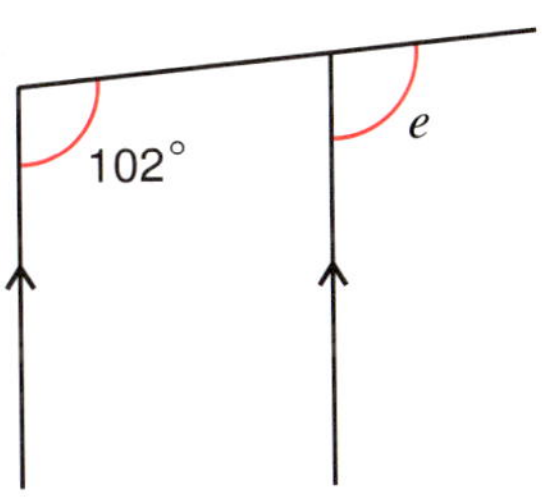

6

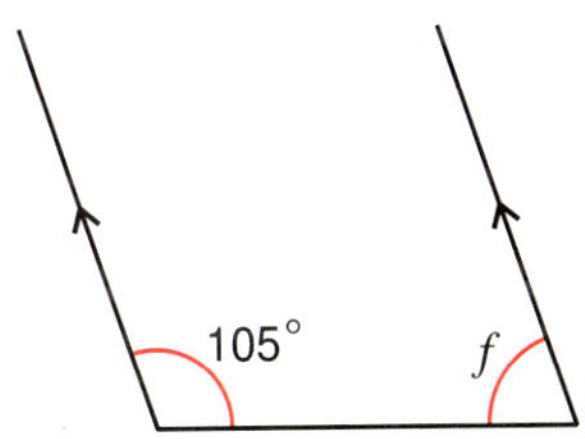

2. Calculate the size of angle a and use your answer to calculate the size of angle b.

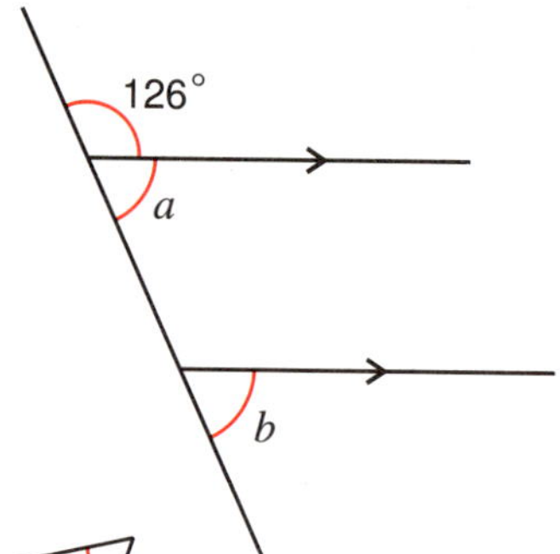

Questions 3 to 10.

Calculate the sizes of the marked angles, giving reasons.

3.

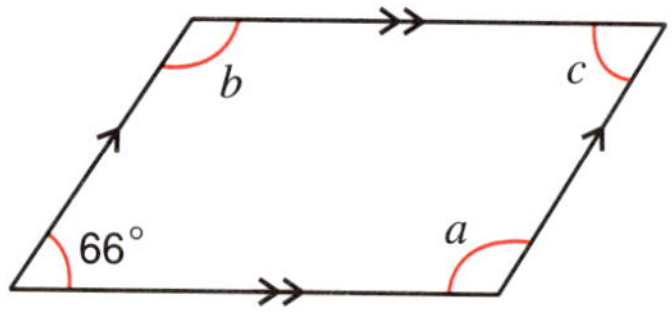

4.

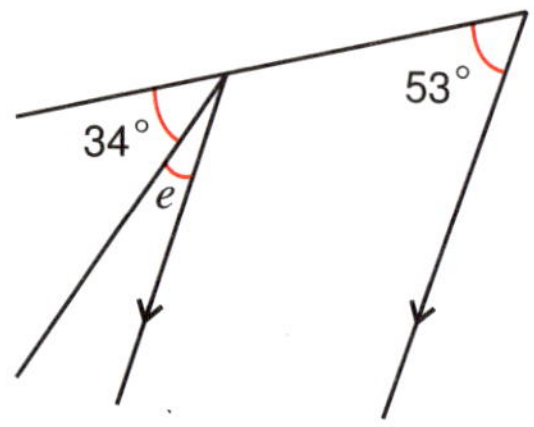

5.

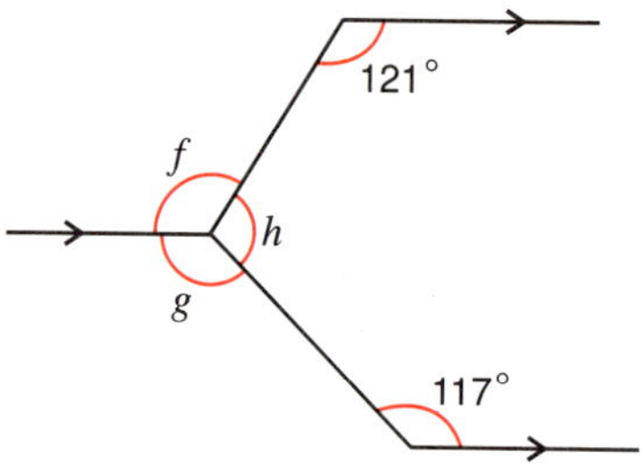

6.

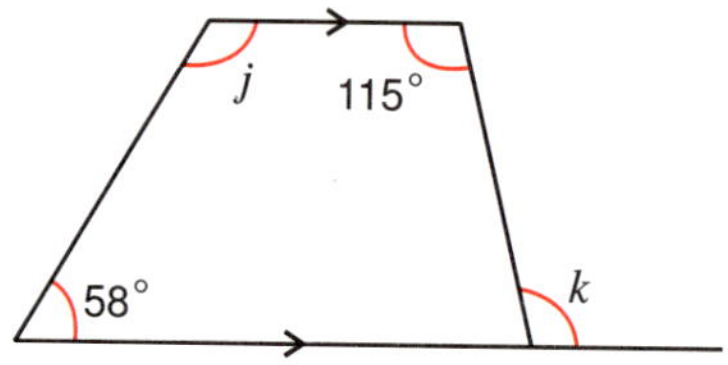

7.

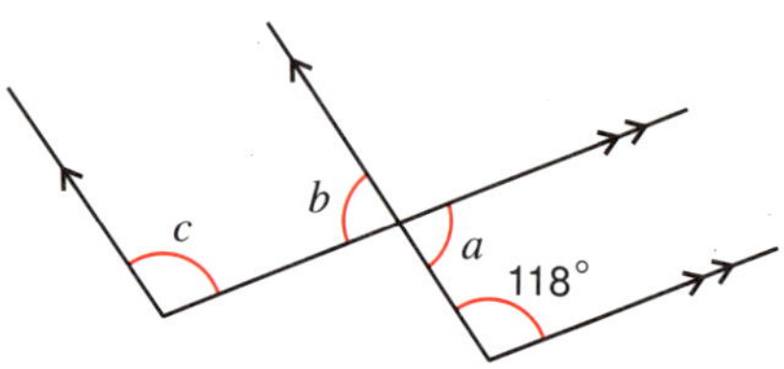

8.

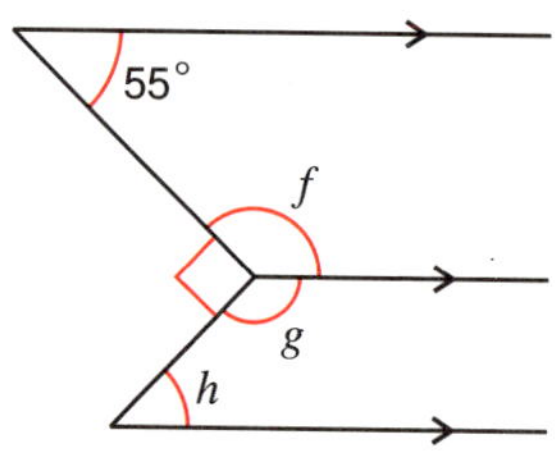

9.

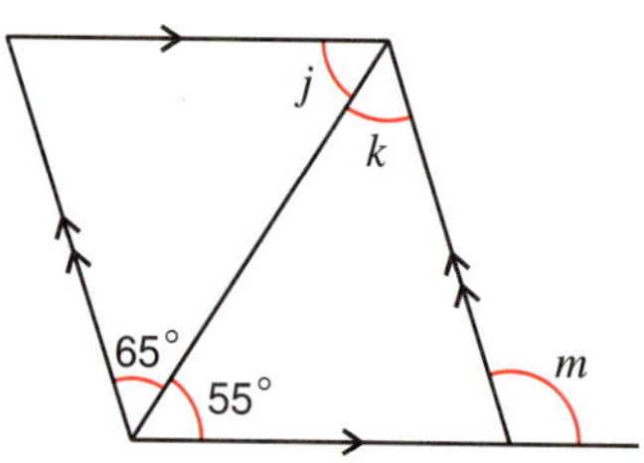

10.

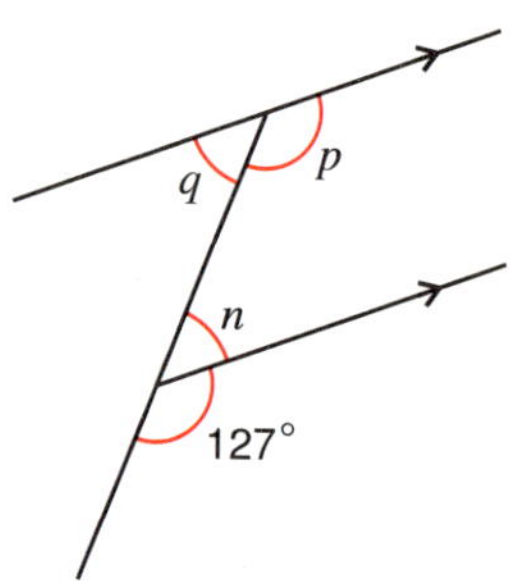

Naming of angles

Sometimes it is not convenient to label angles with small letters.

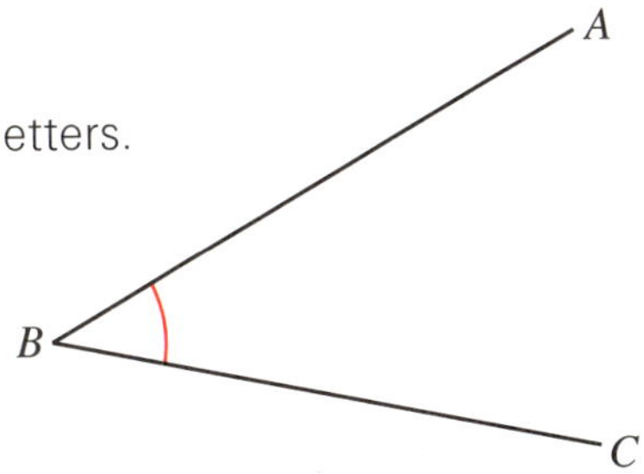

Instead we can label an angle by naming the point where the angle is.
This is angle B, or $\angle B$, because it is at point B.

If there is more than one angle at point B, we need further information.
Here the **marked** angle is called angle ABC, or $\angle ABC$, or $\widehat{ABC}$. It could also be called $\angle CBA$. The middle letter tells us at which point the angle is.
Here it is at B so the middle letter is B.
The other two letters, each with B, tell us the two lines making the angle. Here they are BA and BC.

The unmarked angle is $\angle CBD$ (or $\angle DBC$).
The complete angle is $\angle ABD$ (or $\angle DBA$).

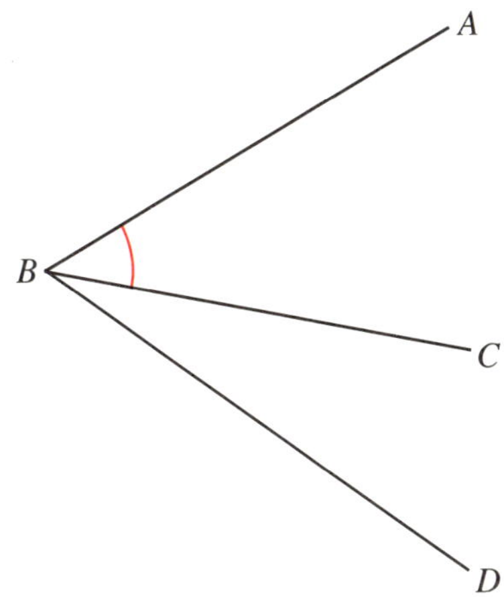

This angle is at F, so the middle letter is F.
The lines are FD and FE, so the angle is $\angle DFE$ (or $\angle EFD$).

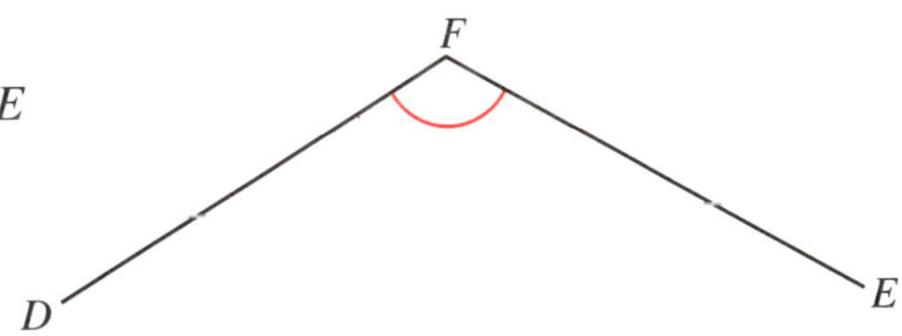

Exercise 15.3

1. Give the small letter names of these angles.
   1 $\angle BAC$ **2** $\angle DCB$ **3** $\angle ADC$

   Name these angles using 3 capital letters.
   4 f **5** d

   6 Name $\angle B$ using 3 letters, in 4 different ways.

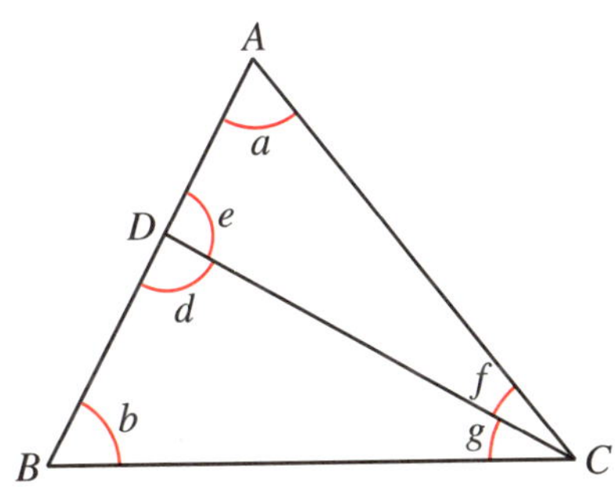

2. In the diagram, the lines AD, BE and CF are parallel.

Find the sizes of

1 $\angle ABE$,

2 $\angle CBE$,

3 $\angle ABC$.

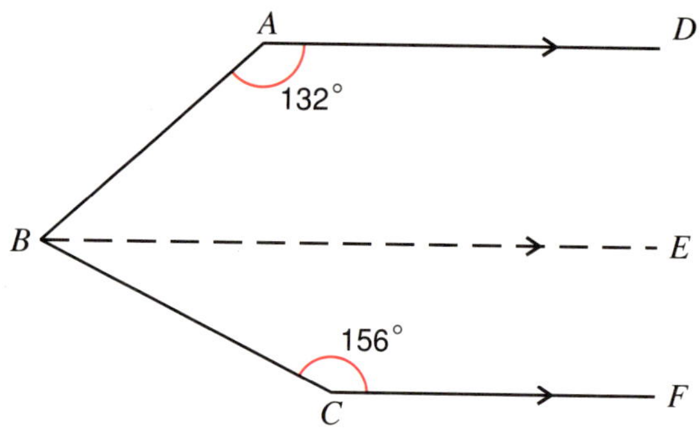

Exercise 15.4 Applications and Activities

1. **Clocks**

1 How long does the hour hand take to make a complete revolution ?

2 Through how many degrees does the hour hand turn in 1 hour ?

3 Through how many degrees does the hour hand turn between 2 pm and 6.30 pm ?

4 What is the size of the obtuse angle between the hands of a clock at 4 pm ?

5 What is the size of the acute angle between the hands of a clock at 4.30 pm ?

6 Through how many degrees does the minute hand of a clock turn in 1 minute ?

7 How many minutes does it take for the minute hand to turn through 150° ?

8 Through how many degrees has the minute hand turned between 8.53 pm and 9.15 pm ?

2. **Angles and symmetry**

In each diagram the dotted line is an axis of symmetry. Decide which angles are equal and then calculate the marked angles.

1

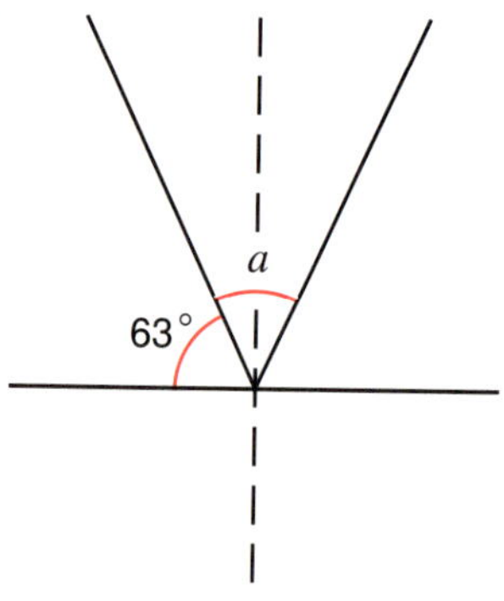

2

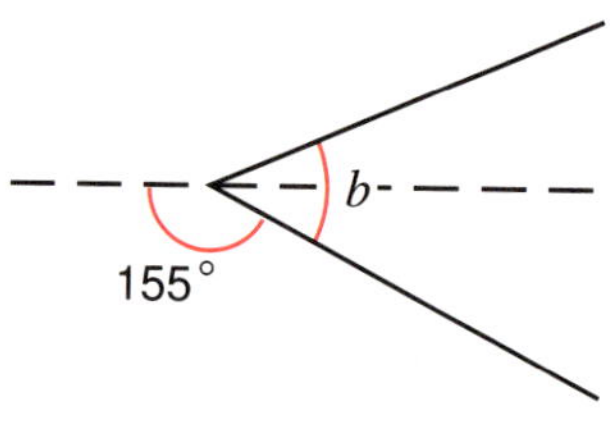

3

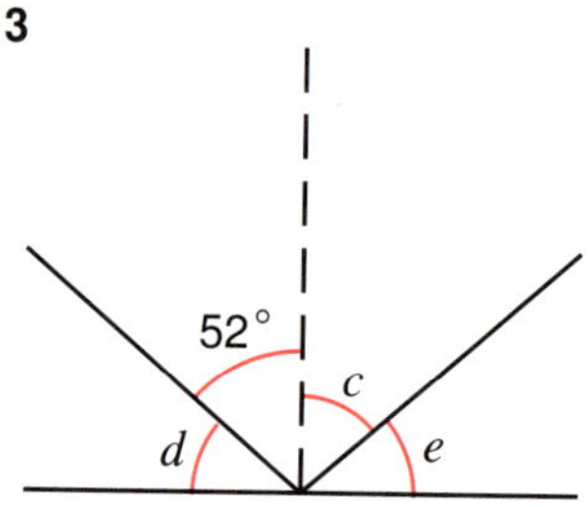

3. **Angles of a triangle**

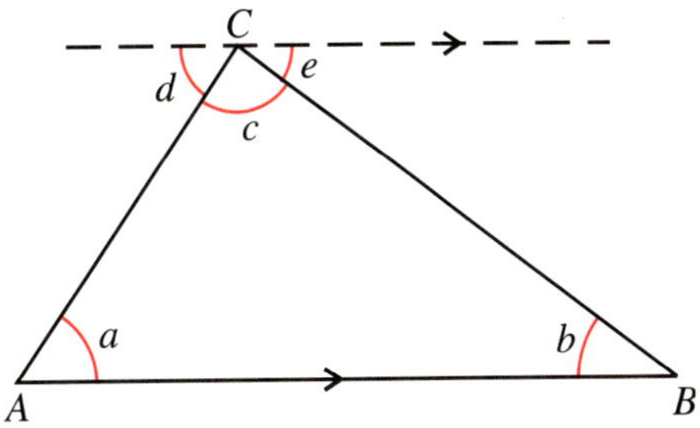

In this diagram the angles of the triangle are a, b, c.
A line parallel to AB is drawn through point C.

What is the sum of the angles $d + c + e$, and why ?
Which angle is equal to d, and why ?
Which angle is equal to e, and why ?
What does this show about the sum of the angles of the triangle, $a + b + c$?

4. **Angles of a parallelogram**

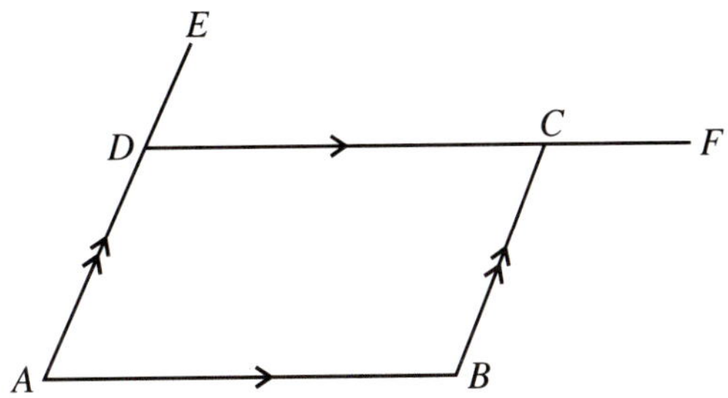

$ABCD$ is a **parallelogram**. That is a 4-sided figure with both pairs of opposite sides parallel.

AD is extended to a point E and DC is extended to a point F.

Name two angles which are equal to $\angle CDE$, and say why they are equal.

Name two angles which are equal to $\angle BCF$, and say why they are equal.

What does this show about the opposite angles of a parallelogram ?

Chapter 15 test

1. **1** If all the angles in the diagram are equal, find the size of angle a.

2 If $a = 80°$ and the other angles are all equal, find their size.

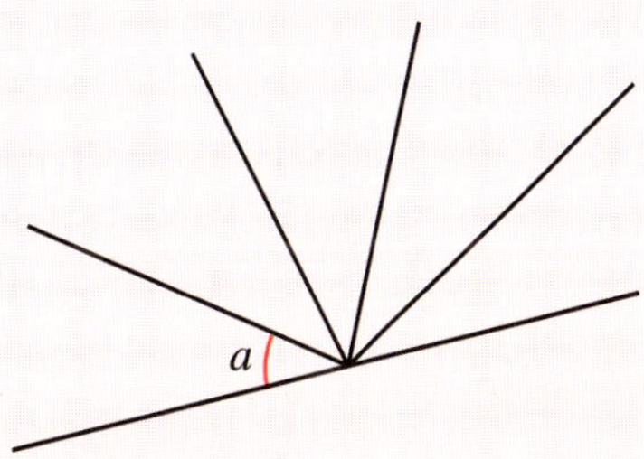

[Turn over]

Questions 2 to 7.

Find the marked angles in these diagrams, giving reasons.
AB and CD are straight lines.

2.

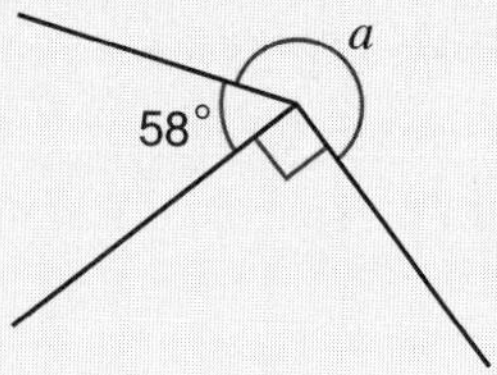

3.

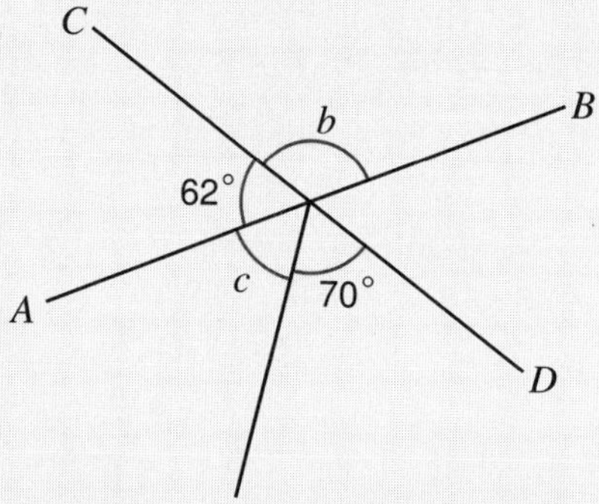

4.

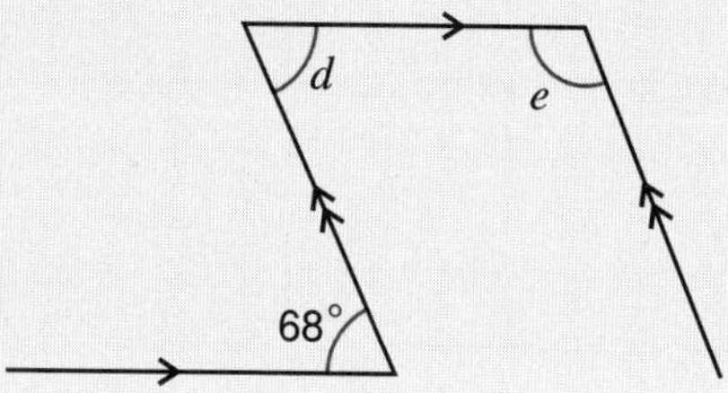

5.

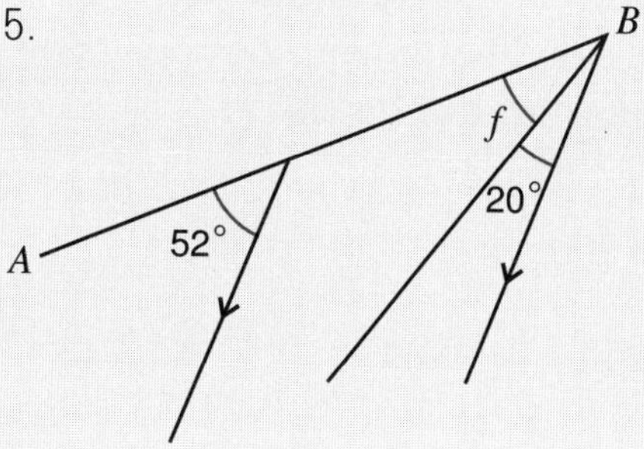

6.

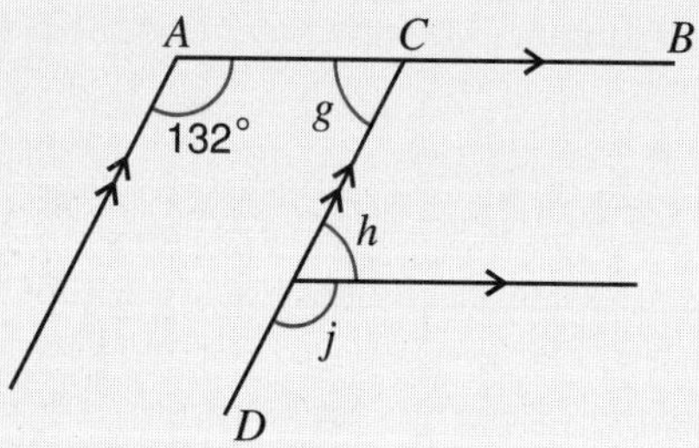

7.

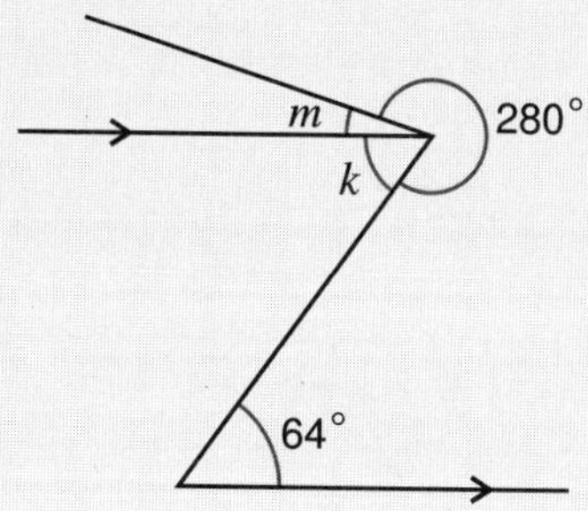

PUZZLES

26. There was a water-lily in a pond. Each day it doubled its size and on the tenth day it completely filled the pond. On which day did it half-fill the pond ?

27. Here is a pattern of triangles. By considering the pattern of numbers, find how many triangles there are in the last two drawings.

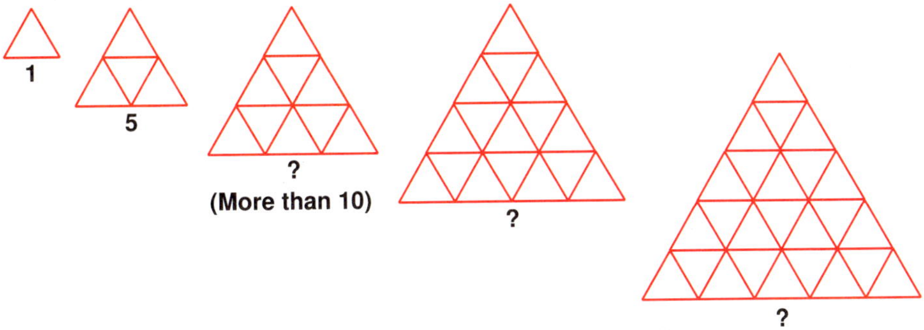

28. Copy the diagram and arrange the 13 letters **A C C E G I L N Q R S T U** in suitable positions in it, so that
the circle contains the letters **C I R C L E**,
the triangle contains the letters **T R I A N G L E**,
and the square contains the letters **S Q U A R E**.

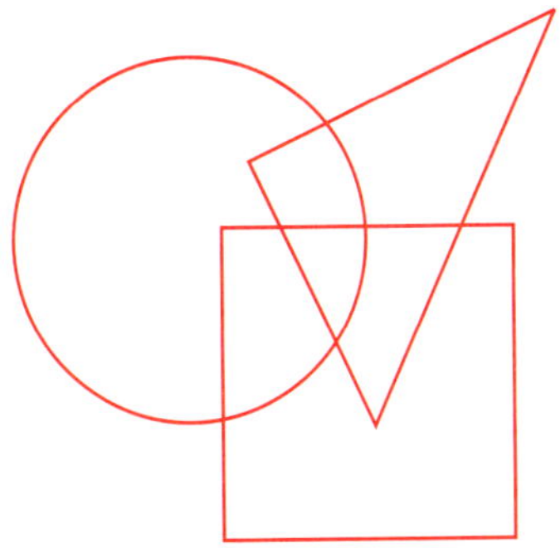

29. **1** What is the next term in the sequence 1, 2, 4, 8, 16 ?

2 A circle is divided into regions, as shown. How many regions are there for the hexagon ?

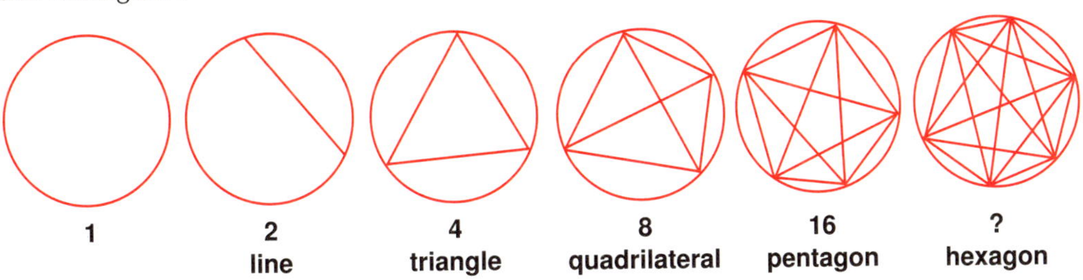

30. A man rode every day to work, on his bicycle. But one day he had a puncture exactly a mile before he reached the factory, and as he did not have a repair outfit with him, and there wasn't one at the factory either, he had to wheel his bicycle the rest of the way to work, and all the way home. How many miles did the man walk **further** than he rode ?

16 Thinking about equations

Equation

Look up the mathematical meaning of the word **equation** in a dictionary. It is derived from the Latin word aequus, meaning 'even'. Find other words beginning with 'equa' or 'equi' which are also related to this word, and write down their meanings.

Simple equations

Try this problem:
A group of people hired a minicoach for a day-out and the organiser worked out that it would cost them £7 each. On the day, 4 extra people turned up so it only cost each of them £5. How many people were there originally ?
Have you solved it ? Check your answer to make sure that it is correct.
Compare your method with those of your friends. How many different methods can you find to solve this problem ?
You do not need to use algebraic equations, but here is one way to solve it, using an equation.
You are trying to find how many people there were originally, so begin by saying 'Let there be x people originally'.
Then, since they had to pay £7 each, the total cost would be £7x.
When 4 extra people turned up, that meant there were $x + 4$ people.
They each paid £5, so the total cost was £5$(x + 4)$.
These two expressions for the total cost are equal, so we can make an equation.
£7x = £5$(x + 4)$
Now we just write down the **numbers** of £'s as they are also equal.
$7x = 5(x + 4)$
The first thing to do with this equation is to work out the brackets.
$7x = 5x + 20$
Now carry on solving the equation. When you have found x, that is the number of people there were originally.
Problems which are solved by simple equations can often be solved instead by other methods. However, you need to practise solving simple equations, so that you can use them when the algebra gets more advanced.
Here is a simple problem:
5 boys share 36p equally among themselves, putting the extra 1p into a charity box. How much do they each get ?
Now if you let each boy get x pence, then you can write down an equation which is $5x + 1 = 36$,
and you can solve it to find x.

Inventing problems

Now can you do some questions the other way round ? Here are the equations. Invent some problems to which they could apply, and then find the solutions.

$2x + 7 = 23$ $\quad 4x + 1 = x + 31$

$7x - 2 = 26$ $\quad \frac{x}{4} + 1 = 10$

$18 - x = x$

Keeping balanced, or else . . . ?

While the marker stays in the centre, the teams are pulling equally.

Chemical equations

Here is an example of an equation in Chemistry

$HCl + NaOH = NaCl + H_2O$

This means

Hydrochloric acid + sodium hydroxide = sodium chloride (salt) + water.

Graphs of equations

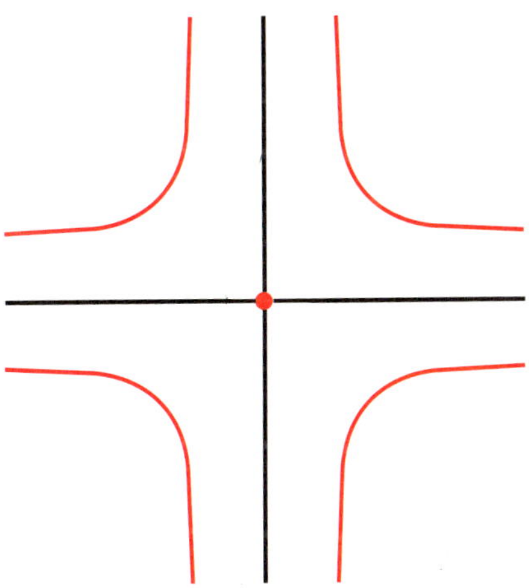

This graph pattern has the equation $x^2y^2 = x^2 + y^2$.

16 Equations

Introduction

1 $x + 3 = 11$ is an **equation**, which we can solve to find the value of x.

Imagine x is a box of unknown weight, on one side of balanced weighing scales together with a weight of 3 units. On the other side is a weight of 11 units.

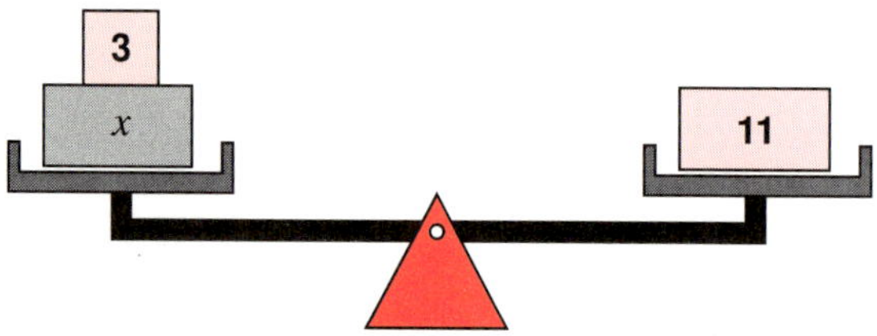

Now the scales will still be balanced if we take 3 units off **both sides**.

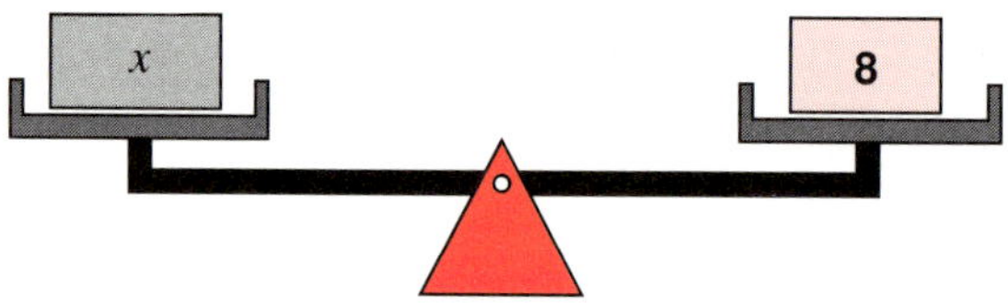

So $x = 8$ units.

This is the method of solving algebraic equations. We deal with both sides equally and the equation will still balance.
Set down the working as shown later (example **1** on page 257).

2 Here is another example worked out on the weighing scales.

$x - 7 = 16$

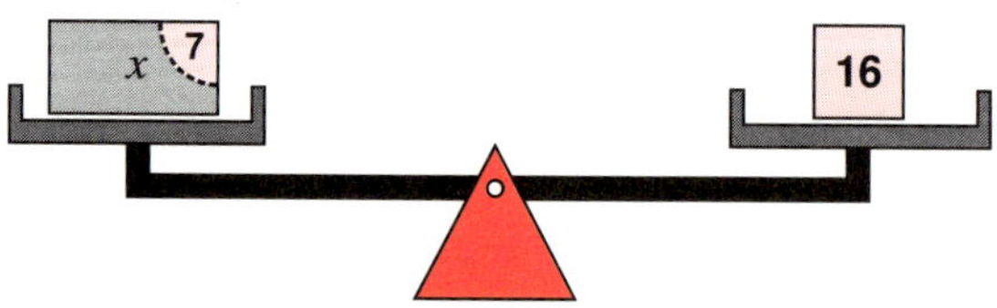

On one side we have a box of unknown weight x with a piece of weight 7 units missing from it. This represents $x - 7$. On the other side balancing it there is a weight of 16 units.

We must fill up the hole where the 7 units is missing so **add** 7 units to both sides.

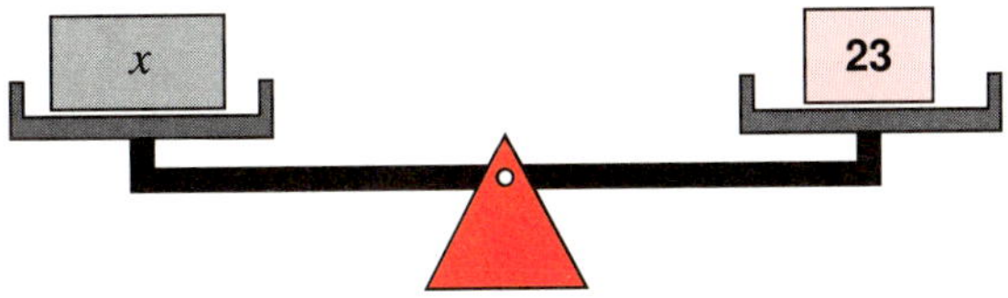

So $x = 23$ units.
The working is shown set down in example **2** on page 257.

Here are two more examples using the weighing scales.

3 $5x = 15$

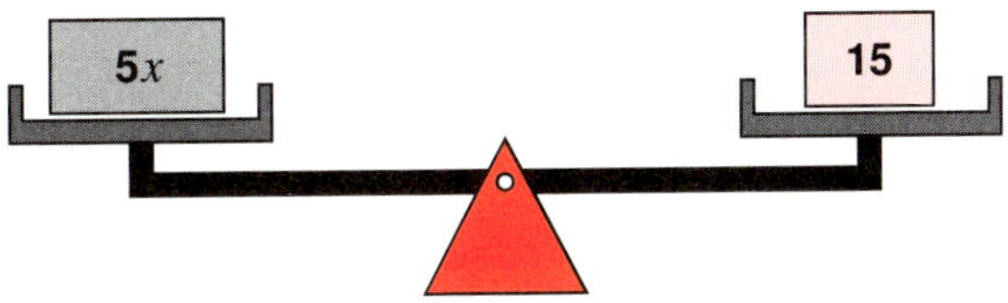

On one side we have a box of unknown weight $5x$ balanced by a weight of 15 units on the other side.
Make $5x$ into 5 separate boxes of x units each.

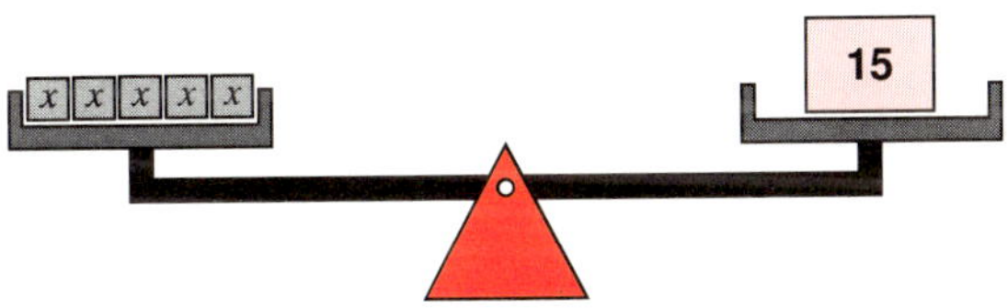

Now by dividing by 5 we leave just one weight of x units on.
It will be balanced if we divide 15 by 5, leaving 3 units on the other side.

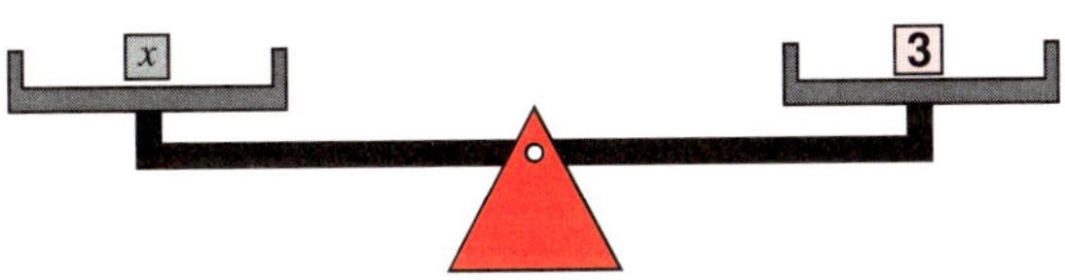

So $x = 3$ units.
The working is shown set down in example **3** on page 257.

4 $\frac{1}{3}x = 8$

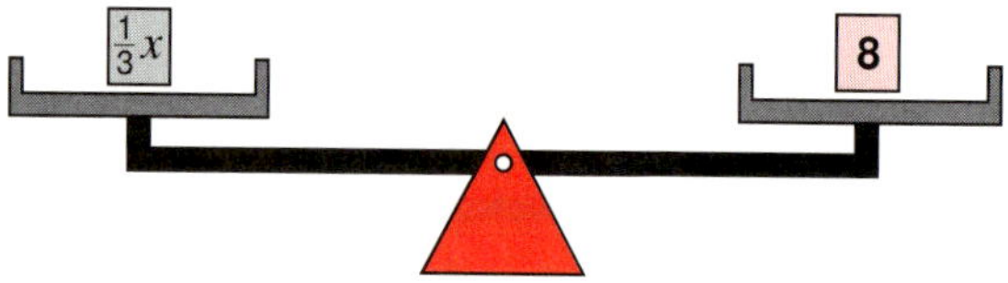

On one side we have a box of unknown weight $\frac{1}{3}x$ balanced by a weight of 8 units on the other side.
Now by multiplying by 3 we make $\frac{1}{3}x$ into x. The weight of x will be balanced if we multiply 8 by 3, giving 24 units on the other side.

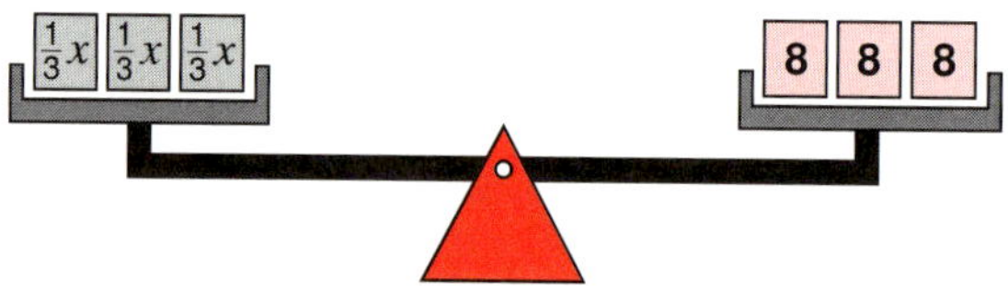

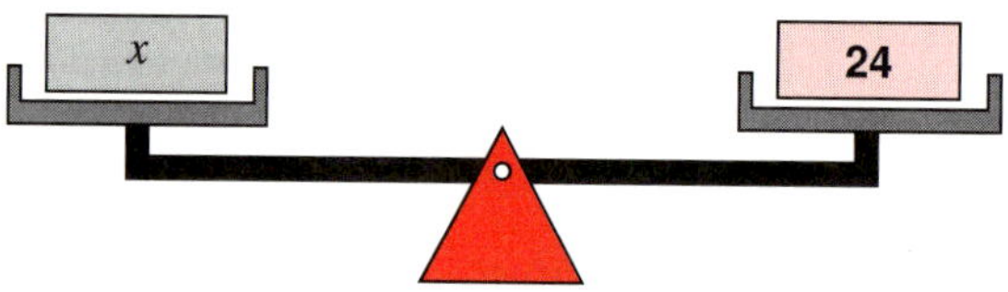

So $x = 24$ units.
The working is shown set down in example **4** on page 257.

Exercise 16.1

1. **1** Write down the equation shown by the weighing scales.
   2 Solve the equation.

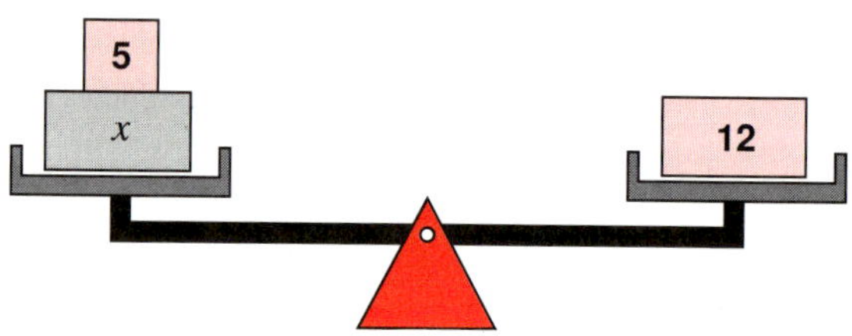

Questions 2 to 10.

Use weighing scales to solve each equation.

2. $4x = 16$
3. $x - 5 = 10$
4. $\frac{1}{2}x = 10$
5. $x + 9 = 18$
6. $3x = 33$
7. $\frac{1}{4}x = 4$
8. $x - 6 = 2$
9. $x + 1 = 15$
10. $7x = 28$

Solving equations

The sides of an equation still remain equal if
1 equal numbers are added to both sides,
2 equal numbers are subtracted from both sides,
3 both sides are multiplied by the same number,
4 both sides are divided by the same number.

Here are the examples **1** to **4** shown earlier, this time written down and solved without using the weighing scales.

1 $x + 3 = 11$
Subtract 3 from both sides.
$x = 8$

2 $x - 7 = 16$
Add 7 to both sides.
$x = 23$

3 $5x = 15$
Divide both sides by 5.
$x = 3$

4 $\frac{1}{3}x = 8$
Multiply both sides by 3.
$x = 24$

Exercise 16.2

1. Solve these equations

1 $x + 12 = 17$
2 $x - 4 = 8$
3 $5x = 40$
4 $\frac{1}{3}x = 5$
5 $x - 6 = 0$
6 $x + 8 = 20$
7 $7x = 42$
8 $x - 16 = 3$
9 $x + 12 = 22$
10 $\frac{1}{9}x = 1$
11 $15 + x = 21$
12 $11x = 121$
13 $12x = 12$
14 $\frac{x}{3} = 6$
15 $5x = 0$
16 $8x = 4$
17 $x + 7 = 7$
18 $16 = 2 + x$
19 $4x = 18$
20 $x - 9 = 0$

2. In the formula $A = 3b$, find the value of b when $A = 21$.

3. In the formula $t = c + d$, find the value of c when $t = 12$ and $d = 5$.

4. In the formula $m = \frac{s}{100}$, find the value of s when $m = 2$.

5. In the formula $k = 2m + n$, find the value of n when $k = 16$ and $m = 3$.

Further examples

5 Here is another example worked out on the weighing scales.
Solve $13x - 20 = 6$.

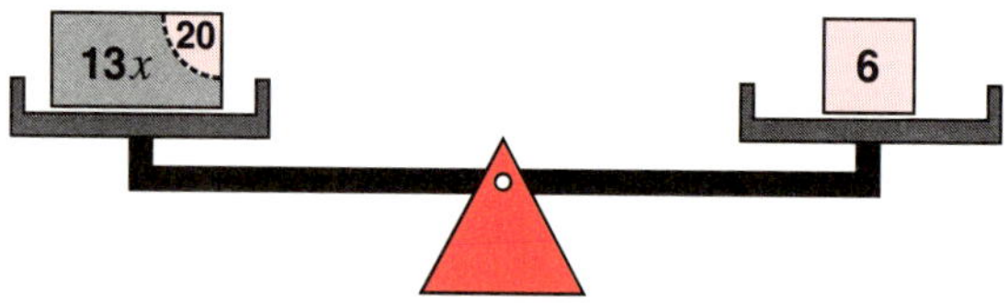

On one side we have a box of unknown weight $13x$ with a piece of weight 20 units missing from it. This represents $13x - 20$. On the other side balancing it there is a weight of 6 units.

The first thing to do is to fill up the hole where the 20 units is missing so **add** 20 units to both sides.

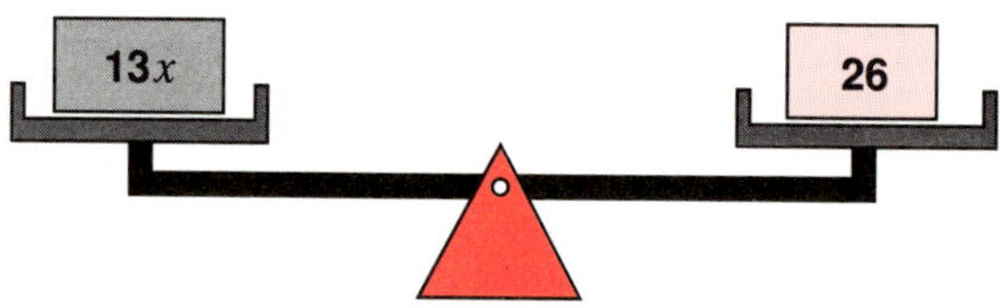

Now we have the unknown weight $13x$ balanced by a weight of 26.
Make $13x$ into 13 separate boxes of weight x units each.

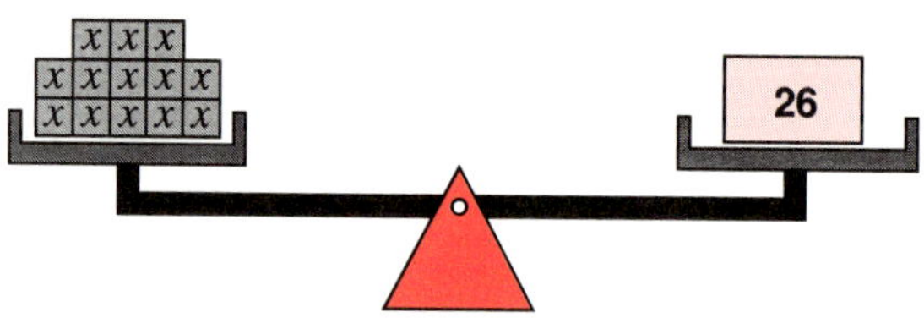

Now by dividing by 13 we leave just one weight of x units on. It will be balanced if we divide 26 by 13, leaving 2 units on the other side.

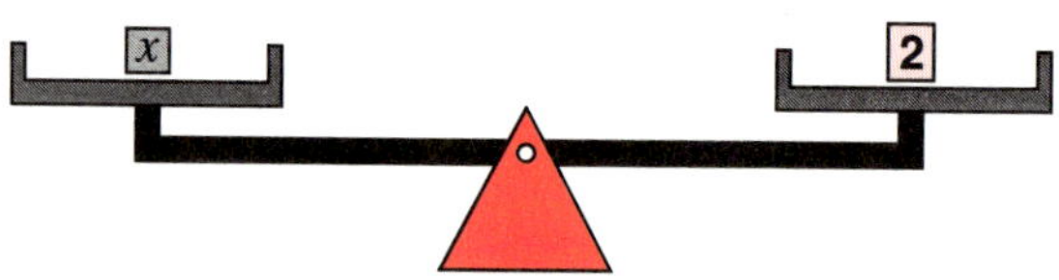

So $x = 2$ units.
The working is shown set down in example **5** on page 261.

6 Here is another example.
Solve $11x = 4x + 28$.

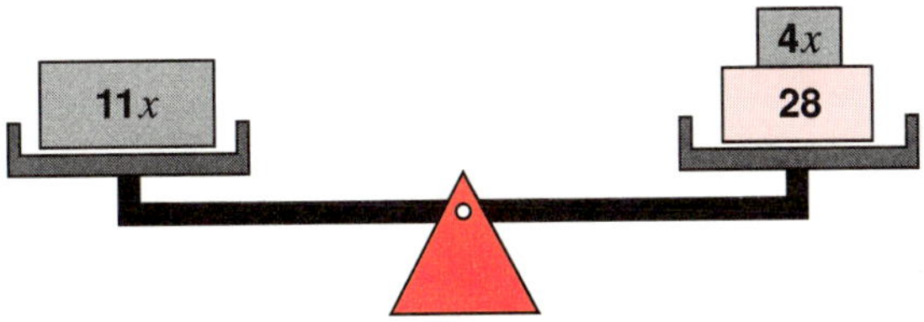

On one side we have a box of unknown weight $11x$ and on the other side balancing it we have a box of weight $4x$ and a box of 28 units.

The scales will still be balanced if we take $4x$ units from both sides.

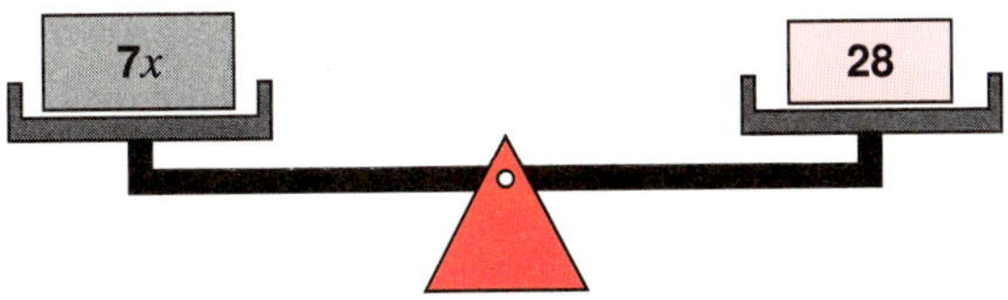

Now we have $7x$ balanced by a weight of 28.
By dividing by 7 we leave just one weight of x on one side of the scales.
It will be balanced if we divide 28 by 7, leaving 4 units on the other side.

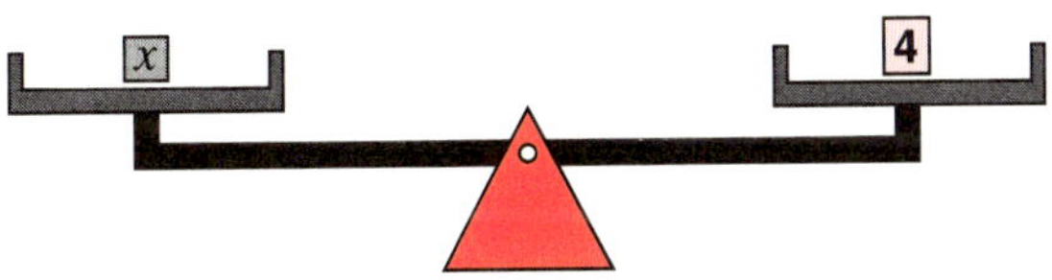

So $x = 4$ units.
The working is shown set down in example **6** on page 262.

7 Here is one more example using the weighing scales.
Solve $7x + 4 = 40 - 5x$.

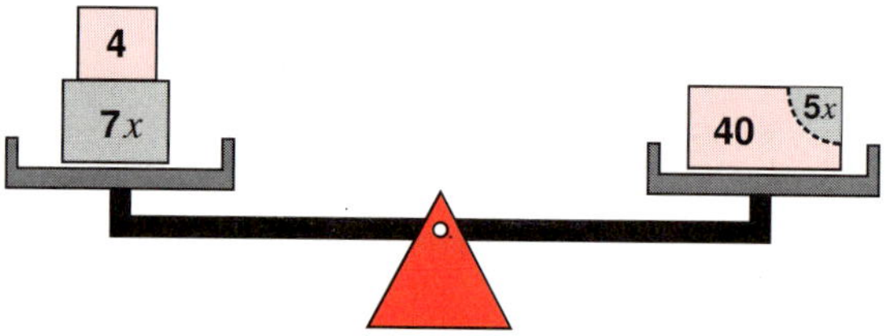

On one side of the scales we have an unknown weight $7x$ and also 4 units. This represents $7x + 4$. On the other side there is a weight of 40 units with a piece of weight $5x$ missing from it. This represents $40 - 5x$.

We can fill up the hole where the $5x$ units is missing, by adding $5x$ to both sides.

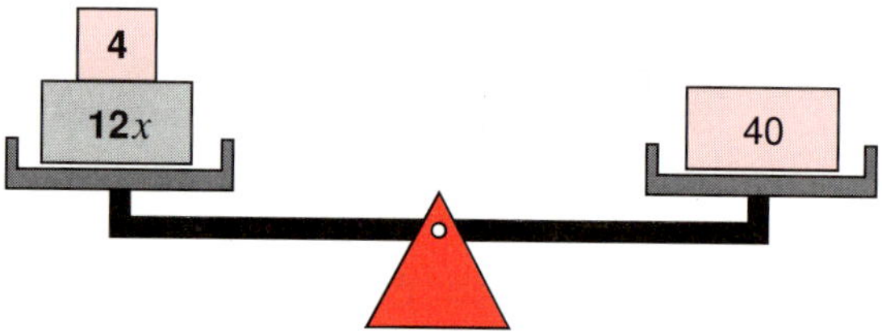

Now we can subtract 4 units from both sides. (It would not have affected the result if we had done this first.)

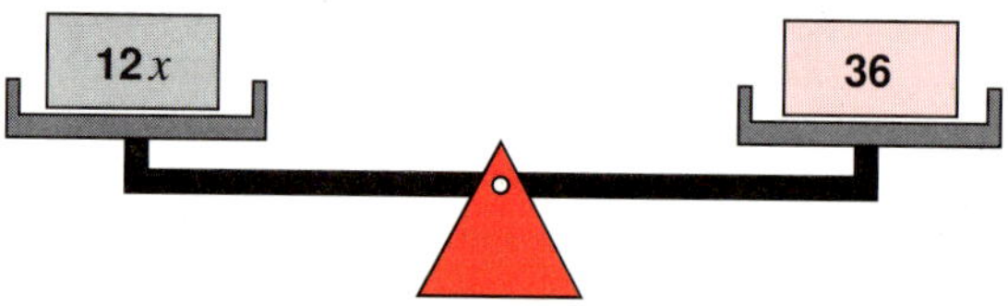

Next we can split the $12x$ weight into 12 weights of x units each, and then divide both sides by 12 to leave just one weight of x on one side, and 3 on the other.

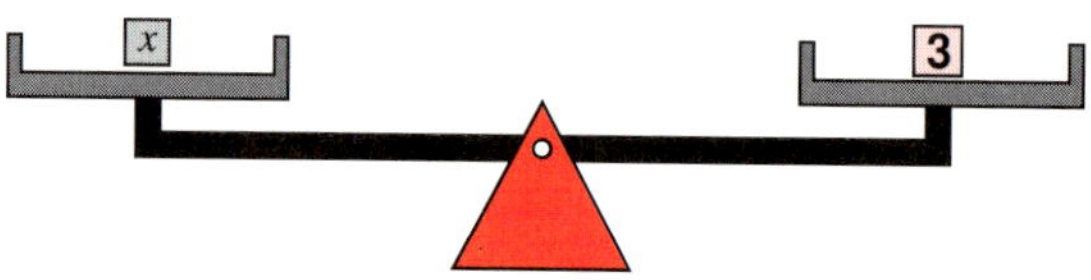

So $x = 3$ units.
The working is shown set down in example **7** on page 262.

Exercise 16.3

1\. **1** Write down the equation shown by the weighing scales.
2 Solve the equation.

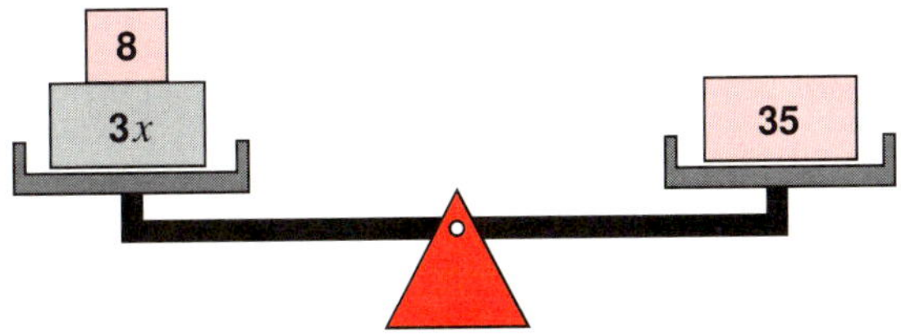

Questions 2 to 10.

Use weighing scales to solve each equation.

2\. $2x - 3 = 21$
3\. $4x = x + 9$
4\. $5x + 1 = 21$
5\. $3x = 2x + 10$
6\. $4x - 5 = 19$
7\. $3x + 5 = x + 11$
8\. $5x - 3 = 3x + 7$
9\. $4x + 6 = 2x + 14$
10\. $4x - 9 = 3x + 13$

Remember:
we can add equal numbers to both sides,
we can subtract equal numbers from both sides,
we can multiply both sides by the same number,
we can divide both sides by the same number,
and the sides still remain equal.

Here are the examples **5**, **6** and **7** shown earlier, this time written down and solved without using the weighing scales.
Also shown is the method for **checking** that the solution to the equation is correct.

5 $13x - 20 = 6$

Add 20 to both sides.
$13x = 26$
Divide both sides by 13.
$x = 2$

To check this equation, substitute $x = 2$ into the left-hand side of the equation.
Left-hand side (LHS) $= 13x - 20 = (13 \times 2) - 20 = 26 - 20 = 6$
Right-hand side (RHS) $= 6$
The two sides are equal, both 6, so the equation checks.

6 $11x = 4x + 28$

Subtract $4x$ from both sides.

$7x = 28$

Divide both sides by 7.

$x = 4$

To check this equation, substitute $x = 4$ into both sides of the equation separately.
LHS $= 11x = 11 \times 4 = 44$
RHS $= 4x + 28 = (4 \times 4) + 28 = 16 + 28 = 44$
The two sides are equal, both 44, so the equation checks.

7 $7x + 4 = 40 - 5x$

Add $5x$ to both sides.

$12x + 4 = 40$

Subtract 4 from both sides.

$12x = 36$

Divide both sides by 12.

$x = 3$

To check this equation, substitute $x = 3$ into both sides of the equation separately.
LHS $= 7x + 4 = (7 \times 3) + 4 = 21 + 4 = 25$
RHS $= 40 - 5x = 40 - (5 \times 3) = 40 - 15 = 25$
The two sides are equal, both 25, so the equation checks.

Exercise 16.4

1. Solve these equations.

1 $3x + 2 = 20$
2 $5x - 7 = 3$
3 $4x - 1 = 19$
4 $7 + 3x = 67$
5 $6x + 15 = 9x$
6 $8x + 6 = 38$
7 $4x + 6 = 50$
8 $3x - 1 = 5$
9 $9x - 16 = 11$
10 $5x + 2 = 37$

Questions 2, 3 and 4.

Solve the equations and then check your answers.

2.
1 $4x = x + 30$
2 $2x + 1 = 15$
3 $2x + 9 = 5x$
4 $6x + 12 = 12$
5 $3x = 5 - 2x$
6 $6x = 15 + x$
7 $12 - x = 4$
8 $15 - 2x = 13$
9 $4x + 3x = 63$
10 $20 = 21 - x$

3.
1 $3x + 1 = 2x + 7$
2 $3x + 18 = 5x + 12$
3 $2x + 7 = 5x - 11$
4 $3x - 5 = x + 3$
5 $4x - 4 = 3x + 5$
6 $3x + 7 = x + 29$
7 $10x + 3 = 4x + 45$
8 $19 + 4x = 3 + 12x$
9 $2x - 4 = 5x - 40$
10 $10x + 1 = 7x + 25$

4.
1 $7x - 11 = 13 - 5x$
2 $20 - x = 2x - 7$
3 $15 - x = 21 - 2x$
4 $5 - x = 11 - 3x$
5 $3x + 7 = 7 - x$
6 $10x - 1 = 6x + 15$
7 $13x - 20 = 8x$
8 $3x - 12 = 0$
9 $3x + 6 = 9x$
10 $15x + 5 + 6x = 47$

5. In the formula $P = 2l + 2b$, find the value of b when $P = 30$ and $l = 7$.

6. In the formula $C = 5n - 7$, find the value of n when $C = 33$.

7. In the formula $S = 2x^2 + 4xh$, find the value of h when $S = 110$ and $x = 5$.

8. For what value of x is the value of the expression $4x - 3$ equal to the value of the expression $x + 12$?

9. If $5x + 6y = 64$,
1 what is the value of x when $y = 4$,
2 what is the value of y when $x = 2$?

Using equations to solve problems

Examples

1 I think of a number, multiply it by 8 then subtract 5 and the answer is 51. What was the original number ?

Let the original number be x.
Then multiplying by 8 gives $8x$.
Subtracting 5 gives $8x - 5$.

So $8x - 5 = 51$.
Add 5 to both sides.
$$8x = 56$$
Divide both sides by 8.
$$x = 7$$

You can check the solution in the problem. I think of the number 7, multiply by 8 getting 56, then subtract 5 getting 51.

2 Stephen has a certain sum of money, Barry has £10 more than Stephen, and Tim has twice as much as Stephen. If together the three boys have £82, how much has each boy ?

Let Stephen have £s.
Then Barry has £$(s + 10)$,
and Tim has £$2s$.
Together they have £$(s + s + 10 + 2s)$, which simplified is £$(4s + 10)$.

So £$(4s + 10)$ = £82
$4s + 10 = 82$ (using the numbers)
Subtract 10 from both sides.
$$4s = 72$$
Divide both sides by 4.
$$s = 18$$
Then $s + 10 = 28$,
and $2s = 36$.
So Stephen has £18, Barry has £28 and Tim has £36.

You can check the solution in the problem.
Barry has £10 more than Stephen, and Tim has twice as much as Stephen.
Together the three boys have £18 + £28 + £36, which equals £82.
So the answer is correct.

Exercise 16.5

Find the answers to these problems by making equations and solving them.

1. I think of a number, multiply it by 4 and add 5. The result is 41. What was the original number ?
(Let the original number be x.)

2. The result of dividing a certain number by 4 and then adding 9 is 11. What is the number ?

3. Julia had a certain number of apples, and when she was given 20 more she had three times as many as at first. How many apples did she have at first ?

4. £70 is divided between Mr Bamber and Mr Craig, so that Mr Bamber receives £18 more than Mr Craig. Find how much each man gets.

5. Rhona and Sally have £49 between them. If Rhona has six times as much as Sally, how much has each girl ?

6. The sum of 3 consecutive numbers is 54. What are the numbers ?
(Let the smallest number be x, then the other two numbers are $x+1$ and $x+2$.)

7. Wayne bought 2 similar toy cars and a toy tractor. The tractor cost 50 pence more than a car and together the three toys cost £2.75 (275 pence). Find the cost of a car, and of the tractor.
(Let a car cost x pence. How much will the tractor cost ? How much will the 3 toys cost altogether ?)

8. In a collecting box there were x 5p coins and three times as many 2p coins. Together the collection totalled £2.86. How many of each kind of coin were there ?
(How many 2p coins were there, and what were they worth ?)

9. A rectangular lawn is three times as long as it is wide. Its perimeter is 56 m. What are its length and its breadth ?
(Let its breadth be b metres.)

10. I think of a number and subtract it from 90. The result is the same as if I multiply the original number by 5 and add 18. What is the original number ?

Further examples of problems

3 Rachel's father was 22 years old when Rachel was born. Now he is three times as old as Rachel. How old is Rachel now ?

Let Rachel be x years old now.
Then her father is $(22 + x)$ years old.
Father's age $= 3 \times$ (Rachel's age).

So $22 + x = 3x$.
Subtract x from both sides.
$22 = 2x$
Divide both sides by 2.
$11 = x$
Rachel is 11 years old (and her father is 33 years old).

You can check the solution in the problem.
If Rachel is 11 years old and her father was 22 years old when she was born, then her father will be 33 years old now. This is three times as old as Rachel, so the answer is correct.

4 Here is a geometry question which can be solved by making an equation.

Write down an equation and solve it to find the value of x.

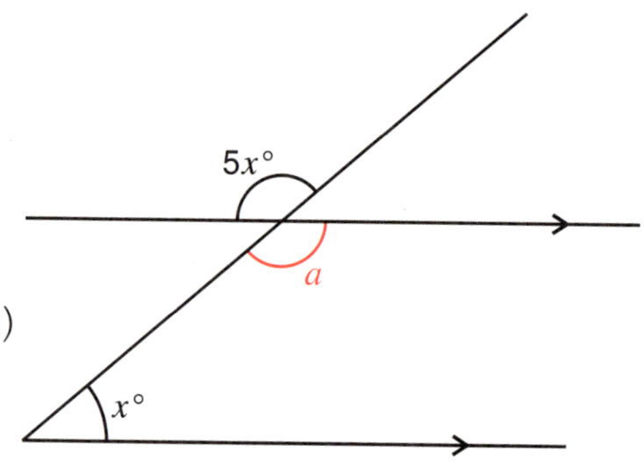

angle $a = 5x°$ (vertically opposite angles)
angle $a = 180° - x°$ (interior angles)

So $5x° = 180° - x°$
$5x = 180 - x$ (using the numbers and leaving out degrees)
Add x to both sides.
$6x = 180$
Divide both sides by 6.
$x = 30$

Exercise 16.6 Applications and Activities

Further problems

1. I think of a number, multiply it by 3 and add 4. The result is 16 less than five times the original number. What was the original number ?

2. Of three painted rods, the red one is twice as long as the blue one, and the yellow one is 5 cm longer than the blue one. The total length of the three rods is 93 cm. Find the length of each rod.

3. In 20 years time Rajesh will be three times as old as he is now. How old is he now ? (Let Rajesh be r years old now.)

4. A carpet seller has a roll of carpet, x metres long, costing £20 per metre. What is its total cost ?
He has a roll of more expensive carpet, which is 12 metres longer than the first roll. Find an expression for its length, in terms of x, and an expression for its cost, if it costs £30 per metre.
The two rolls together are worth £1860. Form an equation in x, and solve it to find x.
How many metres are there in each roll ?

5. Mrs Collins and her two boys together with Mrs Davies and her daughter went together to an adventure park. The total price for admission was £11.20, the three children each being charged half-price. If the cost for a child was x pence, what was the cost for an adult ? In terms of x, what was the total cost for the five people ?
Write down an equation and solve it to find x.
How much was the admission price for an adult ?

6. An exhibition organiser employs 30 temporary workers for a day's work.
He pays x of them £25 each. What is the total amount paid to this group ?
The rest of the workers are paid £20 each. How many workers are there in this group, and what is their total wage ?
If altogether the wages total £630, form an equation in x, and solve it.
How many workers were paid £25 for the day ?

7. A purse contains 24 coins of which some are 10p coins and the rest are 50p coins. Their total value is £8.00. How many 10p coins are there ?

8. Use angle properties to write down an equation involving x and hence find the value of x in these figures.

1

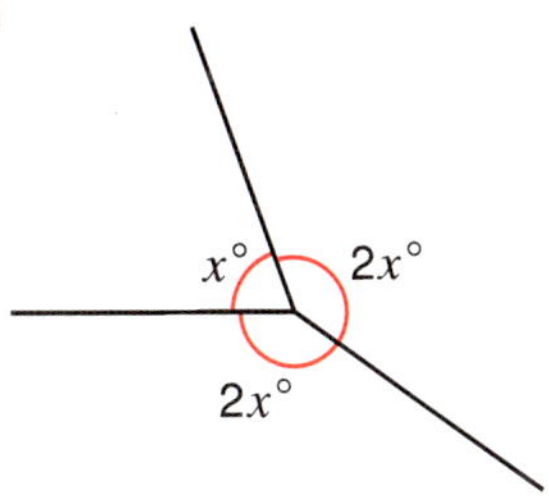

2

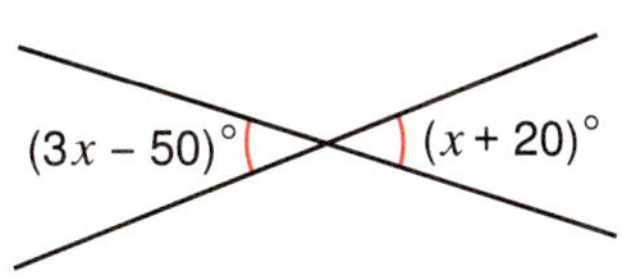

3

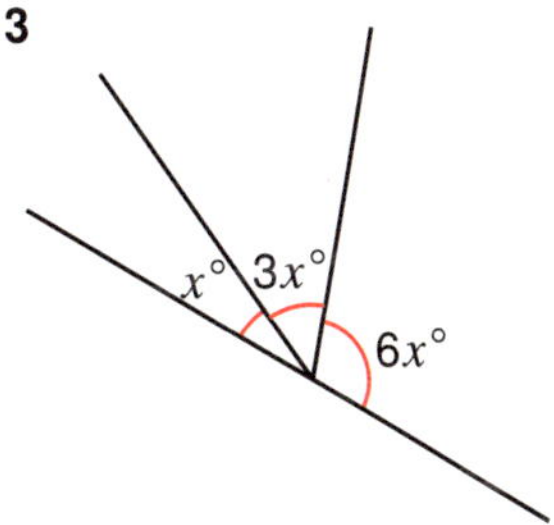

Chapter 16 test

1. Solve the equations.

1 $x - 6 = 17$
2 $6x = 42$
3 $\frac{1}{6}x = 12$
4 $x + 6 = 30$

2. Solve the equations.

1 $5x + 9 = 24$
2 $4x = 49 - 3x$

3. Solve the equations and check your answers.

1 $5x + 18 = 2x + 21$
2 $6x - 15 = 5x + 5$

4. In the formula $A = 3x + y$, find the value of x when $A = 50$ and $y = 8$.

5. If $y = kx$ and $y = 27$ when $x = 3$, find the value of k. With this value of k, find the value of y when $x = 5$.

6. I think of a number. If I multiply the number by 3 and add 48 the result is the same as if I multiply the number by 7 and subtract 12. What is the original number ?

7. Dad gave £24 to his three children. David received twice as much as Simon, and Angela received as much as David and Simon together. How much did each child receive ?
(Let Simon receive £s.)

PUZZLES

31. 'Andrew has joined the navy,' said Beverley.
'No, he's in the RAF,' said Carol.
'Beverley is right,' said Dawn.
'I only know that he's not gone into the army,' said Elaine.
'You're all wrong,' said Fiona.
If only one of these statements was true, and all the others false, which one of the three services had Andrew joined ?

32. If it were possible to take a sheet of paper, a tenth of a millimetre thick, and double it over on itself fifty times, how thick would the resulting wad of paper be ? Approximately 10 cm, 10 m, 1 km, 100 km or 100 000 000 km ?

33. Jodie had £20 to spend on her 4 days' holiday. She kept a total like this:

1st day spent	£8.00	which left her with	£12.00
2nd day spent	£6.50	which left her with	£5.50
3rd day spent	£3.00	which left her with	£2.50
4th day spent	£2.50	which left her with	£0
	£20.00		£20.00

Kevin kept his accounts also:

1st day spent	£8	which left him with	£12
2nd day spent	£6	which left him with	£6
3rd day spent	£3	which left him with	£3
4th day spent	£3	which left him with	£0
	£20		£21

He could not understand why he had an extra £1 in the 2nd column. Can you explain ?

34. On graph paper label the x-axis from 0 to 18 and the y-axis from 0 to 13 using a scale of 1 cm to 1 unit on both axes.
Plot these coordinates and join each point to the next, with a ruler, to make a closed shape. There are 5 shapes altogether. Cut them out, or copy them onto thick cardboard and cut those pieces out.

Rearrange the pieces to make a square,

1 without using the small square piece,

2 using all 5 pieces.

(1) (0,0), (4, 0), (8,4), (4,8), (0,4), (0,0).
(2) (6,0), (14,0), (14,4), (18,4), (14,8), (6,0).
(3) (0,5), (8,13), (0,13), (0,5).
(4) (5,9), (13,9), (9,13), (5,9).
(5) (14,9), (18,9), (18,13), (14,13), (14,9).

35. The diameter of an LP record is 30 cm. The unused centre has a diameter of 10 cm and there is an unused outer edge of width $\frac{1}{2}$ cm around the recording. If there are 100 grooves to 1 cm, approximately how far does the needle move during the playing of the record ?

36. Nine girls were queueing outside the cinema to see a film. Jane was in front of Vicki but behind Mary. Elizabeth was in front of Sarah, and Carol was behind Anna. Sarah was two places in front of Jane. Debbie was six places behind Mary. Louise was three places behind Vicki.
If there were only six seats left, who would be able to see the film ?

17 Thinking about frequency

Frequency distributions and bar-line graphs

We illustrate a frequency distribution with a few variables with a bar-line graph.

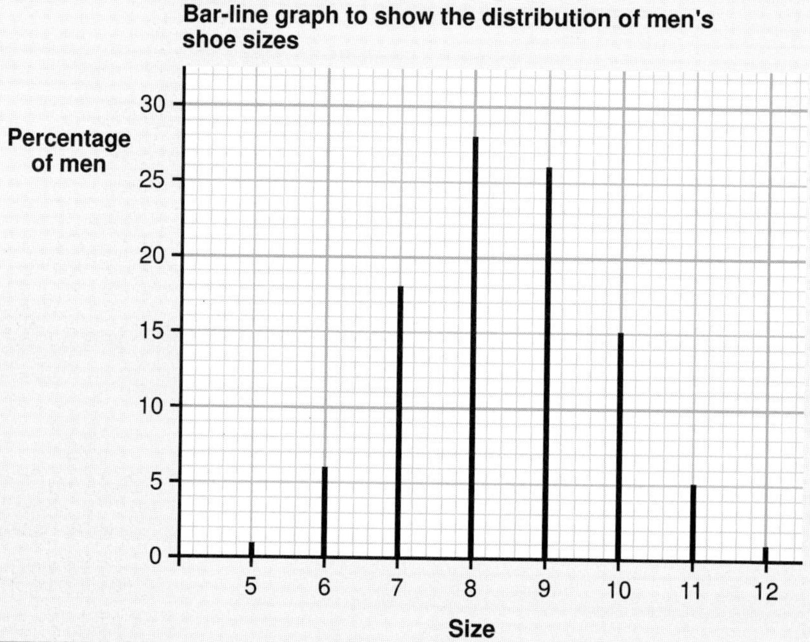

Averages

We can find the average (mean, median or mode) of a frequency distribution.
For the distribution of men's shoe sizes, shown above,
the mean size is 8.4,
the median size is 8, (50% of men take size 8 or less and 50% take size 8 or more),
and the mode size is 8, (the tallest column on the graph).

The average size of women's shoes is size 5.

The average household in the UK has 2.5 people.

distributions

Frequency distributions and histograms

When there are more variables the data is often put into groups, called classes, and a histogram is drawn.
On the right are three histograms. The labelling of the axes is not shown.

We often draw a histogram because we can deduce things from its general shape. Describe the differences in the shapes of these histograms.

In an exam with marks out of 100, grouped in classes of 10, a histogram with the shape of

(1) would indicate that the exam was rather difficult, with many pupils getting low marks and fewer getting good marks,

(2) would indicate that most pupils got average marks with a few getting very high or low marks,

(3) would indicate that the exam was rather easy, with many pupils getting high marks and fewer getting low marks.

(1)

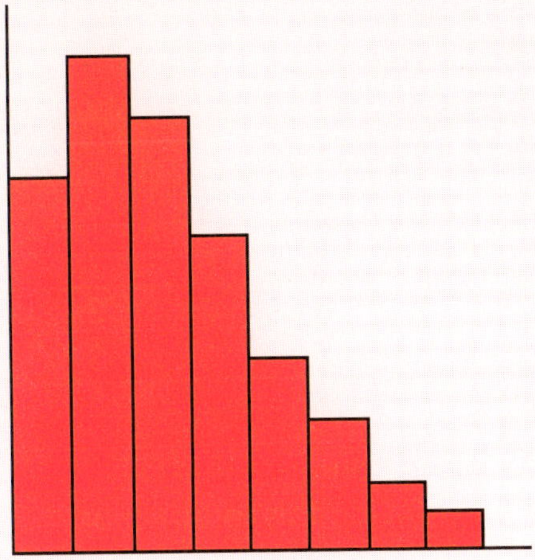

(2)

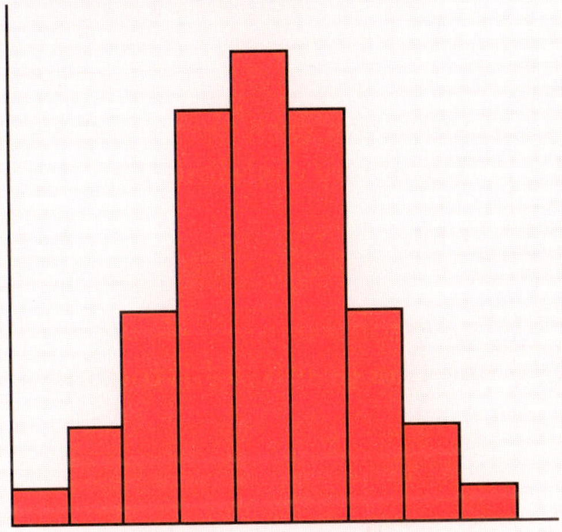

(3)

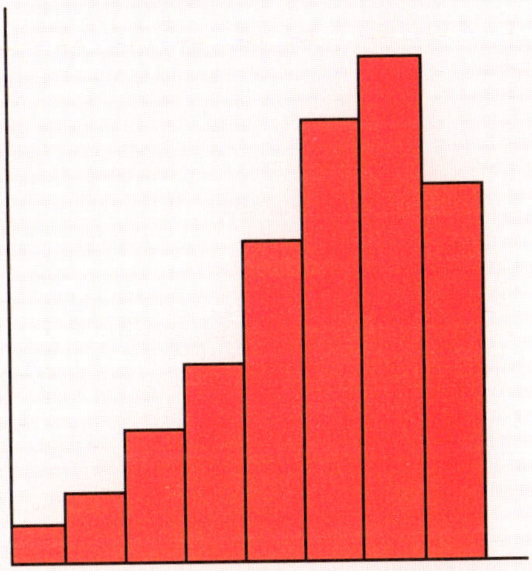

17 Frequency distributions

Example

This list gives information about the size of households, in a sample of 50 households.

1	2	2	4	1	4	3	4	2	4
5	1	3	5	2	5	2	2	2	2
1	1	1	2	3	2	3	4	2	6
2	2	2	3	3	3	2	4	1	3
6	3	4	2	2	2	3	1	5	2

Copy and complete this tally table showing this information.

f is short for **frequency**, the number of times each item occurs. This list showing the frequency of each item is called a **frequency distribution**.

Size of household	Tally	f
1		
2		
3		
4		
5		
6		
		50

The graph we use to illustrate a frequency distribution with a few variables is a **bar-line graph**. A **histogram** is sometimes used.

Bar-line graph to show the distribution of size of household

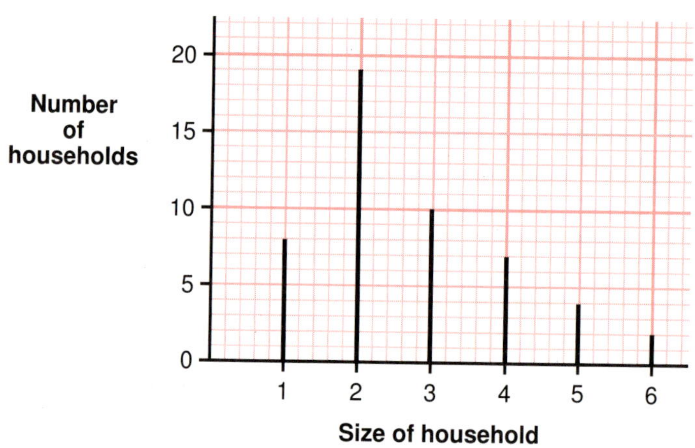

Histogram to show the distribution of size of household

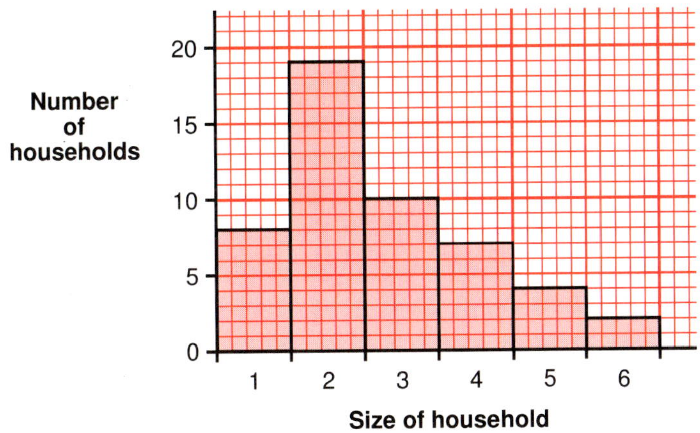

Averages

The mean

To find the mean number of people per household you must first find the total number of people.

1 person in	8 households =	8
2 people in	19 households =	38
3 people in	10 households =	30
4 people in	7 households =	28
5 people in	4 households =	20
6 people in	2 households =	12
	50	136

$$\text{Mean number of people per household} = \frac{\text{total number of people}}{\text{number of households}}$$

$$= \frac{136}{50} = 2.72$$

$$= 2.7, \text{ correct to 1 dec. pl.}$$

You could set down the working to find the mean by putting an extra column on the frequency table, and labelling the first column x.

x	f	fx
1	8	8
2	19	38
3	10	30
4	7	28
5	4	20
6	2	12
	50	136

$$\bar{x} = \frac{\text{sum of } fx \text{ column}}{\text{sum of } f \text{ column}} = \frac{\text{sum}\,(fx)}{\text{sum}\,(f)}$$

$$= \frac{136}{50} = 2.7, \text{ correct to 1 dec. pl.}$$

Note the new formula.

The mode

The mode is the value which occurs most often. From the frequency table it is easy to see that 2 occurs most often, 19 times altogether, so the mode is 2 people.

The median

The median value is the middle value when all the data are arranged in order of size.

If the 50 numbers were arranged in order of size, the middle value would be halfway between the 25th and 26th numbers.

$\underbrace{1\ 1\ 1\ \ldots}_{8\ 1's}\quad \underbrace{2\ 2\ 2\ \ldots}_{19\ 2's}\quad \underbrace{3\ 3\ 3\ \ldots}_{10\ 3's}\quad \underbrace{4\ 4\ 4\ \ldots}_{7\ 4's}\quad 5\ 5\ 5\ 5\ 6\ 6$

The 25th and 26th numbers are both 2, so the median is 2 people.

The range

The range = highest value − lowest value

= 6 − 1

= 5 people

Exercise 17.1

1. The number of people in each car was noted for 100 cars returning from a seaside town on a Saturday evening. The results were:

1	3	2	4	3	4	2	1	1	3
1	2	4	2	1	1	4	3	2	1
1	3	2	1	2	4	3	2	3	2
1	1	3	5	2	1	3	3	2	1
1	1	3	1	1	3	2	4	3	3
1	2	4	2	2	1	5	3	1	1
2	2	1	4	3	1	1	2	4	1
2	4	3	2	2	1	5	3	2	4
2	5	2	4	1	3	2	2	3	3
1	3	5	1	1	1	2	2	3	1

Make a tally table of this information and then represent the frequencies in a bar-line graph or histogram.

Find

1 the mean number of people per car,

2 the median number,

3 the mode number.

2. In an experiment, 10 seeds of a particular vegetable were planted in each of 200 pots, and the number of seeds which germinated was noted for each pot. These results were obtained:

Number of seeds germinating x	0	1	2	3	4	5	6	7	8	9	10
Number of pots f	1	0	1	2	8	20	40	53	46	24	5

Find

1 the mean number of seeds germinating, per pot,

2 the median number,

3 the mode number.

Draw a bar-line graph of the distribution.

3. In a recent Golf Championship, the scores of the players for the first hole are summarized here.

Score for hole x	2	3	4	5	6	7
Frequency f	18	84	146	36	3	1

Find

1 the mean score for this hole,

2 the median score,

3 the mode score.

Draw a bar-line graph of the distribution.

4. A list of surnames of 137 pupils in a year group was obtained, and the number of letters in each surname found.
Here are the results.

Number of letters in surname	2	3	4	5	6	7	8	9	10
Frequency	1	4	14	28	35	22	17	12	4

Find

1 the mean number of letters in a surname,

2 the median number,

3 the mode,

4 the range.

5 Draw a bar-line graph of the data.

Carry out your own survey using the names of pupils in your school and repeat the questions.
Comment on any similarities or differences with the results shown here.

Grouped Frequency Distributions

Data is often put into convenient groups, called **classes**.

Example

The distribution of examination marks of 100 pupils.

Mark	20–29	30–39	40–49	50–59	60–69	70–79	80–89
Number of pupils	3	10	21	25	22	14	5

The data can be represented by a **histogram**.

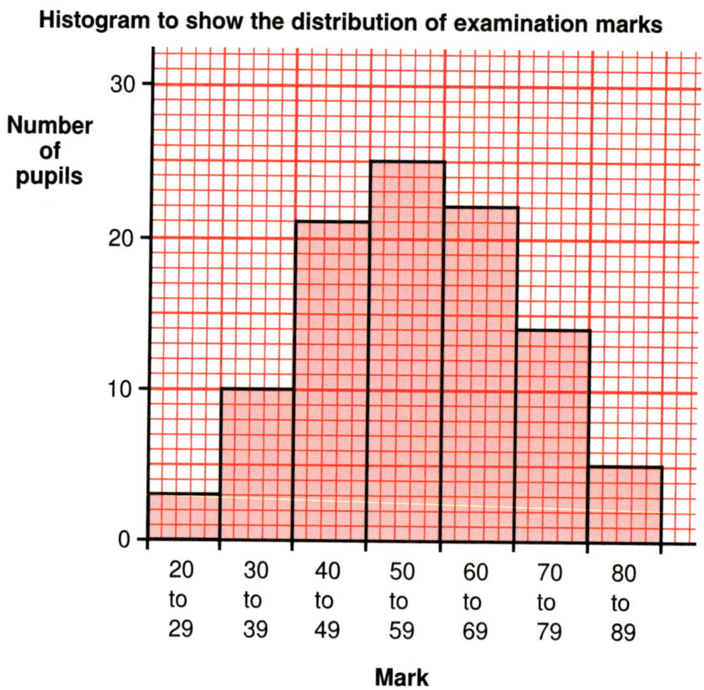

Exercise 17.2

1. In the seven cricket matches played on a Sunday, these were the runs scored by the first five batsmen in each of the teams.

33	8	56	39	3	66	26	5	10	3
8	33	31	1	0	1	31	3	24	22
4	31	38	63	67	46	8	19	46	1
35	0	17	27	39	13	66	7	10	46
7	30	0	5	102	22	24	38	10	1
26	8	24	67	5	17	97	26	20	–
17	21	2	83	56	32	23	19	4	56

(The missing score is because in one team only 4 players batted.)

Group these runs into classes 0–14, 15–29, 30–44, etc. and show the distribution in a table and on a histogram. Comment on the scores.

2. The table gives the frequency distribution of the marks of 60 pupils in an examination.

Mark	Number of pupils
40–49	3
50–59	8
60–69	16
70–79	21
80–89	7
90–99	5

Draw a histogram to represent this information. (Label the blocks on the horizontal axis 40–49, 50–59, etc.)

3. A group of people entering a quiz had scores which are shown in the table.

Score	Number of people
0– 4	3
5– 9	12
10–14	13
15–19	13
20–24	9
25–29	9
30–34	3
	62

Another 8 people entered the quiz later and their scores were as follows:
6, 8, 25, 29, 34, 16, 18, 21.

Copy and amend the frequency table to include these extra 8 scores.

Draw a histogram to represent the complete information.

Exercise 17.3 Applications and Activities

1. The scores in 44 football matches on a particular Saturday were as follows:

Premier	0–0	1–1	4–0	0–1	2–0	3–0	0–0	1–1	1–0	0–0		
Div I	1–0	5–4	1–1	2–2	2–2	1–1	0–0	2–1	2–0	3–2	1–1	
Div II	0–0	1–1	1–0	0–1	0–1	2–3	4–2	1–1	3–0	2–3	0–3	1–0
Div III	0–1	0–0	0–1	4–3	2–2	0–0	0–3	4–1	0–1	0–3	3–3	

Copy and fill in this table showing the **number of teams** in each category.

Number of teams		Goals by home team						
		0	1	2	3	4	5	Total
Goals by away team	0							
	1							
	2							
	3							
	4							
	Total							

Draw two bar-line graphs or histograms, one showing the distribution of goals by the home teams and the other showing the distribution of goals by the away teams.

Find the mean number of goals scored by the home teams and the mean number of goals scored by the away teams.

Comment on the results.

2. Using the table of question 1, make a frequency distribution table of the total scores in each match. Represent these frequencies on a bar-line graph or histogram.

Find the mean, median, mode and range of the distribution.

3. A group of girls in a Youth Club gave information about the number of children in their families. The numbers include themselves.
(The number of girls is given first, so 3, 2 means 3 girls, 2 boys.)
Here is the list:

2,1	2,0	1,1	1,2	1,1	2,0	2,1	2,0	2,1	2,1
2,1	2,1	1,1	4,2	2,1	2,1	2,2	3,2	2,0	1,0
2,0	2,1	2,1	1,1	1,1	1,1	1,0	1,1	3,0	3,1
2,0	5,1	1,1	1,1	2,0	3,1	1,1			

Why must the first number be at least 1 ?
Design a table to show this information.

Make lists showing the frequency distributions of

1 the number of girls in each family,

2 the number of boys in each family,

3 the number of children in each family.

Represent these distributions on bar-line graphs.

For each distribution find the mean, median, mode and range.

Comment on the results.

4. In an experiment with dice, 3 dice were thrown 200 times and the sum of the 3 numbers noted. These sums were:

14	10	17	8	13	10	8	12	9	15
10	13	14	8	13	9	10	14	7	9
13	12	11	13	8	9	7	14	15	8
4	9	8	7	5	13	9	10	12	7
8	3	9	11	8	9	12	8	6	11
12	17	15	4	11	9	12	7	9	14
10	7	11	8	13	11	14	11	9	15
11	8	14	12	9	9	16	11	9	8
8	13	16	12	12	7	6	8	11	8
11	10	11	12	12	13	13	13	18	10
9	14	15	8	8	12	3	12	8	9
13	9	12	11	15	7	15	5	13	6
13	14	12	16	8	15	12	9	12	10
7	13	14	18	4	12	7	18	11	15
12	13	10	7	9	11	10	13	8	11
4	11	12	7	5	13	11	16	7	12
11	10	14	15	11	9	8	10	14	14
10	14	6	12	11	16	9	13	18	10
8	5	14	11	11	12	17	12	13	5
9	10	13	14	13	10	12	12	7	9

Show these sums in a list and draw a bar-line graph or a histogram of the data. Which sum has occurred most ? Which has occurred least ?

Describe the shape of the graph. Are these results what you would have expected, or are they surprising ?

You could try the experiment yourself and compare your results with these.

5. Run a competition using 10 table-tennis balls which have to be thrown into a bucket. Record the scores of competitors (how many out of 10 which land in the bucket) in a tally table. Repeat with the same competitors, but this time they should use the hand they do not normally use, to throw.
Draw bar-line graphs or histograms of the two sets of results.

Find the mean, median and mode of each distribution.
Compare the two distributions.

Perhaps you can plan further competitions of a similar kind.

6. Here is an experiment for you to do.
Put 10 discs in a bag, with two of them coloured differently to the others. (We will call these the red ones.) Take the discs out one at a time, until you get a red one. If it is the first disc out, record that result as 1, if it is the second disc out, record the result as 2, and so on.
Replace the discs in the bag, mix them up, and repeat this process until you have 100 results.

Before you begin it is interesting to guess which result will occur most (the mode result), and to guess the mean of the results.
Put your results in a tally table, and then draw a bar-line graph or histogram.

Find the mean, median and mode of the distribution.
Were your guesses good ones ?

Comment on the results.

7. Do an experiment of tossing sticks over a set of parallel lines.
Use the floorboards of the room if they form parallel lines, otherwise draw equally spaced parallel lines on the floor. Find 10 thin sticks of equal length, with length about $\frac{3}{4}$ of the distance between the lines.

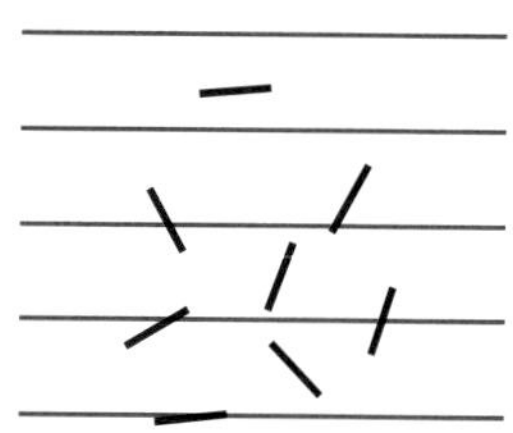

Toss the sticks one at a time, but without taking particular aim. They may either land across (or touching) a line, or land completely between two lines. Record how many of the 10 land completely between lines.
Repeat the experiment until you have 50 results.
Make a frequency distribution table of the results, and draw a bar-line graph or histogram. Comment on the shape of the graph.
Find the mean, median and mode of the distribution.

Repeat the experiment using sticks with length about 0.6 of the distance between the lines.

Compare the results of the two experiments.

8. The number of words per sentence in the 1st 50 sentences of the book 'The Children of the New Forest' are recorded here.

Number of words	Number of sentences
1–10	2
11–20	9
21–30	14
31–40	7
41–50	4
51–60	8
61–70	3
71–80	2
81–90	1

Draw a histogram of the distribution.

Choose a novel by a different author and do a similar survey.
Compare the two surveys and comment on them.
Do you think that the lengths of sentences have some effect on how easy it is to read a book ?
Does this affect your enjoyment of the story ?

9. Get about 120 dried peas, or something similar, and put them in a jar. Ask other people to estimate how many peas there are. (It is best if they do not hear other people's answers first.) Write the results down. Get about 50 results.
Sort the results into groups (called classes). For example, 60–69, 70–79, 80–89, etc.
However, you may have to choose different classes if these do not fit the answers you have. You need about 7 classes with an equal range of numbers in each.
Make a frequency distribution table using these classes and illustrate it with a histogram. Comment on the guesses and the shape of the histogram.

10. Adults sometimes grumble about the amount of coinage they carry around. Mother's purse can get too full of small change, and coins can make a hole, by wear and tear, in father's pocket.
Carry out an experiment to see how much change people have, at the time when you ask them. Record the results. There are two things you can count, the number of coins in purse or pocket, or the amount, in pence, of these coins.
Decide beforehand whether you are going to include £1 coins in your survey.
Since you will have to use adults for this survey, it is best to combine with others in the class so that you can all ask your parents and a few other adults whom you know.
You might do a separate survey of the pupils in your class.
Investigate the results and comment on them.

11. There are many investigations you can do, either in class or at home. You can get data from your class, from families and friends, and from magazines, newspapers and computer databases.
Decide on an investigation on a topic which interests you, and for which you can list the data in a frequency table or tables.
Illustrate your results by drawing suitable diagrams, and possibly finding averages and ranges.
Comment on your results.

Chapter 17 test

1. The number of matches in a sample of 50 boxes is shown.

50 49 50 49 52 50 49 50 50 50 49 50 49 50 48
50 48 50 50 52 48 51 52 49 50 48 49 48 49 48
48 51 49 50 51 51 49 52 50 50 49 49 51 48 47
48 49 51 50 49

Make a frequency table of the data.
Find the mean, median, mode and range of the distribution.
Draw a bar-line graph of the distribution.
The label on the boxes says 'Average contents 50 matches'.
Do your results agree with this statement ?

2. When 5 coins were tossed 250 times the number of heads out of 5 were as follows:

Number of heads	0	1	2	3	4	5
Frequency	4	53	80	70	37	6

Show these results in a bar-line graph or histogram.
Find the mean, median and mode of the number of heads.

3. The marks obtained by 50 pupils in an examination were as follows:

29 48 58 16 61 45 41 66 55 61 49 63 37 85 48
21 74 23 47 63 64 16 77 87 27 48 66 39 67 74
73 41 93 61 58 68 69 49 44 46 41 76 74 29 61
27 61 32 42 82

1 What is the range of the marks ?
2 Group these marks in a tally table into classes 10–19, 20–29, 30–39, etc. and show the frequencies.
3 Show the distribution in a histogram.

PUZZLES

37. 'All of these 9 boxes should contain the same weight of bars of gold,' said the airport cargo officer to his assistant. 'But we have been tipped off that 1 box contains some cheaper metal, and we must identify that box. It will be a bit lighter than the other ones.
As the cargo must go out on the next plane, we have only time to do two weighings and we will have to use the balance scales as the other ones need repairing.'
Can you tell the cargo officer how he can find the wrong box with two weighings ?

38. Here is a letter from a pen-friend in Australia. Work out the sums on your calculator and, remembering that the people in Australia are upside down to us, you should be able to make these answers into words.

$1 - 0.22 - 0.0066$
My name is $(3 \times 4 \times 5 \times 6) - (1 \times 2 \times 3 \times 4) + 1$
I am nearly $\sqrt{444 - 3}$
I like to collect $555555 + 22222 - 444 + 12$
My dog is called $(2 \times 2 \times 3 \times 3 \times 3 \times 5) - 3$
I will put on my $234^2 - 40^2 - 111$ and take him for a walk on the $88^2 - (5 \times 6)$
He digs $54321 - 8^3 - (3 \times 5 \times 7)$ in the $5 \times 29 \times 49$
My sister is called $34567 - 2345 - 678 + 34 - 5$
She is $13 \div 65$
She works for 0.79×0.7
She sells $27^2 - 19$
She says I am a nuisance but $(59 \times 90) + (1469 \div 200)$

39. Mr and Mrs McLean have three household jobs to do before they can set off on holiday.
(1) Their house must be vacuumed. They have one vacuum cleaner, and the task will take 30 minutes.
(2) The lawn must be mowed. They have only one mower, and this task also takes 30 minutes.
(3) Their baby must be bathed, dressed, fed and settled in his carry-cot for the journey. This, too, will take 30 minutes.
How long will it take them to do all these jobs ?

40. Mr English, Mr French and Mr German teach English, French and German. However, not one of them teaches the subject which is the same as his name. If Mr French's wife is the English teacher's sister, what does Mr German teach ?

18 Thinking about triangles

What is a triangle ?

What is a triangle ?
Where is the word derived from ?
What other words begin with the letters 'tri', for a similar reason ?

Why are all these warning signs needed here ?

Triangle facts

You may have made some discoveries about triangles in Chapters 8 and 15. What facts do you already know about them ?

This is a warning symbol used on clothing and other materials. What does it mean ?

Triangles in everyday life

Look for examples of triangles in daily life. The road traffic signs enclosed in triangles are **warning** signs. Can you find any other examples of triangles being used as warning symbols ?
Why in structures like scaffolding are diagonal pieces put in to form triangles ?
Why did a milkmaid traditionally sit on a 3-legged stool rather than a 4-legged one ?

Counting triangles

How many triangles can you find in this drawing ?

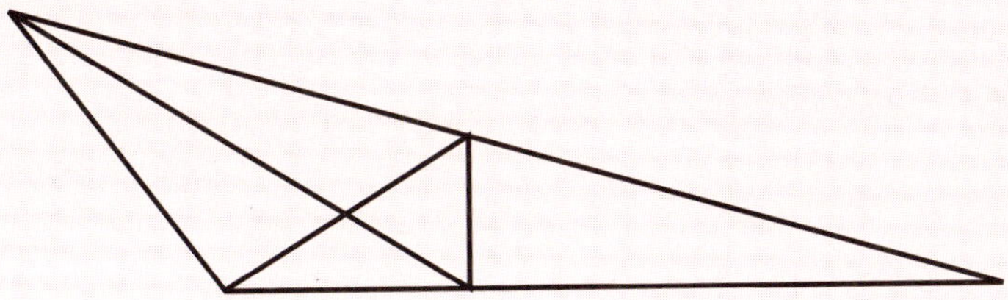

Draw some triangles of different shapes. What different kinds of triangles are there, and what are they called ? Look for some of these in the drawing above.

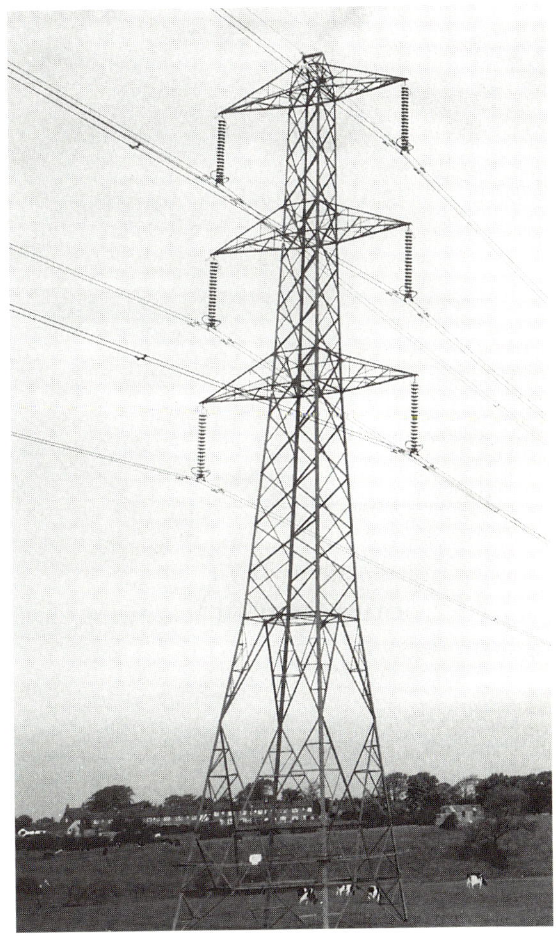

18 Triangles

Triangles

A figure with 3 straight sides is called a **triangle**.

Acute-angled, right-angled and obtuse-angled triangles

These are **acute-angled triangles**, since all their angles are acute angles (less than 90°).

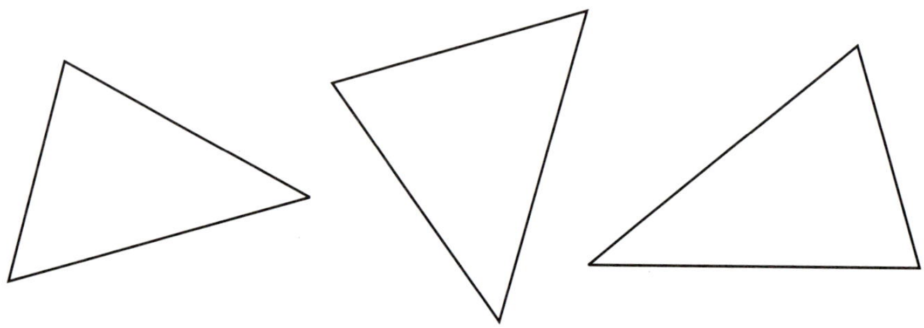

These are **right-angled triangles**, since one of the angles in each triangle is a right angle.

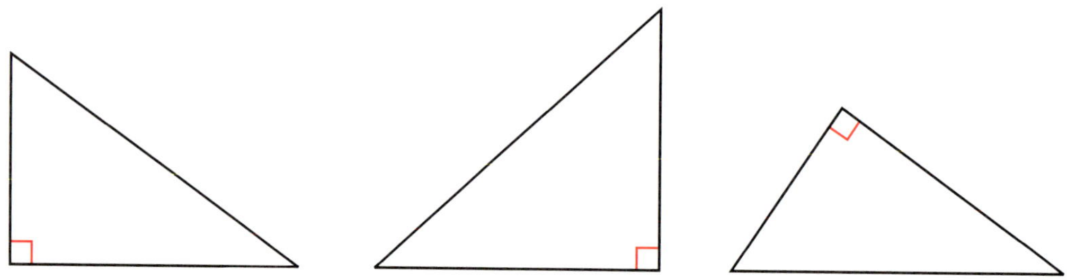

These are **obtuse-angled triangles**, since one of the angles in each triangle is an obtuse angle.

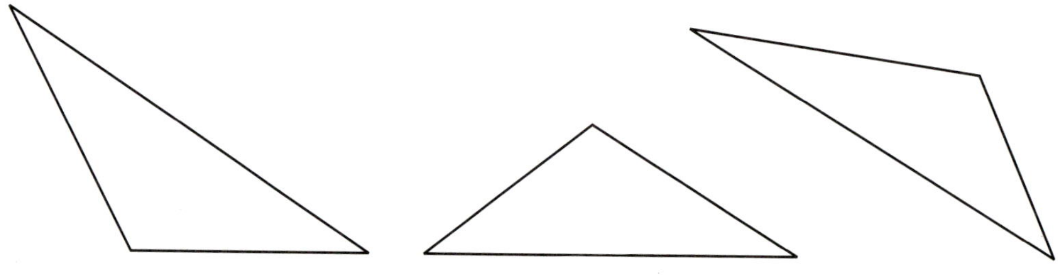

An exterior angle of a triangle

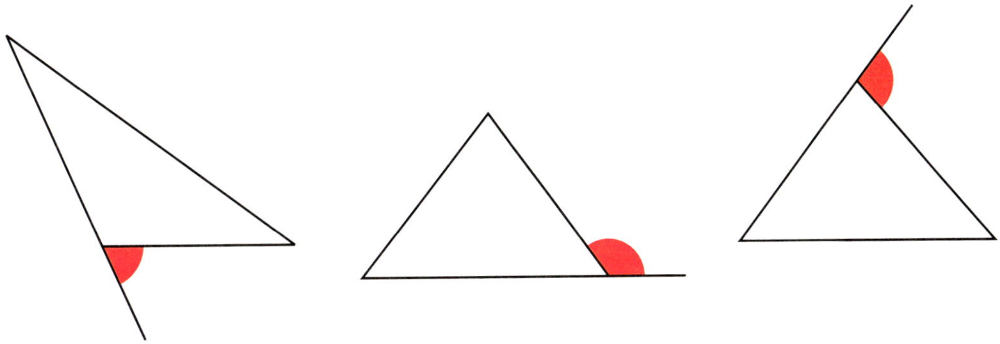

These shaded angles are called exterior angles of the triangles.
They are made by extending one of the sides of the triangle.

Angles of a triangle

1 An exterior angle is equal to the sum of the two opposite interior angles.

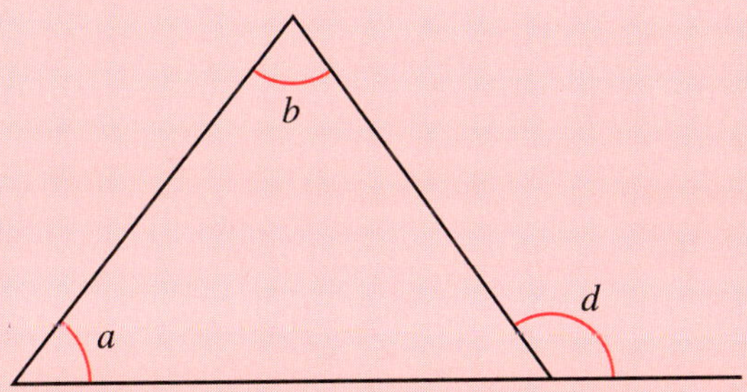

In the diagram, $d = a + b$.

2 The sum of the angles of a triangle is 180°.

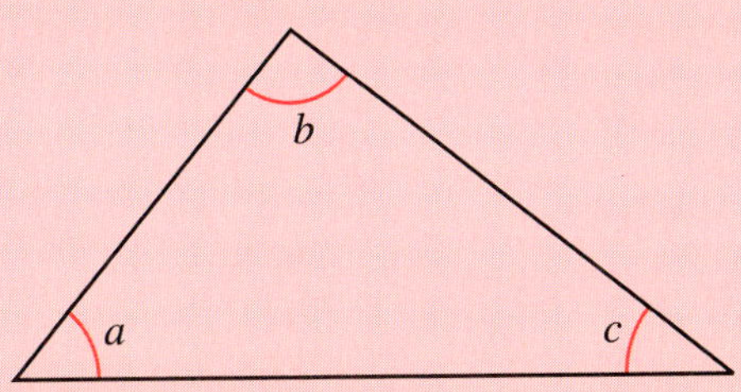

In the diagram, $a + b + c = 180°$.

Naming of triangles

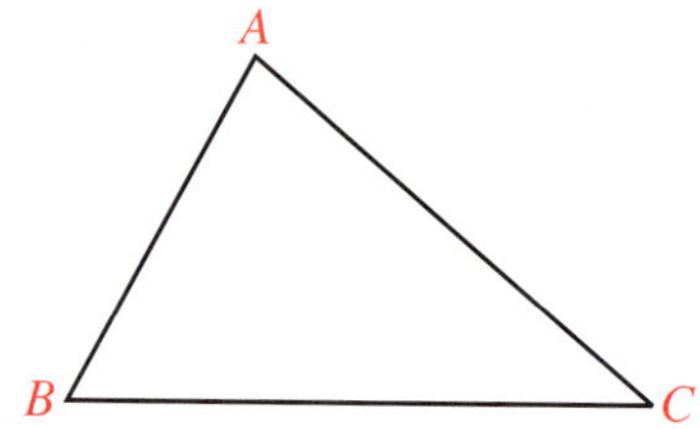

A triangle with vertices at points A, B and C is called triangle ABC.
This can be written as ΔABC.

Examples

1 In the diagram, $b = 42°$, $c = 29°$.
Find the size of angle a.

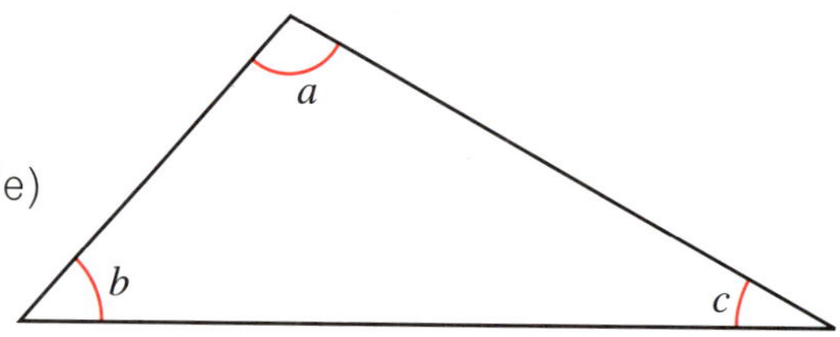

$a + b + c = 180°$ (angle sum of a triangle)

$a + 42° + 29° = 180°$

$a = 180° - 71°$

$= 109°$

2 Find the sizes of angles f and g.

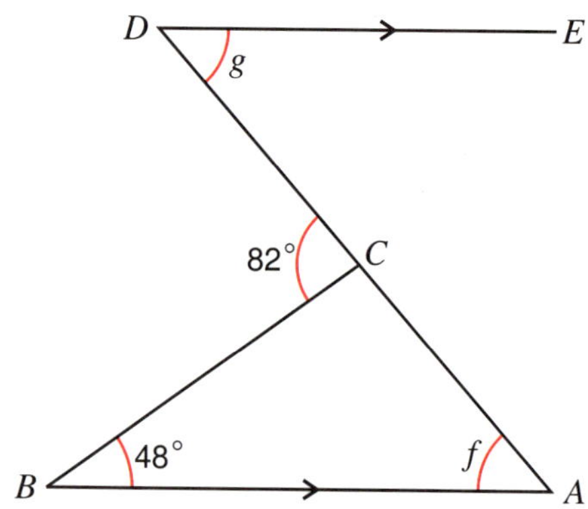

$f + 48° = 82°$ (exterior angle of ΔABC)

$f = 82° - 48°$

$= 34°$

$g = f$ (alternate angles)

$g = 34°$

Exercise 18.1

1. Measure the angles in these triangles, using your protractor. Check that the sum of the angles of each triangle is 180°. (Because you are measuring to the nearest degree, the sum may not be exactly 180°.)

1

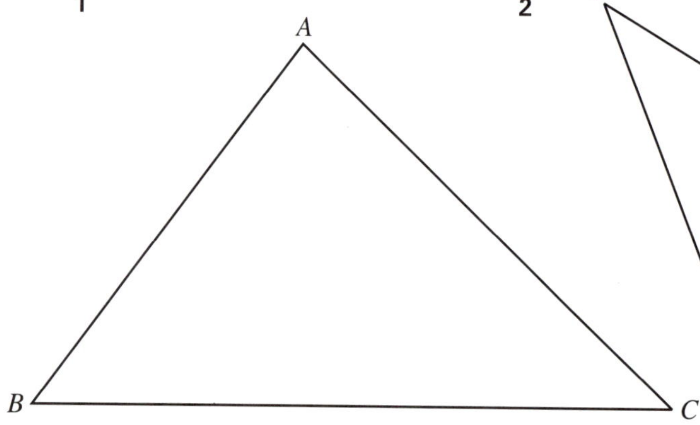

2

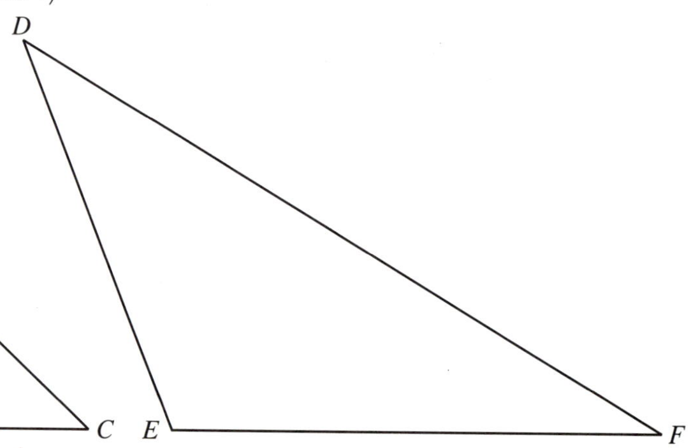

2. Check that two sides in each of these triangles are equal, by measuring in cm, to the nearest mm.
Measure the angles in the triangles, using your protractor. Check that the sum of the angles of each triangle is 180°, and that the angles opposite the equal sides are equal.

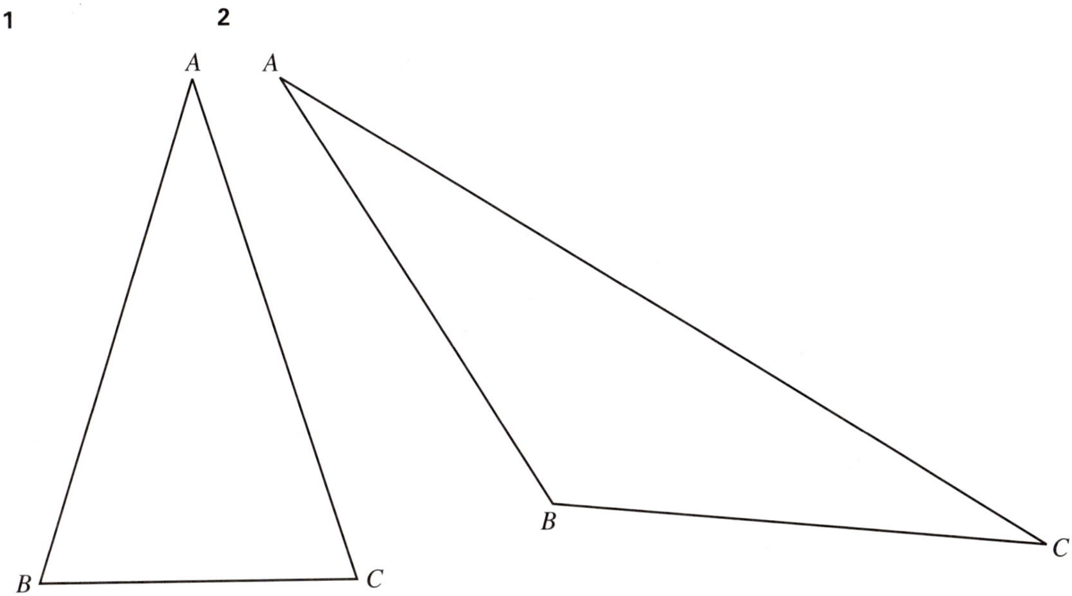

3. Calculate the sizes of the 3rd angles in these triangles.
Say whether the triangles are acute-angled, right-angled or obtuse-angled.

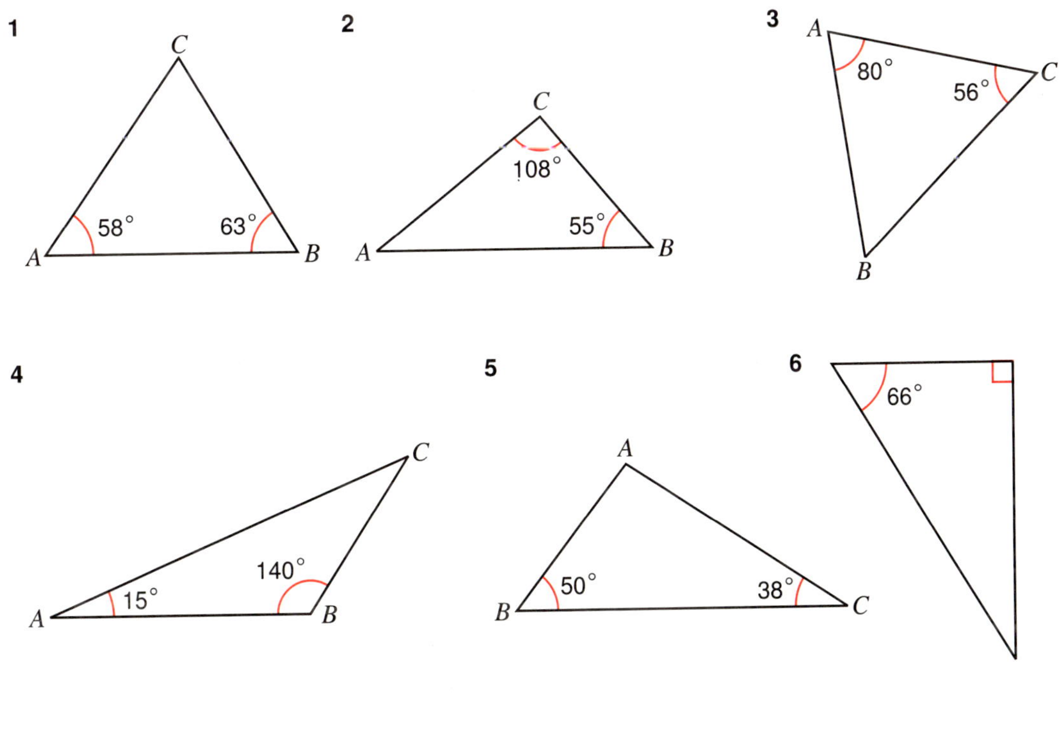

4. Calculate the marked angles in these figures.

1

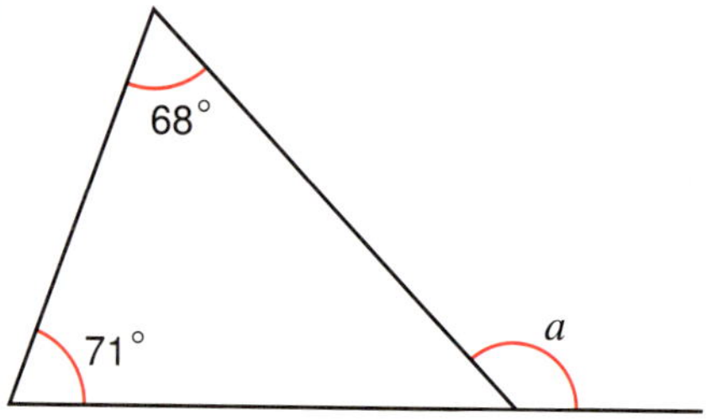

2

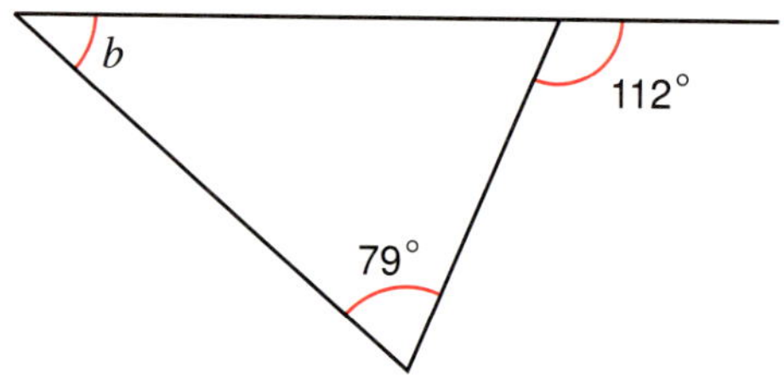

3

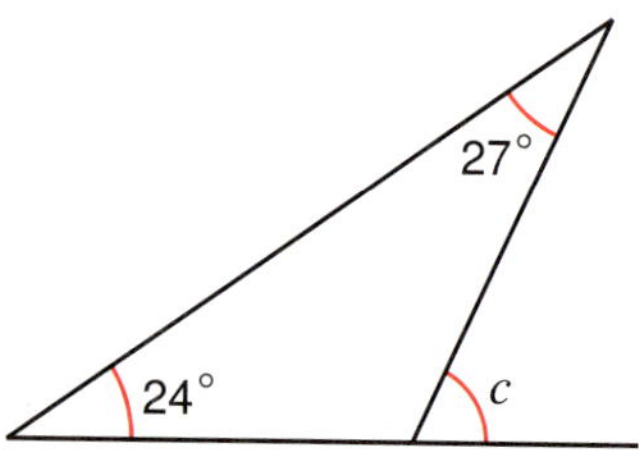

4

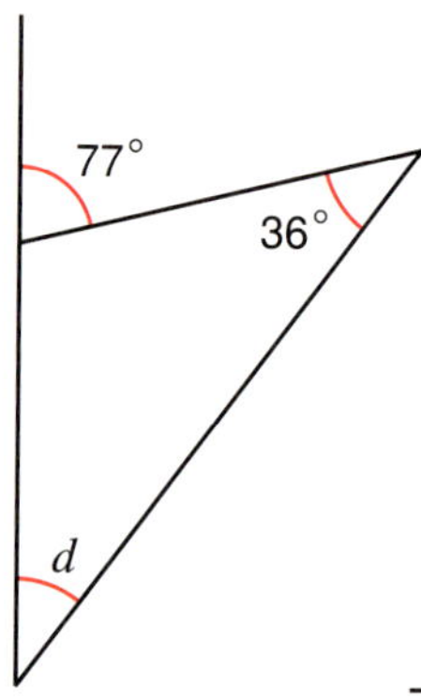

5

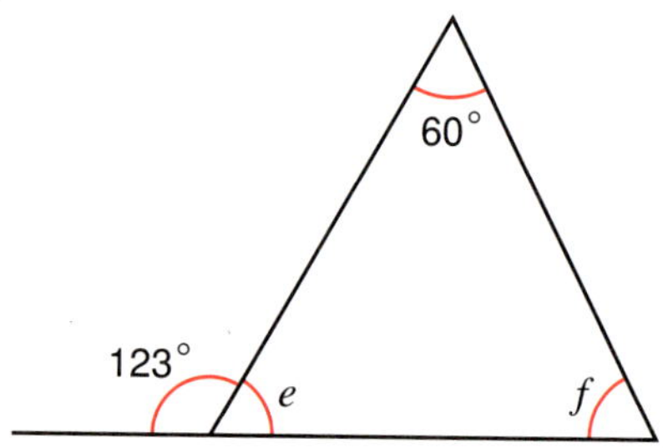

5. Find the sizes of a and b.

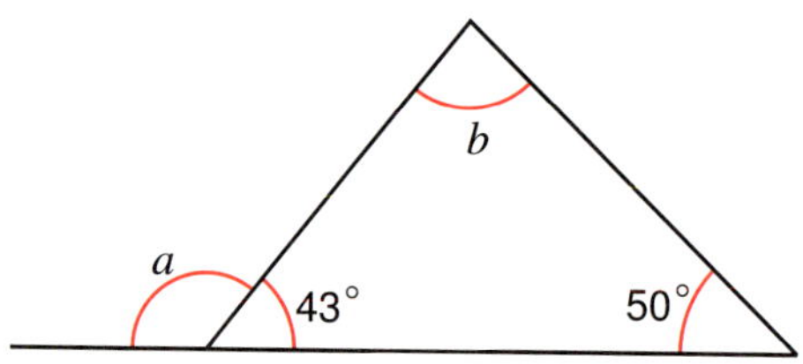

6. Find the size of a, and then find the size of d.

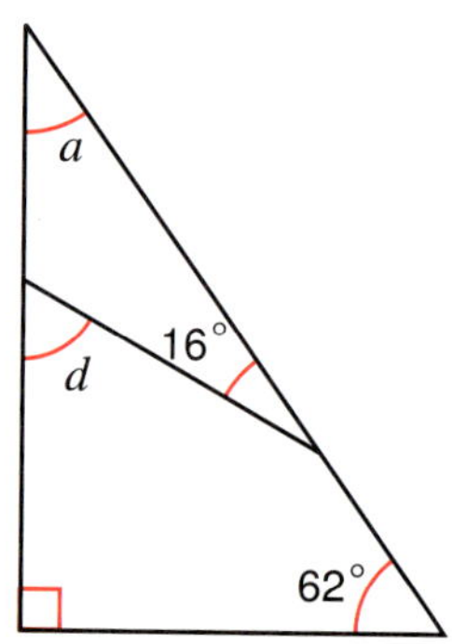

Scalene, isosceles and equilateral triangles

These triangles have all sides of different lengths and they are called **scalene triangles**.

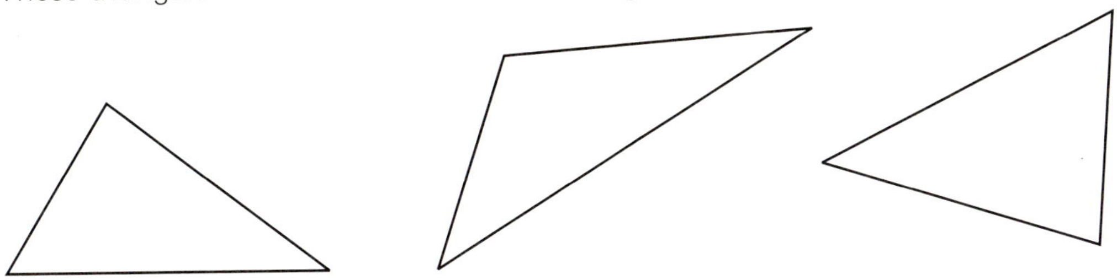

These triangles have two equal sides and they are called **isosceles triangles**.

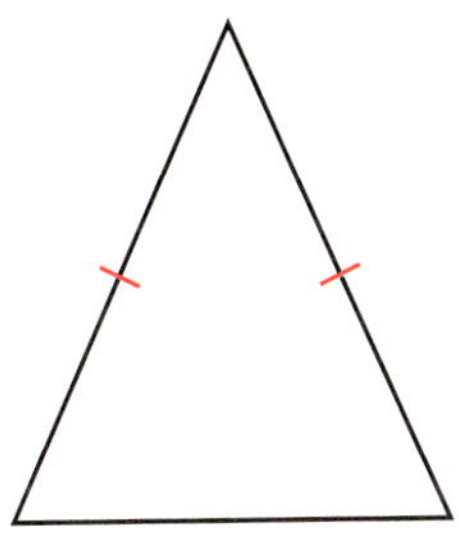

This is an acute-angled isosceles triangle.

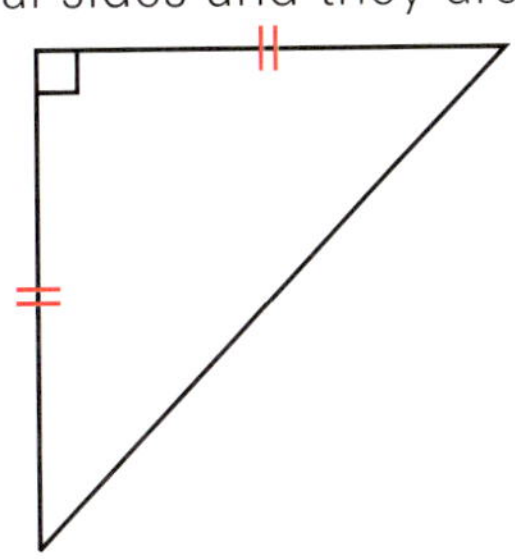

This is a right-angled isosceles triangle.

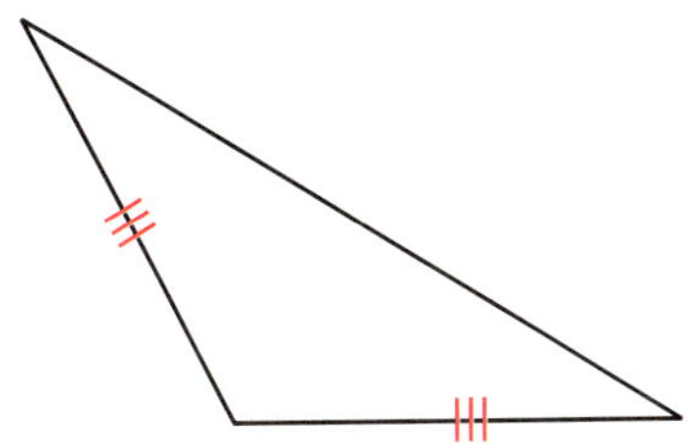

This is an obtuse-angled isosceles triangle.

(The small marks crossing the sides is the sign used to show that those lines have equal length.)

A triangle with all three sides equal is called an **equilateral triangle**.

These are equilateral triangles.

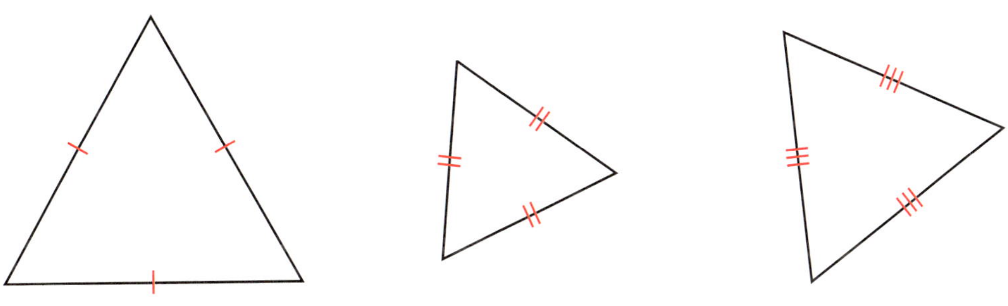

Angles in isosceles triangles

The angles opposite the equal sides are equal.

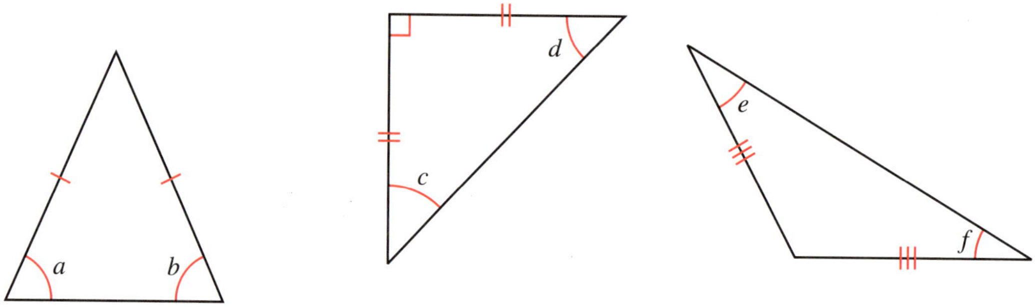

$a = b$ $\qquad$ $c = d$ (and they are 45°) $\qquad$ $e = f$

Angles in an equilateral triangle

Each angle is 60°.

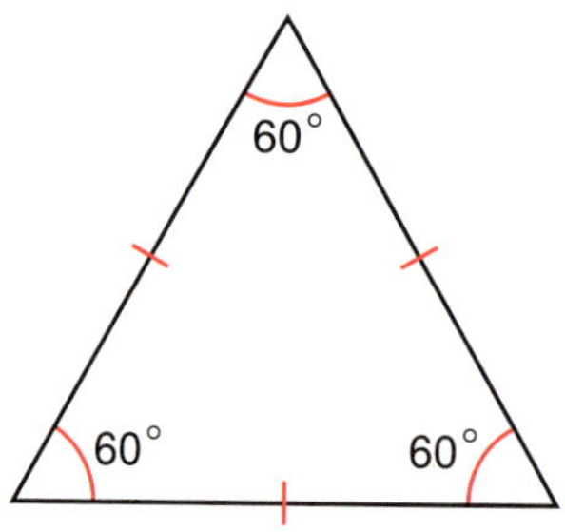

Examples

1 Find the sizes of angles b and c.

ΔABC is isosceles, $AB = AC$, so $b = c$.

$b + c + 44° = 180°$ (sum of angles of a triangle = 180°)

$b + c = 180° - 44°$

$= 136°$

$b = 136° \div 2$

$= 68°$

$c = 68°$

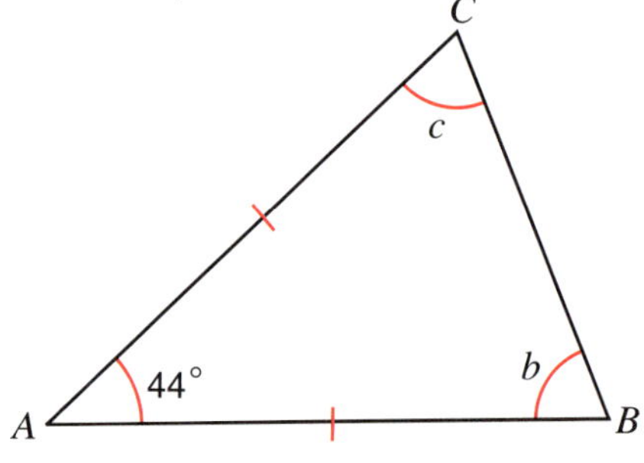

2 Find the sizes of angles d and e.

$d = 76°$ (isosceles triangle, equal angles)

$e = d + 76°$ (exterior angle of triangle)

$= 76° + 76°$

$= 152°$

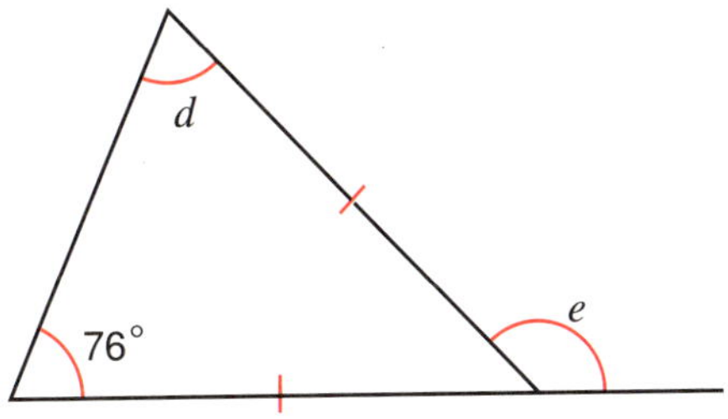

Exercise 18.2

1. Find the sizes of angles a and b.
What sort of triangle is $\triangle ABC$?

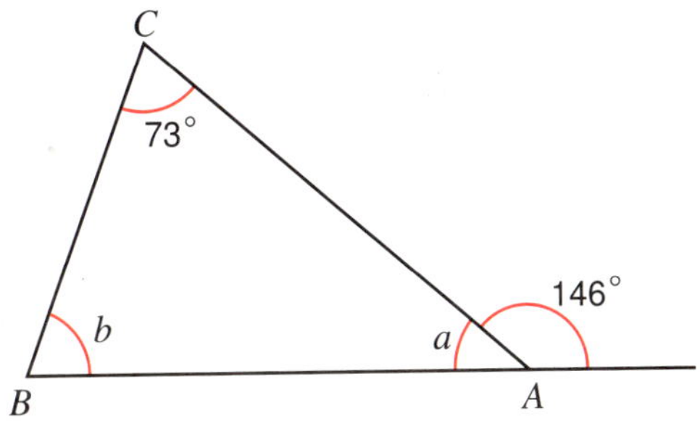

2. Calculate the 3rd angle in these triangles and say whether the triangle is acute-angled, right-angled or obtuse-angled, and if it is isosceles or equilateral.

1 Two angles are 130°, 32°.
2 Two angles are 58°, 32°.
3 Two angles are 60°, 60°.
4 Two angles are 28°, 32°.
5 Two angles are 74°, 32°.

Questions 3 to 8.

Find the marked angles in these diagrams.

3.

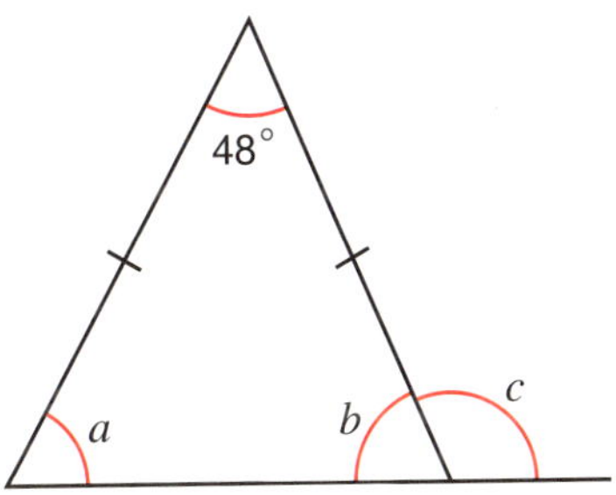

4.

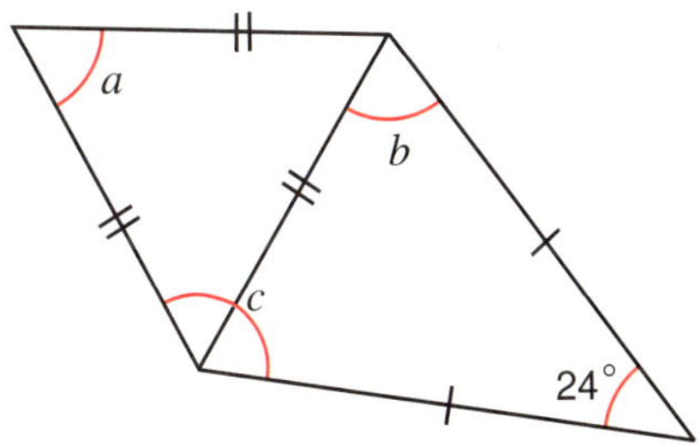

5.

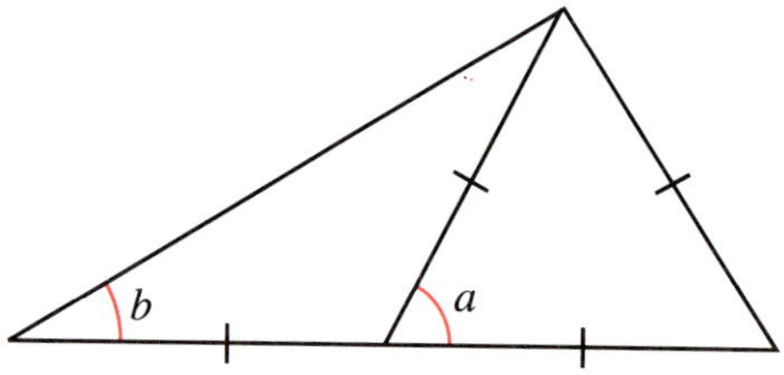

6.

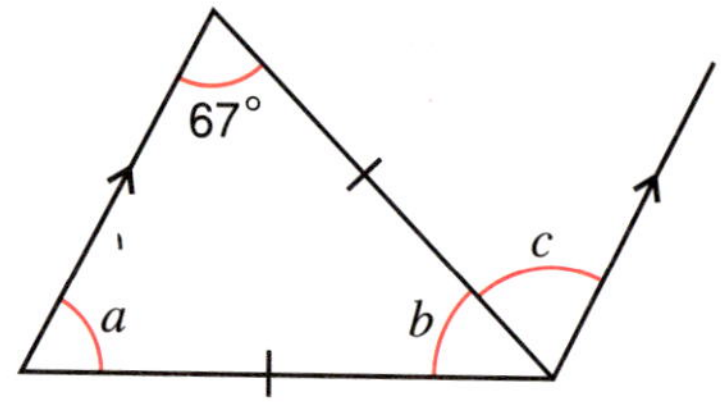

7.

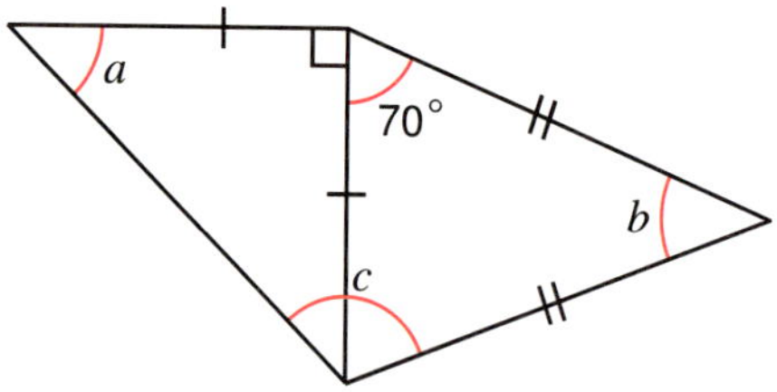

8.

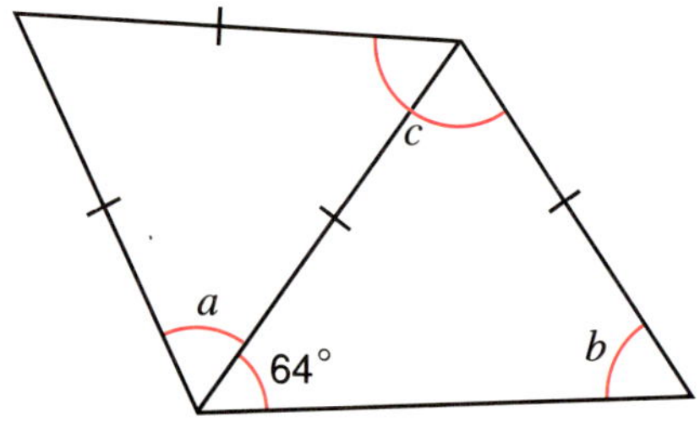

9. **1** If $AB = AC$, which two angles are equal ?

Find the sizes of

2 $\angle ABC$,

3 $\angle BCA$,

4 $\angle ACD$,

5 $\angle CDB$,

6 $\angle BCD$.

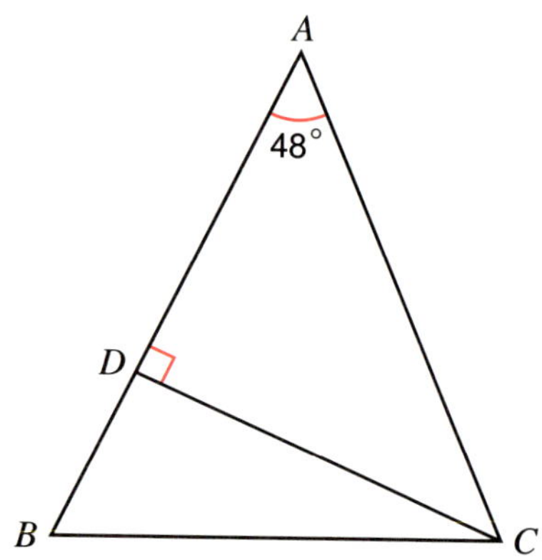

10. ΔABC is a right-angled isosceles triangle with $\angle B = 90°$.
ΔACD is an equilateral triangle.

Calculate the sizes of

1 $\angle BAC$,

2 $\angle CAD$,

3 $\angle BAD$.

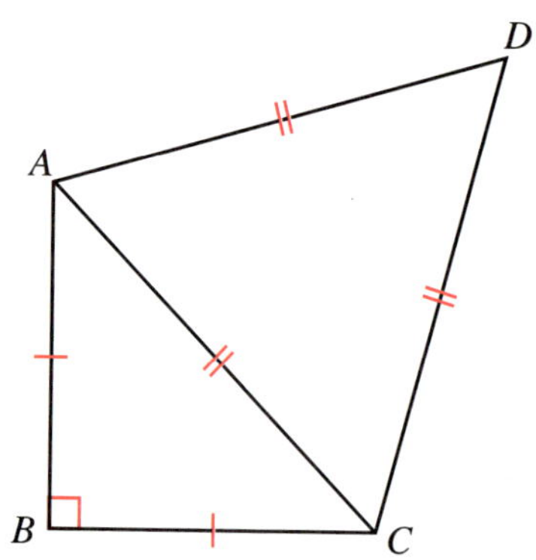

Drawing triangles accurately

Follow the instructions in these examples and draw the triangles yourself.

1. To draw a triangle, given 1 side and 2 angles

Example

Draw a triangle ABC with $AB = 10$ cm, $\angle A = 66°$ and $\angle B = 51°$.

Draw AB, 10 cm long.
Measure an angle of 66° at A and an angle of 51° at B.
Continue these lines until they meet at C.

If instead of being given the size of $\angle B$, you had been told that $\angle C = 63°$, you could have calculated the size of $\angle B$, (how ?), and then you could continue as above.

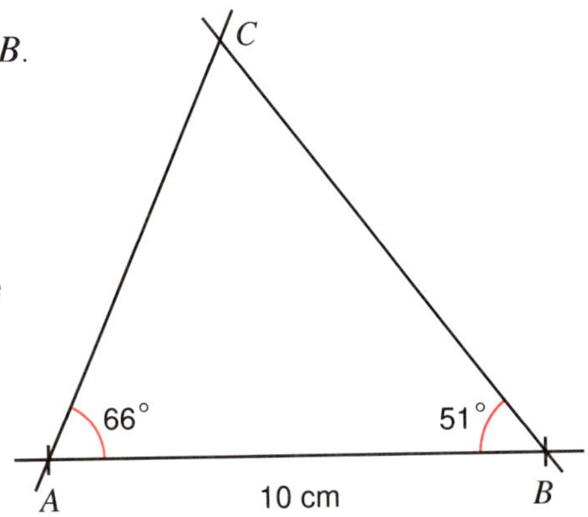

(not drawn full-size)

2. To draw a triangle, given 2 sides and the angle included between these sides

Example

Draw a triangle ABC with $AB = 10$ cm, $\angle A = 66°$ and $AC = 8$ cm.

Draw AB, 10 cm long.
Measure an angle of 66° at A and measure off a distance of 8 cm along this angle line, to give the point C.
Join BC.

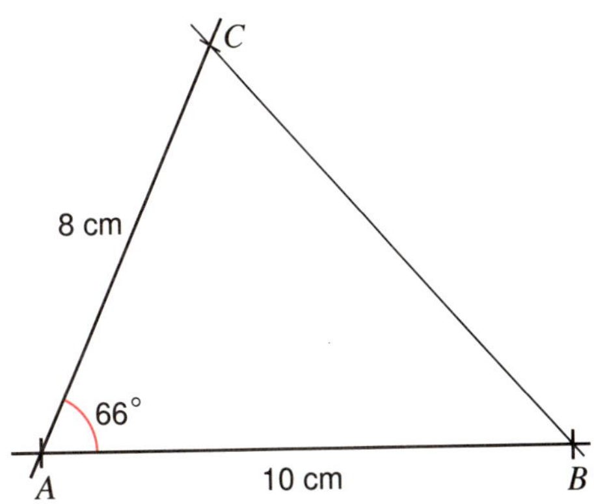

(not drawn full-size)

3. **To draw a triangle, given 2 sides and a non-included angle**

Example

Draw a triangle ABC with $AB = 6$ cm, $\angle A = 37°$ and $BC = 7$ cm.

Draw AB, 6 cm long.
Measure an angle of 37° at A and draw this angle line and extend it.
With compasses, centre B, radius 7 cm, draw an arc to meet this extended line at C.
Join BC.

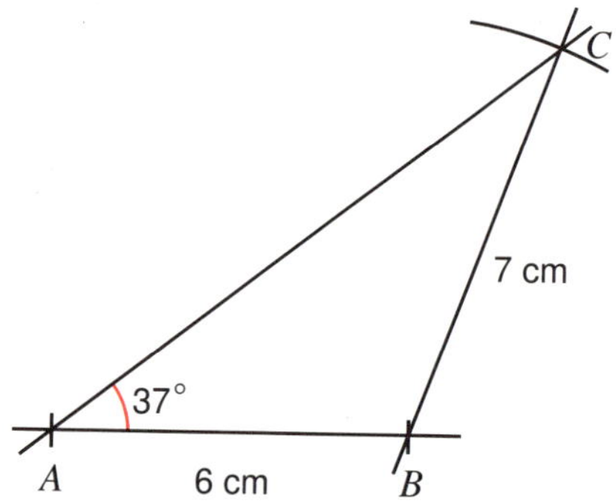

(not drawn full-size)

(In some cases there could be two points where the arc meets the line, so there would be two possible triangles of different shapes satisfying the given data.)

4. **To draw a triangle given 3 sides**

Example

Draw a triangle ABC with $AB = 10$ cm, $BC = 8$ cm and $AC = 7$ cm.

Draw AB, 10 cm long.
With compasses, centre A, radius 7 cm, draw an arc.
With centre B, radius 8 cm, draw an arc to cut the first arc at C.
Join AC and CB.

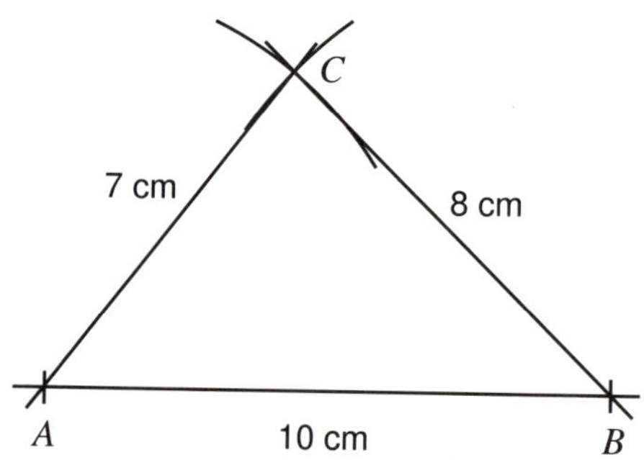

(not drawn full-size)

Exercise 18.3

Using geometrical instruments, construct the triangles full-size.

1. 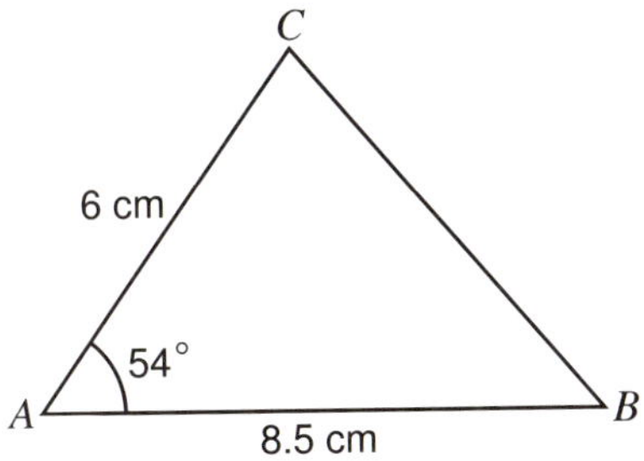

Measure the length of BC and the sizes of $\angle B$ and $\angle C$.

2. 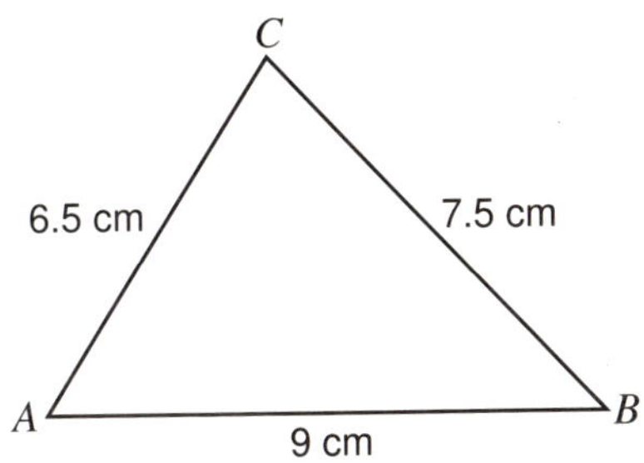

Measure the angles A, B and C.

3. 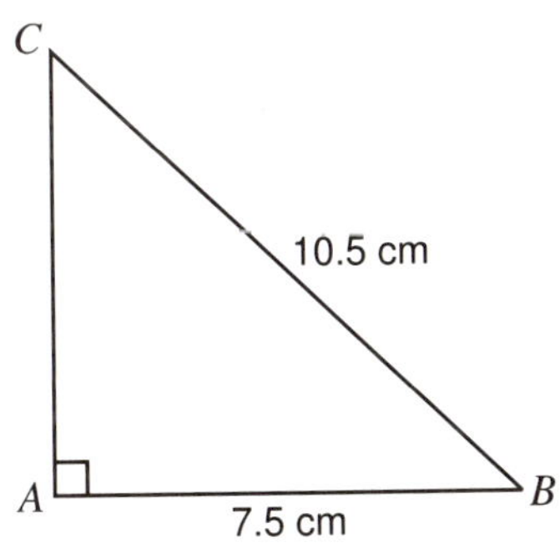

Measure the length of AC and the sizes of $\angle B$ and $\angle C$.

4. 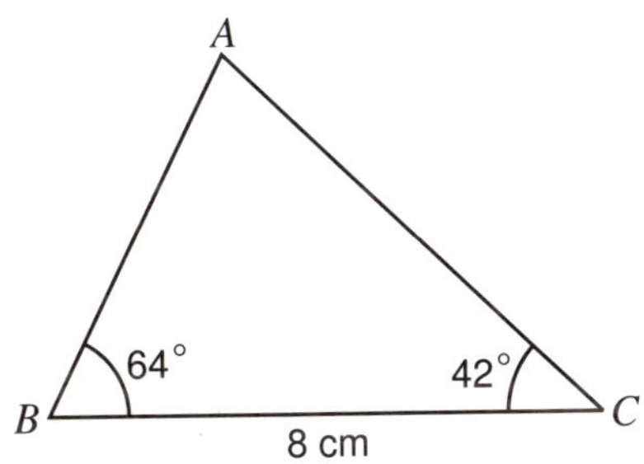

Measure the lengths of AB and AC. Calculate the size of $\angle A$ and check this by measuring it.

Exercise 18.4 Applications and Activities

1. **Triangles and parallel lines**

Find the sizes of the marked angles.

1

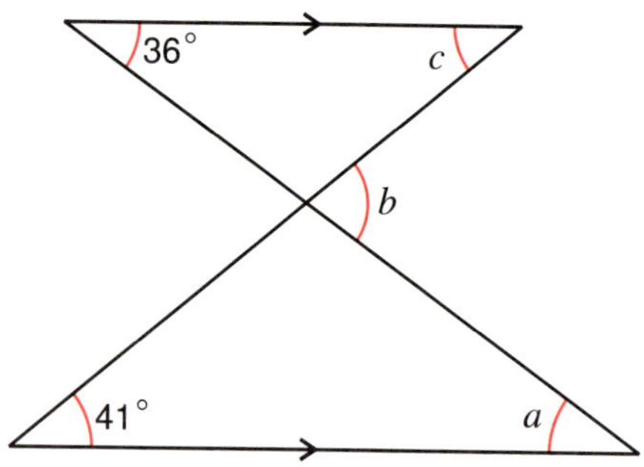

2

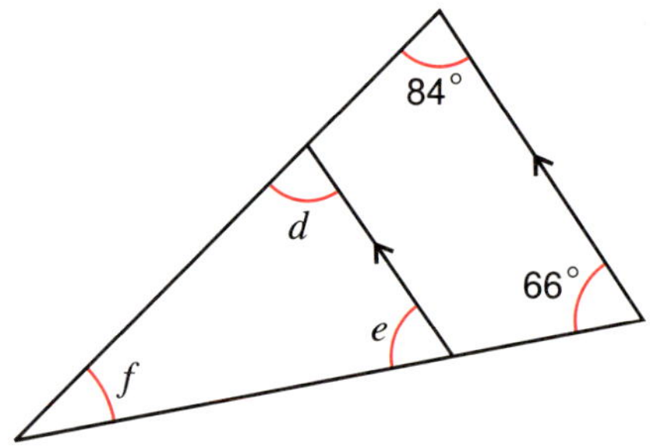

3

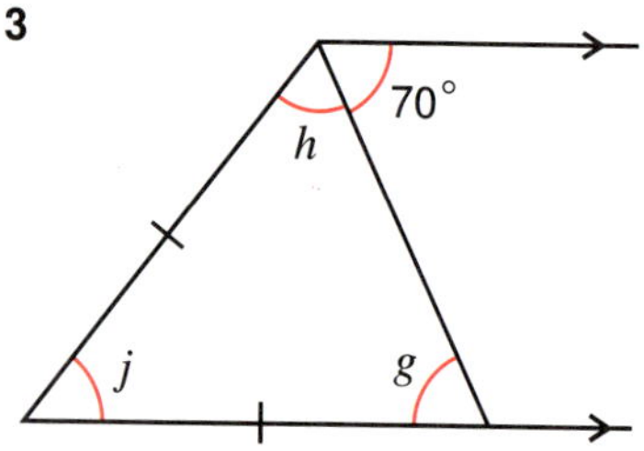

4

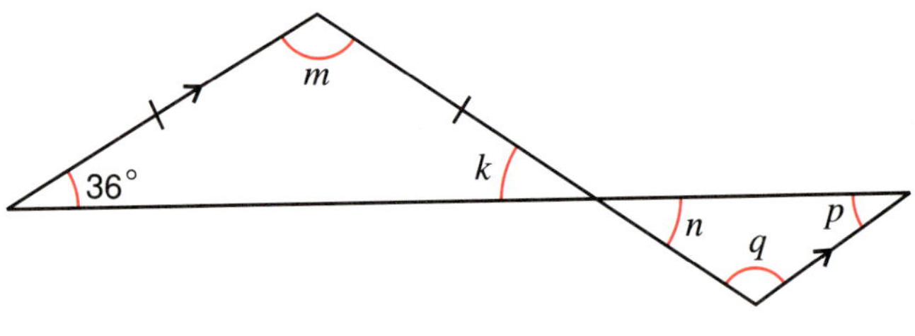

2. **Arranging triangles**

Draw two right-angled triangles of the same size on thin card, and cut them out. Place them together so that they meet completely along one edge. They can be turned over. What different shapes can be made ?

Repeat using two equilateral triangles, then two isosceles right-angled triangles, and then two isosceles triangles which are not right-angled.

3. **To draw an angle of 60°, using ruler and compasses**

Example

To make an angle of 60° at P, on the line PS.

With centre P draw a large arc, to cut PS at Q.
With centre Q and the same radius, draw an arc to cut the other arc at R.
Join PR.
Then angle $QPR = 60°$.

If you joined QR, what sort of triangle would triangle PQR be ?
Explain why this shows that $\angle QPR = 60°$.

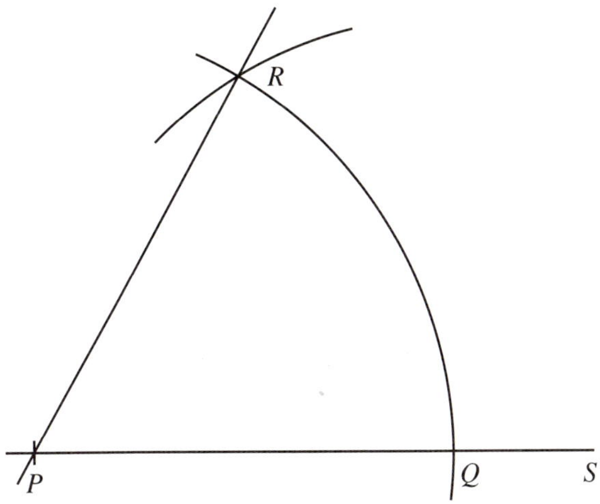

4. **The medians of a triangle**

Construct a triangle ABC with $AB = 6$ cm, $BC = 7$ cm and $\angle B = 95°$.
Measure $\angle A$ and $\angle C$ and the length of AC.

Find the mid-points of the 3 sides of the triangle.
Join each mid-point to the opposite angle of the triangle. These lines are called **medians** of the triangle. Can you discover anything about them ?

5. **Angles of a quadrilateral**

A four-sided figure is called a **quadrilateral**.
The quadrilateral $ABCD$ has been divided by the diagonal BD into two triangles.

What is the sum of the angles $a + b + d$, and why ?
What is the sum of the angles $c + e + f$, and why ?
What is the sum of the angles $a + b + f + c + e + d$?
What is the sum of the angles of a quadrilateral ?

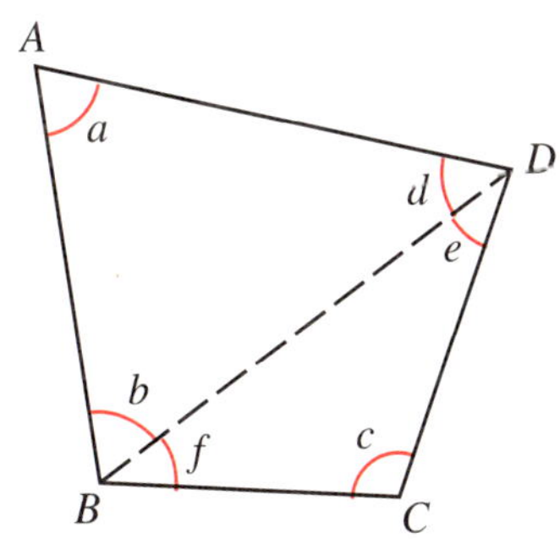

You can also find the sum of the angles of a pentagon, by splitting it into 3 triangles.

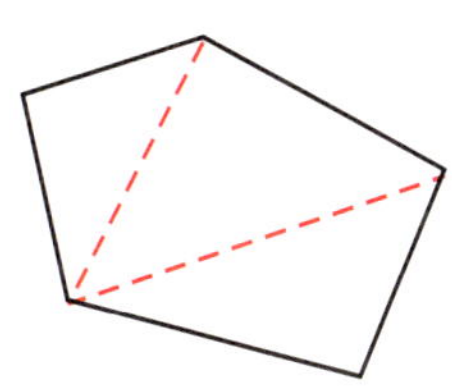

6. **Triangles and equations**

1 Write down an equation involving x and find the value of x.

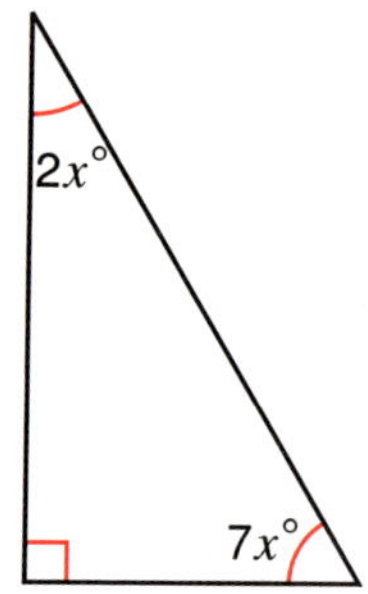

2 Write down an equation involving x and find the value of x. State the sizes of the angles at A and B. What sort of triangle is ΔABC ?

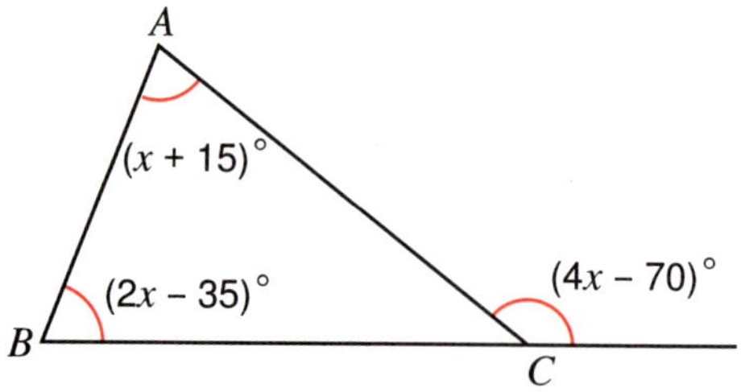

3 Find the values of x, y and z, in that order.

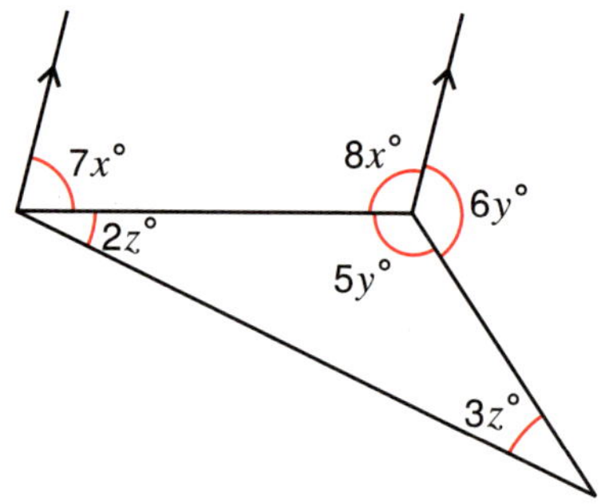

4 The angles of a triangle are $(3x + 12)°$, $(x + 19)°$ and $(2x - 7)°$. Find the value of x, and the sizes of the angles.
What sort of triangle is it ?

Chapter 18 test

1. Find the marked angles in these diagrams.

1

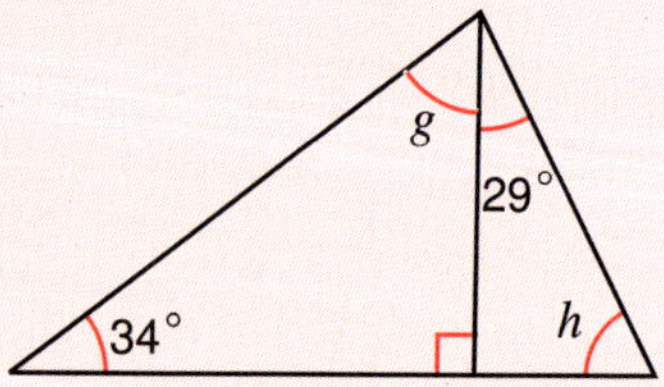

2

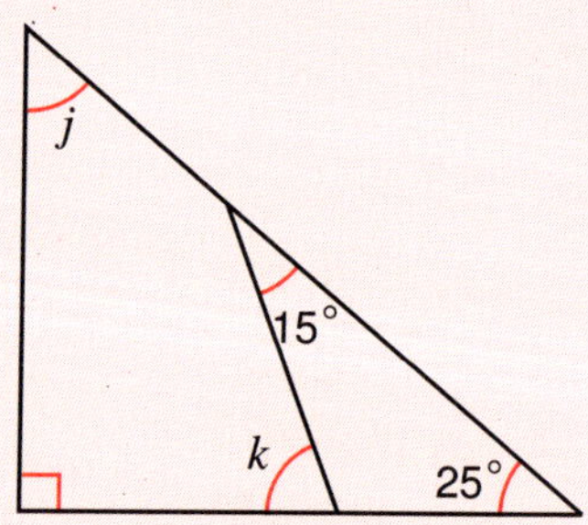

2. In the diagram the line QS bisects the angle PQR. (This means it cuts it exactly in half.) Calculate the sizes of angles a, b and c.

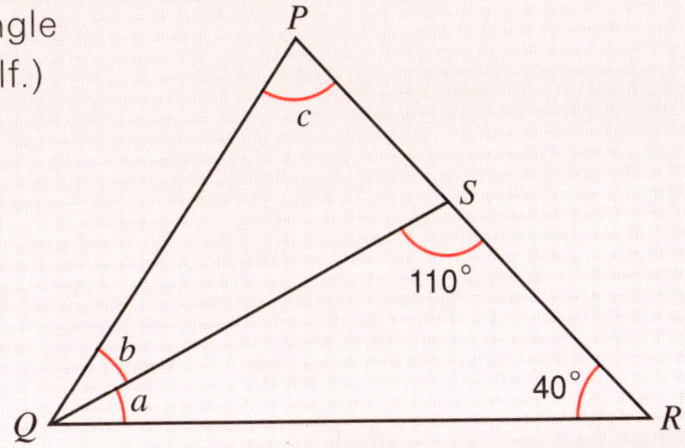

3. ΔABC is equilateral. Find the sizes of angles a, b and c.

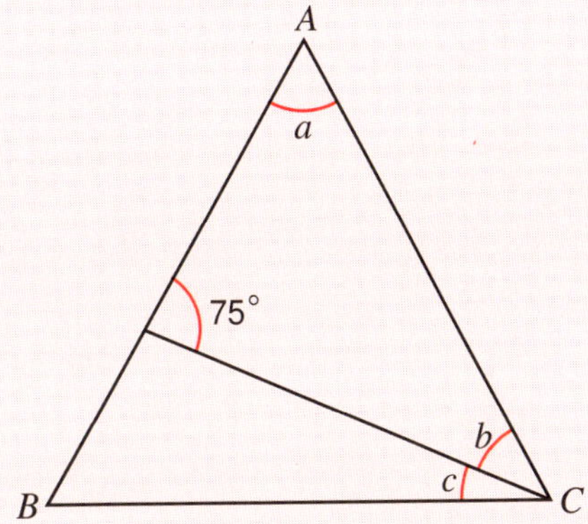

4. Construct a triangle ABC with $AB = 8$ cm, $\angle A = 46°$ and $\angle B = 64°$. Join D, the mid-point of AC, to E, the mid-point of BC. Join BD. Measure the angles ABD and BDE. Comment on your results.

PUZZLE

41. A chess set consists of 16 black pieces and 16 white pieces. All the pieces are put in a bag and 2 pieces are taken out at a time.
If they are the same colour they are put in a pile on the table, if they are different colours they are put away in their box.
What is the probability that there will be equal numbers of black and white pieces on the table after all the pieces have been removed from the bag ?

Miscellaneous Section C

Aural Practice

These aural exercises, C1 and C2, should be read to you, probably by your teacher or a friend, and you should write down the answers only, doing any working out in your head. You should do the 15 questions within 10 minutes.

Exercise C1

1. How many axes of symmetry has an equilateral triangle ?

2. Simplify the expression $6a \times 9b$.

3. Write down the next two terms in the sequence 14, 21, 28, 35, 42.

4. After washing, a roll of cloth shrinks by 10%. If at first it is 60 m long, how long will it be after washing ?

5. If a triangle has one angle of 40° and the other 2 angles are equal, how big are they ?

6. If the temperature is $-4°$ Celsius and it rises in the morning by 3 degrees, what is the new temperature ?

7. A plane left Manchester at 1.50 pm and arrived at Palma at 4.20 pm. How long did the journey take ?

8. Write down an expression for the number of centimetres in d metres.

9. If I turn up the top card of a well shuffled pack of 52 cards, what is the probability that it will be an ace ?

10. There are two adjacent angles on a straight line. One of them is 95°, how big is the other ?

11. What is the value of $a^2 + b^2$ when $a = 4$ and $b = 3$?

12. Roy measured the height of a room as 400 cm. What is this height in metres ?

13. What is the value of x if $5x + 1 = 46$?

14. If the total amount of time represented on a pie chart is 24 hours, what angle is needed for a sector representing 3 hours ?

15. If a gallon is approximately $4\frac{1}{2}$ litres, and I get 6 gallons of petrol, how many litres is this ?

Exercise C2

1. What is 1.23 multiplied by 10 ?

2. Simplify the expression $8c - c$.

3. How many axes of symmetry has a rectangle ?

4. Of the members of a club, 64% are over 18 years old and the rest are under 18. What percentage are under 18 ?

5. If $a = 6$ and $b = 0$, what is the value of $2ab$?

6. Mark is normally paid at the rate of £8 per hour. On Saturdays he is paid at $1\frac{1}{2}$ times this rate. How much does he earn for 4 hours work on a Saturday ?

7. Taking 8 km to be equal to 5 miles, what is 40 km in miles ?

8. Write down a prime number between 32 and 40.

9. In the morning the temperature was $-4°$ Celsius, and later on it was $5°$ Celsius. By how many degrees had the temperature risen ?

10. Write down an expression for each length of ribbon, in cm, if 1 metre of ribbon is cut into r equal parts ?

11. If 2 angles of a triangle are $50°$ and $20°$, what is the size of the other angle ?

12. If I toss a coin properly 8 times and it turns up heads 5 times, what is the probability that next time I toss it, it will show tails ?

13. In the function $y = 8 - 2x$, what is the value of y when $x = 2\frac{1}{2}$?

14. 10 angles meet at a point. How big are they if they are all equal ?

15. A cricketer scored 10, 30, 25 and 15 runs in four innings. What was his average score ?

Exercise C3 Revision

1. If the temperature one morning is $-3°C$, and it rises by 8 degrees during the day and then falls by 12 degrees at night, what is the night's temperature ?

2. Simplify

1 $3a + 3a$ **2** $3a - 2a$ **3** $a^2 + a^2$ **4** $a^2 \times a$ **5** $a \div a$

3. A piece of wire 75 cm long weighs 10 g. A longer piece of the same wire weighs 2 kg. How long will it be ?

4. Azara, Bindoo and Carole weighed themselves. Bindoo weighed 5 kg less than Azara and Carole weighed 12 kg more than Bindoo.
If the weight of Azara is written as w kg, what are the expressions for the weights of Bindoo and Carole ?
Afterwards the girls got on the scales together and the weight shown was 119 kg.
Write down an equation and solve it to find the weight of each girl.

5. This pie chart is drawn accurately.
Measure the angles in each sector to the nearest 10°.
If the whole circle represents a total time of 72 minutes, find the times represented by A, B, C and D.

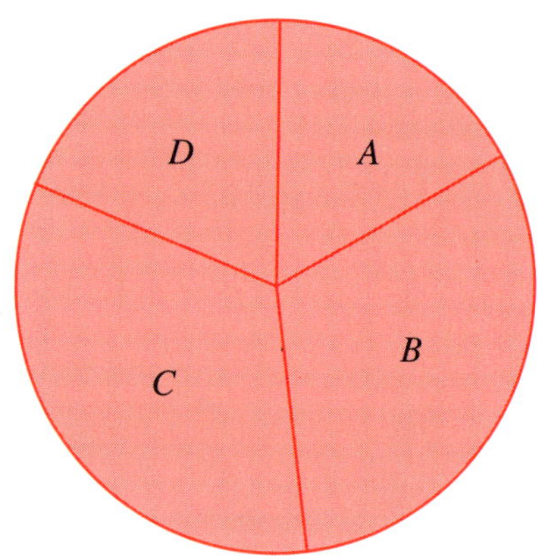

6. Which of the numbers 19, 29, 39, 49, 59 are prime numbers ?

7. Calculate the sizes of angles a, b, c.

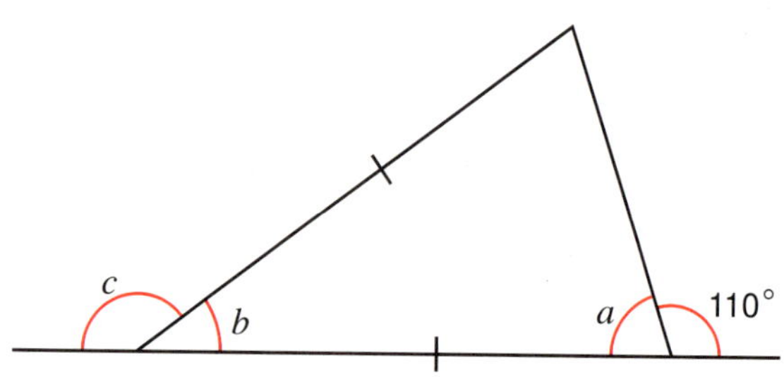

8. A tank containing liquid is $\frac{3}{5}$ full. When 30 more gallons are put in the tank is full. How many gallons does the tank hold altogether ?

9. The numbers of tomatoes on each truss on tomato plants in a greenhouse were counted. Here are the results:

9	8	4	7	7	5	3	5	3	6	5	1	5	6	5
5	4	1	8	6	3	9	5	2	7	4	1	4	7	4
6	3	4	6	4	2	3	4	4	5	2	8	6	4	4
6	6	2	5	7										

Make a frequency table of these results.

1 What is the mode number of tomatoes per truss ?
2 What is the median number ?
3 What is the mean number ?
4 Draw a bar-line graph of the distribution.

10. This is a timetable of the bus service on market days.

Barley Village	dep.	10.40
Thornton Dale	dep.	11.20
Suntown	arr.	12.05
Suntown	dep.	3.55
Thornton Dale	arr.	4.40
Barley Village	arr.	5.15

1 What is the time taken for the journey from Barley Village to Suntown ?
2 How much quicker is the return journey ?
3 Mrs Kenyon uses this service from Barley Village to visit her mother in Thornton Dale. How long can she spend with her mother, if her mother lives 20 minutes walk from the bus stop in Thornton Dale ?

Exercise C4 Revision

1. A farmer had 800 kg of potatoes but $\frac{1}{4}$ of them were bad and had to be thrown away. He kept $\frac{1}{5}$ of the remainder to feed to his pigs and sold the rest. What quantity did he sell ?

2. The diagram shows a thermometer with Celsius and Fahrenheit scales.

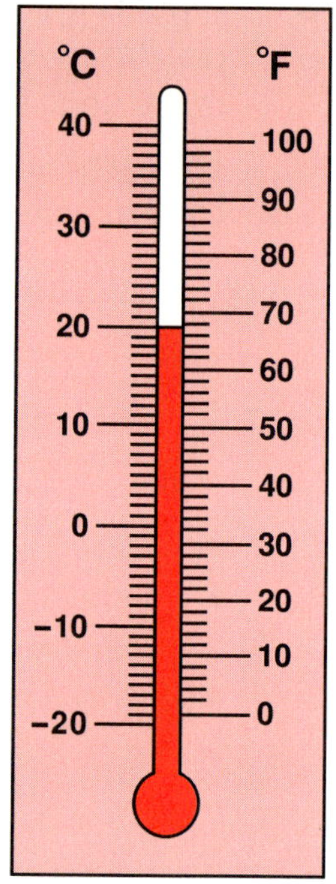

1 What temperature does the thermometer show, in °F, and in °C ?

2 What would be the temperature in °C if it was 90°F ?

3 The classroom should be heated to 16°C. What is this temperature in °F ?

4 A holiday guide gives these temperatures as the average daily maximum temperatures on the Costa Blanca. Change these readings into °F, giving them to the nearest degree.

May	24°C
June	28°C
July	31°C
Aug	31°C
Sept	29°C

3. The ages of 6 boys were 13y 7m, 14y 0m, 14y 0m, 14y 5m, 13y 10m, 13y 2m. Find the mean and median ages, and the range of ages.

4. Calculate the sizes of angles a, b and c.

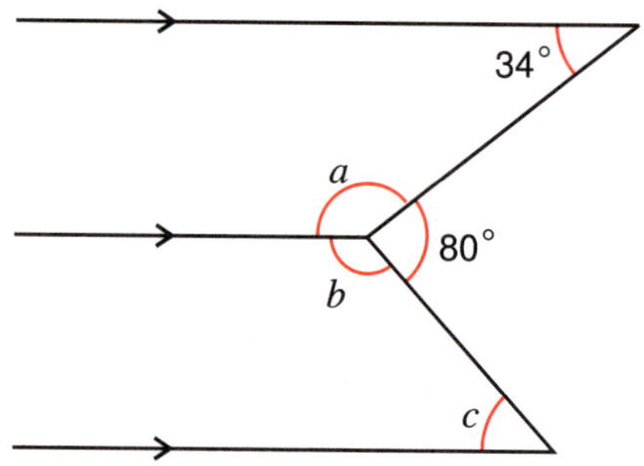

5. If $x = \frac{1}{6}(3a + 2b + c)$, find the value of x if $a = 11$, $b = 8$ and $c = 5$.

6. A card is drawn from a pack of 52 cards and not replaced. It is the Queen of hearts. A second card is drawn. What is the probability that it is another heart ?

7. Construct a triangle ABC with $AB = 6$ cm, $\angle A = 90°$ and $BC = 10$ cm. Measure AC.

8. What is the reading on this dial ? If it rises to 9, by how many units has it risen ?

It then falls 10 units. What is the new reading ?

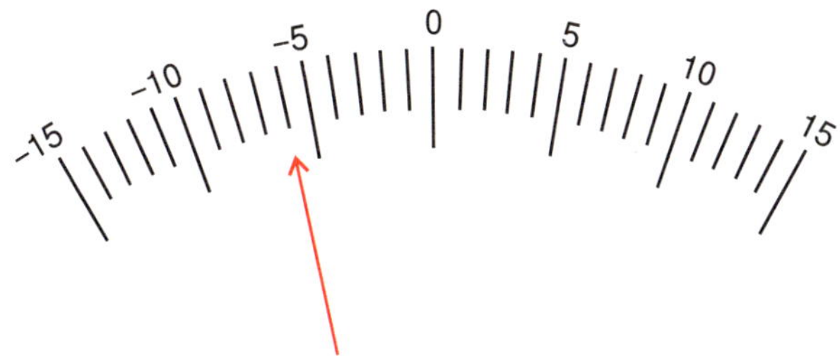

9. The angles of a triangle are $(x+5)^\circ$, $(2x+10)^\circ$, $(3x-75)^\circ$. Write down an equation, and solve it to find the value of x. What are the sizes of the angles ? What sort of triangle is it ?

10. The marks of 94 pupils were as follows:

Marks	Frequency
55–59	3
60–64	13
65–69	37
70–74	29
75–79	10
80–84	2

Six others had marks 76, 61, 68, 63, 83, 78.
Re-write the frequency column to include these figures and draw a histogram of the complete list of the 100 marks.

Exercise C5 Revision

1. A shopkeeper buys an article for £3.60. He then adds onto this price 10% for his profit. How much does he add on ? What would his selling-price be ?

2. Find the sizes of angles a, b, c.

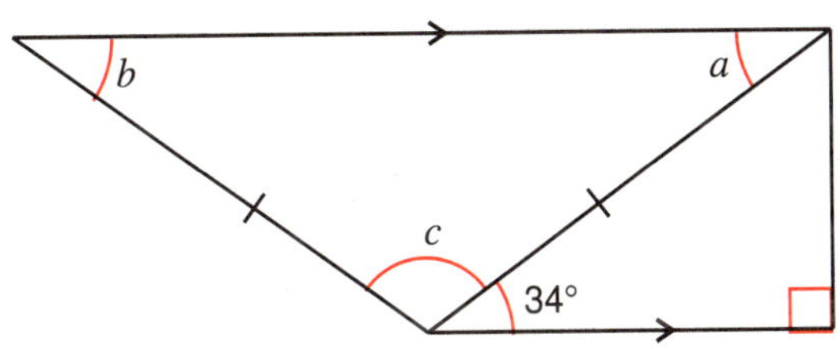

3. The diagram shows the goals scored by some football teams.

   1 How many football teams were there ?

   2 What was the total number of goals scored ?

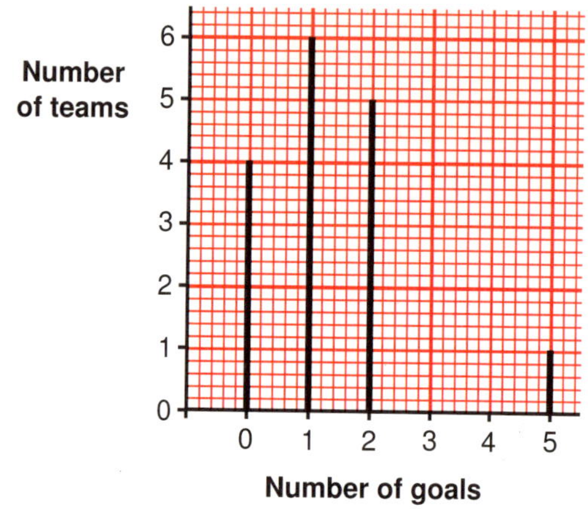

4. The temperature readings taken at noon each day during a winter week in a town are shown in the table.

   1 How much did the temperature rise between Sunday and Monday ?

   2 What was the average daily noon temperature for the week ?

Sun	$-5°C$
Mon	$2°C$
Tues	$-5°C$
Wed	$0°C$
Thur	$3°C$
Fri	$2°C$
Sat	$-4°C$

5. The bar chart shows how some money is divided among 3 charities A, B and C. The bar A is 11 cm long, B is 9 cm and C is 5 cm. If the amount A gets is £165, how much are the shares of B and C ?

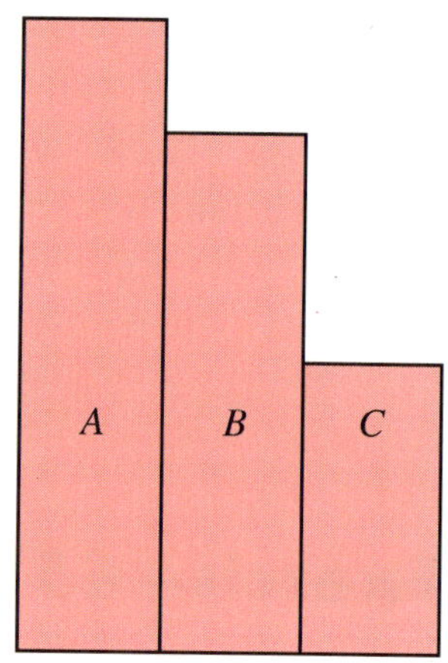

6. How many axes of symmetry have these shapes ?

   1 An equilateral triangle,

   2 a rectangle,

   3 an isosceles triangle,

   4 the capital letter M,

   5 the capital letter N.

7. A holiday is paid for by making an initial deposit of £50 and then paying £30 per month for 10 months. How much has been paid altogether after 3 months ?
   Find a formula for the amount £ A paid after n months (where n is any whole number from 1 to 10).
   Put $n = 10$ in your formula to find the total cost of the holiday.

8. A school has 800 pupils and $\frac{11}{20}$ of them are girls. How many girls are there, and how many boys ?

9. A game is played by picking at random a card from a set of three cards numbered 1, 3, 5 and then picking at random a second card from a set numbered 2, 4, 6.
Copy and complete the table showing the outcomes when the two cards are selected.
What are the probabilities that
1 the sum of the numbers on the cards is 7,
2 at least one of the cards is a 3 or a 6 ?

		1st card		
		1	3	5
2nd card	2	1, 2	·	·
	4	·	·	·
	6	·	·	·

10. The height of Blackpool Tower is $518\frac{3}{4}$ feet. Using 1 foot = 30.48 cm, find this height in metres, to the nearest metre.

Exercise C6 Revision

1. In the diagram, $\angle DBC$ is cut in half by BE. DA is a straight line.
What is the value of x ?

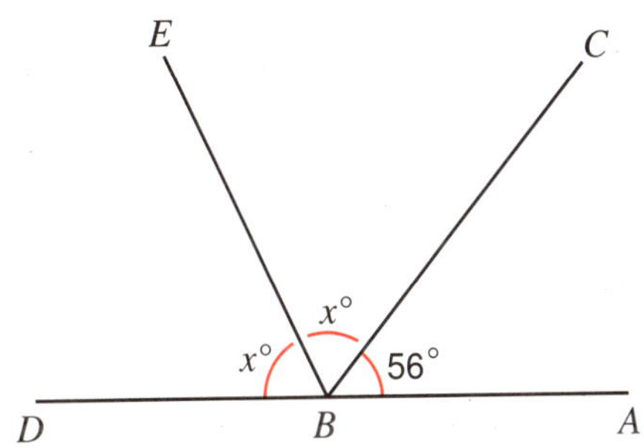

2. One number in each of these sequences is incorrect. Copy the sequences, replacing the wrong number by the correct number.

1 100, 92, 84, 76, 66, 60.
2 1, 3, 6, 9, 15, 21, 28.
3 1, 4, 9, 15, 25, 36.
4 1, $4\frac{1}{2}$, 19, $13\frac{1}{2}$, 18, $22\frac{1}{2}$.
5 1, 6, 27, 64, 125, 216.

3.

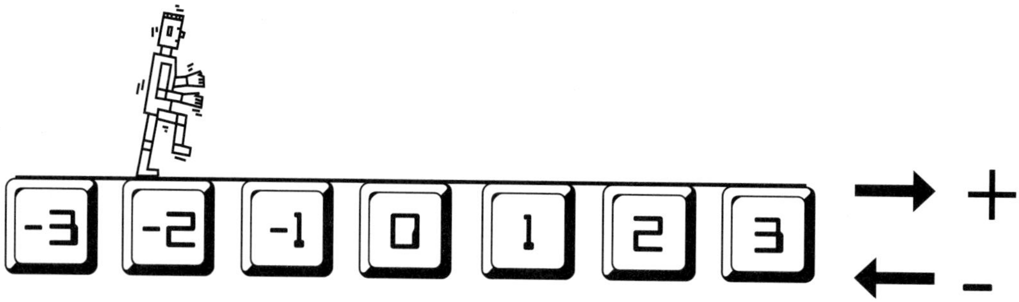

Steve is playing a computer game. To make the robot go to the right he presses the + key. To make the robot go to the left he presses the − key.
e.g. To get from [−2] to [0] he would press +2,
to get from [−1] to [−3] he would press −2.

What must he press to move the robot·
1 from [−2] to [−3].
2 from [0] to [2].
3 from [3] to [−2].
4 from [−1] to [0] ?

Where does the robot end up if
5 it was at [−3] and Steve pressed +6,
6 it was at [0] and Steve pressed −2,
7 it was at [2] and Steve pressed −5 ?

Where was the robot at first if
8 after Steve pressed −3 it ended up at [−1],
9 after Steve pressed +3 it ended up at [0],
10 after Steve pressed −1 it ended up at [2] ?

4. Solve these equations:

1 $a - 8 = 22$
2 $3b + 17 = 26$
3 $9c = 63$
4 $3d + 15 = d + 25$
5 $5e - 8 = 10 - e$

5. From a plank of wood which is 11 ft 4 in long. Alan cuts off 6 lengths of 1 ft 3 in each. He then cuts the remaining piece in half. How long is each half ? (1 foot = 12 inches.)

6. In the diagram, equal lines are marked. Find the sizes of angles a, b, c, d.

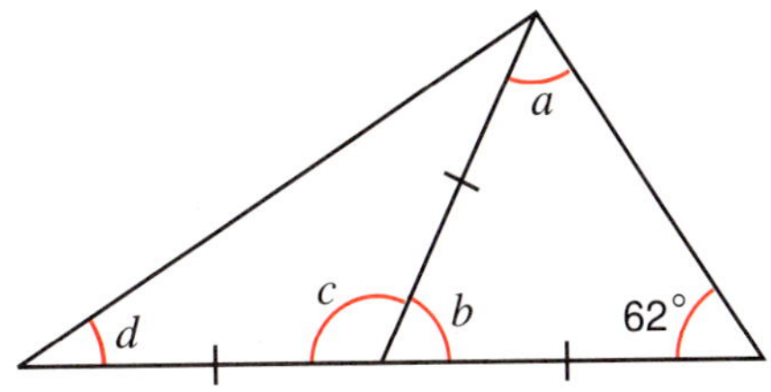

7. In a lottery, there are 2000 tickets sold at 20p each.
There are 4 prizes of £25,
4 prizes of £10,
4 prizes of £5,
40 prizes of £1.

If Charlotte bought a ticket, what is the probability that

1 she will win £25,
2 she will win £1,
3 she will win a prize,
4 she will not win a prize ?

8. How many

1 mm in 6 cm,
2 g in 2 kg
3 m in 3 km,
4 ml in 5 ℓ,
5 cm in 4 m ?

9. The times taken by a plumber to mend 5 bursts were 1 h 20 min, 2 h 25 min, 3 h 10 min, 1 h 10 min, 2 h 45 min. Find the mean time taken for a job, and the range of times.

10. Construct triangle ABC with the measurements given. D is the mid-point of AB. Mark D on your diagram. Through D draw a line parallel to BC. Let this line cut AC at E.
Measure AE and EC.
Comment on your results.

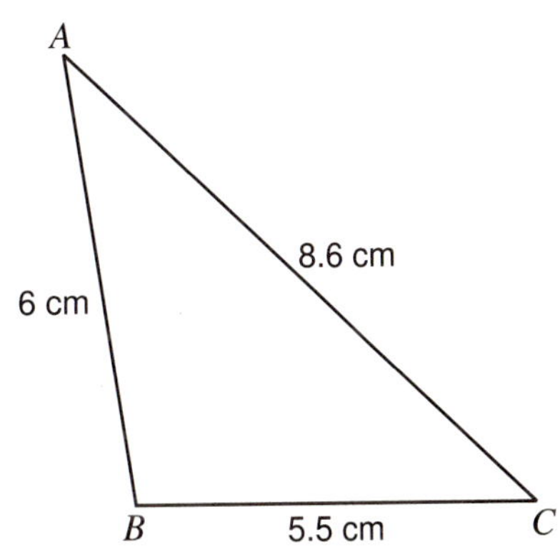

Exercise C7 Activities

1. Planning a day's outing

For the next half-term or main holiday, plan a day-out with some of your friends.

First of all, decide what you would like to do and where you would like to go. Perhaps it will be a visit to the seaside, to a country park, a zoo or one of the theme parks where there are numerous amusements. You may like to visit a city to attend a theatre performance, do a sightseeing trip or a shopping trip.

Find the destination on a map. Decide how you are going to get to the place, by train, bus, coach, car or bicycle. Find the route you will take from your home, and find the approximate distance. Draw a sketch map showing the route.

Make a timetable for the day, including the times of the journeys there and back, and the time for lunch.
Decide whether you are going to buy a meal or a snack for lunch, or whether you will take a packed lunch. Will you be home by teatime or will you need another meal out ?

Calculate an approximate cost for the day, including fares, admission charges, food and drinks, and other spending money.

2. **A display of weighing and measuring instruments**

If everyone in the class helped by bringing things, you could have a good display of weighing and measuring instruments.
(You will have to discuss this with your teacher. You need to have somewhere to show the display, and if parents are willing to lend equipment you must make sure it is looked after carefully.)

You could begin your planning by making a list of instruments available. To begin with, you have rulers and protractors. The home economics department will have weighing scales and measuring jugs. The science department will have more accurate equipment. The PE staff will have longer tape measures, and stop-watches. Think of what other departments in the school might lend to you. Then a letter to parents suggesting what you are looking for might produce other items. Has anyone a gauge for measuring knitting needles, or one for measuring ring sizes ? Don't forget a tyre pressure gauge which a motorist might lend. Can you borrow equipment from a surveyor ?

When you know what items you are going to have in your display, you can print out neat labels. Perhaps you will write notes to put with the more unusual items. Decide how best to arrange your display, perhaps putting all the things which measure length together, then weighing instruments, etc. You could divide the display into British and metric sections.

Take a photograph of the display so you will have a record of it.

3. **Elevens**

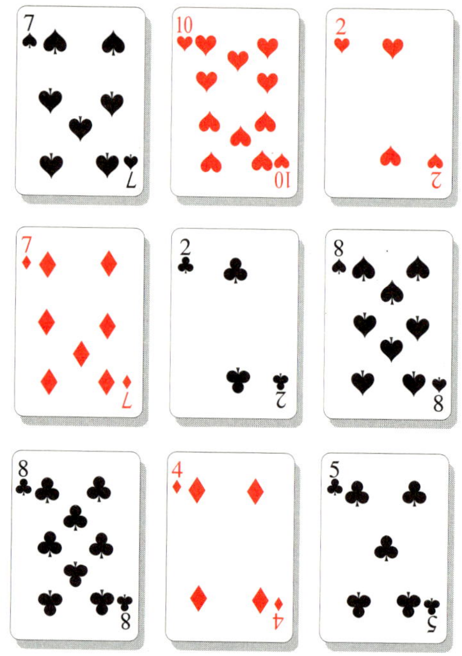

Elevens is a patience game with a pack of cards.
Shuffle the pack of 52 cards and put down 9 cards face upwards (usually in three rows of three, but this is not essential). Keep the rest of the pack in your hand.
Using the next 2 cards from the pack, put cards face upwards to cover any 2 cards whose numbers add up to 11, such as 7 and 4 in the diagram. It does not matter which number 7 you cover up, just choose one of them. Repeat this with other pairs which add up to 11.
You can use the new cards in the same way as the original ones, using only the top card of each pile. Aces count as 1's and pair with 10's.
Do not count the picture cards as numbers. Instead, if a Jack, Queen and King are all visible, cover up all three with the next three cards.
You win the game if you use up all the cards in the pack. If you get to a situation where you cannot find any more pairs, or sets of Jack, Queen, King, you lose.
Try the game a few times and see how many times you win.

Now we are going to change the rules to carry out a statistical experiment.
Amended rules:– If you get to a situation where you cannot cover up any more cards, use the next card from the pack to make an extra pile so that you are now using 10 piles. This extra card may help to get things going again, if not, put another one down so as to make 11 piles, and so on every time you cannot cover any cards up. When you have used all the pack of cards, count how many piles there are. Record this number as the score, on a tally chart. It will be at least 9, and sometimes gets as big as 16. (The smaller, the better.)
Repeat this experiment several times.
Finally, draw a bar-line graph to show the distribution of scores. Comment on its shape, and on the results.

4. **Fourteen**

This is a multiplication square using the numbers 1, 9, 11. Copy this, but instead of putting the actual answers in, if the number is 14 or more then divide by 14 and just write down the remainder. (This is called arithmetic modulo 14.)

×	1	9	11
1	1	9	11
9	9	81	99
11	11	99	121

Comment on the pattern.

Now subtract 1, 9 and 11 from 14 and make a pattern with the new numbers. Can you comment about this one ?
Then combine these numbers to make a table using all the odd numbers under 14, except 7, which is an odd one out.
What about the even numbers ? Begin using 2, 4, 8, and then investigate further. (Dividing by other numbers produces patterns like this, so you can continue your investigations if you have time.)

5. **To bisect an angle using ruler and compasses**

Bisect means 'to cut it exactly in half'.

To bisect $\angle ACB$.

With centre C, draw arcs to cut CA and CB at X and Y.

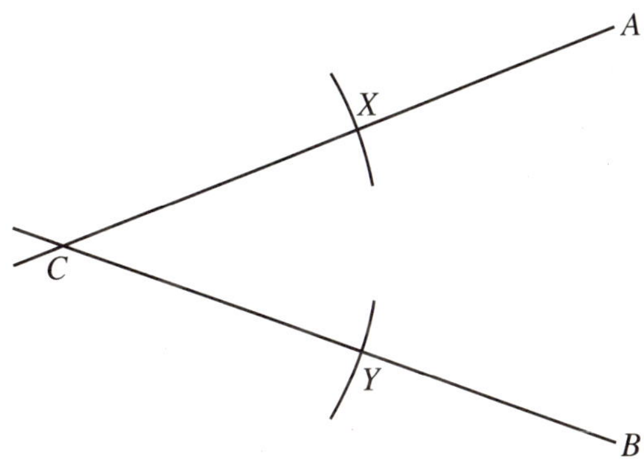

With centres X and Y in turn, and a suitable radius, draw arcs to cut at Z. Join CZ, which is the bisector of $\angle ACB$.

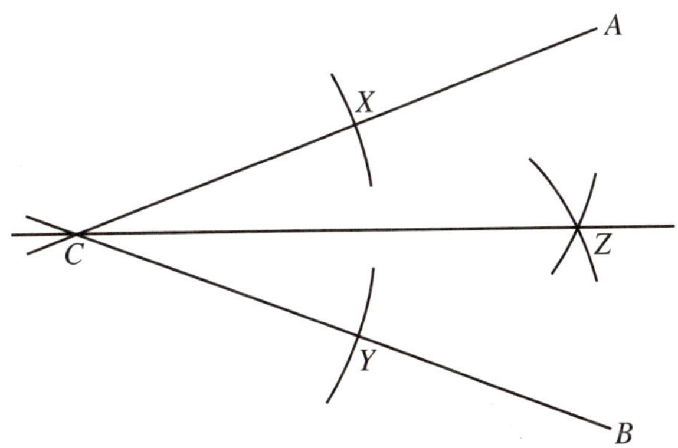

Practise this method, bisecting an acute angle and then an obtuse angle.

6. Nets of solid figures

These are patterns which when cut out and folded will make the figures.

Net of a cube

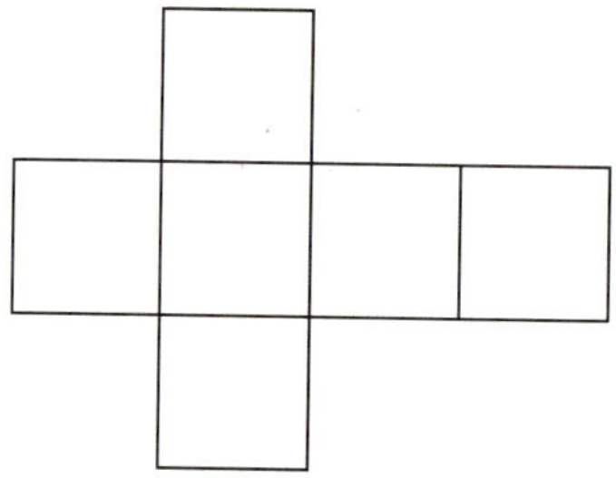

Making models from thin cardboard, using their nets

1 Draw the pattern of the net of the solid figure, on paper. Then place it over thin cardboard, with something underneath to protect the desk or table, and prick through the main points using the point of your compasses. Remove the pattern and join up the marks on the cardboard. (Keep the pattern for future use.)

2 Draw a tab on every alternate edge, i.e. starting at any edge, put tabs on edges 1, 3, 5, 7, . . . in order. Tabs can be drawn freehand. They should be large enough to stick easily.

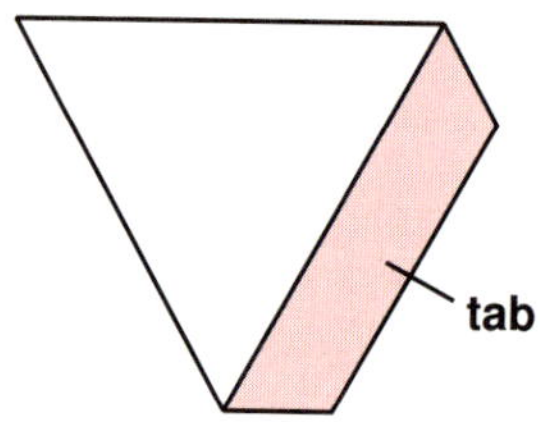

3 Score every line.
This means making a nick in the line so that it folds neatly. Put your ruler along the line and drag your compass point along it. (When you fold the cardboard, always fold **away** from the side you scored on. Do not bend the cardboard backwards **and** forwards.)

4 Cut out the net and fold it along the scored lines.

5 Glue it together, doing one tab at a time and waiting until it has stuck before doing the next one, except at the last face where more than one tab may have to be glued at the same time. You may need to poke your compass point through a corner hole to help to make the last tab stick down properly.

To make a cube

Making the sides of the squares 4 cm long, copy the net of the cube onto paper. (Graph paper or squared paper is useful.)
Carry out the instructions above for making the model.

To make a cuboid

Decide on the measurements your finished cuboid will have, and design and draw the net. Here is the net for a cuboid which will be 8 cm by 3 cm by 2 cm.
Carry out the instructions for making the model.

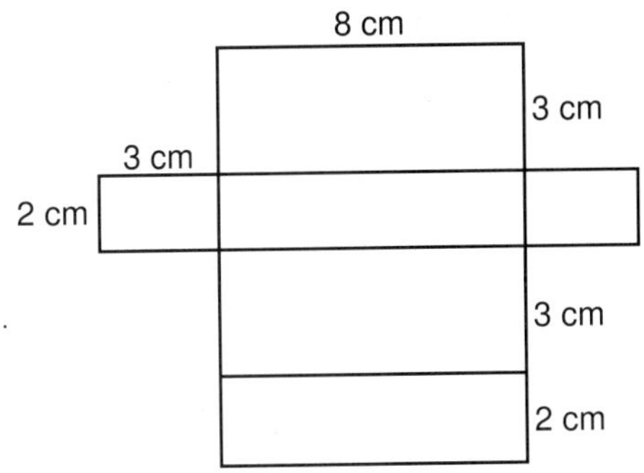

To make a triangular prism

To draw the net, begin by drawing a rectangle, 12 cm by 15 cm, and divide it into the three rectangles shown.
Construct equilateral triangles of side 5 cm on the sides of the centre rectangle. You can do this using compasses or you can make angles of 60° with your protractor.
Carry out the instructions for making the model.

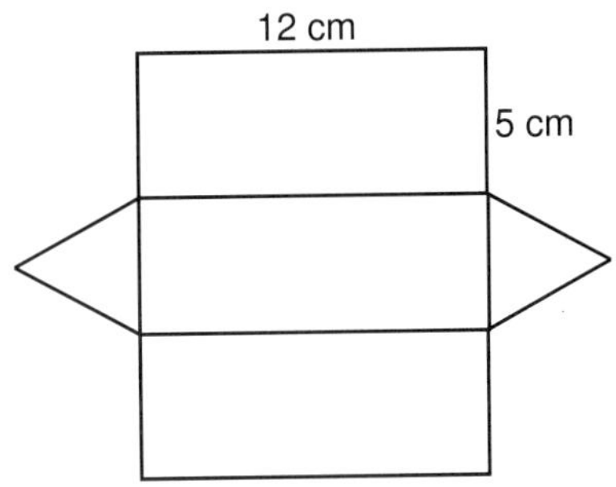

Here are nets for two other figures you can make. Decide which lengths on the nets should be equal.

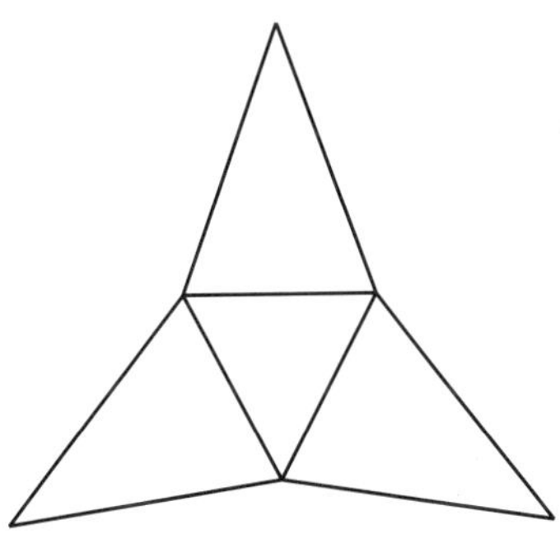

triangular pyramid

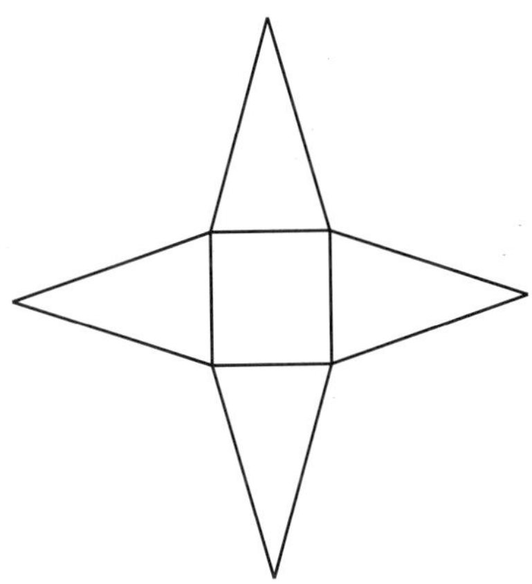

pyramid with square base

7. The Earth

The Earth makes 1 complete revolution about its axis every 24 hours. How long does it take to rotate through 1° ?

London is on longitude 0°, New York is on longitude 74° West. These measurements in degrees correspond to the degrees of rotation. When the sun rises in London, the Earth must rotate another 74° before the sun rises in New York. How much later will this be ?

This is why different countries keep different times. Many countries keep the same time throughout the whole country, but in a large country, such as USA, there is too much difference between the Eastern and Western sides, and the country is divided into different time zones. See if you can find in an atlas a map showing time zones in different countries.

People who have business dealings with another country will need to know the time difference so that they can telephone during working hours. This also matters to anyone who has relations abroad who may not appreciate being woken up by the telephone at 4 am ! Choose 10 cities and make a table showing the times there when it is 9 am, 12 noon, 3 pm and 6 pm in London.

If you visit Greenwich, East London, you can stand on longitude 0°. Why was the 0° line chosen to go through this place ?

Try to find out where the International Date Line is, why it is not a straight line, and what happens when you travel across it. Does it make any difference whether you go eastwards or westwards ?

8. Using a computer database

A computer is a machine that is capable of processing information very quickly, but only in accordance with a given set of instructions, and so it is necessary that information is organised in some way.

A **database program** will put the data in order, and can also make selections of various categories from it. You can imagine how useful such a program is for so many kinds of users, from the small market gardener who keeps a database of the seeds he uses, to a Government department which makes vital decisions from the data it collects.

As an example of a datafile, consider the recording of information on pupils in a school. The school requires a **set of information** which relates to each individual pupil. The collection of all the sets of information is called a datafile. The information needed for each pupil will consist of several items. It could be organised in a table as follows:

Surname	Other names	Sex	Date of birth	Address	Form

The entry for any particular pupil is called a **record**.

The headings listed, such as surname, other names, sex, . . . are called **fields**. In some of them, the entry can be a single letter, e.g. for sex, M for male and F for female. It could be numerical, e.g. 17.10.80 for date of birth. For names and addresses the entry would be much longer. The type of field and its length have to be decided when planning the datafile.

There could be further details entered in other fields, for instance, whether the pupil has school dinner.

By giving the relevant instructions the computer could then be made to select certain pupils. For example, the school might need a list of pupils in each form, in alphabetical order of surname; for a medical inspection the names of all 12 year-old pupils might be needed in two lists, one of boys and the other of girls. If there were transport problems, so that pupils who lived in a certain district had to be sent home early, a list of the names of all the pupils who lived in that district might be needed, together with the forms they were in so that they could be contacted. The computer program would be able to sort out the data and select what was needed in each case.

Here are the fields an employer might have on a payroll datafile.

Employee number	Name	Dept	Job Description	Pay rate	Hours worked

And here are the fields a bookseller might have in the stock datafile.

Book code	Title	Publisher	Author	Category	Price	Copies in stock

A program that will record such data and select from it or sort it into various categories will be quite complicated and so a commercially produced program will probably be used.

If you have such a program available, then you can make use of it to store some data. Think of the sort of data you could keep in a database. Maybe it is data from one of your other school subjects. Maybe you have a hobby for which you collect objects or information, and the details could be stored in a database.

There are problems about storing data which include records relating to people. Those who do this must have a licence to do so. If you intend to include people's real names in your database, you should check with your teacher first, to see if you can do this.

If you would like to practise using your database, here is a simple example you can use. If you have not got access to a computer and a database, you could enter this information on small cards and sort them manually, to answer the questions.

A shop sells watches and classifies them in a datafile as follows. (The names and details are fictitious.)

Cat. no	Name	Type	Price £	Digital (D) or with dial (A)	Special features
89/1	Kiddywatch	childs	6	D	animal picture
89/2	Styletime	ladies	7	D	date
89/3	Sparkletime	ladies	26	A	diamante stones
89/4	Bestime	ladies	20	A	gold plated
89/5	Accritime	gents	12	A	second hand, splashproof
89/6	Tradwatch	gents	10	A	Roman numerals
89/7	Scenetime	ladies	8	A	scene on dial
89/8	Telltime	childs	9	A	fully figured
89/9	Oldytime	gents	11	A	pocket watch
89/10	Sportstime	gents	14	D	stopwatch, alarm

Using the datafile, list the watches in order of price, cheapest first.
List the watches suitable for a lady, together with their prices and any special features.
Meg wants to choose a watch as a birthday present for a child. It should not be a digital watch. Which one is suitable, and how much will it cost ?

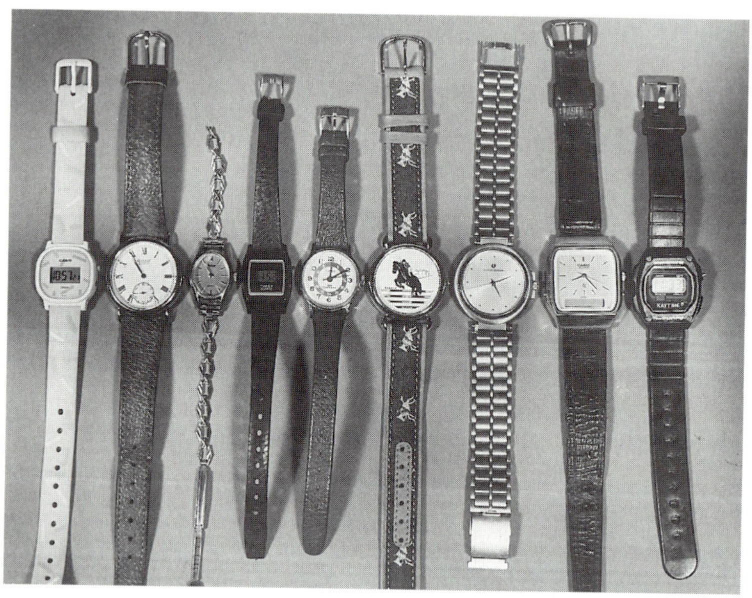

PUZZLES

42. Arrange 6 similar coins like this, each coin touching those next to it.
In 3 moves rearrange the coins into a circle.
A move means moving 1 coin, and finishing the move with it touching at least 2 other coins.

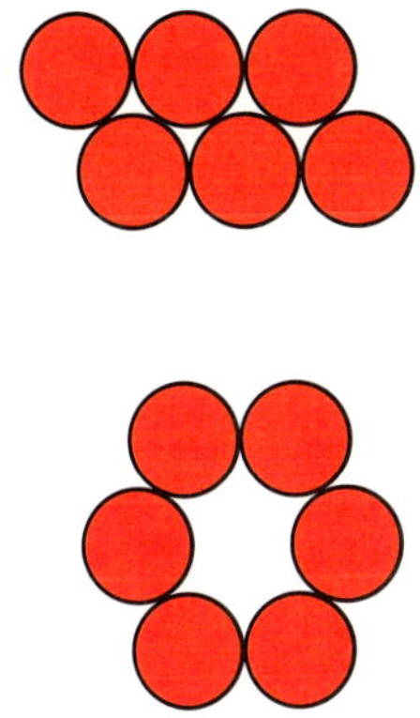

43. Mary and Joan joined the Guides. They gave their names as Mary Bell and Joan Bell, with the same address and the same date of birth. 'So you are twins,' said the leader. 'No, we're not,' they replied together. Can you explain this ? (They are not cousins, either.)

44. The church choirmaster had lost the number cards used to put up the hymn number on the board in the church, but after searching around he found these 5 cards.

Although there are 300 hymns in the hymnbook he must choose one whose number can be made from some of these cards.
How many hymns has he got to choose from ?

45. The five boys, Alec, Benjamin, Christopher, Darren and Eddie took part in a race.

Alec said 'I was not last.'
Benjamin said 'Darren was not first.'
Christopher said 'Eddie was third.'
Darren said 'Benjamin was second.'
Eddie said 'Alec ran slower than Benjamin.'

If the remarks of those who were 1st and 2nd were false, and the rest true, and no-one tied, what was the order ?

Index

accuracy of measurements, 78, 111
acute angle, 122
acute-angled triangle, 286
addition and subtraction in algebra, 184
addition of decimals, 69
adjacent angles, 131, 240, 242
algebra, 180, 182, 252, 254
alternate angles, 245
amounts to the nearest penny, 75
angles, 119, 121, 240, 242, 315
angles at a point, 131, 240, 242
angles of triangles, 137, 249, 287, 292
approximate comparisons, 220
approximations, 20, 39, 71, 75, 76
averages, 167, 273
axis of symmetry, 52

bar chart, 158, 162
bar-line graph, 270, 272
bisecting an angle, 315
brackets in arithmetic, 43
British units, 216, 218

calculations involving negative numbers, 232, 236, 237
calculations with angles, 242, 245
calculations with angles of triangles, 287, 292
calculator, 36, 38, 89, 155, 168, 223, 232
cancelling fractions, 144
capacity units, 106, 108, 218
centre of rotational symmetry, 56
chance, 86, 196
checking answers, 38
checking answers to equations, 261
clocks, 223
collecting information, 171, 172
collecting terms in algebra, 184
computer, 215, 318
computer database, 318
constant function on a calculator, 45
constructing triangles, 295
corresponding angles, 245
cube, 316
cube numbers, 8, 9, 11
cube roots, 8
cubes of numbers, 7, 8, 41
cuboid, 56, 317

database program, 318
decimals, 64, 66
degrees, 121
denominator of a fraction, 142
diagrams in statistics, 158, 161, 164, 270, 272, 273, 276
diameter of a circle, 53
division, 17, 24, 27, 32, 67, 69, 73, 237
division in algebra, 186
drawing an angle of 60°, 299
drawing angles, 126
drawing lines, 120, 134, 210
drawing parallel lines, 134
drawing perpendicular lines, 210
drawing triangles, 295

equally likely outcomes, 196
equations, 252, 254
equilateral triangle, 55, 291
equivalent fractions, 143
estimations, 39, 76, 114, 228
even numbers, 4, 9
expressions in algebra, 181, 182, 189
exterior angle of a triangle, 287

factors of numbers, 4
Farey sequence, 154
formula for probability, 197
formulae (in algebra), 181, 187, 189
fractions, 140, 142
fractions key, 155
frequency, 272
frequency distributions, 270, 272, 276

graphs, 158, 162, 270, 272, 276
grouped frequency distributions, 271, 276

half-turn, 121
hexagonal numbers, 11
histograms, 271, 273, 276

improper fractions, 143
index notation, 7
interior angles (between parallel lines), 245
investigations, 171, 176, 282
isosceles triangle, 55, 291

length units, 106, 108, 218
line of symmetry, 52
line-graph, 162
lines (drawing and measuring), 118, 120, 134, 210
long division, 27
long multiplication, 22

magic squares, 48
mean, 167, 273
measuring angles, 124
measuring lines, 118, 120
measurement units, 78, 108, 112, 120, 124, 218, 222
median, 167, 274
medians of a triangle, 299
memory keys, 43
metric system, 106, 108
metric units, 106, 108

mirror line, 52
mixed numbers, 143
mode, 168, 274
money, 74
multiples, 4, 9
multiplication, 2, 16, 18, 22, 30, 67, 69, 73, 236
multiplication in algebra, 184

naming angles, 129, 247
naming of triangles, 288
negative numbers, 230, 232
nets of solid figures, 316
number chains, 12, 104
numbers, 1, 2, 4, 66, 142, 232
numbers to the nearest 10, 100, 1000, 20
numbers to the nearest whole number, 71
numerator of a fraction, 142

obtuse angle, 122
obtuse-angled triangle, 286
odd numbers, 4, 9
order of rotational symmetry, 56

parallel lines, 133, 241
parallelogram, 59, 249
percentages, 141, 149
perpendicular lines, 129, 210
pictogram, 158, 161
pie chart, 159, 164
plane of symmetry, 54
powers of numbers, 7, 9
prime numbers, 5
prism, 56, 317
probability, 84, 86, 194, 196
probability experiments, 86
probability scale, 84, 196
protractor, 123
pyramid, 56, 317

quadrilateral, 299

random numbers, 89, 209
random selection, 196
range, 169, 274
reading scales, 78, 112
rectangle, 55
reflection, 52
reflex angle, 122
relative frequency, 86
remainder in a division sum, 26, 41
removing brackets in algebra, 184
revolution, 121
right angle, 121
right-angled triangle, 286
Roman numerals, 105
rotational symmetry, 56
rules in algebra, 184, 257

scalene triangle, 291
sequences of numbers, 9
Sieve of Eratosthenes, 12
solid figures, 56, 316
solving equations, 254
spreadsheet programs, 215
square, 55
square numbers, 8, 9
square roots, 8, 41, 81
squares of numbers, 7, 8, 41
statistical calculator, 168
statistical diagrams, 158, 161, 164, 270, 272, 273, 276
statistical investigations, 171, 176, 282
statistics, 158, 160, 270, 272
substitution in algebra, 188
subtraction of decimals, 69
symmetry, 50, 52, 215

tables, 2, 108, 218, 220, 222
tables for statistical data, 161
tally table, 160, 272
temperature, 232
time, 217, 222
time-series graph, 162
triangles, 284, 286
triangular numbers, 1, 9

vertically opposite angles, 132, 240, 242

weight units, 106, 108, 218

Answers

Some answers have been corrected to reasonable degrees of accuracy, depending on the questions.
There may be variations in answers where questions involve drawings or graphs.

Page 3 Exercise 1.1

1.

8	54	49	72	0
30	6	72	4	42
14	0	0	9	132
48	28	2	9	100
25	24	81	63	11
0	45	33	10	24
12	96	84	110	64
88	20	16	12	35
48	77	18	56	70
30	20	144	60	36

2.

11	12	5	9	0
9	6	7	7	9
5	11	5	12	11
12	5	4	8	6
9	6	12	3	9

3. **1** 14 **2** 24 **3** 13 **4** 9 **5** 121 **6** 23 **7** 7 **8** 4 **9** 18 **10** 18

4. **1** 5 r 3 **2** 2 r 4 **3** 5 r 2 **4** 8 r 0 **5** 8 r 4

5. **1** 5 **2** 6 **3** 7 **4** 2 **5** 4

Page 6 Exercise 1.2

1. **1** 213, 415, 677, 717, 725
   2 415, 725, 1000
   3 102, 213, 528, 717, 828

2. **1** 30, 39, 42, 45, 48
   2 30, 35, 45
   3 35, 42, 49

3. **1** 1, 2, 3, 4, 6, 12
   2 1, 2, 3, 5, 6, 10, 15, 30
   3 1, 2, 4, 5, 8, 10, 20, 40

4. 2, 3, 5, 7, 11, 13, 17, 19, 23, 29

5. **1** 1, 3, 9, 27
   2 1, 3, 5, 9, 15, 45
   3 1, 3, 9
   4 9

6. **1** 11 **2** 6 **3** 5 **4** 10 **5** 4 **6** 12 **7** 9 **8** 8 **9** 2 **10** 7

7. **1** 3, 6, 9, 12, 15, 18, 21, 24, 27, 30, 33, 36, 39, 42, 45, 48
   2 7, 14, 21, 28, 35, 42, 49
   3 21, 42
   4 21

8. **1** 20 **2** 36 **3** 35 **4** 24 **5** 30 **6** 33 **7** 18 **8** 6 **9** 28 **10** 4

9. Prime: 71, 73, 79

Page 10 Exercise 1.3

1. **1** 8, 9, 125, 49, 10 000
   2 5^4, 2^7, 11^2

2. **1** 64, 144, 49, 1, 81
   2 6, 2, 11, 5, 10
   3 64, 1, 1000

3. **1** 23, 31 **2** 25, 36 **3** 27, 36 **4** 27 **5** 36

5. **1** 15, 18, 21
   2 32, 24, 16
   3 81, 243, 729
   4 26, 37, 50
   5 125, 216, 343
   6 70, 64, 58
   7 85, 79, 72
   8 160, 320, 640
   9 16, 4, 1
   10 47, 65, 86

Page 10 Exercise 1.4

1.
1 6
2 24
3 41
4 17
5 120

2.
1 55
2 1
3 192
4 15
5 6

Page 14 Chapter 1 test

1.
1 20
2 30
3 11
4 81
5 34

2.
1 4
2 2
3 3
4 1
5 3

3.
1 21, 33, 55, 75, 77
2 55, 75
3 21, 33, 48, 66, 75
4 21, 77
5 33, 55, 77

4. 1, 2, 3, 6, 7, 14, 21, 42

5. 16, 27, 25, 100 000

6. 7^2, 3^4, 2^5

7.
1 36, 121, 1, 100
2 5, 9, 4, 3

8.
1 12, 14, 16, 18, 20
2 16
3 15, 20
4 11, 13, 17, 19
5 12, 15, 20

9.
1 20, 24, 28
2 44, 35, 26
3 32, 64, 128
4 9, 3, 1
5 16, 22, 29

10. 1, 3, 6, 10, 15, 21, 28, 36, 45, 55; sums 4, 9, 16, 25, 36, 49, 64, 81, 100; square numbers

Page 21 Exercise 2.1

1.
1 470
2 84 000
3 601 000
4 120
5 13 500
6 38 000
7 1000
8 8000
9 100 000
10 990

2.
1 210
2 3000
3 27 000
4 800
5 2 100 000
6 450 000
7 160 000
8 300 000
9 280 000
10 24 000

3.
1 168
2 4010
3 344
4 984
5 3661
6 760
7 6687
8 4230
9 6552
10 1900

4. 60, 500, 130, 1040, 290, 90, 1430, 580, 100, 210

5. 600, 500, 500, 1100, 1000, 3100, 9100, 400, 800, 21 000

6. 4000, 15 000, 3000, 28 000, 4000, 56 000, 9000, 81 000, 4000, 10 000

7. 800

8. 2100 m

9. £23 000

10. 2400

11. 2304, 2300

12. 168 cm

13. 300 miles

14. 60 800 feet

15. 1036 kg

16. 2187 cm, 2190 cm

Page 23 Exercise 2.2

1.
1 1372
2 14 911
3 33 354
4 4420
5 22 638
6 2880
7 44 462
8 21 054
9 82 355
10 9882

2. 6912

3. 13 040 m, 13 000 m (13 km)

4. 3000

5. 8060 cm (80.6 m)

6. 3800 kg

7. **1** 224 cm
2 220 cm
3 11 680 cm (116.8 m)
4 11 700 cm (117 m)

Page 26 Exercise 2.3

1. **1** 500 **2** 7 **3** 90 **4** 60 **5** 55 **6** 120 **7** 1000 **8** 196 **9** 10 **10** 25

2. **1** 30 **2** 8 **3** 5 **4** 12 **5** 4 **6** 3000 **7** 20 **8** 120 **9** 50 **10** 350

3. **1** 24 **2** 45 **3** 59 **4** 29 **5** 164 **6** 85 **7** 228 **8** 104 **9** 61 **10** 66

4. **1** 11 r 7 **2** 25 r 2 **3** 36 r 2 **4** 152 r 1 **5** 46 r 6 **6** 20 r 6 **7** 35 r 4 **8** 91 r 2 **9** 56 r 3 **10** 168 r 2

5. 20

6. 0

7. 35

8. 45 boxes, 5 kg

9. 65

10. £38

Page 29 Exercise 2.4

1. **1** 39 **2** 58 **3** 32 **4** 72 **5** 53 **6** 21 **7** 18 **8** 13 **9** 22 **10** 62

2. **1** 13 r 5 **2** 14 r 3 **3** 29 r 2 **4** 33 r 9 **5** 35 r 7 **6** 30 r 21 **7** 25 r 1 **8** 34 r 11 **9** 37 r 9 **10** 12 r 31

3. 13

4. 28 cm

5. 54 pieces, 10 cm

6. 14

7. £75

8. 36

Page 30 Exercise 2.5

2. **1** 4515 **2** 9216 **3** 22 876 **4** 24 840 **5** 26 950

3. **1** 6100 **2** 3200 **3** 11 275 **4** 16 750 **5** 13 225

4. **1** 2010 **2** 4875 **3** 12 150 **4** 7635 **5** 9270

5. **1** 52 272 **2** 47 619 **3** 36 630 **4** 23 661 **5** 11 088

8. **1** 26 **2** 19 **3** 23 **4** 18 **5** 17

9. **1** 21 **2** 15 **3** 18 **4** 33.44 **5** 36.48

Page 34 Chapter 2 test

1. 2400 km

2. **1** 600 **2** 16

3. £1305

4. 46

5. 3816 miles

6. £7056

7. 32

8. 38, 6 ℓ over

Page 39 Exercise 3.1

1. **1** 3326 **6** 36
   2 220 **7** 1779
   3 347 100 **8** 338 085
   4 58 **9** 221
   5 6412 **10** 98

2. **1** 1638 **6** 2989
   2 22 743 **7** 22.5
   3 4659 **8** 135 408
   4 42 662 **9** 21.5
   5 28 **10** 288

3. **1** 761 **4** 35 620
   2 1584 **5** 396
   3 28 836

4. **1** 805 **6** 360
   2 13 **7** 11
   3 180 **8** 9
   4 360 **9** 29
   5 23 **10** 7

5. 2133

6. 37 248

7. £2052

8. 1200

9. 66

10. 64

Page 42 Exercise 3.2

1. **1** 625, 2704, 11 236, 12 321
   2 26, 31, 45, 88
   3 1331, 148 877, 262 144, 857 375

2. **1** 2209 **4** 36
   2 32 **5** 3150
   3 21 952

3. **1**, **4** not square numbers
   2 24, **3** 26, **5** 124

4. **1** 33 r 3 **4** 13 r 25
   2 480 r 4 **5** 59 (r 0)
   3 64 r 8

6. Both 3600

7. 32

Page 44 Exercise 3.3

1. **1** 13 **6** 14
   2 24 **7** 5
   3 5 **8** 16
   4 36 **9** 30
   5 4 **10** 25

2. **1** 328 **6** 11
   2 905 **7** 8432
   3 2992 **8** 1405
   4 108 **9** 1407
   5 8 **10** 5

3. 55 m^2

4. £2128

5. 1 gets £61.80, 14 get £55.80

6. £35

Page 45 Exercise 3.4

1. **1** (1) 243, 271, 292, 320, 509
   (2) 20, 48, 69, 97, 286
   (3) 420, 840, 1155, 1575, 4410
   (4) 4, 8, 11, 15, 42

   2 (1) £8320 (4) £1352
   (2) £11 700 (5) £364
   (3) £4368

   3 (1) 3 (4) 20
   (2) 12 (5) 49
   (3) 35

Page 48 Chapter 3 test

1. 479, 497, 749, 794, 947, 974; sum 4440

2. 15 913 miles

3. £24 386

4. 14, 19; 210 mm by 12 mm

5. **1** 160 **2** 35

6. **1** 38
2 78
3 46
4 88
5 240

7. **1** 19 074 **4** 409
2 240 **5** 19
3 40

8. last column 999, 1998, 2997, etc. to 9990

Page 54 Exercise 4.1

6. **1** 3
2 4
3 2

Page 58 Exercise 4.2

1. **1** 3
2 2
3 5

2. **1** 2
2 2
3 4

3. **1** 2
2 6
3 2

4. **1** 4 **4** 3
2 1 **5** 2
3 0 **6** 0

5. **1** 4 **5** 2
3 3 **6** 5
4 3

6. **1** None
2 Yes, order 2

8. **6** 4 axes, order 4

Page 60 Exercise 4.3

2. **1** 1, 3, 8, 0
2 1, 8, 0
3 1, 2, 5, 8, 0
4 10, 11, 13, 18, 30, 31, 33, 38, 80, 81, 83, 88
5 11, 25, 52, 88
6 11, 22, 55, 69, 88, 96

Page 62 Chapter 4 test

2. **1** **A** 1, **B** 4, **C** 3, **D** 0
2 **B** 4, **C** 3, **D** 2

3. **1** 2, 3, 6
4 1, 4, 5

Page 68 Exercise 5.1

2. **1** 9 **6** 384.2
2 80.2 **7** 1.54
3 341.2 **8** 44.1
4 0.61 **9** 0.052
5 4.5 **10** 6.03

3. **1** 379 **6** 3170
2 15 **7** 23.8
3 1250 **8** 2342
4 3.6 **9** 13
5 70 **10** 8050

4. **1** 1.492 **6** 11.73
2 4.76 **7** 0.138
3 0.208 **8** 0.0059
4 0.03 **9** 8.5
5 0.004 **10** 2.06

5. **1** 0.295 **6** 0.0254
2 0.076 **7** 0.389
3 0.005 **8** 0.007 98
4 0.0358 **9** 0.1402
5 0.019 **10** 0.0025

6. 34 cm

7. 102.6 kg

8. 5.65 kg

9. 3.281 feet

Page 70 Exercise 5.2

1. **1** 7.17, **2** 15.9, **3** 8.22, **4** 1.03, **5** 32.03, **6** 2, **7** 21.87, **8** 11.4, **9** 17.35, **10** 10.71

2. **1** 2.08, **2** 1.07, **3** 7.21, **4** 1.63, **5** 3.48, **6** 2.28, **7** 5.97, **8** 1.86, **9** 18.38, **10** 0.76

3. **1** 56.14, **2** 12, **3** 2.88, **4** 30.1, **5** 0.18, **6** 7.6, **7** 12.3, **8** 1.74, **9** 72.45, **10** 87.9

4. **1** 3.14, **2** 1.92, **3** 0.63, **4** 0.15, **5** 0.008, **6** 0.43, **7** 5.6, **8** 3.02, **9** 2.08, **10** 0.282

5. 42.5 g

6. 19.32 kg

7. 9.95 m

8. 7.37 francs

9. **1** 8.7 cm, **2** 2.9 cm

Page 73 Exercise 5.3

1. **1** 12, **2** 8, **3** 10, **4** 30, **5** 94

2. **1** 5.3, **2** 5.5, **3** 0.4, **4** 1.1, **5** 2.1

3. **1** 3.58, **2** 5.81, **3** 0.70, **4** 6.59, **5** 0.01

4. **1** 1.5, **2** 0.6, **3** 3.7, **4** 2.5, **5** 12.1, **6** 1.6, **7** 0.1, **8** 2.3, **9** 14.4, **10** 10.2

5. **1** 340.866, **2** 78.71, **3** 0.10875, **4** 1.134, **5** 0.1666

6. **1** 0.16, **2** 7.33, **3** 7.40, **4** 2.87, **5** 67.04

7. 232.8 cm (2.328 m)

8. 51.75 cm

9. 10

Page 76 Exercise 5.4

1. **1** £3, **2** £42

2. **1** £7.92, **2** £20.93

3. £4.52, £1.39, 89p, £2.70, £3.27

4. £10.20, £9.80

5. £43.60

6. £391

7. 7.5p

8. £41.67

9. 58, 14p

10. £3.75, £1.95

11. 32

12. 1100 units, £83.40

13. **1** £150, **2** £149.97

Page 79 Exercise 5.5

1. *A* 0.7, *B* 3.3, *C* 6.0, *D* 7.9, *E* 10.5
2. *F* 0.3, *G* 2.1, *H* 3.7, *J* 7.6, *K* 9.9

Page 80 Exercise 5.6

1. **1** 16.82, **2** 2.03, **3** 3.14, **4** 0.67, **5** 0.3, **6** 2.6452, **7** 100, **8** 7, **9** 3.84, **10** 1.03

2. **1** 9.274 **4** 40.835 54
2 6.76 **5** 79.12
3 199

Page 82 Chapter 5 test

1. **1** 11 740 **4** 3.8
2 0.358 **5** 7.37
3 62.88

2. 180.4 m

3. **1** 62 miles
2 2.2 lb

4. **1** 319.64 **4** 20.14
2 48.96 **5** 2.31
3 9.73

5. 185.5 g, 499.53 g (499.5 g)

6. 38.3 miles

7. A 0.09, B 0.27, C 0.40, D 0.68, E 0.94

8. £2.68

9. £28.95

10. 37

Page 89 Exercise 6.1

Theoretical answers. The answers obtained by experiment will not match the theoretical answers although they may come close to them if the number of trials is large.

1. **1** P(head) $= \frac{1}{2}$
Approximately 100 heads in 200 tosses
2 P(2 heads) $= \frac{1}{4}$
Approximately 25 successes in 100 tosses
P(2 tails) $= \frac{1}{4}$
P(1 head and 1 tail) $= \frac{1}{2}$

2. **1** P(six) $= \frac{1}{6}$
Approximately 67 sixes in 400 throws
2 Likely total 7; P(7) $= \frac{1}{6}$
3 P(at least 1 six) $= 0.67$
Approximately 44 times in 66 throws

Page 93 Exercise 6.2

Theoretical answers. (See note above.)

2. P(touch) $= 0.57$

3. P(success) $= 0.68$

4. P(A) $= 0.40$, P(B) $= 0.33$, P(C) $= 0.27$

5. P(success) $= 0.39$

Page 97 Chapter 6 test

1. **1** 0.19 **2** 0.06

2. **1** 0.57 **2** 0.33 **3** 0.07 **4** 0.1

Page 98 Exercise A1

1. 81
2. 1200
3. 8
4. 68.9
5. £1.05
6. 23, 27
7. 9
8. 140
9. 120 cm
10. 2
11. 80p
12. 4 hundredths
13. 0.6
14. 900
15. 40 ml

Page 99 Exercise A2

1. £12
2. 346 (pints)
3. 2
4. 3.5 miles
5. 30
6. 4
7. 5.24
8. 80, 76
9. 16p
10. 35
11. £7.20
12. 27
13. 96
14. 0.7
15. £2.40

Page 100 Exercise A3

1. 31, 37

2. **1** £1.30
2 £1.35

3. **1** 7.18 **4** 46.79
2 6.28 **5** 0.04
3 2029.16

4. 72

5. **1** 4, yes
2 1, no
3 an infinite number, yes
4 2, yes
5 3, yes

6. 10 (weeks)

7. £180

8. **1** 7.6 **2** 3.2 **3** 0.2 **4** 1.2 **5** 200

9. **1** 0.4 **2** 0.514 (0.51) **3** 44

Page 101 Exercise A4

1. 12

2. £97.50

3. **1** 10 400 **2** 7500 **3** 43 300 **4** 3600 **5** 5000

4. **1** 6 **2** 5

5. 25

6. 41.8 kg

7. 28p, £6.16

8. **1** 32 **2** 64 **3** 9 **4** 5 **5** 1 000 000

9. 0.4

10. sum 820

Page 103 Exercise A5

5. **1** XXXVII **2** LXXXIV **3** MCMXC **4** CDLXXV **5** MDCCCXXXIX **6** 2902 **7** 43 **8** 404 **9** 1995 **10** 259

Page 110 Exercise 7.1

1. **1** 80 **2** 4000 **3** 50 **4** 2000 **5** 3000 **6** 5000 **7** 10 000 **8** 1500 **9** 6 **10** 2

2. **1** 2.56 kg **2** 0.25 m **3** 4000 ml **4** 90 mm **5** 230 cm **6** 3500 g **7** 3.6 cm **8** 8 ℓ **9** 3.56 m **10** 750 g

3. 7 kg

4. 50

5. 48, 49 or 50, depending on the pattern

6. 5 rows

7. 550

8. 15 ℓ

9. 54.4 cm

10. 450

11. 301.5 m

12. 18, 62

Page 112 Exercise 7.2

1. **1** 10.46 kg **2** 1 kg 150 g **3** 650 ml

2. **1** 7.8 cm **2** 12.5 cm **3** 4.7 cm

Page 114 Exercise 7.3

2. **1** 1.8 **2** $3\frac{1}{2}$ kg, 35 kg **3** 20 **4** 10 ℓ **5** 250 g

3. 5 m

Page 116 Chapter 7 test

1. 0.9 m

2. 800 g

3. 6 g

4. 50

5. 75 cm

6. 28.6 m, 114.4 m

7. **1** 2.65 kg
2 350 ml

8. **1** 8 m
2 20 cm
3 10 kg
4 300 ml

Page 120 Exercise 8.1

1. $AB = 6.7$ cm, $CD = 8.2$ cm, $EF = 12.1$ cm, $GH = 3.8$ cm

Page 123 Exercise 8.2

1. acute
2. obtuse
3. obtuse
4. acute
5. reflex
6. reflex
7. acute
8. acute
9. reflex
10. obtuse

Page 124 148°

Page 125 52°

Page 128 Exercise 8.3

1. **1** acute, 30°
2 obtuse, 110°
3 acute, 88°
4 acute, 78°
5 obtuse, 138°

Page 130 Exercise 8.4

2. $a = 76°$, $b = 54°$, $c = 92°$, $d = 138°$, sum = 360°

3. $p = 58°$, $q = 104°$, $r = 36°$, $s = 80°$, $t = 82°$, sum = 360°

4. $a = 154°$, $b = 26°$, sum = 180°

5. $c = 147°$, $d = 33°$, sum = 180°

6. $g = 68°$, $h = 112°$, $j = 68°$, $k = 112°$

7. $p = 155°$, $q = 25°$, $r = 155°$, $s = 25°$

Page 134 Exercise 8.5

1. **1** $a = 118°$, $b = 118°$
2 $c = 33°$, $d = 33°$
3 $e = 44°$, $f = 136°$

Page 136 Exercise 8.6

1. **6** 11.0 cm
7 $d = c = 58°$

2. **6** 7.2 cm
7 $d = c = 90°$

3. **6** 6.5 cm
7 $d = 127°$, $c = 53°$

4. **6** 5.6 cm
7 $d = c = 90°$

5. **8** lengths are 2.1 cm

6. **1** $a = 71°$, $b = 47°$, $c = 62°$, sum = 180°; $d = 21°$, $e = 144°$, $f = 15°$, sum = 180°

7. sides 3.8 cm, angles 135°

Page 139 Chapter 8 test

1. **1** a, d, f, h
2 b, e
3 g, j
4 c, k

2. **3** 100°

3. **6** $CD = 8.2$ cm, $DB = 5.8$ cm
7 $b = c = 64°$, $d = 116°$

Page 145 Exercise 9.1

1. **1** $\frac{3}{8}$
2 $\frac{1}{3}$
3 $\frac{1}{3}$
4 $\frac{1}{2}$
5 $\frac{1}{3}$
6 $\frac{3}{4}$

3. **1** $\frac{1}{3}$
2 $\frac{2}{3}$
3 $\frac{3}{4}$
4 $\frac{1}{2}$
5 $\frac{2}{5}$
6 $\frac{1}{4}$
7 $\frac{7}{10}$
8 $\frac{3}{8}$
9 $\frac{3}{4}$
10 $\frac{7}{9}$

4. **1** $\frac{9}{24}$ **2** $\frac{10}{12}$ **3** $\frac{10}{15}$ **4** $\frac{27}{36}$ **5** $\frac{15}{50}$
6 $\frac{3}{6}$ **7** $\frac{8}{20}$ **8** $\frac{42}{48}$ **9** $\frac{6}{27}$ **10** $\frac{8}{32}$

5. **1** $\frac{22}{5}$ **2** $\frac{17}{6}$ **3** $\frac{21}{10}$ **4** $\frac{15}{4}$ **5** $\frac{20}{3}$
6 $\frac{13}{5}$ **7** $\frac{17}{4}$ **8** $\frac{25}{3}$ **9** $\frac{22}{7}$ **10** $\frac{19}{10}$

6. **1** $1\frac{3}{4}$ **2** $2\frac{1}{3}$ **3** $1\frac{5}{12}$ **4** $3\frac{7}{10}$ **5** $4\frac{5}{6}$
6 $11\frac{1}{9}$ **7** $8\frac{2}{5}$ **8** $3\frac{1}{8}$ **9** $5\frac{1}{2}$ **10** $6\frac{2}{3}$

Page 147 Exercise 9.2

1. **1** 30, 10, 22, 5, 40, 8, 17, 35, 28, 100
2 2, 5, 8, 22, 11, 16, 6, 30, 3, 12
3 22, 4, 2, 6, 21, 12, 8, 13, 30, 50
4 2, 14, 50, 12, 66, 40, 8, 30, 18, 20
5 3, 15, 120, 27, 9, 21, 60, 75, 33, 45

2. **1** £2.85 **2** 2.5 km **3** 135° **4** 40 cm **5** 140 g **6** 97p **7** 3.6 ℓ **8** 500 g
9 $1\frac{1}{2}$ hours **10** £100 **11** £1.56 **12** 60 g **13** 80° **14** 15 cm **15** £10.50

3. **1** £4.17 **2** £2.94 **3** 39p
4 £1.92 **5** £17.89

4. **1** 8.75 m **2** 500 g **3** 40 min
4 £47.70 **5** 18 ℓ

5. 120 ℓ

6. 63

7. $\frac{1}{10}$

8. 25 200

9. *A* 630, *B* 1400, *C* 1120;
B won by 280 votes

10. 2 h 30 min, 10.30 am

Page 150 Exercise 9.3

1. **1** $\frac{3}{10}$ **2** $\frac{3}{4}$ **3** $\frac{3}{20}$
4 $\frac{6}{25}$ **5** $\frac{2}{5}$

2. **1** 0.18 **2** 0.95 **3** 0.06
4 0.11 **5** 0.6

3. **1** £2.64 **2** 60p **3** £3.30 **4** £11.40 **5** £18.72
6 £4.80 **7** 28p **8** £10.80 **9** 48p **10** £5.66

4. **1** 12 cm **2** 300 g **3** 18 min **4** 4.5 cm **5** 1.05 ℓ
6 2 m **7** 60 ml **8** 48 s **9** 3 cm **10** 500 g

5. **1** 50 **2** 575

6. **1** £23.40
2 £283.40 (£283)

7. **1** 9 cm **2** 1.41 m

8. 225

9. **1** £3.60
2 £21.60
3 £237.60

10. One gets £15, the others get £11.25 each.

11. **1** 81 **2** 369

12. **1** 40%
2 £96
3 £8

13. **1** £18 **2** £102
14. **1** 42 kg **2** 308 kg
15. **1** 45% **2** 18 kg

Page 152 Exercise 9.4

2. $\frac{4}{9}$; $\frac{2}{6}$, $\frac{3}{9}$, $\frac{4}{12}$; $\frac{2}{3}$; $\frac{3}{7}$; $\frac{2}{5}$

Page 156 Chapter 9 test

1. **1** $\frac{3}{5}$ **2** $\frac{4}{7}$ **3** $\frac{1}{3}$ **4** $\frac{5}{7}$ **5** $\frac{3}{5}$
2. **1** $\frac{51}{8}$ **2** $\frac{14}{3}$ **3** $\frac{11}{4}$ **4** $\frac{17}{5}$ **5** $\frac{15}{8}$
3. **1** $1\frac{5}{6}$ **2** $4\frac{1}{4}$ **3** $5\frac{1}{8}$ **4** $4\frac{2}{3}$ **5** $1\frac{7}{12}$
4. **1** £1.44 **2** 2 m **3** 330 g **4** 1 ℓ **5** 42 min
5. 63, $\frac{9}{40}$
6. £180
7. $\frac{7}{20}$, 0.35
8. **1** 12p **2** 450 g **3** 660 ml **4** 12 m **5** £2.70
9. **1** £14 400 **2** £50 400
10. 198

Page 161 Example 2

40 come by bus,
37 go home by bus

Page 162 Example 3

Monday of the 1st week

Page 163 Exercise 10.1

3. frequencies:
car 17
plane 9
car and ferry 5
coach 2
train 2
canal barge 1
cruise ship 1
total 37

Page 165 Exercise 10.2

1. **1** 36 **2** 10° **3** Science **4** 5 **5** 4 **6** 7
2. 156°, 12°;
bus 11, car 4, cycle 2, walk 13
3. **1** $\frac{1}{2}$ **2** $\frac{1}{3}$ **3** $\frac{1}{6}$
5. £1 represented by 12°
6. frequencies:
blue 10
pink 8
black 6
red 5
yellow 4
green 2
white 1
7. total £1800, £5

Page 170 Exercise 10.3

1. **1** mean 38.3 (38.25), median 38.5, range 10
2 mean 21 km, median 21 km, range 6 km
3 mean 56.9 s, median 55.5 s, range 20 s
4 mean £130, median £129.50, range £41
5 mean 3.8 kg, median 3.7 kg, range 2.3 kg

2. **1** median 11, mode 8, range 9
   2 median 6.5, mode 8, range 9
   3 median 5, mode 4, range 8

3. mean 39.0 kg, median 37 kg, range 18 kg

4. mean 40.94 m, median 41.8 m, range 6.9 m

Page 173 Exercise 10.4

1. RS 15, GS 5, BS 9, RD 16, GD 8, BD 7; totals S 29, D 31, R 31, G 13, B 16; 60

2. men: 320, 308, 276;
   women: 180, 172, 164;
   total: 500, 480, 440; decrease 60

5. **1** A 90°, B 105°, C 165°
   2 120
   3 3°
   4 B 35, C 55

6. $a = 360$, $b = 120$, $c = 80$, $d = 300$, $e = 500$, $f = 100$

8. means in order: 20.7 h, 20.7 h, 23.7 h, 28.1 h;
   medians in order: 16 h, 20.5 h, 23 h, 28 h;
   ranges in order: 32 h, 31 h, 36 h, 43 h

Page 177 Chapter 10 test

3. mean 27°C, range 4 deg C

4. **1** food
   2 extras
   3 $\frac{1}{4}$
   4 food and activities
   5 camp fee and extras

5. £180; food $\frac{1}{3}$, mortgage $\frac{1}{4}$, clothing $\frac{1}{18}$, fuel $\frac{1}{12}$, car $\frac{1}{9}$, other expenses $\frac{1}{6}$

6. men: mean 175.5 cm, median 174 cm, range 24 cm;
   women: mean 159.1 cm, median 158 cm, range 17 cm

Page 183 Exercise 11.1

1. $(8 - b)$ years
2. $5w$ kg
3. $(c + 40)$ pence
4. $(60 - m)$ miles
5. £$(m - 2)$
6. $(2l + 2b)$ cm or $2(l + b)$ cm
7. $(p - 2q)$ metres
8. $(5g + 2h)$ pence
9. pq pence, $(100 - pq)$ pence
10. $(6 + m)$ minutes.

Page 185 Exercise 11.2

1. **1** a
   2 0
   3 cd
   4 e^2
   5 $2fg$
   6 h^3
   7 $3j^2$
   8 0
   9 $3mn$
   10 $4p^2$
   11 0
   12 $6rs$
   13 $7t$
   14 u^3
   15 $12v^2$

2. **1** $2a$
   2 $2b$
   3 0
   4 $5d$
   5 e
   6 $12f$
   7 $6g$
   8 0
   9 $3j$
   10 k
   11 0
   12 $4n$
   13 $6p$
   14 q
   15 r

3. **1** $2a + 4b$
   2 $4c - 4d$
   3 $3e - 6f + 9g$
   4 $5h + 40$
   5 $2j - 8k$
   6 $18k + 24$
   7 $2m - 6n$
   8 $16p + 8$
   9 $7q + 14r$
   10 $9s - 15$

4. **1** $5a + b$
   2 $4c - d$
   3 $3e + 2f$
   4 $3h$
   5 0

5. **1** $7l + 10$
   2 $8m - 6$
   3 $7p$
   4 $10s + 4t$
   5 $8x - 7y + z$

6. $(14a + 6x)$ cm

7. $(8x + 16)$ cm

Page 187 Exercise 11.3

1. **1** a
   2 1
   3 0
   4 $\frac{d}{2}$ $(\frac{1}{2}d)$
   5 $\frac{e}{3}$ $(\frac{1}{3}e)$
   6 $\frac{2f}{5}$ $(\frac{2}{5}f)$
   7 $\frac{5g}{3}$ $(\frac{5}{3}g)$
   8 $\frac{3}{j}$
   9 $\frac{m}{n}$
   10 0
   11 $\frac{4}{q}$
   12 $\frac{2r}{s}$
   13 $\frac{6t}{5}$ $(\frac{6}{5}t)$
   14 $\frac{u}{2}$ $(\frac{1}{2}u)$
   15 0

2. $\frac{d}{20}$ metres or $5d$ cm

3. $\frac{3000}{f}$ square metres

4. $\frac{c}{100}$ metres

5. $\frac{90}{b}$ pence

6. $\frac{q}{p}$ pence

Page 188 Exercise 11.4

1. $E = F + V - 2$

2. $R = \frac{a+b+c+d+e}{5}$

3. $M = \frac{T-D}{24}$

4. $T = 7n + 43c$

5. $d = 5t^2$

Page 189 Exercise 11.5

1. **1** 6
   2 2
   3 15
   4 18
   5 24
   6 5
   7 49
   8 26
   9 27
   10 17

2. **1** 8
   2 6
   3 0
   4 12
   5 13
   6 30
   7 5
   8 5
   9 12
   10 33

3. 260 kg

4. 54

5. 52

6. 180

7. 592

Page 190 Exercise 11.6

1. **1** $2a$
   2 0
   3 a^2
   4 1
   5 a

2. **1** $8b$
   2 $4b$
   3 $12b^2$
   4 3
   5 0

3. 56 pence

4. 280 km

5. 5 litres

6. 144°

7. 8th term 720,
   sum of 8 terms 1980

9. **1** 55
   2 41 616 ($= 204^2$)

10. 13, 23, 31, 37, 41, 43, 43, 41, 37, 31, 23, 13; all prime numbers

Page 192 Chapter 11 test

1. 2 h 20 min, $(20 + 40m)$ minutes

2. $(3 - t)$ metres, 1.8 m

3. **1** $4a$ **2** $4b$ **3** $5c$ **4** 0 **5** e **6** f^2 **7** $4gh$ **8** $4j$ **9** $\frac{k}{3}$ $(\frac{1}{3}k)$ **10** 0

4. **1** $10a - 20b$ **2** $6c + 15d$ **3** $15e + 17$

5. £$\frac{x}{5}$ (£$\frac{1}{5}x$)

6. **1** 25 **2** 0 **3** 2 **4** 1 **5** 50 **6** 16 **7** 31 **8** 44 **9** 7 **10** 1

7. $W = 5a + b$, £242

8. $v = \frac{s}{t}$, 64 km/h

Page 198 Exercise 12.1

1. **1** $\frac{1}{6}$ **2** $\frac{1}{2}$ **3** 50
2. **1** $\frac{1}{3}$ **2** $\frac{1}{4}$ **3** $\frac{1}{4}$ **4** $\frac{1}{3}$
3. $\frac{1}{10}$
4. $\frac{1}{10}$
5. **1** $\frac{1}{8}$ **2** $\frac{1}{4}$ **3** $\frac{1}{2}$ **4** 125
6. **1** $\frac{1}{11}$ **2** $\frac{2}{11}$ **3** $\frac{4}{11}$ **4** $\frac{6}{11}$
7. $\frac{2}{5}$
8. **1** $\frac{3}{10}$ **2** $\frac{4}{5}$
9. **1** $\frac{5}{9}$ **2** $\frac{4}{9}$ **3** $\frac{1}{3}$ **4** $\frac{2}{9}$
10. **1** $\frac{1}{16}$ **2** $\frac{1}{9}$

Page 200 Exercise 12.2

1. **1** $\frac{1}{4}$ **2** $\frac{1}{3}$ **3** $\frac{5}{12}$ **4** $\frac{8}{11}$
2. **1** $\frac{3}{7}$ **2** $\frac{3}{10}$ **3** $\frac{8}{35}$ **4** $\frac{1}{4}$
3. $\frac{1}{7}$, 14
4. P(swim) = $\frac{1}{3}$ then $\frac{4}{7}$
5. **1** 6 **2** $\frac{1}{6}$ **3** 5 **4** $\frac{1}{18}$ **5** 56

Page 202 Chapter 12 test

1. **1** $\frac{1}{13}$ **2** $\frac{1}{4}$ **3** $\frac{1}{52}$
2. **1** $\frac{1}{8}$ **2** $\frac{7}{8}$ **3** $\frac{1}{7}$
3. **1** 4 **2** $\frac{1}{4}$ **3** 8 **4** $\frac{1}{16}$ **5** $\frac{3}{8}$

Page 204 Exercise B1

1. £60
2. acute angle
3. 0.04
4. $12d$
5. 320
6. 2
7. 0.3
8. £18
9. 7
10. 24
11. 5
12. parallel lines
13. £$12x$
14. 15
15. £80

Page 205 Exercise B2

1. £8
2. 4
3. £15
4. obtuse angle
5. 1800 ℓ
6. 1.99
7. b
8. $\frac{1}{6}$
9. 4
10. $(100 - c)$ pence
11. $\frac{1}{5}$
12. $\frac{1}{6}$
13. perpendicular lines
14. 28
15. 3 and 9

Page 206 Exercise B3

1. £13.50
2. $\sqrt{576} + \sqrt{49}$, 6 larger
3. 0.28
4. 13 aprons, 1.6 m left
5. 110°
6. $a = 90°$, $b = 131°$, $c = 67°$, $d = 72°$; $AB = 3.7$ cm, $BC = 4.4$ cm, $CD = 6.8$ cm, $DA = 5.5$ cm
7. $(5x + 3y)$ pence, $c = 5x + 3y$
8. 50
9. 2.7 m

Page 207 Exercise B4

1. **1** $\frac{2}{3}$ **2** $\frac{5}{7}$ **3** $\frac{3}{5}$ **4** $\frac{7}{11}$ **5** $\frac{5}{9}$
2. 300 (grams)
3. **1** 12 **2** 11 **3** 10 **4** 8
4. £60
5. 234 m
6. 640
7. **1** 36° **2** 108° **3** 216°
8. $8x$ pence, $(500 - 8x)$ pence
9. (1, 3), (1, 4), (2, 3), (2, 4);
   1 $\frac{1}{2}$
   2 50
10. $BC = 5.3$ cm; $b = c = 72°$

Page 209 Exercise B5

4. (Answers in order)
   Numbers: 1 000 000, 10^6;
   Pence: £10 000, 1.5 km (1.65 km coins 1992 onwards), 20.3 km, 3.56 tonnes;
   Distance: 1 km, 10 m, 1 m;
   Weight: 1 tonne;
   Time: (impossible ?), about $11\frac{1}{2}$ days, nearly 2 years (1.9 years), 114 years, 2740 years ago;
   London, 8 million, 11 Wembley stadiums
   Sequence: 14 terms

Page 219 Exercise 13.1

1. **1** 75 inches **2** 115 lb **3** 17 pints **4** 36 oz **5** 440 yards **6** 8 feet **7** 3 lb **8** $2\frac{1}{2}$ gallons **9** 3 miles **10** 30 yards
2. **1** 7 st 9 lb **2** $\frac{3}{8}$ pint **3** $3\frac{3}{4}$ inches
3. **1** $\frac{1}{4}$ **2** $\frac{1}{5}$ **3** $\frac{3}{8}$ **4** $\frac{1}{2}$ **5** $\frac{3}{8}$
4. **1** 1 ft 4 in **2** 9 oz **3** 10 pints **4** 6 inches **5** 7 lb
5. 16 inches
6. 155 lb
7. $1\frac{1}{4}$ yards

Page 221 Exercise 13.2

1. **1** 40 km **2** 3 kg or 2.7 kg **3** 2 m **4** 9 ℓ **5** 3 tonnes **6** 96 km **7** 7 kg or 6.3 kg **8** 1.5 m **9** $2\frac{1}{2}$ ℓ **10** 20 m or 22 m
2. **1** 8 inches **2** $2\frac{1}{2}$ gall **3** 20 lb or 22 lb **4** 160 lb or 180 lb **5** 2 lb **6** $2\frac{1}{2}$ yds or 3 yds **7** 5 tons **8** 4.4 gall **9** $\frac{1}{2}$ lb **10** 35 miles
3. **1** 1.2 cm **2** 10 m **3** 20 kg **4** 45 ℓ **5** 200 g
4. 33 lb
5. 1.8 m wide, 3.1 m high, 2.5 m from front to back
6. 12 km
7. £2.86
8. 78.5 kg
9. 7350 km

Page 225 Exercise 13.3

1. 02.10, 19.00, 14.15, 16.05, 23.50
   3.50 am, 7.30 am, 12.05 pm, 6.18 pm, 10.10 pm
2. **1** 2.35 pm **2** 14.35
3. **1** 8 min 27 s **2** 6 hr 35 min **3** 41 hr 12 min **4** 10 min 14 s **5** 67 hr 10 min
4. 2 hr 43 min
5. £56

6. 3.10 pm

7. 3 hr 30 min, 01.50

8. **1** 2 hr 15 min **2** 4 hr 55 min **3** 1 hr 30 min

9. **1** 15.54 (3.54 pm), 25 min, 8 min
2 16.22 (4.22 pm), 32 min

Page 227 Exercise 13.4

1. **1** 8 oz, 4 oz, 2 oz
2 2 lb, 4 oz, 2 oz
3 2 lb, 1 lb, 8 oz, 1 oz

3. **1** 25 lb 5 oz **2** 20 ft 6 in **3** 4 lb 11 oz **4** 1 st 10 lb, 11 st 2 lb **5** 8 **6** 6 lb 15 oz

Page 228 Chapter 13 test

1. 45 miles

2. 55 lb

3. $3\frac{1}{2}$ pints

4. 177.8 cm

5. **1** 4.4 cm or 4.5 cm
2 $3\frac{1}{2}$ inches

6. 40 min

7. $7\frac{1}{2}$ inches

8. 5 hr 30 min

Page 233 Exercise 14.1

1. **1** 0 **2** −2 **3** −11 **4** 3 **5** −5 **6** −1 **7** −1 **8** 0 **9** −2 **10** −4

2. **1** down 3 **2** up 7 **3** down 5 **4** down 3 **5** up 4 **6** down 6 **7** up 3 **8** up 1 **9** up 4 **10** down 8

3. **1** 9 **2** 3 **3** −5 **4** −1 **5** −4

4. **1** −2, 4, 5 **2** −5, −3, 0 **3** −5, 3, 6 **4** −4, −3, 1 **5** −8, −7, −6

5. **1** +11° **2** −3° **3** +2° **4** −7° **5** −6° **6** −14° **7** +2° **8** 0° **9** +1° **10** −4°

6. **1** risen 4° **2** fallen 2° **3** risen 3° **4** risen 1° **5** risen 2° **6** fallen 5° **7** fallen 4° **8** fallen 5° **9** risen 5° **10** risen 8°

7. **1** 8 min past 1 **2** 10 min to 2 **3** 2 min past 3 **4** 5 min to 4 **5** 10 min past 5

Page 235 Exercise 14.2

1. **1** +6 **2** −2 **3** −5 **4** +7 **5** +2 **6** step 1 **7** step 3 **8** step −4 **9** step −1 **10** step −3

2. **1** £250 **2** £120 **3** £60 **4** £180 **5** overdrawn £70

3. **1** 0, −5, −10 **2** −2, 0, 2 **3** 9, 12, 15 **4** −2, 3, 8 **5** 2, −2, −6

4. **1** 0 **2** −35 **3** −10 **4** 0 **5** 30 **6** −28 **7** 20 **8** 5 **9** −80 **10** 0 **11** −6 **12** −60 **13** 27 **14** 0 **15** 48

5. **1** 3 **2** −7 **3** −9 **4** 5 **5** 0 **6** −8 **7** 6 **8** −9 **9** 9 **10** −7 **11** 0 **12** 7 **13** −6 **14** 12 **15** −8

Page 237 Chapter 14 test

1. **1** −5° **2** 11° **3** 15° **4** −7° **5** −3°

2. **1** 12
2 −1
3 0
4 −2
5 down, 4

3. **1** 17
2 20
3 15
4 9
5 20

4. **1** 0
2 4
3 −9
4 −2
5 4

Page 243 Exercise 15.1

1. 90°
2. 155°
3. $c = 18°$, $d = e = 162°$
4. 145°
5. 112°
6. $h = 150°$, $j = 30°$, $k = 18°$
7. 72°
8. $k = m = 48°$
9. $a = 135°$, $b = 225°$
10. $a = 28°$, $b = 332°$

Page 245 Exercise 15.2

1. **1** 72°
2 117°
3 48°
4 57°
5 102°
6 75°
2. $a = 54°$, $b = 54°$
3. $a = b = 114°$, $c = 66°$
4. 19°
5. $f = 121°$, $g = 117°$, $h = 122°$
6. $j = 122°$, $k = 115°$
7. $a = b = 62°$, $c = 118°$
8. $f = 125°$, $g = 145°$, $h = 35°$
9. $j = 55°$, $k = 65°$, $m = 120°$
10. $n = q = 53°$, $p = 127°$

Page 247 Exercise 15.3

1. **1** a
2 g
3 e
4 $\angle ACD$ ($\angle DCA$)
5 $\angle BCD$ ($\angle CDB$)
6 $\angle ABC$, $\angle DBC$, $\angle CBA$, $\angle CBD$

2. **1** 48°
2 24°
3 72°

Page 248 Exercise 15.4

1. **1** 12 hours
2 30°
3 135°
4 120°
5 45°
6 6°
7 25 min
8 132°

2. **1** $a = 54°$
2 $b = 50°$
3 $c = 52°$, $d = e = 38°$

3. $d + c + e = 180°$;
$d = a$, $e = b$;
$a + b + c = 180°$

4. $\angle CDE = \angle DAB = \angle DCB$;
$\angle BCF = \angle ADC = \angle ABC$;
opposite angles are equal

Page 249 Chapter 15 test

1. **1** 36° **2** 25°
2. 212°
3. $b = 118°$, $c = 48°$
4. $d = 68°$, $e = 112°$
5. 32°
6. $g = h = 48°$, $j = 132°$
7. $k = 64°$, $m = 16°$

Page 256 Exercise 16.1

1. **1** $x + 5 = 12$
2 $x = 7$
2. $x = 4$
3. $x = 15$
4. $x = 20$
5. $x = 9$

6. $x = 11$
7. $x = 16$
8. $x = 8$
9. $x = 14$
10. $x = 4$

Page 257 Exercise 16.2

1.

1 $x = 5$	**11** $x = 6$
2 $x = 12$	**12** $x = 11$
3 $x = 8$	**13** $x = 1$
4 $x = 15$	**14** $x = 18$
5 $x = 6$	**15** $x = 0$
6 $x = 12$	**16** $x = \frac{1}{2}$
7 $x = 6$	**17** $x = 0$
8 $x = 19$	**18** $x = 14$
9 $x = 10$	**19** $x = 4\frac{1}{2}$
10 $x = 9$	**20** $x = 9$

2. 7
3. 7
4. 200
5. 10

Page 261 Exercise 16.3

1. **1** $3x + 8 = 35$
   2 $x = 9$
2. $x = 12$
3. $x = 3$
4. $x = 4$
5. $x = 10$
6. $x = 6$
7. $x = 3$
8. $x = 5$
9. $x = 4$
10. $x = 22$

Page 262 Exercise 16.4

1.

1 $x = 6$	**6** $x = 4$
2 $x = 2$	**7** $x = 11$
3 $x = 5$	**8** $x = 2$
4 $x = 20$	**9** $x = 3$
5 $x = 5$	**10** $x = 7$

2.

1 $x = 10$	**6** $x = 3$
2 $x = 7$	**7** $x = 8$
3 $x = 3$	**8** $x = 1$
4 $x = 0$	**9** $x = 9$
5 $x = 1$	**10** $x = 1$

3.

1 $x = 6$	**6** $x = 11$
2 $x = 3$	**7** $x = 7$
3 $x = 6$	**8** $x = 2$
4 $x = 4$	**9** $x = 12$
5 $x = 9$	**10** $x = 8$

4.

1 $x = 2$	**6** $x = 4$
2 $x = 9$	**7** $x = 4$
3 $x = 6$	**8** $x = 4$
4 $x = 3$	**9** $x = 1$
5 $x = 0$	**10** $x = 2$

5. 8
6. 8
7. 3
8. 5
9. **1** 8 **2** 9

Page 265 Exercise 16.5

1. 9
2. 8
3. 10
4. Mr Bamber £44, Mr Craig £26
5. Rhona £42, Sally £7
6. 17, 18, 19
7. car 75p, tractor £1.25
8. 26 5p coins, 78 2p coins
9. length 21 m, breadth 7 m
10. 12

Page 266 Exercise 16.6

1. 10
2. red 44 cm, blue 22 cm, yellow 27 cm
3. 10 years
4. £$20x$, $(x + 12)$ metres, £$30(x + 12)$,
   $x = 30$;
   rolls 30 m and 42 m
5. adult $2x$ pence, total $7x$ pence, $x = 160$;
   adult price £3.20
6. £$25x$, $(30 - x)$ workers, £$20(30 - x)$,
   $x = 6$;
   6 workers were paid £25
7. 10 10p coins

8. **1** $x = 72$
2 $x = 35$
3 $x = 18$

Page 268 Chapter 16 test

1. **1** $x = 23$
2 $x = 7$
3 $x = 72$
4 $x = 24$

2. **1** $x = 3$
2 $x = 7$

3. **1** $x = 1$
2 $x = 20$

4. 14

5. $k = 9$, $y = 45$

6. 15

7. David £8, Simon £4, Angela £12

Page 274 Exercise 17.1

1. frequencies in order:
32, 28, 23, 12, 5, total 100
1 2.3
2 2
3 1

2. **1** 6.9
2 7
3 7

3. **1** 3.7
2 4
3 4

4. **1** 6.3
2 6
3 6
4 8

Page 277 Exercise 17.2

1. frequencies in order:
26, 17, 12, 6, 5, 1, 2

3. frequencies in order:
3, 14, 13, 15, 10, 11, 4

Page 278 Exercise 17.3

1. totals for goals by home teams:
(0) 16, (1) 11, (2) 8, (3) 4, (4) 4, (5) 1, total 44;
totals for goals by away teams:
(0) 16, (1) 15, (2) 5, (3) 7, (4) 1, total 44;
mean goals by home teams 1.4;
mean goals by away teams 1.1

2. frequencies:
(0) 7, (1) 10, (2) 9, (3) 6, (4) 4, (5) 4, (6) 2, (7) 1, (8) 0, (9) 1, total 44;
mean 2.5, median 2, mode 1, range 9

3. frequencies:
girls: (1) 13, (2) 18, (3) 4, (4) 1, (5) 1, total 37;
boys: (0) 10, (1) 23, (2) 4, total 37;
children: (1) 2, (2) 17, (3) 12, (4) 3, (5) 1, (6) 2, total 37;
girls: mean 1.9, median 2, mode 2, range 4;
boys: mean 0.8, median 1, mode 1, range 2;
children: mean 2.7, median 2, mode 2, range 5

4. frequencies:
(3) 2, (4) 4, (5) 5, (6) 4, (7) 14, (8) 22, (9) 23, (10) 17, (11) 23, (12) 26, (13) 22, (14) 16, (15) 10, (16) 5, (17) 3, (18) 4, total 200;
most 12, least 3

Page 282 Chapter 17 test

1. frequencies:
(47) 1, (48) 9, (49) 14, (50) 16, (51) 6, (52) 4, total 50;
mean 49.6 (49.58), median 50, mode 50, range 5

2. mean 2.4, median 2, mode 2

3. **1** 77
2 frequencies in order:
2, 6, 3, 13, 3, 13, 6, 3, 1, total 50

Page 288 Exericse 18.1

1. **1** $\angle A = 84°$, $\angle B = 53°$, $\angle C = 43°$
   2 $\angle D = 37°$, $\angle E = 112°$, $\angle F = 31°$
2. **1** $AB = AC = 6.9$ cm; $\angle A = 36°$, $\angle B = \angle C = 72°$
   2 $AB = BC = 6.8$ cm; $\angle A = \angle C = 26°$, $\angle B = 128°$
3. **1** 59°, acute-angled
   2 17°, obtuse-angled
   3 44°, acute-angled
   4 25°, obtuse-angled
   5 92°, obtuse-angled
   6 24°, right-angled
4. **1** 139°
   2 33°
   3 51°
   4 41°
   5 $e = 57°$, $f = 63°$
5. $a = 137°$, $b = 87°$
6. $a = 28°$, $d = 44°$

Page 293 Exercise 18.2

1. $a = 34°$, $b = 73°$, isosceles (acute-angled)
2. **1** 18°, obtuse-angled
   2 90°, right-angled
   3 60°, acute-angled, equilateral
   4 120°, obtuse-angled
   5 74°, acute-angled, isosceles
3. $a = b = 66°$, $c = 114°$
4. $a = 60°$, $b = 78°$, $c = 138°$
5. $a = 60°$, $b = 30°$
6. $a = 67°$, $b = 46°$, $c = 113°$
7. $a = 45°$, $b = 40°$, $c = 115°$
8. $a = 60°$, $b = 64°$, $c = 112°$
9. **1** $\angle B = \angle ACB$
   2 66°
   3 66°
   4 42°
   5 90°
   6 24°
10. **1** 45°
    2 60°
    3 105°

Page 297 Exercise 18.3

1. $BC = 6.9$ cm, $\angle B = 44°$, $\angle C = 82°$
2. $\angle A = 55°$, $\angle B = 45°$, $\angle C = 80°$
3. $AC = 7.3$ cm, $\angle B = 44°$, $\angle C = 46°$
4. $AB = 5.6$ cm, $AC = 7.5$ cm, $\angle A = 74°$

Page 298 Exercise 18.4

1. **1** $a = 36°$, $b = 77°$, $c = 41°$
   2 $d = 84°$, $e = 66°$, $f = 30°$
   3 $g = h = 70°$, $j = 40°$
   4 $k = n = p = 36°$, $m = q = 108°$
3. ΔPQR is an equilateral triangle
4. $\angle A = 47°$, $\angle C = 38°$, $AC = 9.6$ cm
5. $a + b + d = 180°$, $c + e + f = 180°$, $a + b + c + d + e + f = 360°$
   sum of angles of a quadrilateral = 360°, sum of angles of a pentagon = 540°
6. **1** $x = 10$
   2 $x = 50$; $\angle A = \angle B = 65°$, isosceles (acute-angled) triangle
   3 $x = 12$, $y = 24$, $z = 12$
   4 $x = 26°$; angles 90°, 45°, 45°; isosceles right-angled triangle

Page 300 Chapter 18 test

1. **1** $g = 56°$, $h = 61°$
   2 $j = 65°$, $k = 40°$
2. $a = b = 30°$, $c = 80°$
3. $a = 60°$, $b = 45°$, $c = 15°$
4. $\angle ABD = \angle BDE = 27°$

Page 302 Exercise C1

1. 3
2. $54ab$
3. 49, 56
4. 54 m
5. 70°
6. −1°C
7. $2\frac{1}{2}$ h (2 h 30 min)
8. $100d$ (cm)
9. $\frac{1}{13}$
10. 85°
11. 25
12. 4 m
13. 9
14. 45°
15. 27 ℓ

Page 303 Exercise C2

1. 12.3
2. $7c$
3. 2
4. 36%
5. 0
6. £48
7. 25 miles
8. 37
9. 9 (°C)
10. $\frac{100}{r}$ cm
11. 110°
12. $\frac{1}{2}$
13. 3
14. 36°
15. 20

Page 304 Exercise C3

1. −7°C
2. **1** $6a$ **2** a **3** $2a^2$ **4** a^3 **5** 1
3. 150 m
4. Bindoo $(w-5)$ kg, Carole $(w+7)$ kg; $w+w-5+w-7=119$, $w=39$; Azara 39 kg, Bindoo 34 kg, Carole 46 kg
5. angles: A 60°, B 110°, C 120°, D 70°; times: A 12 min, B 22 min, C 24 min, D 14 min
6. 19, 29, 59
7. $a=70°$, $b=40°$, $c=140°$
8. 75 galls
9. frequencies for 1 to 9: 3, 4, 5, 11, 9, 8, 5, 3, 2, total 50
   1 4
   2 5
   3 4.8
10. **1** 1 h 25 min
    2 5 min
    3 4 h 40 min

Page 305 Exercise C4

1. 480 kg
2. **1** 68°F, 20°C
   2 32°
   3 61°F
   4 75°F, 82°F, 88°F, 88°F, 84°F
3. mean 13 y 10 m
   median 13 y 11 m
   range 1 y 1 m
4. $a=146°$, $b=134°$, $c=46°$
5. 9
6. $\frac{4}{17}$
7. $AC = 8.0$ cm
8. −6, risen 15, −1
9. $x+5+2x+10+3x-75=180, x=40$; angles 45°, 90°, 45°; right-angled isosceles triangle
10. frequencies in order: 3, 15, 38, 29, 12, 3

Page 307 Exercise C5

1. 36p, £3.96
2. $a=b=34°$, $c=112°$
3. **1** 16
   2 21
4. **1** 7°C
   2 −1°C
5. B £135, C £75
6. **1** 3 **2** 2 **3** 1 **4** 1 **5** 0
7. £140; $A=50+30n$; £350
8. 440 girls, 360 boys
9. **1** $\frac{1}{3}$ **2** $\frac{5}{9}$
10. 158 m

Page 309 Exercise C6

1. 62
2. **1** 100, 92, 84, 76, $\underline{68}$, 60
   2 1, 3, 6, $\underline{10}$, 15, 21, 28
   3 1, 4, 9, $\underline{16}$, 25, 36
   4 $\underline{0}$, $4\frac{1}{2}$, 9, $13\frac{1}{2}$, 18, $22\frac{1}{2}$
   5 1, $\underline{8}$, 27, 64, 125, 216

3. **1** -1 **2** $+2$ **3** -5 **4** $+1$ **5** 3 **6** -2 **7** -3 **8** 2 **9** -3 **10** 3

4. **1** $a = 30$ **2** $b = 3$ **3** $c = 7$ **4** $d = 5$ **5** $e = 3$

5. 1 ft 11 in

6. $a = 62°$, $b = 56°$, $c = 124°$, $d = 28°$

7. **1** $\frac{1}{500}$ **2** $\frac{1}{50}$ **3** $\frac{13}{500}$ **4** $\frac{487}{500}$

8. **1** 60 **2** 2000 **3** 3000 **4** 5000 **5** 400

9. mean 2 h 10 min, range 2 h

10. $AE = EC = 4.3$ cm

Page 312 Exercise C7

7. 4 minutes for 1°, in New York 4 h 56 min later